W9-BEV-580

Getting the Expert Edge from SAP

Whether you are just beginning to work in R/3 System management, or you would like to improve your grasp of the subject, you will benefit from the first-hand, practical experience and information in these books.

Gerhard Oswald
Member of the Executive Board, SAP AG

Dr. Uwe Hommel
Executive Vice-President, SAP AG
R/3 Technical Core Competence

SAP R/3 System Administration:

The Official SAP Guide

SAP® R/3® System Administration:
The Official SAP Guide

Liane Will

SYBEX®

San Francisco • Paris • Düsseldorf • Soest

Associate Publisher: Amy Romanoff
Contracts and Licensing Manager: Kristine Plachy
Acquisitions & Developmental Editor: Melanie Spiller
Editor: Vivian Perry
Project Editor: Raquel Baker
Translator: Paul Read
Book Designer: Kris Warrenburg
Graphic Illustrator: Tony Jonick
Desktop Publisher: Adrian Woolhouse
Production Coordinator: Susan Berge
Indexer: Nancy Guenther
Companion CD: Ginger Warner
Cover Designer: Calyx Design
Cover Photographer: Courtesy of West Stock

Library of Congress Card Number: 98-86865
ISBN: 0-7821-2426-7

Manufactured in the United States of America

10 9 8 7 6 5 4 3 2 1

To the memory of Dr. Gerhard Paulin,
who encouraged me to write my first
book, and to my family, for their
generous support and understanding.
—Liane Will

FOREWORD TO THE SAP EXPERT KNOWLEDGE BOOK SERIES

Enabling you to operate your R/3 System at a minimum cost is of the utmost importance to SAP. You can attain this *lowest cost of ownership* both by implementing R/3 efficiently and quickly with *AcceleratedSAP*, and through optimized and secure production operation. *TeamSAP* exists to provide you with active and close support. TeamSAP brings together the most important resources: *people, processes,* and *products.* SAP acts as the central contact in this team, and shares its knowledge with partners and customers.

To keep your knowledge up to date, TeamSAP conceived this book series, which offers you a detailed overview of the technical issues and concepts of R/3 System management. The books cover subjects ranging from the technical implementation project to R/3 System and database operation.

Whether you are just beginning to work in R/3 System management or you would like to improve your grasp of the subject, you will benefit from the first-hand, practical experience and information in these books. This book series also supports you in your efforts to prepare for a Certified Technical Consultant exam for R/3 Release 4.0. However, this book series cannot, and makes no claim to, be a substitute for your own experience in working with the R/3 System. The authors provide recommendations for your daily work with R/3.

With the increase in R/3 installations, there is an increased need for qualified technical consultants. Through certification, SAP has been setting high standards for many years now. Certification not only confirms whether you are familiar with R/3 System administration for a particular R/3 release, it also establishes whether you can administer one of the database systems and the extent to which you are familiar with one of the supported operating system platforms.

Upgrades to the R/3 System regularly introduce new challenges and solutions for R/3 System management. A certification can therefore only be valid for specific R/3 releases, and must be renewed with every major revision.

Gerhard Oswald
Member of the Executive Board, SAP AG

Dr. Uwe Hommel
Executive Vice-President, SAP AG
R/3 Technical Core Competence

Walldorf, July 1998

ACKNOWLEDGMENTS

I have now spent many months doing intensive research, testing, correcting, reading, and writing. My colleagues also had their share of the work. There was hardly anyone I didn't have questions for, or who didn't get a section of the manuscript to read or test. I would like to thank each of them for their magnificent support. Many minds have contributed to this book; my only task was to write it all down. I would also like to thank Paul Read for translating the original German manuscript into English. A very special thank you goes to Klaus Schläger, who made it possible for me to investigate the new R/3 4.0A Release at an early stage in its development. It was he who made it possible for this book to be published to coincide with R/3 Release 4.0. All information, menu paths, and screen captures are based on R/3 Releases 4.0A and 4.0B. Unfortunately, there is no way to avoid occasional slight discrepancies between the information provided in this book and future R/3 Releases. I ask readers to please make allowances for this when you are working with the R/3 System.

This book contains the collected knowledge of R/3 System administration. If you have not yet gained any experience working with R/3 and R/3 administration, you will soon realize how complex the subject of R/3 is. It would please us to know that this book accompanied you on your way to becoming a certified Basis consultant or R/3 System administrator for R/3 Release 4.

If you already have some experience of R/3 System administration with Release 3.x, you will see that R/3 Release 4.x incorporates numerous changes and enhancements. This book is intended to help you to quickly gain a compact comprehensive familiarity with the innovations in R/3 System administration.

Liane Will
Berlin, October 1998

CONTENTS AT A GLANCE

TABLE OF CONTENTS

INTRODUCTION

With over 16,500 R/3 installations worldwide, SAP has achieved a market penetration without parallel in the Enterprise Resource Planning (ERP) area. Currently, over 9,000 customers with approximately 3.2 million users in over 95 countries rely on R/3. The product SAP R/3 has effectively become an industry standard in the area of ERP software. The reason for this is certainly R/3's powerful integrated functionality, which is implemented using state-of-the-art information technology. SAP's software development efforts are preceded by a precise study of the potential market. Customer specifications and technical expertise have been combined to produce the comprehensive functionality and flexibility of R/3, with all the benefits of standard software. Thousands of people are currently working on the technical implementation of customer specifications. Not surprisingly, it is a challenge to get up-to-date information on effectively using R/3 at the same rate that R/3 is developed.

This book is the first in the SAP Expert Knowledge series and provides an introduction to the technical aspects of R/3 System Administration. Other subjects are covered in the other books in this series. These books cannot—and are not intended to—substitute for SAP's own product documentation. This book describes practical processes and activities in the context of their use, rather than providing complete descriptions of tool functionality.

How This Book Is Organized

This book is divided into 15 chapters and six appendices. Chapter 1 focuses on the basics of R/3 architecture. It takes a look at the technical implementation of client/server architecture in R/3 and introduces important concepts from the R/3 world.

Chapter 2 familiarizes you with general handling procedures, such as starting and stopping the system and logging on. In this chapter, you learn about the important basic functions in the R/3 System.

Chapter 3 focuses on the Online Service System (OSS) that provides support for R/3 customers. You learn how the connection to the OSS is established using an SAProuter and what features the OSS offers.

Chapter 4 explains the concepts of the new installation procedure for R/3 Release 4.0. The chapter covers the requirements for an R/3 installation, the basic procedures, and how to check a completed installation.

Chapter 5 describes the steps necessary to build an R/3 System landscape. The chapter looks at two- and three-system landscapes.

Chapter 6 focuses on Software Logistics in multi-system landscapes. You learn about the new Transport Management System.

Chapter 7 covers copying and maintaining clients. Managing clients is important when you implement R/3 and build a system landscape.

Chapter 8 explains in detail how to define R/3 users, and discusses the R/3 authorization concept. In addition to the basics such as authorization objects, individual authorizations, and authorization profiles, this chapter explains how to work with the Profile Generator.

Chapter 9 focuses on background processing. R/3 allows you to schedule and execute operations in the background, as well as use dialog processing.

In addition to synchronous data processing, changes can be made asynchronously to R/3 data, using the update service. Chapter 10 describes the tasks of an R/3 System administrator, in particular monitoring the update and what to do in error situations.

Chapter 11 explains your options of output configuration and managing output requests.

Greater volumes of data require increased management efforts. At the same time, some data age—and frequently do not need to be available for direct access. Data archiving, which is described in Chapter 12, allows you to store data outside of the R/3 database.

Chapter 13 focuses on Application Linking and Embedding (ALE), including the methods and technology used by R/3 to support distributed business processes. The basics of Batch Input are also described. (This is the procedure used to quickly import data into an R/3 System.)

Chapter 14 describes the management and maintenance of R/3 parameters. You can define operation modes to allow the R/3 System to adapt to changes in user requirements. The chapter also describes how logon groups are used to balance the logon load between the instances.

Chapter 15 introduces you to the tools used by system administrators to monitor R/3 and analyze errors. If you're already familiar with this topic, you can use this chapter to deepen your knowledge of how to use familiar tools. The chapter concludes with an overview of the routine tasks of an R/3 System administrator.

In the appendices at the end of book you'll find lots of information that will help you carry out the tasks of an R/3 administrator, as well as further your knowledge of R/3. Appendix A lists important Transaction codes, and Appendix B is a compilation of profile parameters. The glossary of abbreviations and terms in Appendix C should prove helpful as you gain familiarity with the workings of the R/3 System. Appendix D lists titles of other books and resources you may want to consult to broaden your knowledge of this topic and related topics. Appendix E shows the menu structure for the main Basis administration tasks in R/3 4.0.

Finally, Appendix F is a list of the review questions in each chapter with their corresponding correct answers.

About the CD-ROM

The CD-ROM is a timed test engine containing practice questions and answers from each chapter of the book. The questions are designed to review the concepts presented in each chapter. The test engine simulates the SAP exam and allows you to determine which chapters you may need to review in more detail.

For details on how to install the test engine, see the inside cover of this book, or take a look at the readme file included on the CD-ROM.

CHAPTER
ONE

1

Technical Implementation of Client/Server Architecture in R/3

The architecture of R/3 is based on three-tier client/server software technology. This technology is now successfully used in many complex software systems. This chapter provides an overview of R/3 architecture and explains how its components work together.

The first section of this chapter deals with the implementation of this technology in R/3 from the viewpoint of the R/3 System administrator. This section explains how the three-tier client/server architecture manifests itself in R/3 and in what ways you can influence the system setup. Details on how to do so are given in later chapters that address these issues in detail. You should have thought through the reasons for using the three-tiered system before you begin the technical implementation of the R/3 System.

NOTE   In this book I assume that the basic principles and benefits of client/server technology are familiar to the reader. You may want to consult some of the books available on this topic. Thorough descriptions of this technology can be found, for example, in *SAP R/3 System: A Client/Server Technology,* by Rüdiger Buck-Emden and Jürgen Galimow. (Addison-Wesley, 1997).

Client/Server Architecture in R/3

From the viewpoint of the software, the three-tier client/server architecture consists of a presentation layer, an application layer, and a database layer (see Figure 1.1). From the hardware perspective, these three layers can run separately on different computers or all together on the same computer. R/3 also allows the distribution of the presentation and application layers over multiple computers.

All variants of the central system and three-tier configuration are feasible. Running a central system—all three layers of the client/server architecture on a single computer—cancels out the advantages of the three-tier architecture. Such a central system can adequately serve a maximum of 10 users. For this reason, this single-computer central instance configuration is normally used only for demonstration or test purposes.

FIGURE 1.1:

Client/server architecture in R/3

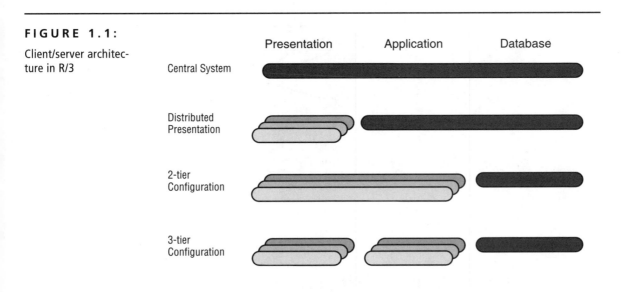

Distributed Presentation

For smaller R/3 Systems, the most frequently chosen constellation is a distributed presentation, as shown in Figure 1.2. On the presentation layer, PCs are used or, less frequently, UNIX servers with X-Terminals may be used. When using X-Terminals, it is best to only have to maintain the central presentation server. In contrast, when using PCs, you must ensure that each PC works properly. This is usually the task of the administrator, who either performs this task manually, which is time consuming, or with the help of additional software. A PC running one of the standard operating systems offers greater functionality than an X-Terminal, a factor which is often central in the decision to use PCs.

FIGURE 1.2:

Distributed presentation

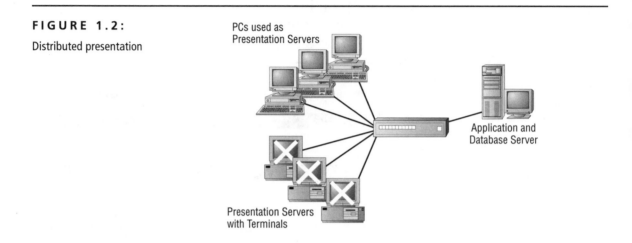

PCs used as
Presentation Servers

Application and
Database Server

Presentation Servers
with Terminals

Three-Tier Architecture

The distributed presentation of the R/3 System satisfies only user requirements for a system with up to about 200 front ends, or users. If there are more than 200 users, bottlenecks occur on the central application and database server. To improve the performance of the R/3 System, the application layer can be distributed over multiple servers. This configuration is shown in Figure 1.3. A part of the application layer could still run on the database server. This configuration also makes it possible to mix the layers from the hardware viewpoint. A system distributed in this way can serve more than 5,000 users, depending on the performance of the specific hardware used.

NOTE   Each additional computer increases the work needed to administer the R/3 System.

FIGURE 1.3:

Three-tier architecture
using multiple servers

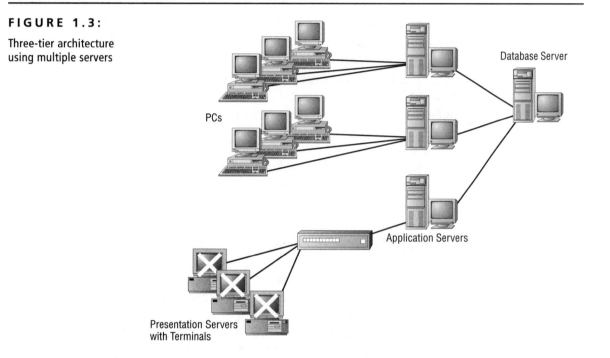

One of the most important decisions to be made in the early phases of R/3 implementation is which hardware architecture to use. Within guidelines, the system administrator must set up the system to best satisfy the requirements of the users. If it becomes apparent only during R/3 production operation that the architecture chosen does not satisfy the requirements, the result will frequently be increased costs and additional organizational work.

The software implementation, which is described in the following sections, is the basis for the technical hardware variations.

Presentation

For users working with the R/3 business functionality, only the presentation layer is relevant. The presentation layer in R/3 consists of the *SAP Graphical User Interface* (SAPGUI). The SAPGUI accepts the user input and passes it to the next layer, the application layer, for further processing. The SAPGUI accepts data from the application layer and presents this data to the user. Each R/3 session is performed through a SAPGUI, and each SAPGUI consists of a process on the operating system level of the front ends. The R/3 administrator defines how many SAPGUI processes, or user sessions, can be started from the front ends.

Multiple R/3 user sessions can be coordinated using the *SAP Session Manager.* The SAP Session Manager provides an overview of the sessions in one or more different R/3 Systems.

The Application Layer

User requests are passed from the presentation layer to the R/3 application layer. This is where the actual calculations and evaluations are performed. Data that is needed to perform these calculations and evaluations is requested from the database layer. Incoming data is processed by the application layer and passed to the database.

The application layer is the control center of an R/3 System. This means that the application layer is one of the central points on which an R/3 System administrator exerts influence. The tools used for R/3 System administration are, for the most part, fully integrated into R/3, which means that the R/3 System can be administered through a SAPGUI user interface.

Instance

The application layer can be made up of multiple computers. On each computer in the application layer, a number of processes perform tasks. These processes make up an *instance* of an R/3 System. The R/3 System administrator configures the number and the types of these processes, and monitors their status while the system is running.

The Database Layer

The database layer consists of a *Relational Database Management System* (RDBMS). Data is exchanged between the application processes and the RDBMS through the SQL interface. The data in an R/3 System is stored in one database on one computer. The name of the database determines the name of the R/3 System. This name must consist of three characters—either uppercase letters and/or numbers, for example, D10, K11, K4K, DDD. (The first character must be an uppercase letter.) The abbreviation SID (short for System Identifier) is normally used as a placeholder for the R/3 System name. Sometimes the name SAPSID (for SAP System Identifier) is used.

When using an R/3 System, the administrator must perform the usual database administration tasks. These tasks include:

- Database backups and data restoration if errors occur
- Configuration
- Flow control and optimization
- Memory management
- Data reorganization
- Software maintenance and installation

SAP provides both the integrated R/3 tools for the database administrator and, for some database systems, special tools for use on the database server.

If the database and the application layer are distributed over at least two computers, this is known as a *distributed R/3 System.*

Network Technology

Standard network technology is used between the layers that are distributed over multiple computers, within the layers, and to connect the R/3 System to the outside world. TCP/IP is the transport protocol. For each dialog step, between 2 and 4KB of data are transferred between a front end in the presentation layer and an application server. For this reason, it makes sense to have a WAN connection based on X.25 and ISDN between the presentation computers and the application servers. For each dialog step, 20–40KB is transferred between the database server and the application server, that is, 10 times as much as the transfer between the presentation layer and the application layer. For this reason, these database servers should only be connected through a LAN.

An R/3 System can be connected to a mainframe system through IBM's SNA (*Systems Network Architecture*) protocol LU6.2.

Internet Transaction Server

The R/3 System is connected to the Internet through the *Internet Transaction Server* (ITS). The ITS consists of two software components: the A-gate process (*Application Gate)* and the W-gate process (*Web Gate*). The A-gate process establishes the connection to an R/3 application server. The W-gate process establishes the connection to the Web server. Both components communicate with each other using the TCP/IP protocol (see Figure 1.4). The ITS converts requests from the WWW into requests as they are formulated by the standard SAPGUI, based on the *Dynamic Information and Action Gateway* protocol (DIAG). ISAPI is the abbreviation for Microsoft Information Server API, NSAPI is the abbreviation for Netscape Server API. The ITS enables the execution of *Internet Application Components* (IACs), R/3 transactions that are compatible with the Internet.

FIGURE 1.4:

The structure of ITS

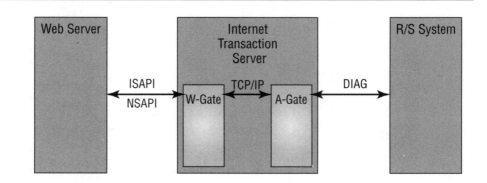

The Presentation Layer

This section deals with the use of the R/3 presentation layer, which is the interface to the user. The R/3 presentation layer serves all kinds of R/3 users, that is, both the R/3 System administrator and the business manager. This places high demands on the user interface. Demands might include:

- Simple ergonomic use
- User-specific configuration
- Simple management
- Flexible, location-independent access

- Multilingual ability
- Portability between different hardware and operating systems with identical functionality and appearance

To meet all these requirements, SAP provides R/3 users with the following programs that build on each other:

- SAPGUI (SAP Graphical User Interface)
- SAPLOGON
- SAP Session Manager

SAPGUI

SAPGUI creates a Single-System/Single-Task environment. When a SAPGUI is executed, the user defines the R/3 System to log on to in a possible system landscape. Under Windows operating systems, you can create a special icon to call the program. The SAPGUI is mouse- and menu-driven. The user navigates in the menus, thus working sequentially. To perform steps in parallel, an additional SAPGUI or a new window (*session*) must be started. As far as the technical processes are concerned, a new session is most similar to an additional SAPGUI.

SAPLOGON

For all the R/3 Systems available in a system landscape, the R/3 user can either create program icons or start the SAPGUI and enter the appropriate information. This individual access would quickly increase clutter, especially in extensive system landscapes. SAPLOGON therefore allows you to define in advance all possible connections from SAPGUIs to the R/3 Systems that will be available in your system landscape. SAPLOGON also supports uniform load distribution over all the computers belonging to the R/3 System. The user can choose from these pre-defined settings.

SAPLOGON then causes a SAPGUI to start with the appropriate parameters.

SAP Session Manager

Unlike the SAPGUI, the SAP Session Manager supports a Multi-System/Multi-Task environment. You can use this program to log on in parallel to multiple R/3 Systems and work in these systems simultaneously in multiple windows. The Session Manager opens and closes windows, which are ultimately SAPGUIs. The Session Manager supports individual configuration of the user interface. You can choose between the SAP default menu, a company-specific menu, and a user-specific menu for each available R/3 System.

Figure 1.5 shows the initial screen of the SAP Session Manager. The lower part shows the list of known R/3 Systems. You can extend or change this list using the pushbuttons. You enter information in the upper part of the screen when you log on to a system. This information consists of your user name, password, client name, and the abbreviation for the language you will be using.

FIGURE 1.5:

The initial screen of the SAP Session Manager

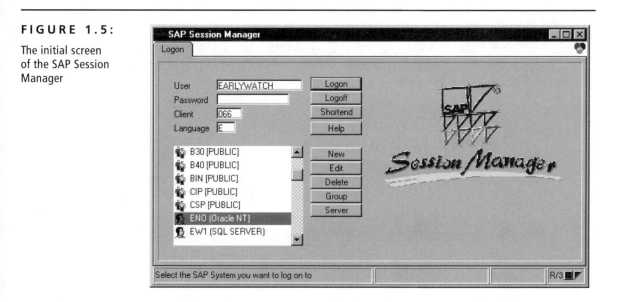

Client

A client is an independent business unit within the R/3 System. The client key is used to separate all user-specific data within a table. The technical administration data in the R/3 System, like programs, are client-independent. Multiple clients are mostly used within one R/3 System for organizational reasons. Using multiple clients, you can perform tests or hold training exercises using separate data within the same system.

Default Clients

The R/3 System contains the default clients 000, 001, and 066. You should not make any changes to these clients. Client 000 is used specifically for R/3 release upgrades and to import certain R/3 configuration settings. Settings made in this client are usually valid throughout the whole R/3 System. Simple test structures for all applications are also provided.

Client 001 is a copy of client 000. All the settings made in this client are only valid in this client. Client 001 contains test data for working with the ECU (European Currency Unit) currency. Client 066 is reserved for the special SAP EarlyWatch Service, which checks your R/3 System to avoid bottlenecks that can affect performance. Client 066 is preconfigured specifically for the EarlyWatch Service.

Default Users

Just as there is a default client, every installed R/3 System contains default users that have specific predefined authorizations. (These default users and their passwords are shown in Table 1.1.) Users in the R/3 System are client-dependent, that is, a user is only valid in the client in which it was created.

TABLE 1.1: Default Users and Their Predefined Passwords

Client	User	Default Password
000	SAP*	06071992
000	DDIC	19920706
001	SAP*	06071992
001	DDIC	19920706
066	EARLYWATCH	SUPPORT

 The passwords for the default users can be changed at any time, but in R/3 release 4.0, users cannot be deleted.

If you try to delete the users SAP* and DDIC, the password is reset to the password in the R/3 kernel, PASS. The users themselves are retained. This constitutes a gap in security.

For production operation, a new client must be created. This process is described in detail in Chapter 7.

Figure 1.6 shows the active SAP Session Manager. In this figure, the connection to the R/3 System QO1 is active. The user has logged on with user WILL to client 000. The application Tools was chosen.

All the subentries are displayed on this screen to the right of the selected menu tree, which is highlighted. You can copy frequently used actions to a "favorites" list below the menu entry. Double-click the action in the menu tree or the favorites list to open a new SAPGUI window for this action, and to branch to this window. If you have completed your work and leave the SAPGUI window, this window is automatically closed and you are returned to the active menu tree of the SAP Session Manager. If you switch from one R/3 System to another, all the SAPGUI windows for the first system are hidden and the windows of the new system are displayed (if any are active).

The SAPGUI interface is based on the Windows Style Guide and the EG 90/270 and ISO 9241 standards on interface ergonomics. SAPGUI is available for multiple platforms, including the following:

- Microsoft Windows 3.*x*
- Windows 95
- Windows for Workgroups
- Windows NT (Intel processor) 4.0, 3.51
- Apple Macintosh
- OS/2 Presentation Manager
- OSF Motif
- Java

SAPGUI has the same characteristics on each platform. The only difference is that sometimes there is a variation in the integration of familiar, platform-specific user elements that are embedded in a platform. This means that users do not have to do any relearning after switching to a new platform. This portability of the R/3 interface can be achieved because only data and logical information for generic graphical display based on the DIAG protocol are exchanged between application and presentation. The actual presentation of the data is handled by the programs in the presentation layer using platform-specific resources.

A SAPGUI window is divided into several areas. The name of the window is displayed in the title bar. (See Figure 1.7.)

FIGURE 1.7:

The SAPGUI

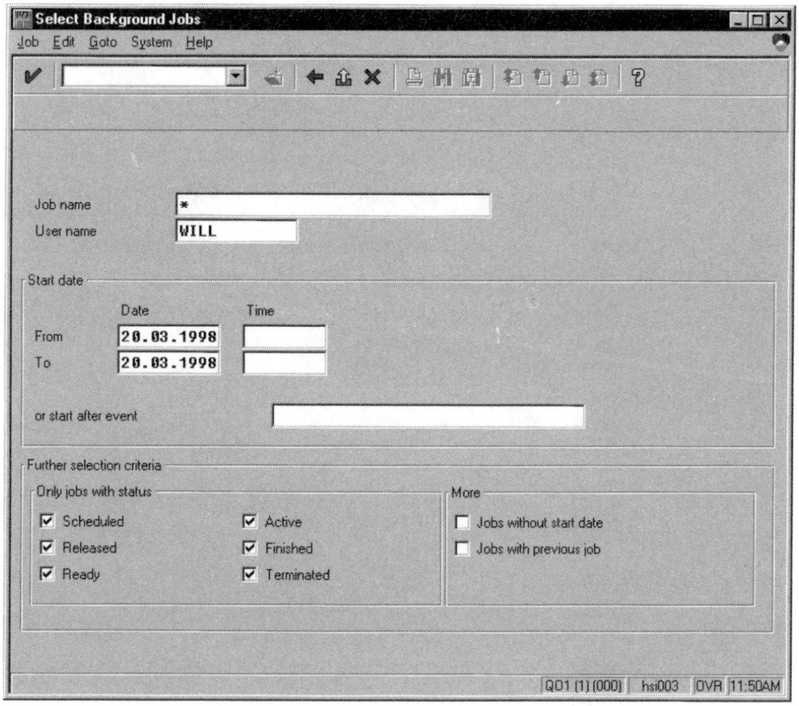

Menu Bar

The menu bar is below the title bar. Within the SAPGUI, you can use the functionality accessed through the icon on the right of the menu bar to change color, font, and size of the text in the menus. Each menu bar contains the menus System and Help. The menu System contains important functions such as those for creating or deleting a session, and processing lists, as well as utilities and information on the system status. The Help menu lets you access R/3 documentation and context-sensitive help.

Button Bar

Frequently used functions can be executed using standardized icons. Table 1.2 shows the meanings of the most important icons. Context-sensitive pushbuttons may be displayed in addition to these icons.

TABLE 1.2: Important R/3 Icons and What They Mean

Icon	Function Key	Meaning
	Ctrl+S	Save
	F3	Back
	Shift+F3	Exit
	F12	Cancel
	Enter	Confirm

TABLE 1.2: Important R/3 Icons and What They Mean *(Continued)*

Icon	Function Key	Meaning
	Ctrl+P	Print
	Ctrl+F	Find
	Ctrl+Page Up	First page of a list
	Page Up	Previous page of a list
	Page Down	Next page of a list
	Ctrl+ Page Down	Last page of a list
	F1	Help
	F8	Refresh
		Copy
		Create
		Delete
		Display
		Generate
		Change

TABLE 1.2: Important R/3 Icons and What They Mean *(Continued)*

Icon	Function Key	Meaning
		Check
		Execute

Transaction Code

The icon bar contains a field called the *command field* that is used to enter commands. Because the functionality offered by R/3 is complex, the R/3 menu tree is also complex and not always strictly hierarchical. All R/3 transactions are assigned a *transaction code,* which you can enter to call a R/3 transaction directly without having to navigate throughout the menus. A transaction code can be prefixed by /n or /o. /n interrupts the current work step and calls the transaction in the same window. Using /o calls the transaction in a new window or session.

Although this procedure may at first appear antiquated, it does have its enthusiasts in practice, particularly among experienced R/3 users. When I describe particular functionality, the transaction code will be specified in addition to the assigned transaction code, if appropriate. If you are using the Session Manager, you can reduce the number of menu steps and the use of transaction codes, as the functions can be accessed directly.

Status Bar

The last bar in the SAPGUI window is the status bar. The status bar displays important information about the R/3 System that the user has logged onto, as well as information, messages, or error messages about a workflow.

Between the top area and the last bar of a SAPGUI window is the R/3 user's actual work area. The structure and functionalities in this area depend on the user's task.

Multilingual Capability

The multilingual capability of SAPGUI derives from the fact that all text elements displayed are stored separately. You can select a language either when you log onto an R/3 System or by setting an R/3 parameter. However, the selected language must already be installed; that is, the text elements for the language you choose must be imported into the R/3 database. English and German are available by default in every system. Currently, over 20 different languages can be installed, including Japanese and Mandarin.

Since R/3 release 3.1, an Internet version of SAPGUI is also available. Since R/3 release 4.0, there is also an Internet version of the SAP Session Manager. The handling and appearance of both programs are almost identical, whether you are working with the Internet or not. (See Figure 1.8.)

This was possible because of R/3's open client/server architecture R/3. (See Figure 1.9.) SAPGUI and the SAP Session Manager are embedded in the Java-enabled Web browser. The Web browser and the R/3 instance communicate through the Internet Basis components, which convert the requests of the Internet SAPGUI to the DIAG protocol. This means that there is no apparent difference for the R/3 instance between the Internet SAPGUI and the standard SAPGUI.

The benefits of Internet technology are clear. When you work with the Internet SAPGUI, all the R/3 application transactions are automatically Internet-enabled without the need for SAP or the customer to customize any program code.

From the administrator's viewpoint, there is one especially important benefit that should be emphasized: Administration of the R/3 client software on the client is no longer necessary. To exchange the client software, you only need to update the software in the defined *Uniform Resource Locator* (URL). With the standard SAPGUI and the standard Session Manager up to R/3 release 3.1, it was necessary to update the software on the client. The larger the number of clients used in the presentation layer, the greater the effort required, unless special administration software was used. With R/3 Release 4.0, SAP provides software components based on *Client Components Enabling Technology* (CET) that automatically update the R/3 software components on the client.

FIGURE 1.9:

Architecture of the Internet front end

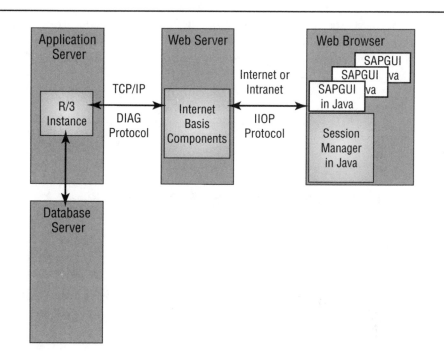

Component Manager

The Component Manager manages the individual R/3 components (SAPGUI, SAP Session Manager) on the client. It is sufficient to install the software once, at the time R/3 4.0 is installed. The system then automatically recognizes when the client components need to be upgraded. This is usually after the R/3 software in the application and database layer has been updated. For this purpose, the software for the clients is managed centrally in the R/3 database. When a component is called, it is automatically installed and registered on the client. This is known as the *Self Upgrading Software Environment* (SUSE), which runs on all computers in the application layer.

NEW! Release 4.0 also includes a Data Provider to convert various standard Internet file formats, known as *Multipurpose Internet Mail Extensions* (MIME). MIME enables all the data in one of the MIME formats to be displayed directly from the R/3 client, the standard SAPGUI, or the Internet SAPGUI. Any necessary conversion is performed automatically and is transparent to the user.

The Application Layer

This section focuses on the structure of the application layer and describes the R/3 processes that run in this layer and their interaction. It also covers the interfaces to the presentation and database layer. R/3 administrators will learn which processes they can and must influence.

Unlike the presentation layer in which each front end runs independently of the other front ends—and possibly on separate computers—all R/3 processes in the application layer—possibly on different computers—make up a logically closed unit. While the SAP Session Manager can be started as many times as required and used to log on to one or more R/3 Systems, when the processes in the application layer are started, they are assigned to one R/3 System.

The application layer of an R/3 System provides the following services:

Dialog service   (D)

Update   (V)

Lock management (Enqueue)   (E)

Background processing (Batch)   (B)

Message Server   (M)

Gateway   (G)

Spool service   (S)

As the application layer can consist of multiple instances, these services can be distributed over the individual instances in keeping with different considerations.

The name of an instance contains the name of the R/3 System and the letter for each service provided. A central R/3 System with one instance offering all services will have the name *<SID>_ DVEBMGS<TCP/IP Port>*. Replace *<SID>* with the 3-character system name that is unique in the system landscape. Replace *<TCP/IP Port>* with the last two numbers of the TCP/IP port used for the connection.

Message Server

Within the application layer there is one instance among the instances which offers the single message server. This process is for communication between the instances of an R/3 System. The message server monitors and assigns free process resources on the application layer. The instance on which the message server is running is known as the *central instance* of the R/3 System. The tasks of the central instance are described later in this chapter.

Dispatcher and Work Processes

The dialog service, lock management, update, background, and spool service are provided by the work processes. The work processes are coordinated by the dispatcher process, of which one runs on each instance. For this purpose, an *Advanced Program to Program Communication* server (APPC) is part of the dispatcher. The work processes and the dispatcher are one and the same program, which is started depending on function and parameters.

Depending on the requirements and available resources, the administrator must define which and how many processes implement a service throughout the whole system and in a specific instance. The dispatcher starts and manages these processes. If the dispatcher fails, the whole instance fails as a consequence. The dispatcher works at the interface between the presentation layer and the application layer. All the requests that come from the presentation layer, that is the SAPGUI, are received by the dispatcher and assigned to a work process available in this instance. (See Figure 1.10.)

FIGURE 1.10:

The role of the dispatcher in the R/3 instance

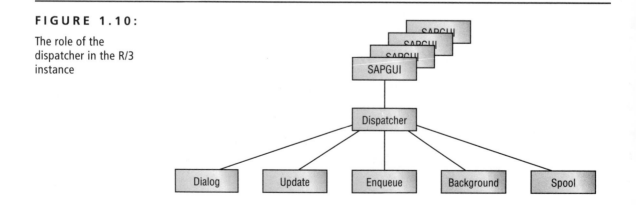

If we look more closely at the structure of a work process, we see that the Screen Processor, ABAP Processor, SQL interface, and Taskhandler work together using special main memory areas. The Taskhandler coordinates the activities within the work process. Depending on the task, processing is passed to the Screen Processor (which processes screens), the ABAP Processor (which programs in SAP's programming language ABAP), or the SQL interface to exchange data with the database.

Dialog Service

The work processes are distinguished by their tasks. Dialog processes implement requests from active user sessions. Each R/3 instance must provide at least two dialog processes to process the necessary internal R/3 procedures.

The dispatcher does more than assign one user (SAPGUI) to a dialog process. For each dialog step, the instance's dispatcher assigns the task to an available dialog process. The user data needed for the processing that is being done, such as authorizations, is stored as user context in the main memory areas available to the work processes. In R/3, a dialog step is seen as one screen. When a screen is opened, the dialog step starts; when the screen is closed, the dialog step ends. For the database, a dialog step is seen as one transaction. This mechanism enables a dialog process to serve multiple users.

Background Service

Tasks that need to be executed in the background are executed by the background work processes. It makes sense to process protracted tasks that do not need any online data entry in the background. You can schedule the programs to be executed, known as *jobs*, to run at a specific time or at a time determined by an event.

The background service must be supported by at least one instance with at least one appropriate work process.

Update Service

The update service makes asynchronous changes to the database. This service is used if changes to the data are not time-critical, that is, they do not need to be made immediately, or synchronously. An R/3 user has no influence over when the update service is used. This decision is made when the business application is developed. An example is order entry: each order must be entered quickly online in dialog mode. The actual update is performed in the background with a slight delay, without the user having to wait for the transaction to be completed.

There must be at least one update service on one instance available in an R/3 System to handle asynchronous data changes.

Spool Service

Output requests are passed to the spool service, which stores them temporarily in the temporary sequential objects (TemSe) until they are output. The R/3 System administrator must decide whether the *TemSe objects* should be stored in the database using the RDBMS security mechanisms, or in the file system using operating system management.

At least one spool process must be available in the system. Each instance can provide any number of spool processes.

NOTE   Until R/3 release 3.1, no more than one spool process could be started for each instance. That meant that frequent extensive and lengthy output requests could cause performance bottlenecks. A possible solution was to install two instances of the same R/3 System on one application server, using one instance for the spool service.

The spool processes coordinate all the output processes, such as print and fax requests. Depending on the configuration, output requests can be either passed directly to the output medium or processed using the operating system spool system. In both cases, output is monitored. System messages are recorded in the R/3 System logs.

Enqueue Service

Lock management plays a special role among the services. Lock management is a system-wide service like the Message Server; that is, only one instance can provide this service for the whole system. The service is normally provided by one process, which is why the term *Enqueue Server* is used synonymously for both the instance that provides the service and the service.

R/3 Transaction

The Enqueue Server and the Message Server should, where possible, run on the same instance because the Enqueue Server and the Message Server work together closely. The Enqueue Server manages the logical locks for the R/3 transactions. An R/3 transaction is made up of a sequence of functionally and logically connected work steps that are consistent from an enterprise management point of view. An R/3 transaction usually consists of multiple dialog steps. From the database perspective, each dialog step makes up a physical and logical unit, the database transaction. The RDBMS can only coordinate this database transaction with its lock management. This is not sufficient from the R/3 point of view. For this reason, *Logical Units of Work* (LUW) were introduced to R/3. R/3 supports the *ACID* maxim for these LUWs as defined for transactions within the RDBMS. The following rules apply to a Logical Unit of Work:

> **Atomic**—LUWs make up a unit. Either the whole LUW is executed or no single part is executed.

Consistent—A LUW converts a consistent database state into a new consistent state, that is, after a LUW is completed, a logically correct state is achieved.

Isolated—LUWs are independent of each other; they can run in parallel. They can only run sequentially if multiple LUWs attempt to process the same sources.

Durable—The result left by successfully completed LUWs is permanent. For example, the result is not affected by any system errors that may occur.

To meet these requirements, the Enqueue Server is needed. Lock requests from an R/3 Transaction are passed to the Message Server, which has them executed by the Enqueue Server. To reduce additional load on the network, it makes sense to make the Enqueue Server and the Message Server available on the same instance. The Enqueue Server manages these locks in a separate main memory area. An Enqueue Server failure would thus cause the loss of all R/3 locks, which would result in an automatic rollback of all affected LUWs. If the Enqueue Server fails, the Dispatcher immediately attempts to start a new Enqueue work process.

Gateway Service

Each R/3 instance also needs a Gateway Service to perform tasks that extend beyond the local instance. These include:

- Communication between different R/3 Systems
- Remote Function Call (RFC)
- Common Programming Interface for Communications (CPIC)
- Connection of external systems such as MAPI server, EDI systems, external fax devices, and Telex service

The Gateway process exists once for each instance, and is activated automatically—without the system administrator's intervention—when an instance is started.

Table 1.3 shows the rules for the number of R/3 processes in the application layer.

TABLE 1.3: Rules for the Type and Number of Processes in the Application Layer

Service	R/3, System-Wide	For Each R/3 Instance
Dialog	>=2	>=2
Update	>=1	>=0
Enqueue	1	0 or 1
Background	>=1	>=0
Message	1	0 or 1
Gateway	>=1	1
Spool	>=1	R/3 3.1;0 or 1 Since R/3 4.0: >=0

The Message Server is kept informed about which instances and which services are available. It is the system control unit. If the Message Server fails, the R/3 System can no longer function. Within an instance, the Dispatcher is the control unit. If the Dispatcher fails, the instance can no longer function. However, if work processes fail, the Dispatcher can start new ones. Each work process can perform any task.

Based on the standards set by the R/3 administrator, the Dispatcher determines which task a work process has. For an administrator to accomplish these tasks, the administrator must be aware of the requirements placed on the R/3 System. These requirements must be resolved during the R/3 technical implementation phase. Later phases deal with issues concerning system extensions or refining a defined configuration.

The coordination of the application layer is one of the main activities of the R/3 System administrator. It is the responsibility of the administrator to decide on the type and number of the instances and their processes, the size of the main memory areas of the instances, and other characteristics and settings.

The possible configurations of an R/3 System, especially of the application layer, are very complex. With central systems, that is, when the application layer consists of only one instance, the number of processes and the size of their main memory areas must be configured. Main memory areas are used for purposes such as buffering frequently used table contents, factory calendars, ABAP run-time objects, and user context. With distributed systems, that is, multiple instances within one R/3 System, instances can be defined that only provide one service, like the update server, background server, or spool server. These decisions are usually motivated by system performance or administration. These areas are discussed in greater detail in Chapter 14.

The Database Layer

The database layer of an R/3 System is implemented on a central computer by using a central RDBMS. This section examines the database layer in R/3 in greater detail. It explains how the RDBMS is used for R/3 purposes and which administration activities are to be expected.

Native and Open SQL

Figure 1.11 shows the interfaces between the RDBMS and the work processes. The application layers and the database layer communicate exclusively through SQL. In spite of the SQL standard, each RDBMS supported by R/3 offers its own SQL dialect, which extends beyond the SQL standard. To enjoy the greatest possible independence from these kinds of manufacturer- and release-specific extensions and modifications, the R/3 work processes normally only support the Open SQL interface. ABAP Open SQL corresponds to the Entry Level in accordance with the SQL2 standard. Within the database interface that is integrated into the work processes, this Open SQL is converted, if necessary, into the Native SQL of the RDBMS.

FIGURE 1.11:

The database interface

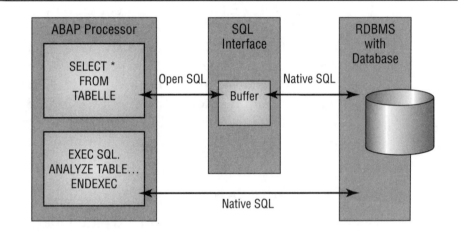

You can also use the special SQL language features of the RDBMS within ABAP programs. As these language features are vendor-specific, the modules are encapsulated within the R/3 applications. Their use is reduced to an "absolutely essential" level. However, appropriate areas of use are specific applications such as database monitors. The following statements are used to encapsulate native SQL statements into ABAP programs:

```
EXEC SQL.
    <Native SQL Statement>
ENDEXEC.
```

Table Types

Data is stored in tables of the RDBMS. All the application data is mapped 1:1 to *transparent tables.* This data could, in theory, also be accessed using other SQL- or vendor-specific tools. Technical R/3 administration data is also stored in other types of tables. From the RDBMS perspective, they are still tables.

R/3 sometimes groups multiple small tables into one table in the RDBMS. This table container is known from the R/3 viewpoint as a *table pool.* The tables in a table pool are only visible for R/3. The main benefit of table pools is the reduction of the total number of tables, from the RDBMS viewpoint. Within the table pool, the individual tables are identified using their unique names and their specific record keys. A table in a table pool is known as a *pool table.* The structure and the storage method used for individual pool tables means that it is considerably more complicated to access data from each of them without R/3 tools.

Example: Table Pools

Table ATAB is an example of a typical table pool. It contains multiple R/3 control tables. The control tables themselves are quite small and their content is relatively constant, which means that it is possible and makes sense to buffer the entire table pool. Table ATAB is defined as shown in Table 1.4.

TABLE 1.4: Definition of the Table Pool ATAB

Field Name	Meaning	Key	Type	Length
TABNAME	Name of the pool table	X	CHAR	10
VARKEY	Key of the pool table	X	CHAR	50
DATALN	Length of the record in the pool table		FIXED	5
VARDATA	Record in the pool table		RAW	452

Table ATAB contains, for example, a table called TCOLL, which in turn contains the execution plans for the programs to collect statistical data for R/3 performance analysis. The structure of table TCOLL from the perspective of R/3 is shown in Table 1.5.

TABLE 1.5: Definition of Pool Table TCOLL

Field Name	Meaning	Key	Type	Length
RNAME	Program to be started	X	CHAR	40
RENUM	Number of repetitions		CHAR	1
SYTYP	System type		CHAR	1
ALTSY	Alternative system		CHAR	20
DAYOW	Weekday for run		CHAR	7
TIMEOD	Start time		CHAR	24

From the perspective of RDBMS, table TCOLL does not exist. The data in table TCOLL can only be deciphered using R/3 tools. The corresponding records in table ATAB could look like Table 1.6.

TABLE 1.6: Excerpt from the Contents of the Table Pool ATAB from the RDBMS Viewpoint

TABNAME	VARKEY	DATALN	VARDATA
TCOLL	RSDBREV	-32731	Data in bytes
TCOLL	RSEFA350	-32735	Data in bytes
TCOLL	RSHOSTDB	-32730	Data in bytes

The keys are the name of the pool table and the key of this table, which is the program name in this example. From the R/3 viewpoint, the pool table TCOLL would have the contents shown in Table 1.7.

TABLE 1.7: Excerpt from the Pool Table TCOLL

RNAME	RENUM	SYTYP	ALTSY	DAYOW	TIMEOD
RSDBREV	1	C		'XXXXXXX'	'X X X X X X X X X X X X'
RSEFA350	1	C		' X '	' X '
RSHOSTDB	1	*		'XXXXXX '	'XXXXXXXXXXXXXXXXXXXXXXXX'

Table clusters and their logical *cluster tables* are a similar case. Cluster tables do not exist as independent tables in the RDBMS. Multiple cluster tables are grouped in a table cluster, also known simply as a *cluster*. Normally, multiple rows in the cluster table are grouped into a record in the cluster under a shared key. Unlike the table pool, where a record is assigned a record in the pool table, a record is made up from multiple records in the cluster table. The records are concatenated and a cluster key is added. This technique is used mostly in the area of documentation.

Example: Clusters

Table DOKCLU is just such a cluster. It is used only for storing table DOKTL, which contains lines of text from different pieces of documentation. Table 1.8 shows the definition of table DOKCLU.

TABLE 1.8: Structure of Cluster DOKCLU

Field Name	Meaning	Key	Type	Length
ID	Document class	X	CHAR	2
OBJECT	Document object	X	CHAR	60
LANGU	Documentation language	X	CHAR	1
TYP	Documentation type	X	CHAR	1
DOKVERSION	Documentation module version	X	CHAR	4

TABLE 1.8: Structure of Cluster DOKCLU *(Continued)*

Field Name	Meaning	Key	Type	Length
PAGENO	Page number		INT2	5
TIMESTMP	Timestamp		CHAR	14
PAGELG	Page length		INT2	5
VARDATA	Text		RAW	3800

The cluster table DOKTL is managed in table DOKCLU with the structure shown in Table 1.9.

TABLE 1.9: Definition of the Cluster Table DOKTL from the R/3 Viewpoint

Field Name	Meaning	Key	Type	Length
ID	Document class	X	CHAR	2
OBJECT	Document object	X	CHAR	60
LANGU	Documentation language	X	CHAR	1
TYP	Documentation type	X	CHAR	1
DOKVERSION	Documentation module version	X	CHAR	4
LINE	Line number within the documentation text	X	CHAR	6
DOKFORMAT	Documentation format		CHAR	2
DOKTEXT	Text line of the documentation		CHAR	72

The field LINE was added to the key for table DOKTL with regard to the cluster DOKCLU. Each record in table DOKTL represents one line of a documentation text in one language. All the lines of a text are grouped together into one record under the key of the documentation text in table DOKCLU. This achieves a certain level of object orientation, a documentation object corresponds to one record in a cluster.

Availability

An R/3 System 4.0A consists, at the database layer, of approximately 12,700 tables and 14,900 indexes. From the R/3 viewpoint, there are approximately 15,000 tables.

The database and the RDBMS play a central role in R/3 operation. All the data that the user enters, including the R/3 administration data, is managed there. Administration is also important, particularly backing up this data. In the broadest sense, these activities are part of R/3 System administration. With larger systems, the database administration tasks can sometimes fully occupy one person or a group of people. However, this task area is marked by many RDBMS-specific characteristics.

This book deals only with generally used procedures. For more detailed questions, you'll want to refer to a book about specific aspects of RDBMS administration. At the time of this writing, the RDBMSs and operating systems available with R/3 are those listed in Table 1.10. Adabas D is only delivered to existing customers and is no longer available to new customers.

TABLE 1.10: RDBMS and Operating System Availability for R/3

	Oracle	Informix	DB2	MS SQL Server	Adabas D
HP-UX	x	x			x
AIX	x	x	x		x
Reliant/UNIX	x	x			x
Digital UNIX	x	x			x
Solaris	x	x			x
NT4.0 Intel	x	x	x	x	x
NT4.0 Alpha	x	(planned)	x	x	
OS/400			x		
OS/390			x		

Network

Network services are used between the individual layers of the client/server architecture. The protocol layers used in R/3 Systems are shown in Figure 1.12. Communication between the R/3 components, and with other systems, is based on the TCP/IP protocol.

FIGURE 1.12:

The R/3 Systems protocol layers

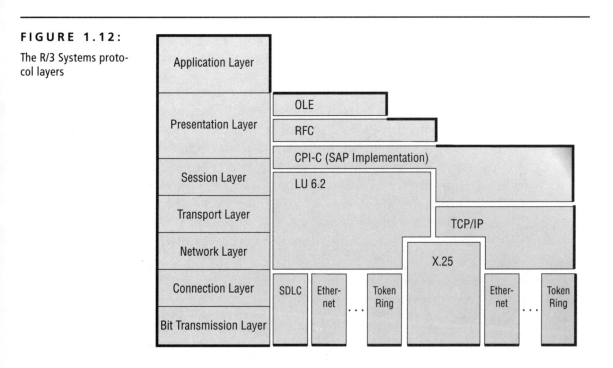

R/3 provides various services to facilitate communication. The R/3-specific *Common Programming Interface-Communication* interface (CPI-C) is used from one ABAP program to another, which ensures that the communications interface is consistent and standardized. CPI-C corresponds to the SAA standard, which was first defined by IBM in 1987. This standard covers:

- Establishing communication
- Controlling communication

- Exchanging information

- Closing the communication connection

The SAP Gateway is responsible for converting the CPI-C calls. The CPI-C interface is always used for communication between different R/3 Systems, or between R/3 and R/2 Systems, or when programs outside of R/3 are executed. The Message Server processes short messages. When larger volumes of data are exchanged, the service responsible specifically for this purpose (the SAP Gateway based on TCP/IP or LU6.2) is used. The CPI-C language is an integral part of the R/3 programming language ABAP in the Starter Set, which includes additional data conversion functions.

To save users from having to write their own CPI-C communication routines, R/3 provides the *Remote Function Call* interface (RFC). RFC contains a separate protocol to execute both internal and external function modules that are managed in the R/3 function library. You can use the parameter *Destination* to execute a function module on any computer in the same R/3 System or on other R/3 or R/2 Systems. RFC supports asynchronous and synchronous communication (see Figure 1.13).

FIGURE 1.13:

Remote Function Call (RFC)

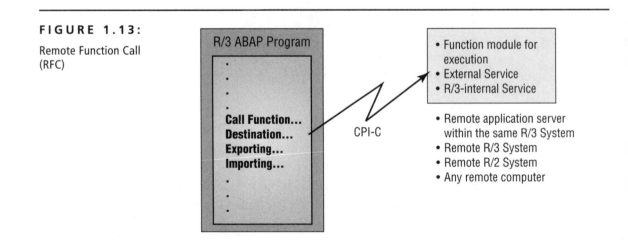

Synchronous communication has the disadvantage that a remote program can only send a call if the partner is active. If the recipient is very slow, there can be delays with the sender. If the recipient is suddenly lost, it may be necessary to perform a recovery on both systems. However, asynchronous communication can ensure transaction consistency. RFC calls are made with the addition *IN BACKGROUND TASK*. If processing in the target system is started manually or if the target computer is temporarily unable to fulfill the requests, data is first placed in queues. The administration mechanism for this is the *Queue-Application Programming Interface* (Q-API).

Above RFC is *Object Linking and Embedding* (OLE). OLE is used to connect PC programs to the R/3 System. OLE commands within ABAP programs are passed as RFCs to the SAPGUI and the relevant PC software. This enables data exchange with programs such as MS Word or MS Excel.

From the administrator's viewpoint, the technical requirements, such as stable network connections, must be met. At the same time, security precautions, such as setting up a firewall, must be taken. In practice, these tasks are normally performed by the technical support service. In large systems, it is advisable to entrust these tasks to a network administrator, who will define and check the necessary R/3 connections.

The Operating System

Now that the structure of the individual layers of the R/3 client/server architecture and the network technology between them has been examined, this section will deal with the embedding of the R/3 System into the operating system. Of particular interest is the interaction between the R/3 kernel and the operating system on the application servers.

The SAPGUI software and its components are installed in the typical way for PCs—once in a directory on the front end or remotely—and then maintained manually or automatically with each new R/3 release. The procedure is described in Chapter 4. In the database layer, the operating system embedding is heavily dependent on the RDBMS and is not universally applicable. As the main task of the R/3 System administrator is the coordination of the R/3 application layers—the R/3 kernel—this section focuses mainly on that area.

Directory Structure

In much the same way as the individual R/3 processes in the instances that make up an R/3 System form a unit, the R/3 directory structure is made up of branches on the connected instances, independently of whether the instances are running on Windows NT or UNIX systems. Figure 1.14 shows the general structure of the directory tree.

<SID> stands for the unique R/3 System name, which is the same as the database name. SIDs always consist of three letters and/or numbers. Below that, the directory tree branches into directories SYS and the directories named after the instances, for example, DVEBMGS00 for a central instance with number 00. For Windows NT, two additional Windows NT shares, *sapmnt* and *saploc*, are stored in the root directory \usr\sap. For UNIX, this is only done for directory /sapmnt using links. Directory SYS is made up of the following directories:

profile	The instance profile
global	Data and logs relevant throughout the entire R/3 System
gui	SAPGUI program packets
exe	Executable programs

FIGURE 1.14:

The directory tree

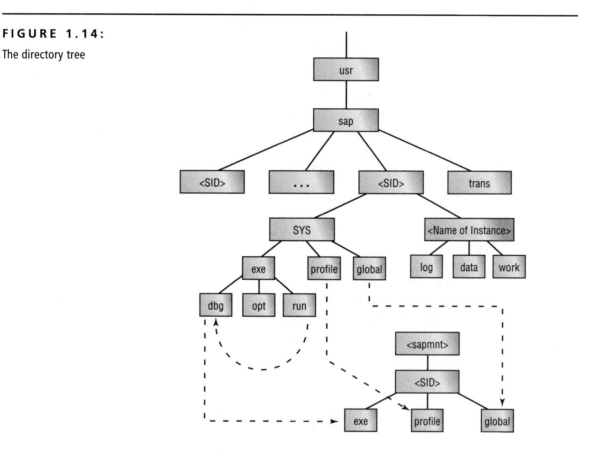

The **exe** directory is divided into the directories **dbg**, **opt**, and run. It contains the R/3 System's executable programs. UNIX systems have the programs optimized for production operation, as well as having executable versions of the programs for debug purposes. When the R/3 System is started, the programs referenced by directory **run** are always executed. This directory is normally mapped by a link to the directory **opt**. To execute the program versions intended for debugging, which are slower, reset the link to directory **dbg** and then restart the R/3 System.

From the logical viewpoint, node /usr/sap/<SID> has a directory for each instance in the R/3 System consisting of the directories log, data, and work. The directory log contains the system log for the R/3 instance. Trace and error information on the R/3 processes in an instance is stored in the directory work. The directory data contains files from the Memory Management of the R/3 processes. Physically, these directories are localized on each application server in an instance. They are visible logically on the central instance using NFS Mount. The directory trees /usr/sap/<SID>/SYS are also linked to the directory tree of the central instance.

Users

On the operating system level, special users are needed for R/3. The environment needed for them—authorizations, settings, and the corresponding database users—is created during R/3 installation.

UNIX

For each R/3 System, the UNIX operating system has the users <sid>adm and <RDBMS><sid>. <sid> stands for the R/3 System name in lowercase letters and <RDBMS> stands for the RDBMS used, for example, *ora* for Oracle and *inf* for Informix. Both users cover substantially different task areas, and therefore also have different authorizations. The operating system user <sid>adm is for R/3 administration purposes in the broadest sense. Administration tasks in the RDBMS are part of the task area of <RDBMS><sid>, but there are overlaps between the users.

In Windows NT systems, all the tasks described are performed with user <sid>adm. The R/3 processes themselves are run as services under user SAPService<SID>.

On the database side, user SAPR3 is available to the R/3 System. All the database tables in the R/3 System belong to this user.

Other database users that may exist do not have authorization to access these tables.

Review Questions

1. Which services does the application layer provide?

   A. Communication service

   B. Dialog service

   C. Spool service

   D. Update service

   E. Message service

   F. Transport service

   G. Gateway service

   H. Network service

   I. Enqueue service

   J. Background service

   K. Change service

2. Which of the following statements is correct?

   A. The Dispatcher and the dialog processes should not run on the same instance.

   B. The Enqueue Server and the Message Server work together closely and should therefore run in one instance.

   C. The background service and the update service work together closely and should therefore never run on different instances.

3. What is the Gateway service for?

   A. Communication between the R/3 processes

   B. Communication between R/3 Systems and instances of an R/3 System

   C. Communication with the operating system spool

   D. Connection of external programs such as MAPI, EDI, and Telex service

   E. Communication with R/3 Systems

4. How many Message Servers are active in an R/3 System?

   A. 0

   B. 1

   C. 2

5. How many update services can be active in each instance?

   A. 1

   B. 2

   C. The number is changed automatically by the R/3 System depending on requirements.

   D. Any number depending on the available resources. The number must be determined in advance by the administrator.

6. Which clients and users are delivered in the standard R/3 System?

   A. Client 000 and users SAP* and DDIC

   B. Client 001 and user MUSTER

   C. Client 001 and users SAP* and DDIC

   D. Client 066 and user SUPPORT

   E. Client 066 and user EARLYWATCH

CHAPTER

TWO

First Steps

This chapter introduces the basic tasks and procedures you'll need to master in order to administer an SAP system. The tools described are fundamental to SAP and are among the equipment used by every SAP system administrator.

Starting the Database and R/3 Instances

An R/3 System is started in several steps. In UNIX or Windows NT, starting the R/3 System is the task of the operating system user, who uses <*sid*>adm. The following steps are performed during the start-up procedure. To collect statistical information on the workload of the computer and its operating system, the procedure starts a special program called saposcol if it is not already active. Then the main work of the R/3 System start-up procedure begins.

The most basic element of the R/3 System is the database, which must be activated before much else can happen. After that is done, the central instance of the R/3 System must be activated. Other instances can only be started when the Message Server and the Enqueue Server are active. The R/3 startup procedure is then complete.

It is only possible for users to work with the R/3 System once the front ends have been started. Front ends can be started separately, at any time, and independently of each other. For this reason, starting the front ends is not part of the R/3 start-up procedure. Except for the front ends, the individual steps of the R/3 start-up procedure are usually performed together automatically.

Windows NT

In this section I'll discuss the steps you take to start the database in Windows NT. If you use Windows NT as a back end, there is a program group SAP R/3 that includes the SAP R/3 Service Manager. When you choose Start from the SAP Service Manager dialog box, the Service Manager first checks whether the RDBMS is already active with the R/3 database. (See Table 1.10 in Chapter 1 to find out which RDBMS to use.) If the R/3 database is not already active, it is started automatically at this point.

NOTE   It is common to refer to an *R/3 database* or just a *database* if you mean the collection of data. To refer to the software that manages the data, you'd say RDBMS. For example, Oracle is an RDBMS. R/3 has a database which you could manage with an RDBMS like Oracle.

The R/3 processes in the central instance are started next by calling the script `sapstart` automatically. A traffic light indicates the status of the two main processes, the Message Server and the Dispatcher. The Dispatcher is the gatekeeper process for all the other work processes. If the Dispatcher is activated, you must wait until the Dispatcher starts the other work processes. Only then is the R/3 System operational.

The traffic light in the *SAP Service Manager* indicates the status of only the Message Server and the Dispatcher (see Figure 2.1). The color of the traffic light indicates the status of the processes as follows:

Gray . . . . Not running

Yellow . . . . Starting

Green . . . . Active

Red . . . . Terminated after error

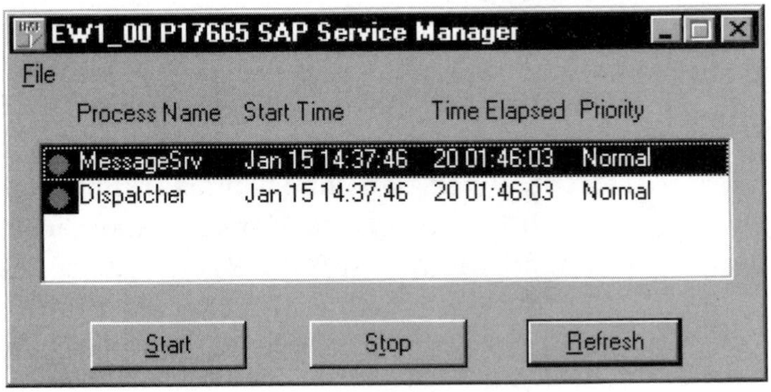

FIGURE 2.1:

SAP Service Manager
for Windows NT
systems

UNIX

In UNIX systems, starting the R/3 System requires an additional step not required in Windows NT systems. The user *<sid>*adm can use the shell script startsap in the home directory of the R/3 administrator *<sid>*adm. The file startsap includes a link to a file called startsap_*<hostname>*_*<instance number>*.

Except for the shell script, the start-up procedure is almost identical to that under Windows NT. Calling startsap starts—in the sequence described at the beginning of this chapter—the collector saposcol, the RDBMS with the R/3 database, and finally the R/3 System if the components are not already active. startsap also offers these options:

    startsap db

which executes the script only up to the start of the database, and

    startsap r3

which assumes that the database is already active.

NOTE   These options are specific to UNIX; they are not available under Windows NT.

Instances

You can start additional instances in a distributed R/3 installation using the same tools we used to start the central instance. Under Windows NT, you use the SAP Service Manager, which in this case only has one traffic light for the Dispatcher. You'll notice that there is no traffic light for the Message Server because there is only one Message Server, which is on the central instance and must already be started in order to add Instances.

In UNIX environments the shell script startsap with option R/3 is also used to start additional instances, but not the Message Server or the RDBMS.

If no R/3 instance is active on the database server, you can activate the database using either RDBMS-specific tools or startsap db as described in your RDBMS-specific literature.

Using Logs

Logs of the start-up procedure are stored in the file system. If problems occur during startup, these logs provide you with valuable information, like the error code or the problem descriptions. In UNIX systems, the logs must be evaluated manually. The home directory of user <*sid*>adm (\users\ <*sid*>adm in Windows NT systems, or /home/<*sid*>adm in UNIX systems, contains the following logs for the start-up procedure:

```
startdb.log
startsap_<computer name>_<instance number>.log
```

You can use the SAP Service Manager to view the start-up logs. Select File ➤ View ➤ Trace, and enter the information in the dialog boxes that appear. In the example that follows, the log comes from the UNIX system QO1 on computer hsi003, and shows the individual start-up phases of the R/3 instance.

Report 2.1:

```
Trace of system startup/check of R/3 System Q01 on Tue Jan 27
22:35:05 MET 1998
Called command: /home/qo1adm/startsap_hsi003_00
Starting SAP-Collector Daemon
-----------------------------
 saposcol already running
Checking SAP R/3 Q01 Database
-----------------------------
Database is not available via /usr/sap/Q01/SYS/exe/run/R3trans -d
-w
Starting SAP R/3 Q01 Database
-----------------------------
  Startup-Log is written to /home/qo1adm/startdb.log
  Database started
Checking SAP R/3 Q01 Database
-----------------------------
  Database is running
Starting SAP R/3 Instance
-----------------------------
SAP-R/3-Startup Program V1.7 (92/10/21)
---------------------------------------
Starting at 1998/01/27 22:35:53
Startup Profile:
/usr/sap/Q01/SYS/profile/START_DVEBMGS00_hsi003
Execute Pre-Startup Commands
----------------------------
(19301) Local: /usr/sap/Q01/SYS/exe/run/sapmscsa -n
pf=/usr/sap/Q01/SYS/profile/Q01_DVEBMGS00_hsi003
/usr/sap/Q01/SYS/exe/run/sapmscsa: SCSA is attached and useable.
/usr/sap/Q01/SYS/exe/run/sapmscsa: finished.
(19301) Local: ln -s -f /usr/sap/Q01/SYS/exe/run/msg_server
 ms.sapQ01_DVEBMGS00
(19301) Local: ln -s -f /usr/sap/Q01/SYS/exe/run/disp+work
dw.sapQ01_DVEBMGS00
(19301) Local: ln -s -f /usr/sap/Q01/SYS/exe/run/rslgcoll
co.sapQ01_DVEBMGS00
```

```
(19301) Local: ln -s -f /usr/sap/Q01/SYS/exe/run/rslgsend
se.sapQ01_DVEBMGS00
Starting Programs
-----------------
(19327) Starting: local ms.sapQ01_DVEBMGS00
pf=/usr/sap/Q01/SYS/profile/Q01_DVEBMGS00_hsi003
(19328) Starting: local dw.sapQ01_DVEBMGS00
pf=/usr/sap/Q01/SYS/profile/Q01_DVEBMGS00_hsi003
(19329) Starting: local co.sapQ01_DVEBMGS00 -F
pf=/usr/sap/Q01/SYS/profile/Q01_DVEBMGS00_hsi003
(19330) Starting: local se.sapQ01_DVEBMGS00 -F
pf=/usr/sap/Q01/SYS/profile/Q01_DVEBMGS00_hsi003
(19301) Waiting for Child Processes to terminate.
Instance on host hsi003 started
```

R/3 Startup Log *startsap_hsi003_00.log*

After the system checks whether the collector saposcol is active (and starts it if necessary), the system checks whether the database system is operational. The preceding log shows that the database was not ready, and was therefore started in the next step. After that, the processes of the R/3 kernel were activated. The log shows that the profile START_DVEBMGS00_hsi003 was used. The configuration of an R/3 instance—for example, the type and number of processes, R/3-specific main memory size, memory management, main memory, and options—are controlled using profiles, as is common for many software products. R/3 has three types of profiles:

```
DEFAULT.PFL
START_<instance><instance number>_<computer name>
<SID>_<instance><instance number>_<computer name>
```

All profiles are stored in the directory \usr\sap\<SID>\SYS\ profile during the R/3 installation. This directory can be read by all instances in an R/3 System using the share or mount method.

DEFAULT.PFL

Only one copy of the profile DEFAULT.PFL exists in the R/3 System, and it contains settings that apply to the entire system. These settings include, for example, the system name, the database computer, and the name of the Enqueue Server. This profile is read first by each R/3 instance in the system when it is started.

Start Profiles of the Instances

Both the other profiles (START_<*instance*><*instance number*>_<*computer name*> and <*SID*>_<*instance*><*instance number*>_<*computer name*>) are instance-specific. The name of an instance is determined by its active processes (see Chapter 1).

Let's look at the profile START_DVEBMGS00_hsi003. The first segment of the expression, START, tells you that the following segment is the start profile of the instance. The underscore separates the type of profile from the name of the profile. Next, the DVEBMGS represents the services of the instance and the name of the instance. It is a central instance because it includes the message service. The digits, 00, are the last two numbers of the port number of the Dispatcher's TCP/IP port. The next underscore separates the name of the instance from the name of the computer, hsi003, on which it runs. (For more on the naming conventions, see Chapter 1).

The profile determines how, where, and under what name the individual R/3 services or processes are started. For example, the profile excerpt that follows starts the Message Server in the instance DVEBMGS00_hsi003.

```
#------------------------------------------------
# start message server
#------------------------------------------------
_MS             =ms.sapQ01_DVEBMGS00
Execute_01      =local ln -s -f $(DIR_EXECUTABLE)/msg_server $(_MS)
Start_Program_01=local $(_MS)
   pf=$(DIR_PROFILE)/Q01_DVEBMGS00_hsi003
#------------------------------------------------
```

Instance Profiles

The instance profile defines the parameters and options for an instance and has the following naming conventions:

$$<SID>\_<instance><instance\ number>\_<computer\ name>$$

In this example, we'll use the profile Q01_DVEBMGS00_hsi003. This profile determines how many work processes of a particular type are started. In the excerpt below, we'll look at four dialog processes (parameter rdisp/wp_no_dia=4). An important part of this instance profile is the definition of the size of the main memory areas of the R/3 System. The profile also contains settings such as logon parameters and log sizes.

Report 2.2:

```
SAPSYSTEMNAME           =Q01
INSTANCE_NAME           =DVEBMGS00
SAPSYSTEM               =00
rdisp/wp_no_dia=4
rdisp/wp_no_vb=1
rdisp/wp_no_vb2=0
rdisp/wp_no_enq=1
rdisp/wp_no_btc=1
rdisp/wp_no_spo=1
#.********************************************************
#.*       Instance Profile                              *
#.*                                                     *
#.*       Version                  = 000000             *
#.*       changed at               = Installation       *
#.*                                                     *
#.*       Generated for usage of 0192 MB memory         *
#.*       and average number of  0010 active users      *
#.********************************************************
em/initial_size_MB=200
rdisp/PG_SHM=0
rdisp/ROLL_SHM=0
rdisp/ROLL_MAXFS=16384
rdisp/PG_MAXFS=16384
```

```
abap/buffersize=49000
#---------- Shared Memory (Key=14) ---------
zcsa/presentation_buffer_area=6600000
sap/bufdir_entries=6600
#---------- Shared Memory (Key=19) ---------
zcsa/table_buffer_area=12000000
zcsa/db_max_buftab=2000
#---------- Shared Memory (Key=31) ---------
rdisp/elem_per_queue=2000
rdisp/wp_ca_blk_no=1000
#---------- Shared Memory (Key=33) ---------
rtbb/buffer_length=10000
rtbb/max_tables=200
#---------- Shared Memory (Key=34) ---------
enque/table_size=500
```

When an R/3 System is installed, the required profiles are created using default values, based on the user's specifications. When the system is first up and running, it is frequently necessary to change settings manually. Chapter 14 describes in greater detail how this is done and which parameters are available. In this chapter, we will assume that the profiles are available when we start the R/3 database and the R/3 instance.

Stopping the Database and R/3 Instances

An R/3 System is stopped in the reverse order from how it was started. In a Windows system, you choose the appropriate function (Start or Stop) from the SAP Service Manager's menu. In a UNIX system, you use the shell script stopsap with parameter r3 as follows:

```
stopsap r3
```

Here, only the R/3 instance would be stopped while the database system remains active. The shutdown procedure is logged in the same way as the start-up procedure. UNIX systems use the files `stopdb.log` and `stopsap_<computer name>_<instance number>.log` in the home directory of user `<sid>adm`.

At this stage, we will assume that the central instance of the R/3 System is active.

Starting the Front End

When the software for the presentation layer is installed, data on possible target R/3 Systems is requested, and icons are created to access them. The SAPGUI call concealed behind the icons is structured like this:

```
sapgui /H/<computer name>/S/sapdp<instance number>
```

For a front end to be able to establish a connection to an R/3 instance, the computer name and the instance number must be sent to the R/3 instance. You could create an icon in Windows NT for each SAPGUI call to each available R/3 instance of possible R/3 Systems. Because a large number of similar icons quickly becomes difficult to work with, it is more efficient to use the program SAPLOGON. SAPLOGON allows you to create all possible connections and to choose their names. If there were, say, 400 possible connections, you could just name them all sequentially and have them waiting for use, even if only 14 will be active in the near future. Typically, there are about three R/3 Systems in a landscape. After creating an icon, you choose the appropriate connection from the list of names, and a corresponding SAPGUI call is generated. The connection data is saved in the following files:

- `saplogon.ini`
- `sapmsg.ini`
- `saproute.ini`

These configuration files can be transferred to other front-end computers. This considerably reduces the work needed, compared to entering the connection data manually. Naming all the possible connections in advance saves you the effort of creating a new icon for each possible connection. You'll find this pre-naming system even more convenient when you're working with load distribution over all instances of an R/3 System simultaneously. And when you're looking at load distribution, you'll find that this way of naming and saving the file information will also make maintenance easier because you can identify all the connections quickly. For this purpose, the Message Servers of an available R/3 System are stored in the file `sapmsg.ini` as follows:

```
<SID>=<computer name of the Message Server>
```

The TCP/IP port for communication between the front end and the message server is saved in the services file (in UNIX: `/etc/services`). The Message Server has all the information on the instances in an R/3 System. The administrator can set up sub-groups of instances, for example, for specific areas such as Materials Management or Financial Accounting. SAPLOGON users then select the instance groups relevant to their requirements. Based on the available statistical information, the Message Server selects the instance with the lowest load from this instance group. A SAPGUI is started for this instance at the requester's computer. The logon load is distributed based on logon groups. The definition procedure for creating logon groups is described in detail in Chapter 14.

In this chapter, we will assume that logon groups have already been defined. If the system is new, all the available instances make up the logon group `Space`. When you select this group, a SAPGUI is automatically started for one of the instances.

The most convenient R/3 presentation-level tool to use is the SAP Session Manager because it uses the same files and data as the SAPLOGON program. You can add a new R/3 System by selecting New from the menu of the SAP Session Manager. Figure 2.2 shows this for the example system QO1 on computer hsi003, instance number 00. You could also call a SAPGUI directly using the following command:

```
sapgui /H/hsi003/S/sapdp00
```

Performing General Administration Tasks

All administration tasks can be performed within the R/3 System when the central R/3 instance and a front end are started. The user decides which front end to use when logging onto the R/3 System. Before getting into the details, you should be aware of some fundamental functions in R/3.

Checking the Status

From anywhere in R/3, you can display the most important status information by choosing System ➤ Status. In addition to information on the R/3 System, such as release number, installation number, and validity of the license, you'll see the name of the database server and the RDBMS used, the current user name and the transaction code, and the program of the currently active transaction (see Figure 2.3).

FIGURE 2.3:

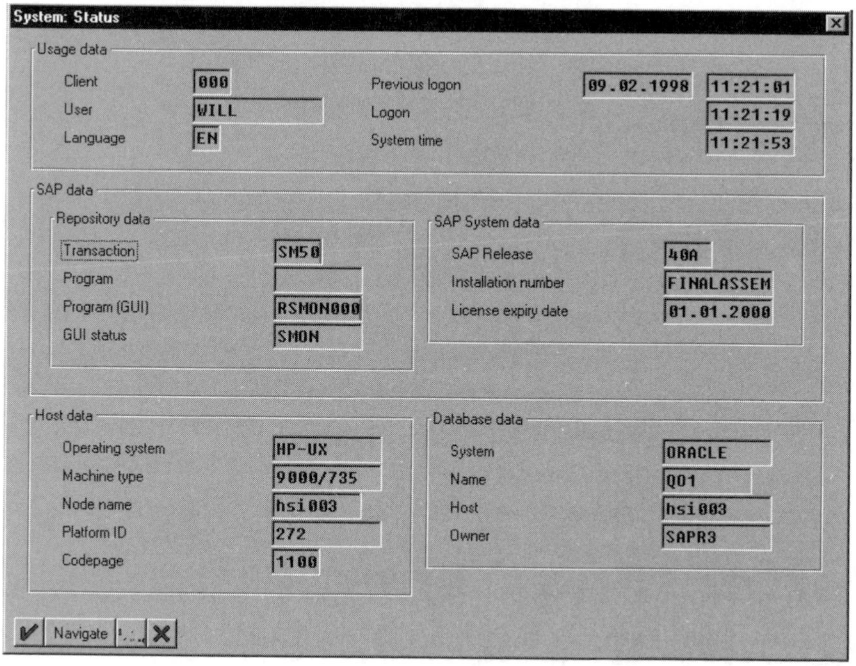

The Status dialog box provides a lot of information.

Monitoring the System

System monitoring is one of the most important tasks performed by a system administrator. Many monitors are available for this purpose and will be described throughout the book. You can display an overview of the instances and processes active in the application layer. Choose Tools ➤ Administration ➤ Monitoring ➤ System ➤ Monitoring ➤ Servers or use transaction code SM51 to display a list of the active instances and their services (see Figure 2.4). Chapter 1 introduces how and where to enter transaction codes.

FIGURE 2.4:

Displaying the active instances

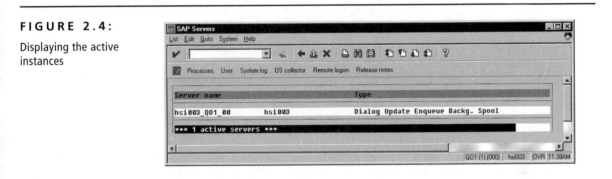

By choosing **Processes** or **User** for a selected instance, you display an overview of the active work processes or users for that instance. Important information on the status of the work process is also provided. The process overview (Transaction code SM50) in Figure 2.5 shows that four dialog processes (DIA), one update process (UPD), the Enqueue process (ENQ), one background process (BTC), and one spool process (SPO) are active on the selected instance. This instance is the central instance.

NOTE   For more details on the central instance and how to identify it, refer to Chapter 1.

You can see in Figure 2.5 that dialog processes 0 and 2 are busy executing reports for user WILL. The administrator can use the process overview to estimate the current activities and the resulting load on an instance. The process overview is a key part of system monitoring. The system administrator can display a wide variety of information (described in detail in Chapter 15), and if necessary, cancel work processes by selecting Process ➤ Cancel with Core or without Core. (Every operating system has a core.)

Canceling a work process does not seriously affect the functioning of the instance. Open transactions get rolled back when a work process is canceled, and the instance's Dispatcher recognizes the cancellation and immediately attempts to start a new work process of the same type. The user overview (Transaction code SM04) offers similar functions, but the display is user-oriented. These functions are explained in more detail in Chapter 15.

Displaying a Process Overview with Operating System Tools

On the operating system level, the administrator can use a tool similar to the operating system user, `<sid>adm`.

```
dpmon pf=<instance profile>
```

displays a character-based process overview for an instance, as shown below. The initial screen displays a brief statistical summary of the I/O load, as shown in this example.

Report 2.3:

```
dpmon pf=Q01_DVEBMGS00_hsi003
Dispatcher Queue Statistics
==============================
Type      Now    High   Max    Write   Read
NOW       0      6      2000   2663    2663
DIA       0      4      2000   961     961
UPD       0      3      2000   2       2
ENQ       0      0      2000   0       0
BTC       0      0      2000   0       0
SPO       0      2      2000   349     348
UP2       0      0      5      0       0


    q - quit
    m - menu
```

In UNIX environments, this display is updated at short intervals; in Windows NT environments, the display must be obtained manually. You can use *m* to choose from the monitors in the following example.

Report 2.4:

```
Dispatcher Monitor Menu
-----------------------
d - dispatcher queue statistics
p - work process admin table
l - work process admin table (long)
t - trace level/components for wp
w - wp_ca blocks
a - appc_ca blocks
q - quit
```

NOTE   **dpmon** with option I is essentially the same as the process overview within the R/3 System.

The listing that follows is from a UNIX system. At the time of the snapshot, only dialog processes 0, 1, and 2 were active. On this level, a work process can only be canceled using operating system tools.

Report 2.5:

```
Work Process Table
NoTyPid Status Cause Start Err Sem CPU Time Program Cl User
-----------------------------------------------------
0 DIA 9972 Run        yes       17       SDB1FORA 000 WILL
1 DIA 9973 Run        yes        3       SAPMSSY0 000 DDIC
2 DIA 9974 Run        yes        1       SAPMSSY6 000 SAPSYS
3 DIA 9975 Wait       yes
4 UPD 9976 Wait       yes
5 ENQ 9977 Wait       yes
6 BTC 9978 Wait       yes
7 SPO 9979 Wait       yes

   q - quit
   m - menu
```

Obtaining Information with Other Operating System Tools

You can use other operating system tools to obtain information about R/3 processes. In Windows NT systems, the *Task manager* is the main tool to use. You can also use the program pmon to display a process overview; it is essentially the same as the command ps used in UNIX environments. However, the information provided by these tools will not be as comprehensive and specific as the information provided by the R/3 System, because the R/3 System contains additional information about its own processes.

The listing that follows was created in a UNIX environment on a central instance using the Oracle RDBMS command `ps -efa`. To make it clearer, the overview was manually sorted and restricted to the R/3 processes and Oracle processes. The first process in the overview is the program `saposcol`. The next process, `sapstart`, is activated when the shell script `startsap` is executed, and it starts the individual R/3 processes. In other words, sapstart is the script that startsap calls to start the R/3 processes.

A process that collects and writes the central system log of an R/3 System is started using `co.sap<SID>_<instance>`. The counterpart process is `se.sap<SID>_<instance>`, which transmits the information to the system log. (For more on the counterpart process, see Chapter 1.) These processes are activated directly by the start script, which is indicated by the same process number (column PID) of the program `sapstart` and the parent process number (column PPID) of the other processes. The Message Service is indicated by `ms`. All work processes in an instance are listed under `dw`. This stands for `disp+work`, which means Dispatcher and work processes.

The parent process number of the Dispatcher is the same as the process number of the start script, as only the Dispatcher is activated directly by the start script. All the other work processes are started by the Dispatcher. Therefore, their parent process number is the same as the process number of the Dispatcher. In the listing that follows, Message Server and Dispatcher are printed in bold type so they are easy to identify.

```
UID     PID    PPID   C    COMMAND
qo1adm  29278  1           saposcol
qo1adm  9941   1      0    /usr/sap/Q01/SYS/exe/run/sapstart
            pf=/usr/sap/Q01/SYS/profile/Q01_DVEBMGS00_hsi003
qo1adm  9969 9941   0    co.sapQ01_DVEBMGS00 -F
            pf=/usr/sap/Q01/SYS/profile/Q01_DVEBMGS00_hsi003
```

```
qo1adm   9970   9941   0 se.sapQ01_DVEBMGS00 -F
                pf=/usr/sap/Q01/SYS/profile/Q01_DVEBMGS00_hsi003
qo1adm   9967   9941   0 ms.sapQ01_DVEBMGS00
                pf=/usr/sap/Q01/SYS/profile/Q01_DVEBMGS00_hsi003
qo1adm   9968   9941   0 dw.sapQ01_DVEBMGS00
                pf=/usr/sap/Q01/SYS/profile/Q01_DVEBMGS00_hsi003
qo1adm   9974   9968   0 dw.sapQ01_DVEBMGS00
                pf=/usr/sap/Q01/SYS/profile/Q01_DVEBMGS00_hsi003
qo1adm   9976   9968   0 dw.sapQ01_DVEBMGS00
                pf=/usr/sap/Q01/SYS/profile/Q01_DVEBMGS00_hsi003
qo1adm   9977   9968   0 dw.sapQ01_DVEBMGS00
                pf=/usr/sap/Q01/SYS/profile/Q01_DVEBMGS00_hsi003
qo1adm   9973   9968   0 dw.sapQ01_DVEBMGS00
                pf=/usr/sap/Q01/SYS/profile/Q01_DVEBMGS00_hsi003
qo1adm   9975   9968   0 dw.sapQ01_DVEBMGS00
                pf=/usr/sap/Q01/SYS/profile/Q01_DVEBMGS00_hsi003
qo1adm   9971   9968   0 gwrd -dp
                pf=/usr/sap/Q01/SYS/profile/Q01_DVEBMGS00_hsi003
qo1adm   9978   9968   0 dw.sapQ01_DVEBMGS00
                pf=/usr/sap/Q01/SYS/profile/Q01_DVEBMGS00_hsi003
qo1adm   9972   9968   0 dw.sapQ01_DVEBMGS00
                pf=/usr/sap/Q01/SYS/profile/Q01_DVEBMGS00_hsi003
qo1adm   9979   9968   0 dw.sapQ01_DVEBMGS00
                pf=/usr/sap/Q01/SYS/profile/Q01_DVEBMGS00_hsi003
qo1adm   9890      1   0 ora_reco_Q01
qo1adm   9875      1   0 ora_pmon_Q01
qo1adm   9884      1   0 ora_lgwr_Q01
qo1adm   9880      1   0 ora_dbwr_Q01
qo1adm   9888      1   0 ora_smon_Q01
qo1adm   9882      1   0 ora_arch_Q01
qo1adm   9886      1   0 ora_ckpt_Q01
```

The Gateway process is indicated by `gwrd`. This process is also started by the Dispatcher. (See Chapter 1 for more about the Dispatcher.) The IDs of the processes, as they appear on operating system level, are given by the operating system during the start process of the instance. You cannot determine further details, such as the current task of a process within R/3. This can only be done using R/3 tools.

Checking the System Log

All the important events that happen during system operation are recorded in the system log of an R/3 System or in an instance. Checking the system log is therefore one of the tasks of the system administrator. To obtain information about messages in the system log select Tools ➤ Administration ➤ Monitoring ➤ System Log or use Transaction code SM22 in the R/3 System, as described in Chapter 1. If there is an error situation in the R/3 System, start a detailed analysis of the system by consulting the system log.

NOTE   Chapter 15 provides a detailed description of how to use the system log.

Sending System Messages

It is useful for the system administrator to be able to send messages to all R/3 users or to only selected users. For example, communication is essential when imminent maintenance work will impede system operation. To send a message, choose Tools ➤ Administration ➤ Administration ➤ System Messages ➤ Create. You will see the screen labeled Create System Messages.

NOTE   You don't have to be a system administrator to send a message; anyone can do so.

You can send a message to all the users in a particular instance or to all the users in the R/3 System. You can also restrict the time that a message is valid, so that users only receive the message if they are working in the system during a particular period or in a particular instance. When the user starts the next dialog step, the message appears in a separate window. It is useful to send a system message if, for example, a particular instance has to be shut down. It is always advisable to give users advance notice.

NOTE   In this chapter, I present the information you'll need to understand system messages. At this point, it is essential to know where the system log is found. On the other hand, due to the nature of the R/3 System, you need more detailed information about R/3 and its structure to understand the information. I'll cover those details in the chapters that follow.

Using Lists

All displays that do not require any interactive input from users are referred to as *lists*. Lists can be printed by the R/3 System to local files on the presentation computer or sent to other R/3 users. You can access the functions needed by choosing System ➤ List. You can also enter commands in the command field. *%sc* lets you search for character strings and position the cursor in the list. *%pc* lets you save a list to a local file on the front end.

In the area of system administration, lists are used for working with such things as statistics, logs, and evaluations. System administrators frequently have to analyze lists, so it is important to be familiar with them.

Using Table Maintenance Tools

Many R/3 administration tables can—and sometimes must—be modified using the table maintenance tools integrated into R/3. For example, the TSTC table that every R/3 System has contains all the transaction codes available in the R/3 System. To create new transaction codes in R/3, a developer or system administrator must include those new transaction codes in the TSTC table. This is an example of a task where table maintenance tools are used. R/3 provides three such tools that are accessed in the following ways:

- From the ABAP Workbench (Tools ➤ ABAP Workbench), choose Overview ➤ Data Browser, or use Transaction code SE16.

- From any R/3 window, access the standard table maintenance tool by choosing System ➤ Services ➤ Table Maintenance. Alternatively, use Transaction code SM31.

- To access the extended table maintenance tool, choose System ➤ Services ➤ Extended Table Maintenance, or use Transaction code SM30.

In future R/3 releases, the standard table maintenance tool will be replaced fully by the extended table maintenance tool. Extended and standard table maintenance tools can be used on a table if an appropriate interface has been generated for it. (For more on this interface, see the ABAP/4 Development Workbench documentation.) The appearance of the table maintenance tool depends on the interface created for each table. By default, a table maintenance interface is provided for all tables delivered by SAP that may need to be modified, including Table TSTC. The first step in maintaining this table is always to enter the Transaction code. The corresponding ABAP program and the initial screen are maintained for each Transaction code (see Figure 2.6) using the Display Dialog Transaction screen. You call up the screen in Figure 2.6 by following these steps:

1. Choose System ➤ Services ➤ Table Maintenance.

2. Select the table named TSTC.

3. Choose Maintain.

4. Select the transaction code SM31 and choose Display.

The table maintenance tool in the ABAP Workbench is independent of the table contents and the meaning of the table. The maintenance tool is primarily used to display the table contents.

FIGURE 2.6:

Table maintenance (Transaction code SM31) using the Display Dialog Transaction dialog box

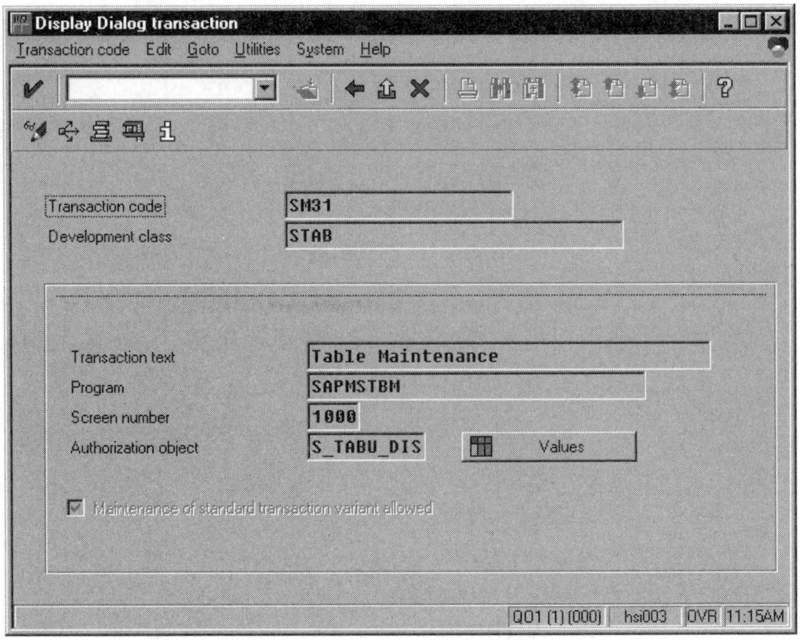

You can record changes made to table contents with R/3 tools. You must activate this option in the Dictionary of the R/3 System for each table. For more details, please refer to ABAP/4 Development Workbench documentation.

Review Questions

1. Which tools can you use in the operating system to start your R/3 System?

   A. Task Manager

   B. SAP Service Manager

   C. start SAP

   D. startsap

2. Which tools can you use to stop the R/3 System (depending on the operating system)?

    A. Task Manager

    B. SAP Service Manager

    C. kill

    D. `stopsap`

3. Which profiles are used for the configuration of R/3?

    A. R/3 Profile

    B. Instance profile

    C. Application server profile

    D. `DEFAULT.PFL`

    E. Start profile

    G. Stop profile

4. In which logs does R/3 document the system start?

    A. `startdb.log`

    B. `startsap_<computer name>_<instance number>.log`

    C. `startsap.log`

    D. `r3start.prot`

5. How could an SAPGUI to R/3 System QO1 instance 00 on computer P311 be started?

    A. `sapgui -p3111/00`

    B. `sapgui /H/QO1/I/3200`

    C. `sapgui /H/P311/S/sapdp00`

CHAPTER
THREE

The Online Service System

The support service that SAP provides for its customers has as its base the *Online Service System (OSS)*. All SAP customers and their R/3 and R/2 Systems are registered in this R/3 System, which is physically located at SAP in Germany. The OSS supports customers by providing extensive services including:

- Providing Notes, information, and solutions for problems.

- Processing information about errors reported by customers and finding solutions to them.

- Making available *Hot Packages.* (This is the term SAP uses for corrections to the R/3 System.)

Customers can also use special functions that are integrated into the OSS that allow SAP employees time-limited remote access to the customer's R/3 System to help resolve a problem. Since R/3 release 3.0, all SAP customers need a network connection to the OSS. This chapter shows how the OSS access is set up and how the OSS can be used as a central information pool.

Security Issues

There are obvious security risks involved in establishing connections from a local network to external systems. Access to the local network and its computers should only be permitted to authorized persons. Normally, firewalls are used to secure access. For communication between remote R/3 Systems, there is a special program called *saprouter*.

You can use saprouter to control and log all inbound and outbound connections to your local R/3 Systems. Saprouter runs on one computer, which is connected to the WAN. All the other computers, in particular the R/3 application server and the database server, do not need separate access; they just connect to the computer that is running `saprouter`. That single computer running `saprouter` represents the local network's interface to external systems and can be regarded as a special firewall extension for R/3 Systems. The administration effort is concentrated in one location.

The SAProuter Connection

The computer on which the `saprouter` program runs must be accessible through an official IP address. The term *SAProuter* is frequently used to refer to the computer on which the program is running, although the `saprouter` program is usually only one of the multiple functions of this computer. An analysis of costs and benefits will determine which type of connection from the local network to remote systems you will choose for your R/3 System. Possible choices are commonly used connections such as those based on X.25, ISDN, and Frame Relay. You should consider that this connection is not used solely for brief connections for support from SAP, but also to transmit data such as software corrections, Notes (hints on how to prevent or solve a problem in R/3), and documentation.

The connection to customer sites is organized at SAP in a manner similar to the one used by the customer. SAP's firewall and the `saprouter` program are run on permanently dedicated computers. Every customer intending to establish a connection to the OSS system must first register their R/3 System with SAP.

To register an R/3 System, you need to send SAP information on the IP addresses of your R/3 computers and the computer with the SAProuter, as well as a list of the people who will need access to OSS. SAP stores the customer IP addresses and information about who is permitted access to the OSS. SAP notifies the customer which SAProuter and which IP address to use at SAP. The currently available SAProuters are shown in Table 3.1.

TABLE 3.1: Available SAProuters Maintained by SAP

Computer	Location
sapserv3	Walldorf (Germany)
sapserv4	Foster City (San Francisco, USA)
sapserv5	Tokyo (Japan)
sapserv6	Sydney (Australia)
sapserv7	Singapore (Singapore)

The number of SAProuters at SAP is frequently increased due to the continued growth in the number of R/3 installations. Figure 3.1 shows how a connection is established between a customer system and SAP.

FIGURE 3.1:

Using SAProuters

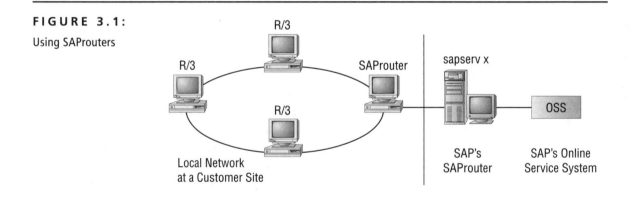

To use a SAProuter, you need to be able to establish a physical connection between the SAProuter at the customer's site and the SAProuter at SAP, sapserv<x>. You should first check this using the operating system command ping as follows: ping <IP address>.

Saprouter and *Saprouttab*

The `saprouter` program is available for every R/3 installation (for both Windows NT and UNIX systems) in the directory `\usr\sap\<SID>\exe\run`. From this directory, you can copy the program to the directory `\usr\sap\saprouter` on the computer you choose. It is recommended that you do this. The `saprouter` program bases its access control on a `routing table`, which by default is called `saprouttab` and is normally in the same directory as the `saprouter` program. The table `saprouttab` is defined in accordance with specific rules. Entries in table `saprouttab` must take the following form:

```
[P|D] <IP address of the external system> <local system>
[<password>]
```

where

D stands for *deny* access

P stands for *permit* access

```
D     194.3.*.*     host1
```

which denies all computers from network 194.3.*.* access to the local computer `host1`. It is only necessary to grant access to someone if they need to log on to the customer R/3 System. After their need is met, you would deny access. In another case, if there were a user who needed permanent access to your system, you would make a permanent entry in the `saprouttab`.

Access to the local computer can also be protected by a password. The following example would permit access to the R/3 System on `host2` with the password "Hans":

```
P     195.7.8.102    host2   Hans
```

If you make multiple entries in the routing table for a connection, the first matching entry is used. You can use multiple routing tables and start the `saprouter` program when it is needed for access. To start and stop the `saprouter` program use the following commands on the operating system level:

    saprouter -r

starts saprouter

    saprouter -s

stops saprouter.

Table 3.2 shows the main `saprouter` options.

TABLE 3.2: Options for the Program `saprouter`

Option	Meaning
-r	Start `saprouter` using the default routing table `saprouttab` in the `start` directory
-n	For a running `saprouter` program, re-read and activate the routing table
-l	List the currently active connections through SAProuter
-t	Write a log file, by default to file `dev_root`.
-T *<file>*	Write a log to file `<file>`. Use option -T to change the name of the log file
-R <saprouttab>	Assign a routing table other than the default table
-c *<id>*	Cancel a specific connection with ID `<id>`. You must first determine the ID using option -l.

Establishing a Connection

Before you can use the connection from a local R/3 System to the OSS, you must configure the technical settings. Choose System ➤ Services ➤ SAP Service ➤ Parameter ➤ Techn. Settings ➤ Change, or use Transaction code OSS1. First configure the settings for the SAProuter recommended by SAP. Choose SAP ➤ Router at SAP from the menu.

You must enter the data for your local SAProuter. Two SAProuters can be implemented in succession, in which case information about both SAProuters must be entered when connecting your R/3 System to the OSS. A SAPGUI is used to work with the OSS. Enter the location of this program on the front end in the lower part of the screen (see Figure 3.2).

FIGURE 3.2:

Entering the technical settings

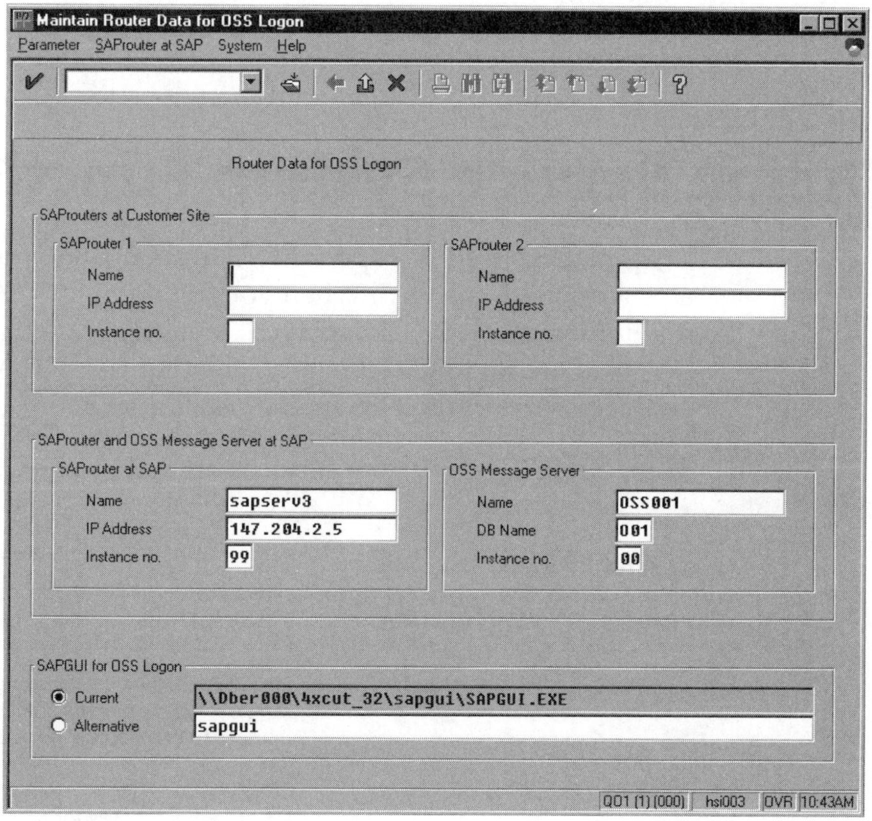

When you have saved your settings, you can establish a connection to the OSS by choosing Log On to the Online Service System from the OSS menu. The connection to the local SAProuter is then opened internally and a SAPGUI to the OSS is started. The SAPGUI call looks like this:

```
Sapgui /H/<local saprouter>[/H/<2nd local saprouter>]/H/<Router
at SAP>/H/<OSS>/S/<instance number of OSS>
```

The easiest way to establish the connection using `saprouter` is to add an entry like this:

```
P <saprouter at SAP> <local system>
```

and then manually call a SAPGUI to the OSS.

Online Service System Functions

The OSS itself is a special R/3 System, and you use SAPGUI to work with the OSS. When you log on to the OSS, a list of the most important news is displayed. Messages that have already been read are highlighted in a contrasting color. The next step is to access the initial OSS menu (see Figure 3.3).

Table 3.3 shows the services offered by the OSS.

TABLE 3.3: OSS Services

Area	Function	What It Does
SAP OSS	Registration	SSCR (SAP Software Change Registration) Registers R/3 developers and assigns an object key for changes to original SAP objects (see Chapter 6). CD Assigns an access key for SAP products that require registration on the CD, such as Knowledge Products.

TABLE 3.3: OSS Services *(Continued)*

Area	Function	What It Does
	Message	Is used to enter and track customer error messages. Messages are automatically forwarded to the SAP Service, processed, and replied to with a suggested solution.
	Administration	Maintains OSS users.
	Service	Opens connections for SAP support to the local R/3 System for a customer number. Is used to download R/3 software corrections (Hot Packages).
General Functions	Notes	Notes administration for release-specific problems, new features, installations, upgrades, migrations from R/2 to R/3, etc., with extensive search functions.
	General Functions	Provides an overview of training courses offered by SAP and offers course registration. Provides order documentation.
Company Messages	Messages	Enters and processes problem messages within your company group.

Working with the OSS is relatively easy and is described in detail in the user manual. For this reason, this section only covers the most important aspects of working with OSS.

Messages

You can use the OSS to enter information about problems that occur in your R/3 Systems and send them to the SAP Hotline (select Messages ➤ Create). The problem messages are processed by SAP. Solutions are also sent to you using the OSS. In fact, all customer messages are administered by the OSS. Each new message is assigned a unique number. You can use this number to find and display messages—even processed messages.

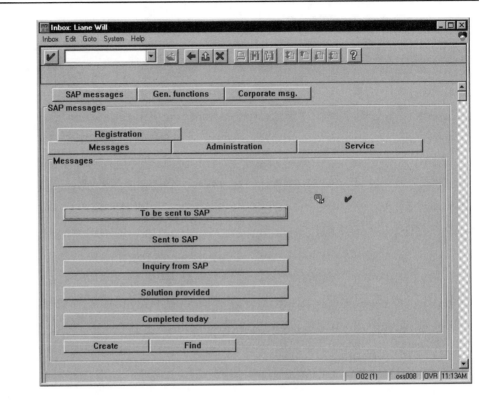

Data on the originator of the message and general data on the R/3 installation are of importance to SAP. For example, the particular R/3 release may be an important indication of the cause of a problem. SAP can also check whether similar problems have occurred in other customer systems with the same R/3 release and find out what solutions were applied. When a message is created, the tracking data is automatically taken from the customer data stored in the OSS.

You must also enter your R/3 release number and the purpose for which the system is being used (Test, Production) when you send your problem message to SAP. You can provide more precise details about the problem area by assigning a component. And the priority assigned should reflect the urgency of the problem.

The highest priority should only be used for a production system brought to a standstill.

A status indicator is assigned to each message depending on the stage of processing. For example, when you create a new message, it is automatically given the status *To be sent to SAP*. You must send the message to SAP so that SAP can process it. When you send the message, its status is automatically changed to *Sent to SAP*. If SAP needs any additional information, the message status is changed to *Query from SAP*. When SAP finds a solution, the message status is changed to *Solution proposed by SAP*. The message is closed only when you accept it, and then the status is changed to *Completed today*. An overview screen lets you track message processing.

Figure 3.4 shows the screen for entering a message.

FIGURE 3.4:

Creating a message

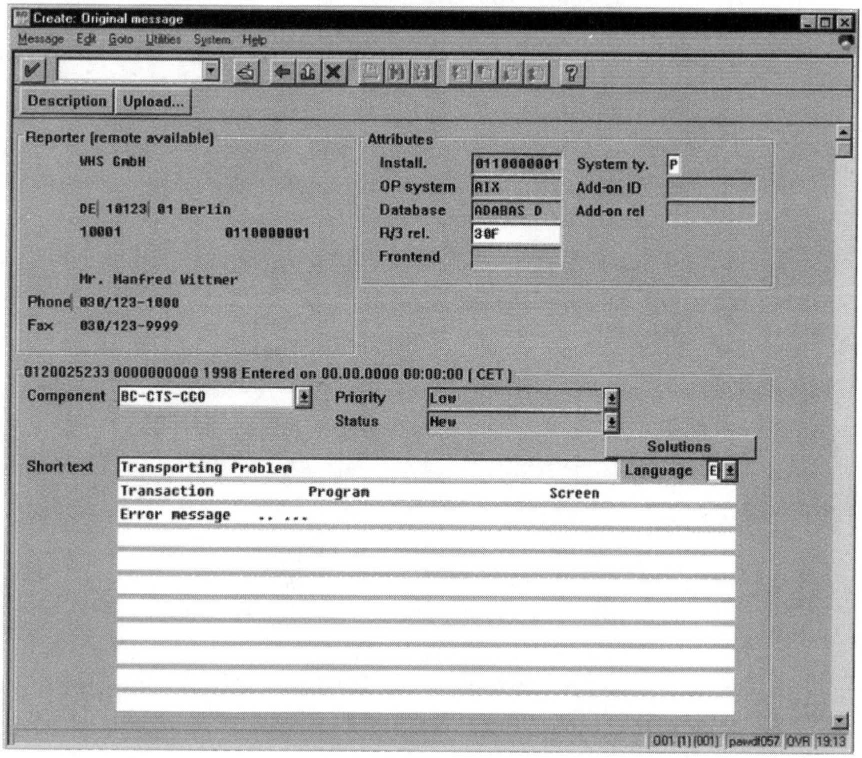

Service Connections

To process a problem, SAP often needs to perform a detailed analysis of your R/3 System. For service engineers from SAP and partner companies to be able to log on to your system, you must explicitly open a connection to your system from the OSS. This means that you temporarily activate the corresponding SAProuter entries. The R/3 System data must be maintained correctly for this to work. Figure 3.5 shows how general data is entered for a customer who can be reached by choosing SAP OSS ➤ Service ➤ Service Connection ➤ Create System, or Choose System ➤ Change.

FIGURE 3.5:

Maintaining connection data

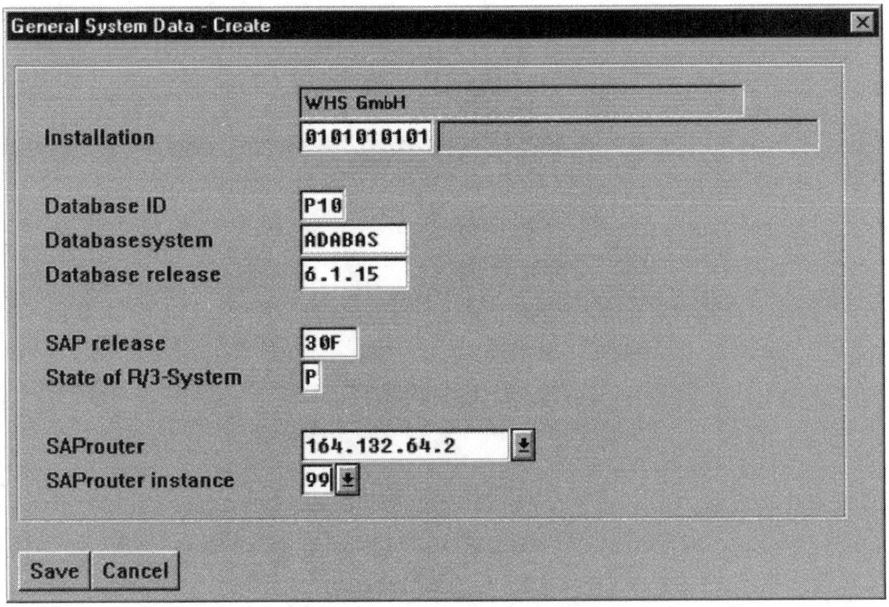

You can open a connection entered in this way for a specified time by choosing SAP OSS ➤ Service ➤ Service Connection ➤ Choose System ➤ Edit ➤ Open. An overview of the status of the connections for an R/3 System is then displayed (see Figure 3.6).

FIGURE 3.6:

Overview of service
connections

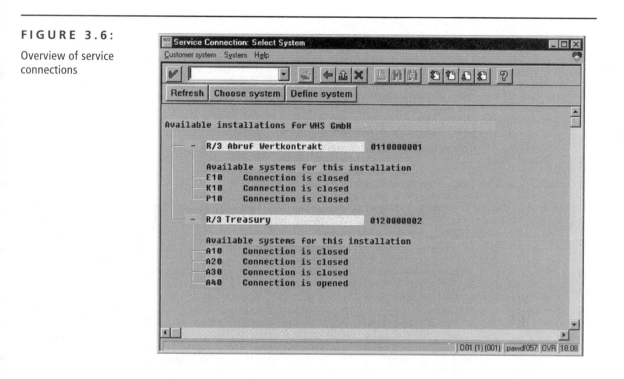

To obtain more detailed information on a connection, choose
Create/Open from the Service Connection: System Maintenance
screen (see Figure 3.7).

Notes

The Notes area of SAP's OSS offers SAP customers access to all
the known problems, their solutions, and information about how
to prevent them, as well as about the handling of individual components of R/3. Each Note has a unique number. The validity of
each Note is defined by the relevant R/3 releases, operating system environments, and RDBMS versions.

Customers can also use the functions in the OSS to search for
information on specific problems. A solution to the problem in

question will frequently already be there. It is advisable to search the OSS at fairly regular intervals for important new information, in particular when you are using a new R/3 release. In that way, you can often prevent initial errors.

The OSS is the most important source of information and assistance for SAP customers. You should therefore ensure that you have a permanent and reliable connection to the OSS.

FIGURE 3.7:

Information on a connection

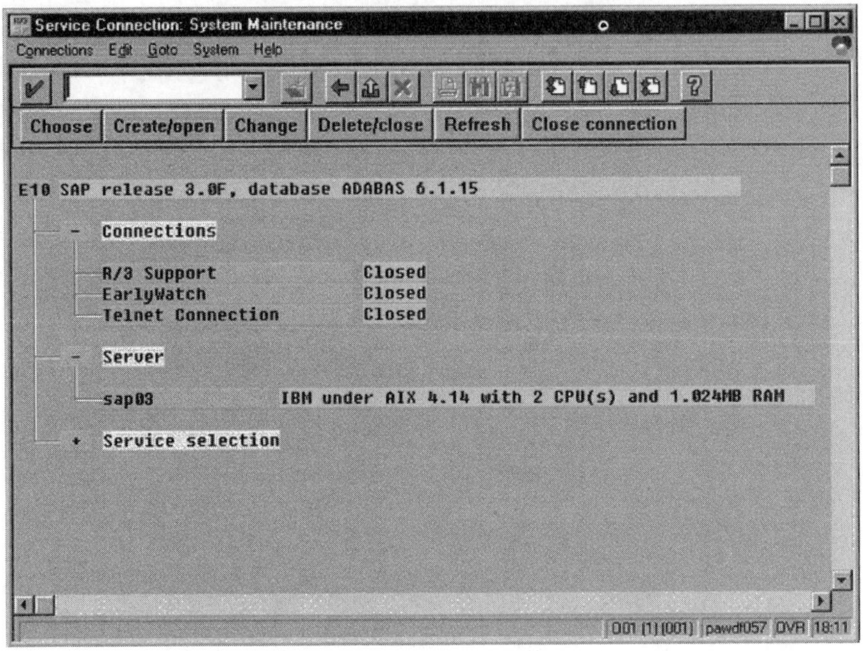

Review Questions

1. What is `saprouter` used for?

   A. It replaces a firewall.

   B. It is used to control the establishment of remote connections to application servers in an R/3 System.

   C. It is used to establish connections between front ends and the application servers in an R/3 System in the local network.

2. In what file do you normally maintain the SAProuter routing data?

   A. `saprouttab`

   B. `DEFAULT.PFL`

   C. `autoexec.bat`

3. What requirements must be met in order to establish a service connection from SAP to a customer's R/3 System?

   A. The R/3 System must be registered in the OSS System.

   B. The connection data for the application computers in the R/3 System and the SAProuter in the customer's system must be maintained.

   C. The connection must be opened by the customer.

# CHAPTER FOUR

Installation Concepts

The architecture of the R/3 System is reflected in the order in which the different phases of installation are carried out. During installation, the database, then the instances—beginning with the central instance—and finally the front ends are created step by step. This chapter describes the requirements and the basic procedure for an R/3 installation. In this chapter you'll also find background information to help you understand the processes. We've left the highly technical discussion of this topic to the relevant manuals (see the SAP R/3 Installation Guide).

Preparing for Installation

Before you can begin the actual installation, decisions concerning hardware and software must be made. This section discusses the decisive factors.

Sizing

One of the most important points in planning an installation is estimating the expected size of the future R/3 System. The size of an R/3 System is greatly affected by the following parameters:

- Number of users, both the total number and the number of concurrently active users
- R/3 modules used and the number of users per module
- Volume of data to be entered and retention times for data
- Number and size of requests for background processing
- Demands of data exchange through interfaces
- Number and size of output requests

SAP's Internet site provides a *Quick Sizing* tool that estimates sizes based on the information you provide. The planned number of users per application module and the estimated level of activity in the R/3 System (low, medium, or high) are of primary importance.

NOTE   Prospective R/3 users may find the Quick Sizing tool helpful in evaluating the product. It is available on the Internet at **www.sap.com**.

Hardware Requirements

The next step in preparing for installation is to choose the appropriate hardware, the operating system (UNIX, Windows NT, OS/390, or AS400), the RDBMS software, and the peripheral hardware, etc. The planning phase should not be approached lightly, as bad decisions at this stage can only be rectified later with additional cost and effort. These issues are discussed in detail in *SAP R/3 Implementation with ASAP: The Official Guide* by Hartwig Brand (also published by Sybex, 1998). For the purposes of this book, let's assume that you've already resolved these issues and that hardware and R/3 software are in place.

Checklist

An important early step before installation is to use the checklist supplied with the installation package to check whether the requirements have been met. This checklist includes the most important requirements for each RDBMS and operating system. For R/3 Release 4.0A, approximately 15GB of disk space is needed for the central instance of the R/3 database without application data. The disk space requirements vary between the different operating systems and RDBMS.

The central instance computer also needs enough space to include "swap space" (3* RAM in computer + 500MB, and at least 1.25GB), and some room in RAM for the various activities to take place (256MB RAM), although that could be an associated computer rather than the central instance. In addition, you need another computer on which the work areas live (256MB RAM and 800MB disk space). You might also want more space on the work area computer or another computer altogether, which could contain the central transport directory.

> **NOTE**   These figures are based on R/3 Release 4.0A. Later releases will have higher requirements due to the increased range of functions.

Software Requirements

In addition to the hardware requirements, there are also software requirements, such as NFS (Network File System), the appropriate operating system version, or TCP/IP. R/3 requires the English version of Windows NT. Software requirements vary depending on operating systems and RDBMS, especially among different R/3 releases. You should therefore check them thoroughly using the checklist.

Disk Design

When you have checked the requirements, the next step is to plan the distribution of data over the individual disks. (See Figure 4.1.) Security always has higher priority than performance, which provides some basic rules. Independently of the RDBMS software used, the actual data area and the log area should be on separate disks, if possible, with separate controllers, so that a disk failure will not affect the log area and the data area simultaneously.

FIGURE 4.1

Disk configuration

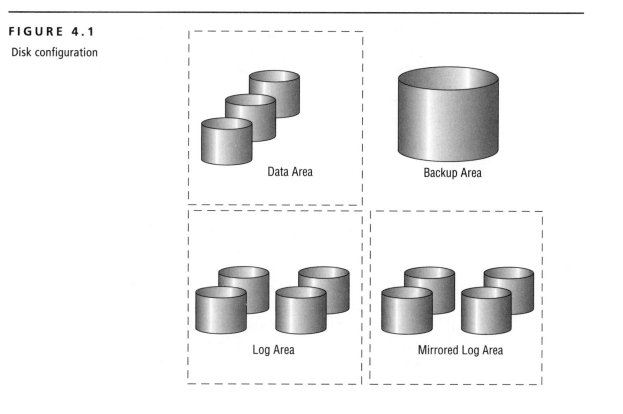

Due to the importance of the data in the R/3 database, the usual procedure is to use mirroring for the log areas. You should create the individual log areas on different disks. Otherwise, the failure of one disk would result in the complete loss of the data in the log areas. You should have at least one extra disk for backups of log areas and data areas to the file system of the computer, or for use with the Oracle Archiver. Not observing these guidelines could easily result in security risks and loss of performance. There are complicated reasons that these guidelines must be followed, and they have to do with the nature of the RDBMS architecture, a topic which is beyond the scope of this book. For more information, please refer to the specific RDBMS literature, for example, *Oracle 8 DBA Handbook* by Kevin Loney (Osborne McGraw-Hill, 1997).

WARNING Failure to observe backup and archiving safety rules could result in security risks, loss of performance, and loss of data.

For a minimal R/3 installation for test purposes, you need at least three hard disks.

RAID

RAID (Redundant Array of Inexpensive Disks) systems are used effectively in the R/3 environment. Oracle's online redo log area and offline redo log area, or the transaction log or archive log of other RDBMSs, must be assigned to different logical disk volumes in RAID 1 areas (disk mirroring). It is also advisable to use a logical disk volume based on RAID 1 for the data areas. You can also use RAID 5 systems (block interleaved striping with parity) for the R/3 database. RAID 5 systems are not appropriate for the log areas of an RDBMS, because the greatest I/O load normally occurs in the log areas of the RDBMS. The performance of RAID 5 systems is about 10 percent less than RAID 1 systems. If a disk fails, a RAID 1 system restarts considerably more quickly than a RAID 5 system. For technical details, please refer to the hardware vendor's literature, for example, *An Introduction to RAID* by Pete McLean (published by DEC Company, 1991), or on the Internet at `www.unix.digital.com/products/raid-paper`. You can find useful Notes on recent changes and installation instructions in the OSS (the Online Service System described in Chapter 3). The current Notes numbers for installations are also given in the installation manuals. You should study these Notes as part of your preparation for installation.

R3Setup

There are some special considerations in preparing for an R/3 installation, depending on the R/3 release and the operating system being used. The procedure described here is for R/3 Release 4.0A for UNIX systems. With this R/3 release, SAP introduced a new, and more flexible, installation tool. The previous tool, R3INST, was replaced by the tool *R3Setup*, which is based on client/server technology. R3Setup can only be used on Windows NT systems from the next R/3 release, 4.0B.

At the time of this writing, preparation for an R/3 installation also includes creating the temporary installation directory /tmp/install and the RDBMS directory, for example, /oracle or /informix. In addition, the required operating system users and groups must be created as described in the installation manual.

In Windows NT environments, similar preparations are necessary. Use the installation directory \users\<*sid*>adm\install.

UNIX

When working with a UNIX installation, you need to modify the UNIX kernel parameters using the operating system tools. Informix uses raw devices to store data in UNIX systems. These raw devices must be available before you can start the R/3 installation.

Architecture of the Installation Tool

With R/3 Release 4.0, the installation procedure has been completely reworked. UNIX and Windows NT systems and the individual RDBMSs sometimes differed considerably in terms of appearance and procedures. The installation procedure sometimes required a detailed knowledge of the components used. The new installation tool was designed to simplify the procedures, making them clearer and, above all, uniform. The result is an installation procedure that takes advantage of client/server technology. To use the installation tool, you need the *InstGUI* on any computer that has a TCP/IP connection to the target computer (see Figure 4.2). InstGUI is available for different Windows interfaces. The actual installation program, R3Setup, is located on the server. R3Setup can be executed both by an InstGUI and in the background when all the parameters are passed.

FIGURE 4.2:

The architecture of the installation tool

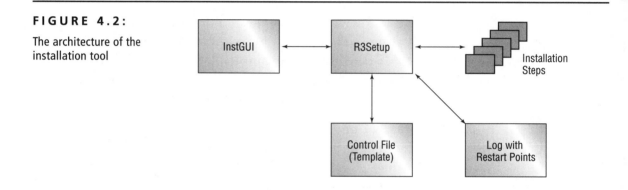

When an InstGUI is used, confirmation messages from each installation step are sent to the user at the front end. If an error occurs, the problems can be resolved, and you can continue the installation from the point at which the error occurred.

The main benefit of this architecture is not only the uniform appearance for the user in the form of the InstGUI. Differences in the procedures between UNIX, Windows NT, and the RDBMS are no longer an issue and do not affect the way the software is handled. They are administered by R3Setup. The split into front end (InstGUI) and server (R3Setup) means that you are no longer tied to the computer that has the R/3 instance installed. That is, when you install R/3, you can also log on to R3Setup from another computer after starting R3Setup on the target computer.

With later R/3 releases it will also be possible to establish WAN connections using SAProuters. There will also no longer be a limit of just one InstGUI per R3Setup, which will make it possible to activate additional InstGUIs for an R3Setup for monitoring purposes, in addition to an active InstGUI. The new installation tools for UNIX installations are available with R/3 Release 4.0A. For Windows NT systems, the installation procedure is the same as for R/3 Release 3.1.

Installation Procedures

In the first phase of the installation, you are asked to supply customer-specific configuration data for the R/3 System to be installed.

You can choose from the following components:

- Central instance with RDBMS and database

- Central instance

- RDBMS and database

- Additional dialog instances

- Front ends

- Stand-alone gateways for instances that are only used as gateways to other R/3 and R/2 Systems

NOTE   For a complete definition of the central instance, see Chapter 1.

When a new R/3 System is installed, the installation proceeds from the back end to the front end. First, the RDBMS and database are installed on the database server, and then the central instance is installed on the selected application server. If the database server and the central instance are installed on the same computer, these two steps can be combined. In a case like that, additional instances can be installed. The last step is the installation of the front end.

User entries of the operating system are required depending on the component to be installed. In UNIX environments, this is currently done using a shell script that is assigned to each component. You execute the corresponding script on the target computer, for example, centraldb.sh for the central instance with the database. Then, you are asked to enter information, including:

- The name of the database
- The name of the database computer
- Users, UID and GID
- TCP/IP ports for the Message Server and the instance

NOTE In a later release, this procedure will be replaced by an easier-to-use wizard. Check the installation manuals for the latest information.

The information specified is formatted and saved in a text file (template). This template is used as a control file for the R3Setup program, which is then started. For example, for a central instance with a database, template CENTRDB.R3S is generated in the installation directory of the target computer. The templates are structured according to special rules, but an experienced user will be able to make manual changes to these files. The example that follows shows an excerpt from the template CENTRDB.R3S.

```
[Z_ORACREATETSP]
PSAPBTABD=@Z_SAPDATAPATH=SAPDATA4@;400
PSAPBTABI=@Z_SAPDATAPATH=SAPDATA6@;400
PSAPCLUD=@Z_SAPDATAPATH=SAPDATA5@;40
PSAPCLUI=@Z_SAPDATAPATH=SAPDATA4@;20
PSAPDDICD=@Z_SAPDATAPATH=SAPDATA6@;345
```

```
PSAPDDICI=@Z_SAPDATAPATH=SAPDATA6@;165
PSAPDOCUD=@Z_SAPDATAPATH=SAPDATA1@;28
PSAPDOCUI=@Z_SAPDATAPATH=SAPDATA2@;28
PSAPEL40AD=@Z_SAPDATAPATH=SAPDATA1@;600
PSAPEL40AI=@Z_SAPDATAPATH=SAPDATA6@;43
PSAPES40AD=@Z_SAPDATAPATH=SAPDATA3@;2000!@Z_SAPDATAPATH=SAPDATA5@
;500
PSAPES40AI=@Z_SAPDATAPATH=SAPDATA2@;1200
PSAPLOADD=@Z_SAPDATAPATH=SAPDATA6@;20
PSAPLOADI=@Z_SAPDATAPATH=SAPDATA1@;20
PSAPPOOLD=@Z_SAPDATAPATH=SAPDATA1@;550
PSAPPOOLI=@Z_SAPDATAPATH=SAPDATA4@;550
PSAPPROTD=@Z_SAPDATAPATH=SAPDATA1@;79
PSAPPROTI=@Z_SAPDATAPATH=SAPDATA5@;33
PSAPROLL=@Z_SAPDATAPATH=SAPDATA1@;300
PSAPSOURCED=@Z_SAPDATAPATH=SAPDATA5@;100
PSAPSOURCEI=@Z_SAPDATAPATH=SAPDATA4@;100
PSAPSTABD=@Z_SAPDATAPATH=SAPDATA6@;800
PSAPSTABI=@Z_SAPDATAPATH=SAPDATA5@;900
PSAPTEMP=@Z_SAPDATAPATH=SAPDATA4@;300
PSAPUSER1D=@Z_SAPDATAPATH=SAPDATA5@;8
PSAPUSER1I=@Z_SAPDATAPATH=SAPDATA6@;5
SYSTEM=@Z_SAPDATAPATH=SAPDATA2@;200
```

SAP Naming Conventions

The preceding section of the template defines the sizes of the tablespaces for an Oracle system. Each line contains the name of the tablespace, followed by a parameter for the path to the file, and then the size of the tablespace. By default, all the Oracle files are stored in the root directory /oracle/<SID>/, which is used as a mount point. This directory contains the individual tablespace paths called SAPDATA<x>. The SAP naming conventions are similar for other RDBMSs. For example, the Informix data areas are stored in the directory /informix/<SID>/sapdata. As Informix uses raw devices in UNIX environments, links to the raw devices are created in this directory. Similar naming conventions apply to the log areas. Depending on the RDBMS, directory /<RDBMS>/<SID>/ has subdirectories, such as *saparch* or `saplog`, which in turn contain files or links into raw devices.

In situations where pre-installation planning has been thorough, and where no problems occur, the installer's activities are normally limited to changing the installation CDs and installing the RDBMS software. For observation purposes, the installer starts the InstGUI from a computer. When the InstGUI is called on a front end, it finds a TCP/IP port available for communication with the R3Setup to be started; it then displays the command line needed to start R3Setup on the target computer (see Figure 4.3).

FIGURE 4.3:

InstGUI initial screen

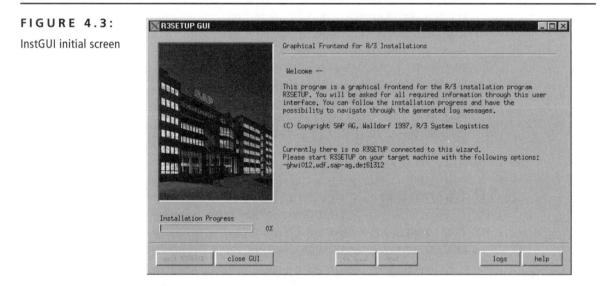

If you start R3Setup with these options on the target computer, InstGUI establishes a connection to R3Setup. If this is successful, what is displayed on the screen changes (see Figure 4.4).

R3Setup first checks the requirements on the target computer, such as authorizations and available disk space. You can monitor the details using the InstGUI function LOGS. Figure 4.5 shows what happens if the space required for the installation is not available on the target computer.

FIGURE 4.4:

Establishing the connection to R3Setup

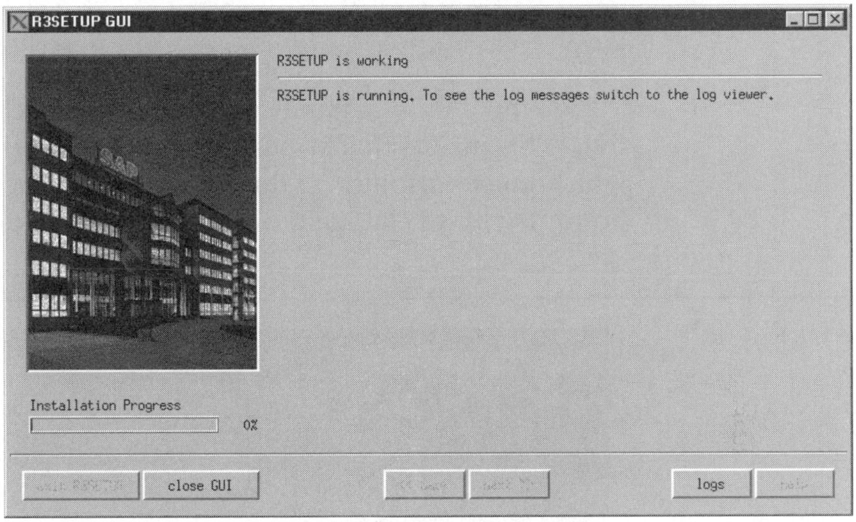

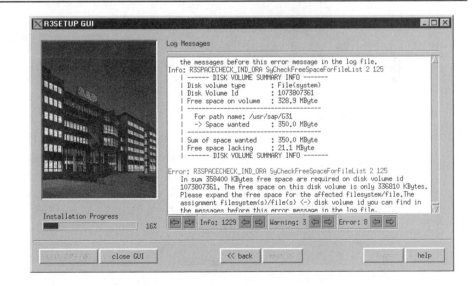

FIGURE 4.5:

An error in the disk check

If this error occurs, R3Setup is canceled. When the problem is resolved, you can start R3Setup again. The individual steps are logged, which means that the installation can be restarted from the point that installation was stopped. R3Setup goes back to the point where it left off. A graphical progress indicator lets you keep track of the installation status from start to finish.

The whole R/3 installation package currently consists of seven CDs. This means that you have to change CDs during installation, which must normally be done by an operator. The InstGUI prompts you to change the CD (see Figure 4.6).

FIGURE 4.6:

You'll be prompted to change the CD.

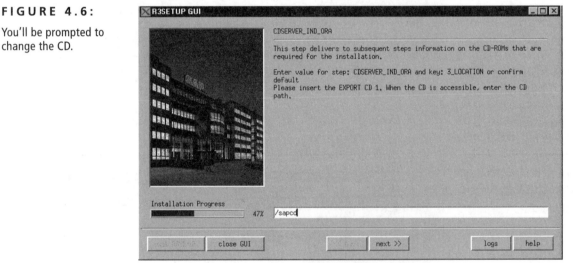

It is necessary to interrupt R3Setup to install the RDBMS software. You'll need to do this using the RDBMS-specific installation tool (see Figure 4.7). For Oracle in UNIX environments, you'll need to use the `orainst` tool found in the directory `/oracle/<SID>/orainst_sap`.

You can then continue the R/3 installation by starting R3Setup. The installation step that takes the most time is importing the data into the R/3 database. The data for that is stored on two

CDs. Depending on how powerful the computer is, this step can take several hours. To avoid having to change the CD during this time, you can copy the contents of the first CD to the hard disks of the target computer. The entire data import into the database can be completed without you having to do anything else. This installation step takes a long time and is normally done during the night.

FIGURE 4.7:

If appropriate, you'll be prompted to install the Oracle software.

```
R3SETUP GUI                                                                _□×

                    EXITORAINST_IND_ORA

                    At this point, you can exit R3SETUP to install the database software. You
                    can also install the database software in a separate window and then choose
                    to continue R3SETUP.
                    See the installation guide on how to install the database software.

                    Enter value for step: EXITORAINST_IND_ORA and key: EXIT or confirm default
                    YES: exit R3SETUP
                    NO: continue R3SETUP



  Installation Progress
  ▬▬▬▬▬▬▬        54%  │YES│

         close GUI                  next >>                  logs   help
```

ABAP Program Loads

After the database import, you can import the ABAP Program Loads, which are computer-specific, processable intermediate ABAP code. ABAP programs are not processed directly by the R/3 System. Instead, intermediate code is generated and processed. This intermediate code is stored in special tables so that it does not need to be generated a second time if the ABAP program is executed again.

To keep the generation of intermediate code for ABAP programs to a minimum in a freshly installed R/3 System, the intermediate code of the most important ABAP programs is imported during the installation. This means considerable performance benefits during subsequent R/3 System usage, because you do not need to import the ABAP Program Loads into a test system (in which performance is less important). As a consequence, the intermediate code must first be generated when a report is first called. After the ABAP Program Loads are imported, adjustments must be made to the central instance, such as changing the default passwords for the standard users.

The installation steps carried out by R3Setup are mostly hidden, unless you unexpectedly need to resolve an error. Table 4.1 summarizes the most important steps in the installation of a central instance for a UNIX system with an Oracle database. Depending on the operating system and the RDBMS used, the sequence of the phases and the tools may differ, but the type and number of phases remain the same. (Phases that run automatically and do not normally require operator intervention are marked with an asterisk.)

TABLE 4.1: Installation Phases for a Central Instance and Database

Phase	What Is Done
Check using the checklist	Check whether hardware and software meet the requirements

Manual preparation	Create directories
	  /tmp/install
	  /usr/sap/trans or mount this directory
	  /sapmnt
	Create UNIX users
	  ora<*sid*> and <*sid*>adm
	Set up logical disk volumes and file systems
	Create the necessary Oracle directories
	Make UNIX kernel adjustments
	Configure the swap spaces

Create the R/3 configuration parameters by running the appropriate shell script	Prompt for:
	  Database name
	  Database computer
	  Users
	  TCP/IP ports

TABLE 4.1: Installation Phases for a Central Instance and Database *(Continued)*

Phase	What Is Done
Start R3Setup on the target computer	Automatic generation of the start commands for InstGUI
Start InstGUI as specified by R3Setup	
Check the requirements*	Contact the InstGUI
	TCP/IP ports
	Group IDs
	User IDs
	Authorizations for directories
	Links to directories
	Check the available disk space
Unpack the R/3 software*	Distribute the software over the appropriate directories
Set the work environment for the users*	
Unpack the Oracle software*	Store in the appropriate directories
Stop R3Setup*	
orainst	Install the Oracle software
Start R3Setup	
Create the R/3 database*	Check the size of the database files
	Create an empty Oracle database
	Create the database users
	Import the data
If required, import the ABAP Program Loads	
Create a temporary R/3 license*	
Start the R/3 System*	
Make manual adjustments	

Additional R/3 instances are installed in the same way, but are easier and quicker to install because shared files have already been installed.

After Installation

When the actual R/3 software installation with R3Setup is complete, you need to indicate some settings in the R/3 System and the RDBMS so that the R/3 System can operate. This phase is known as the *follow-up*.

SAP License Key

It is particularly important to apply for the SAP license key for the new system. To find out the system serial number on the central instance computer, use the command

```
saplicense -get
```

The ID is transmitted to SAP, which then assigns and sends your license ID. To activate the SAP license, use the command

```
saplicense -install
```

You are then prompted to set the required parameters.

Installation Check

To check the R/3 installation, you should stop and restart the entire R/3 System. Perform the installation check integrated into the R/3 System. Log on to the R/3 System, client 000, as one of the standard users, and choose Tools ➤ Administration ➤ Administration ➤ Installation Check, or use Transaction code SM28.

The installation check primarily checks the installed software for completeness and compatibility of versions, for example, compatibility between the R/3 release and the operating system version. The availability of the Message Server is also tested as part of the installation check. The system checks whether all types of work processes (dialog, background, update, spool, and enqueue) are available in the installed R/3 System. The system also checks whether the information generated on the Enqueue Server and the update service conforms to reality.

It is important to change the passwords for the standard users to protect the new R/3 System from unauthorized access. You can do this when you log on by choosing the New Password button on the logon screen of SAPGUI.

Backing Up

In the RDBMS, you have to define the desired back-up media for your system. Starting and stopping the RDBMS provides a degree of security, because it generates a backup. You should frequently make a complete backup of the database.

In Windows NT systems, you should also save the entries in the Registry, using the command `rdisk /s`. To ensure high availability of a Windows NT System, it is a good idea to install a second Windows NT operating system on a separate hard disk. If the hard disk with the operating system fails, you can restart the computer using the second operating system (*dual boot*). At the very least, you should set up an *emergency repair disk*, from which the computer can be started in an emergency without access to the operating system on the hard disk. You can also use the command `rdisk` to do this.

NOTE For reasons of performance and security, neither the R/3 database server nor the application servers should be used as primary domain controllers or back-up domain controllers.

Performing a Language Import

English and German language options are integrated into the standard installation of R/3. When you log on, you can choose between English and German. If you need additional languages in an R/3 System, you must perform a *language import*. During a language import, all the necessary language elements for a language are imported into tables in the R/3 database. The R/3 database must have sufficient space for each new language. For a more detailed description of the procedure, please refer to the appropriate manual, in this case the SAP R/3 Installation Guide.

The follow-up phase, which is described only briefly here, actually has many more steps. The most important steps are described in the installation guide. When these steps are completed, the R/3 System can function, but the work doesn't end there. For example, its role within the system landscape still needs to be defined, the correction and transport system needs to be initialized, users need to be set up, etc. These tasks are described in the following chapters.

Review Questions

1. Which statement is correct? During an R/3 installation with Oracle,

   A. Multiple tablespaces are created according to the R/3 naming conventions.

   B. Exactly one tablespace is created, which is large enough to store all R/3 data.

   C. No Oracle-specific storage structures are established.

2. Which statement is correct? The R/3 naming conventions

   A. Can be changed using operating system tools.

   B. Are a permanent part of various R/3 tools and therefore cannot be changed arbitrarily.

   C. Help the user find logs and messages quickly.

3. Which statement is correct?

   A. Using RAID systems increases security in case of R/3 System failure.

   B. Running the R/3 database in a RAID system is not recommended because it causes a loss in performance.

   C. RAID systems are only recommended for the data areas of the R/3 database. For performance reasons, log areas should not be run with RAID systems.

4. What programs are used to perform an R/3 installation?

   A. R3up

   B. InstGUI and R3Setup

   C. Sapinstall

   D. Setup

CHAPTER

FIVE

5

Setting Up a System Landscape

When the R/3 license is installed and the installation check is carried out, the installation of the R/3 System is complete. All the necessary data and programs are available. The next step is to maintain all the customer-specific technical settings. You should not work with the system before this has been done. In particular, no business settings (*Customizing*) should be made. When preparing a freshly installed R/3 System, it is particularly important to initialize the correction and transport system (*Change and Transport Organizing, CTO*). This provides the basis for interaction with other systems. When the CTO of the R/3 System is configured for the first time, it becomes operational.

This chapter discusses the theoretical possibilities for setting up an R/3 System landscape and how they would be implemented technically. It will enable you to configure the system landscape required for your company.

Tasks of a System Landscape

Every installed R/3 System contains the resources to cover the entire spectrum of R/3 functionalities. These are not only business-related tasks, but also such tasks as software development and administration, and quality assurance for custom R/3 components. It is not advisable to perform all these tasks with only one R/3 System. A single system would only be adequate for training or demonstration purposes. The reasons for this lie in the different requirements of, for example, a production system and a test system:

- All the changes to the repository affect the entire run-time environment of the R/3 System and, in turn, production.

- Developers have access to all the tables in the R/3 System. In a one-system landscape, developers therefore have access to production data.

- Development activities negatively affect the performance of a system. For example, if programs are being processed in debugging mode for test purposes, a dialog work process cannot be assigned to another user during this time. This dialog work process works exclusively for that user. Training courses that are being held at the same time in a single R/3 System also negatively affect the performance of the production processes.

It is therefore advisable to distribute the tasks over different systems and only to transfer changes from the test system to the production system after ensuring that they function correctly. This is referred to as *transporting* the changes. The CTO is used to manage all the modifications and software development in the systems, as well as to transport them between the systems.

Two-System Landscapes

SAP recommends that you install a system landscape with at least two systems. Only a three-system landscape adequately meets the requirements if you develop your own applications in the R/3 System. For example, transports cannot be tested in a two-system landscape.

From the technical viewpoint, a two-system landscape comprises:

- Integration system
- Consolidation system

From the application viewpoint, the *integration system* plays the part of the development and quality assurance system. If the software has attained an acceptable development status, you can transport the changes into the next system, the consolidation system. The consolidation system takes on the role of the production system (see Figure 5.1).

FIGURE 5.1:

A two-system
landscape

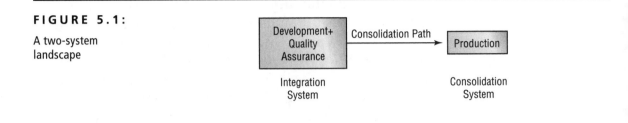

Three-System Landscapes

Software and changes to ABAP programs and many system settings are valid throughout the R/3 System. For example, you cannot test an intermediate version of an ABAP program while work
is still being done on the same object. This single use of an object
invariably causes a bottleneck in a two-system landscape, in
which development and quality assurance must be done in one
system. The only solution is a three-system landscape. From the
technical point of view, the three systems are:

- The integration system, which acts as the development system

- The consolidation system, which acts as the quality assurance
  system

- The delivery system, which acts as the production system

The roles of the development, quality assurance, and production systems are strictly separate. Software can only be tested in a
separate system before it is used in the production system. The
transport paths between the systems are fixed, and cannot be
changed without taking specific steps (see Figure 5.2).

The relationship of costs and benefits with regard to the system
requirements is a decisive factor in your decision regarding a system landscape. With the benefits offered by a three-system landscape comes increased administration due to the complexity of the

system landscape. You must weigh those requirements against the costs.

FIGURE 5.2:

A three-system landscape

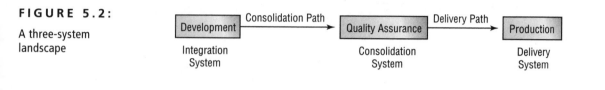

Multisystem Landscapes

There are configurations in which it makes sense for a system landscape to comprise more than three systems. For example, it may be appropriate to have multiple, geographically separate production systems in order to separate different subsidiaries of a company. The technical distinction between the systems—integration, consolidation, and delivery systems—is retained in these system landscapes, as the technical functions remain the same. These system landscapes comprise multiple systems of the same type working in parallel. The roles of the systems cannot then be defined so precisely. To a certain extent, each system plays a dual role. Figure 5.3 shows an example of a multisystem landscape. The entry point is a central integration system, which is used for international software development tasks. A subordinate consolidation system is used for quality assurance for this software. Independent system landscapes are connected for country-specific software development.

Technical Implementation

This section explains how the theoretical concept of setting up a landscape system is put into practice.

FIGURE 5.3:

An example of a multi-system landscape

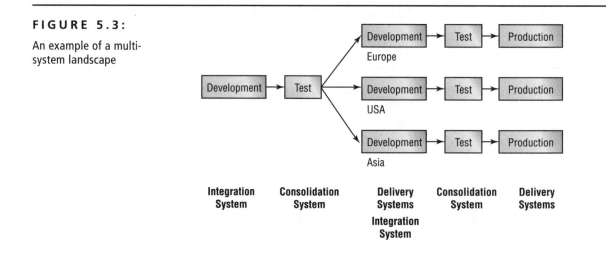

Initialization

To initialize an R/3 System:

1. Log on to client 000 as user DDIC.

2. Choose Tools ➤ Administration ➤ Transports ➤ Installation Follow-up Work, or use Transaction code SE06 (see Figure 5.4).

3. To initialize the system, choose R/3 Standard Installation or Database Copy or Migration, depending on the origin of the system.

4. Choose Execute. Any open change or transport requests in the copied system are closed (see Chapter 6), and the initialization is started.

Initialization is now complete. If you want to build a system landscape or integrate a new system, further measures are necessary.

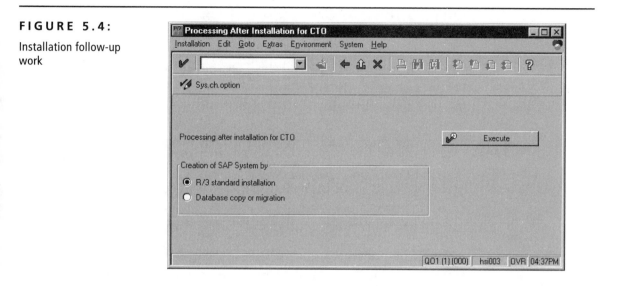

Transport Domain and Transport Domain Controller (TDC)

Administration of settings and transports has been improved considerably in the area of software logistics. The R/3 *Transport Management System* (TMS) is used for this. R/3 Systems, which logically form one unit, can be grouped together into a transport domain. A logical unit is formed by systems between which data is transported. There are defined transport paths between the systems, so it is advisable to control and administer transport activities for these systems centrally from one system. This system is the *Transport Domain Controller* (TDC).

Communication between the TDC and the other R/3 Systems in the domain is based on RFC (Remote Function Call) connections between the application servers. The application servers are only used as a basis for communication for the RFC connections to be generated. The *TMS* and the TDC are available on every application server. All the necessary system settings, such as the definition of the transport paths, are made on one application server using the Transport Domain Controller. The necessary RFC connections are generated automatically by the TDC based on this information. When activated, the information is distributed over all systems in the transport domain.

NOTE In earlier R/3 releases, these settings had to be made separately for each R/3 System in the landscape, which of course required much greater effort. Users had to make sure that the settings were consistent throughout the system.

The Transport Domain Controller should be an application server with high availability and good security in an R/3 System from the landscape. The R/3 System should be as recent a release as possible. Therefore the production and quality assurance systems are normally better suited for TDC than are test systems. The load generated by the Transport Management System in an R/3 System is low and does not represent an impact on performance.

Creating the Transport Domain

When you create the transport domain and its domain controllers:

1. Decide which systems should be grouped into one domain, and which R/3 System and which application server are best suited for use as the TDC.

2. If possible, log on to the chosen application server of the chosen R/3 Systems to client 000 as user DDIC.

3. Choose Tools ➤ Administration ➤ Transports ➤ Transport Management System, or use Transaction code STMS.

   • If the TMS is not defined, you are notified and prompted for a domain name.

- If you have not logged on to the application server, which will subsequently be used as the communication point of the TDC, you can explicitly name an application server by choosing F5, Address.

4. Choose New Domain.

5. Enter the name and the description of the domain.

NOTE   The domain name must not contain blanks.

---

6. Save your entries.

WARNING   Once you have chosen a domain name, you can only change it by reconfiguring the TMS.

The domain and its controller are now defined. You can check this definition by choosing Overview ➤ Systems. When systems are defined and integrated into a domain, the system automatically makes preparations for subsequent functionality in the R/3 System:

- The configuration data is not only saved in the database, but also in files on operating system level.

- The user TMSADM is created in the R/3 System. This user is simply a CPI-C user, which is only permitted to call one function module from a function group.

- R/3 has automatically generated the RFC connections relative to the chosen application server.

Integrating Additional Systems

If the TDC and the transport domain are defined, additional systems can be integrated. For each system to be integrated, the installation follow-up work must already be performed (Transaction code SE06). Proceed as follows:

1. As user DDIC, log on to the system to be integrated in client 000 of the application server that was chosen for the TMS.

2. Call TMS by choosing Tools ➤ Administration ➤ Transport ➤ Transport Management System, or use Transaction code STMS. The system automatically recognizes that it is not assigned to a domain and prompts you to define a new domain.

3. Use function key F6, Other Configuration, to switch to the screen to enter the TDC application server.

4. Enter the computer name and the number of the TDC instance. Information on the desired transport domain is automatically read from this computer.

5. Save. The new system is made ready to be included in the desired domain.

Next, the TDC has to confirm that the new system is included for it to be fully integrated into the domain. Proceed as follows:

1. As user DDIC, log on to client 000 of the TDC R/3 System.

2. Go to the initial screen of the TMS (Transaction code STMS).

3. Choose Overview ➤ Systems. You see a list of the R/3 Systems registered with the TDC. The new system appears in this list, and must be confirmed. This is indicated by this icon:

4. Choose the system, and include it in the domain with function key F7, Accept.

Integrating Multiple Systems into the Domain

Once this is done, the configuration change can be distributed to all systems in the domain. Only then is the new system known throughout the entire domain. To integrate multiple systems into the domain at the same time, it is a good idea to first accept all configuration changes and then make them known to the domain in one step. To distribute the configuration data in the system landscape:

1. From the TMS of the TDC, choose Extras ➤ Distribute TMS Conf.

2. Go to the TMS of the new system to check the settings made to the new system in the domain.

3. Choose Overview ➤ Systems to display the list of systems. The status of the system is indicated by an icon:

If errors occurred during configuration, details of the errors are displayed on the screen. Also, an error history with possible causes and solutions is available in the Alert Monitor of the TMS. To call the Alert Monitor, choose from the initial screen of the TMS: Monitoring ➤ Alert Monitor, or use function key F7.

To integrate a system in a domain, both the TDC and the system to be integrated must be available. This is to prevent, for example, the administrator of another R/3 System spontaneously causing the system to be included in an existing domain without checking with colleagues, and thereby allowing transports into this domain. When a system is included in the domain, all the configuration settings, such as transport paths between the systems, can and must only be made by the TDC.

If settings for the assignment to a domain or even the TDC have to be changed, you can delete the settings from the initial screen of the TMS by choosing Overview ➤ Systems ➤ Extras ➤ Delete TMS Conf. Some settings still remain active and may need to be overwritten with new settings. For a single system, you need to delete the settings both in the system itself and in the list of available systems of the TDC by choosing Overview ➤ Systems, marking the system, and then choosing R/3 System ➤ Delete.

> **NOTE**   Beginning with R/3 Release 3.1H, a system could be integrated into a transport domain. However, the TMS in these systems could only be accessed using Transaction code STMS. Older R/3 releases do not have the functionality needed for integration into a transport domain.

Virtual Systems

To allow data to be made available for transports into older R/3 Systems, which do not have the functionality necessary for full integration into the transport domain, you can define *virtual systems* in the domain. Virtual systems cannot be controlled by the TDC. However, the transport paths to these systems can be defined, thus preparing transports. This data is then transported into the systems using the transport control program `tp`. These processes are not controlled by the TMS.

Virtual system entries are sometimes useful when planning complex system landscapes if not all the planned systems were installed but, for example, you want to set the transport paths between the system. If the system is installed later, you can delete the virtual entry and create a proper entry. To define a virtual system, from the initial screen of the TMS on the TDC, choose Systems ➤ R/3 System ➤ Create ➤ Virtual System.

External Systems

In addition to the virtual system definitions, entries for *external systems* are also possible. External systems are a special type of virtual system, which also do not exist physically in the transport domain. Entries for external systems are required if you want to:

- Transfer data between different transport domains, that is, from one system to a system in a different transport domain, or

- Import or export transport data to or from a removable medium

As for a virtual system, create an external system by choosing Systems ➤ R/3 System ➤ Create ➤ External System. The R/3 System, from which you want to administer the external R/3 System, is called the *communication system*. You can use the display function for these systems from the defined communication system, which is normally the TDS. For external systems, the transport directory must be made known relative to the communication system. The transport directory stores all the data and logs needed for transports from or to the external systems.

The default directory used to store the transport data and logs is the central directory \usr\sap\trans, which was created during installation. Figure 5.5 shows the structure of this directory.

FIGURE 5.5:

The transport
directory tree

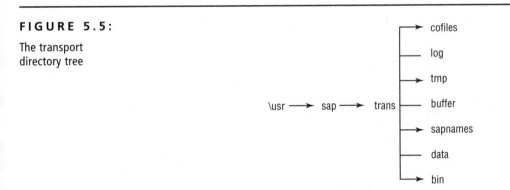

It is not necessary for each R/3 System to have its local directory tree, but it is sensible to make the transport directory tree available globally using operating system tools (Share, Mount, NFS Link). Systems that have special security restrictions can be assigned their own local transport directory with reduced access authorizations. Figure 5.6 shows the transport processes in a three-system landscape with a global transport directory.

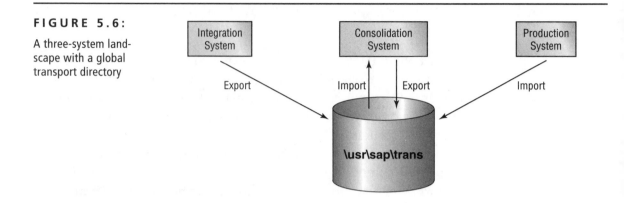

FIGURE 5.6:

A three-system landscape with a global transport directory

Transport Groups

The R/3 Systems that share a common transport directory tree form a *transport group*. A transport domain can comprise multiple transport groups.

The Transport Control Program *tp*

The program tp on the operating system level is used for the actual control and execution of transports between systems. By using tools such as the transport program R3trans on the operating system level and other tools integrated into R/3, tp both exports data from an R/3 System and imports data into other systems.

To perform these tasks, you must next enter all the systems defined in the TMS, including the virtual and external systems, in the tp program's parameter file TPPARAM. TPPARAM is normally in the directory \usr\sap\trans\bin. Add the new entries to this file using an operating system editor. By default, after installation, a file called TPPARAM.TPL is in the directory \usr\sap\<SID>\SYS\ exe\run\INSTALL, and can be used as a template. If there are multiple transport groups within a transport domain, and in turn multiple \usr\sap\trans directory trees, you must ensure that a TPPARAM exists in each \usr\sap\trans\bin directory, each with a different transport directory definition.

The following rules apply to the definition of the TPPARAM file:

- The parameter transdir defines the global transport directory of the group, normally in the form:

  transdir = \usr\sap\trans\

- The parameter

  dbname = $(system)

  is used to pass the name of the R/3 database, for which tp is called.

- At least the database server must be defined for each R/3 System defined in the domain.

  <SID>/dbhost = <Server name>

Parameters that are valid for a particular R/3 System are indicated by the prefix of the R/3 System name. Global settings have no prefix to the name.

NOTE   In Windows NT systems, the transport directory must also be made known in the instance profile using the parameter DIR_TRANS, for example, DIR_TRANS = \usr\sap\trans. Please note the differences in the naming conventions: In file **TPPARAM**, the transdir path is passed ending in "\"; with parameter **DIR_TRANS** in the instance profile, there is no "\".

A TPPARAM file for a system, QO1, should at least have the following contents:

Report 5.1:

```
#@(#) TPPARAM.sap          20.7   SAP        97/10/09
##################################################
#     Template of TPPARAM for UNIX              #
##################################################
# First we specify global values for some       #
# parameters,                                    #
# later the system specific incarnation of      #
# special parameters                            #
##################################################
#              Global Parameters                #
##################################################
transdir              = \usr\sap\trans\
dbname                = $(system)


##################################################
#          System-specific Parameters           #
##################################################
QO1/dbhost            = bhsv003
##################################################
# Example            T11                         #
##################################################
#T11/dbhost           = my_hostname
```

Numerous other parameters allow adjustments for operating-system– and database-specific requirements. Placing *<cpu2>* as follows

```
<cpu2> := aix | hp-ux | osf1 | sinix | sunos | wnt
```

in front of a parameter allows you to make settings specific to the operating system. For example, the entry

```
wnt0transdir = \\trans02\trans
```

means that the transport directory for Windows NT systems is expected on computer \\ trans02, directory \trans. In the same way, the prefix

```
<db> := ora | inf | ada | sql
```

defines database-specific settings.

All actions made by `tp` are logged to the subdirectory `\usr\`
`sap\trans\log`. By default, file `ALOG` contains all the entries for
transport requests, for which the `tp` program was used. The file
`SLOG` records the start time, work steps, duration, and the completion time of each transport. If you want to use file names other
than the default, change the definitions of parameters `alllog` and
`syslog` in TPPARAM. For example, the following

```
alllog = ALOG$(syear).$(yweek)
```

writes a new log file for each year and each week of the year in the
form ALOG<YY> <WW>. Table 5.1 shows which prefixes can be used.

TABLE 5.1: Macros for Parameter Definitions in TPPARAM

Macro	Meaning
$(cpu)	CPU name (alphaosf I hp I rm600 I sun I wnt)
$(cpu2)	Operating system (aix I hp-ux I osf1 I sinix I sunos I wnt)
$(dname)	Weekday (SUN, MON...)
$(mday)	Day of month (1-31)
$(mname)	Name of month (JAN, FEB...)
$(mon)	Month (01-12)
$(system)	SAP system name
$(wday)	Weekday (00-06, 00 is Sunday)
$(yday)	Day of the year (001-366)
$(year)	Year expressed in 4 figures
$(syear)	Year expressed in 2 figures
$(yweek)	Calendar week (00-53)

The system also keeps a log file ULOG<*Year*>_<*Number*>, in which each executed tp call is recorded with its parameters and operating system user. <*Year*> stands for the last two numbers of the year and <*Number*> for the current quarter.

To display the tp parameter file TPPARAM from the TMS, select a system from the system display by choosing Goto ➤ TP Parameters.

Transport Paths

After the R/3 Systems available in the landscape have been made known throughout the system, the last step is to define the transport paths between the systems. It is assumed that the R/3 administrators have agreed on which roles each system will play, and that these issues are not being considered now for the first time. Let's assume that the configuration goal is known, and look at how to make the settings needed for a two-system and a three-system landscape.

Editors

The transport paths and the roles of systems are controlled by entries in specific tables. In earlier R/3 releases, it was the duty of the administrator to make the entries in these tables manually for each R/3 System. This situation has been improved.

Two tools are now available to define the transport paths: the hierarchical list editor and the graphical editor. These editors relieve the administrator from this task. The administrator now only has to decide which technical settings the role of the system requires (integration, consolidation, or delivery system). All the necessary table entries are generated automatically by the R/3 System. It is enough to define the roles of the systems only once in the TDC, and the definition is passed on to all the systems. For the following ways to define transport paths, it is assumed that you have logged on to client 000 of the TDC R/3 System as user DDIC.

List Editor

To use the hierarchical list editor to create transport paths between systems:

1. From the initial screen of the TMS, choose Overview ➤ Systems.

2. Choose Environment ➤ Transport Paths to display the hierarchical tree with the links. Initially, only all the defined systems are displayed as individual systems with their configuration status (see Figure 5.7).

3. To make changes, choose Configuration ➤ Change.

FIGURE 5.7:

The tree before configuration

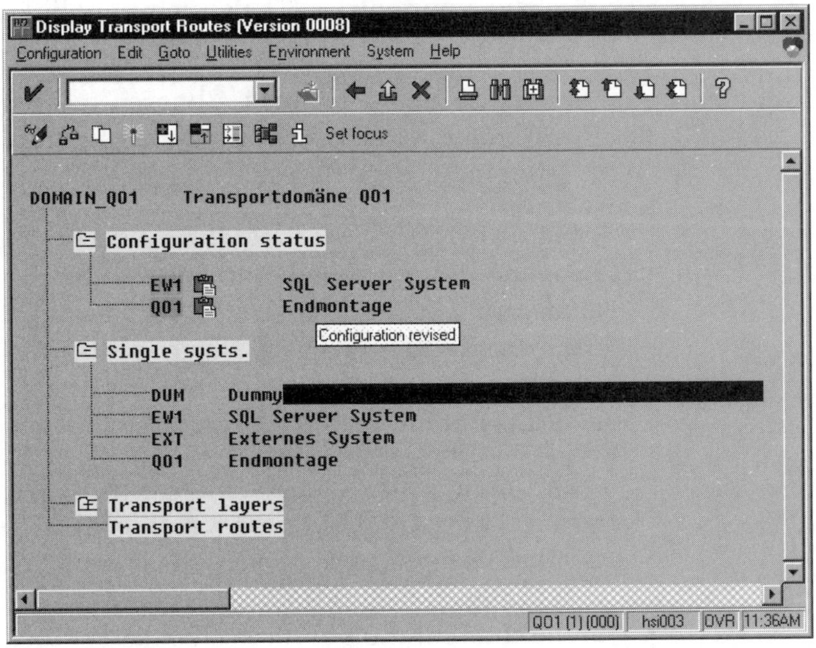

4. Choose Configuration ➤ Standard Configuration to select a one-, two-, or three-system landscape, and assign a role to each system (see Figure 5.8).

FIGURE 5.8:

Choosing the configuration

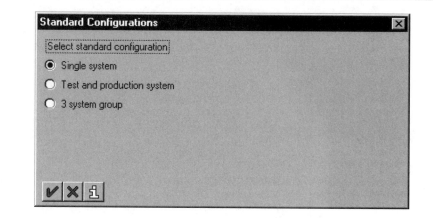

5. Save your entries. The systems are linked automatically, and the necessary table entries are generated automatically.

6. Distribute the settings. Choose Configuration ➤ Activate ➤ Domain, or first activate the configuration locally by choosing local, then choose Configuration ➤ Distribute.

Figures 5.9 and 5.10 show the hierarchy tree after the tasks for a two- and three-system landscape are completed. The two-system landscape also has a system DUM, a dummy system, and an external system EXT, neither of which is integrated into the system landscape. The three-system landscape has a single system DUM, which is not integrated into the system landscape.

The implemented version management is used to log the configuration changes and to restore an older version. When the configuration has been made and saved, it is numbered automatically, which is indicated in the title of the screen. If subsequent changes are made to the configuration of the system landscape, the version number is increased with each saved variant.

FIGURE 5.9:

A two-system
landscape

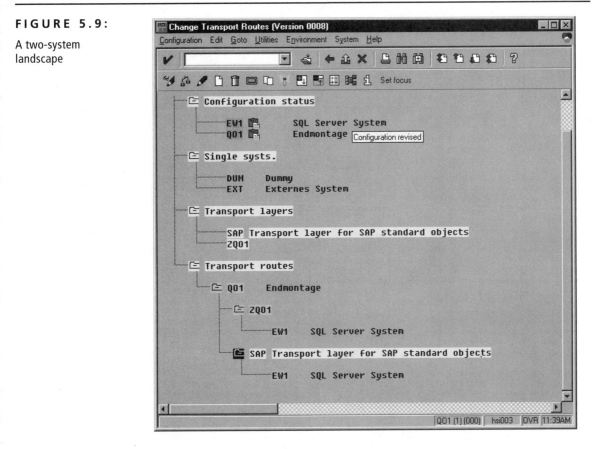

Transport Layer

You will also notice that a transport layer called Z<Integration system> is generated between the integration system and the consolidations system. A transport layer always describes the transport path for data being moved from a development system. This path is also known as the *consolidation path*. The transport path from a consolidation system to a delivery system is also known as the *delivery path*. A delivery path can only exist in a system landscape that consists of at least three systems. A two-system landscape has no delivery system from a technical viewpoint, as explained with Figures 5.1 and 5.2.

FIGURE 5.10:

A three-system landscape

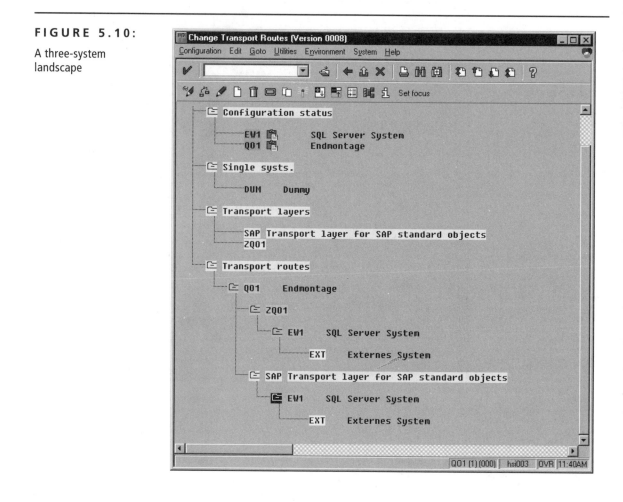

NOTE In a two-system landscape, the consolidation system takes on the role of the production system.

In addition to the transport layer between the integration and consolidation system, the SAP transport layer is automatically generated in the systems. This transport layer allows changes made to objects delivered by SAP to be imported into the systems.

NEW! To find out which entries were generated, choose Utilities ➤ Display Conversion (see the listing in this section, which shows the log of generated settings for a three-system landscape). In R/3 releases prior to 4.0, these entries in the displayed tables had to be maintained manually.

Report 5.2:

```
|----------------------------|
| Known Systems (Table TSYST):                  |
| System    Transp.layer   Short Description    |
|----------------------------|
| DUM                       Dummy               |
| EW1                       SQL Server System   |
| EXT                       External System     |
| Q01     ZQ01              Final Assembly       |
| SAP     SAP               Delivery System SAP  |
|----------------------------|
| Deliveries (Table TASYS):                     |
| Delivery system supply by cross-transport     |
| permitted?                                    |
|----------------------------|
| EXT             EW1                      X     |
|----------------------------|
| Consolidation paths (Table TWSYS):            |
| Source system Consolidation system Target system |
|----------------------------|
| Q01             EW1              EW1           |
| Q01             SAP              EW1           |
|----------------------------|
|----------------------------|
| Transport layers (View V_DEVL):               |
| Name Int. System Cons. System Short description |
|----------------------------|
|Development layer for local software dev.      |
|                              (no transport)   |
```

```
| SAP     SAP           SAP                              |
|                       Transport layer for objects     |
|                                 in the SAP standard    |
| ZQ01    Q01           EW1    Development                |
```

Graphical Editor

The same configuration can be made using the graphical editor:

1. From the display or maintenance of transport paths, call the graphical editor by choosing Goto ➤ Graphical Editor. If no settings have been chosen, all the available systems are displayed as insertable objects in the upper part of the screen (see Figure 5.11).

FIGURE 5.11:

Before the configuration of settings

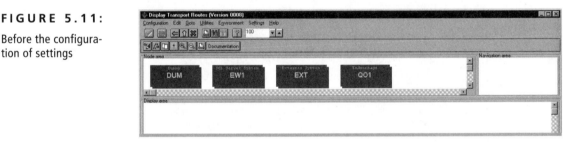

2. Choose Configuration ➤ Standard Configuration to select a system landscape and assign roles to each system (see Figure 5.12).

3. Save your settings by choosing Configuration ➤ Save. The table entries are generated automatically and displayed in a flow diagram (see Figure 5.13 for an example of a three-system landscape)

4. Distribute the configuration throughout the domain either by choosing Configuration ➤ Activate ➤ Domain-wide or Configuration ➤ Activate ➤ Local, and then Distribute.

FIGURE 5.12:

Definition of the transport path

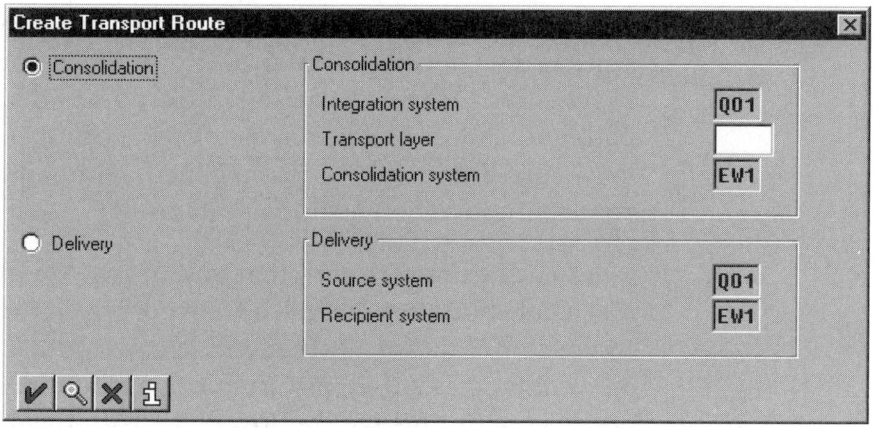

Create Transport Route

- ● Consolidation

  Consolidation

  Integration system   Q01

  Transport layer

  Consolidation system   EW1

- ○ Delivery

  Delivery

  Source system   Q01

  Recipient system   EW1

FIGURE 5.13:

A configured three-system landscape

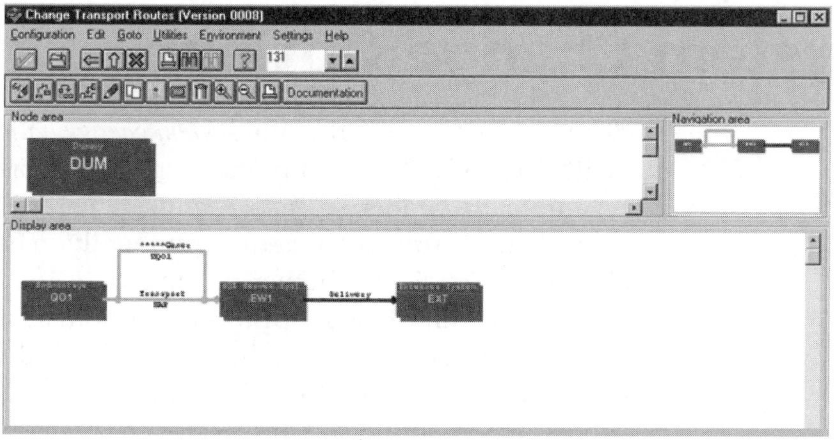

The advantage of the graphical editor lies mainly in its clear presentation, which is particularly important in very complex landscapes that do not conform to a standard. In these cases, use the mouse first to move the available R/3 Systems from the area with the insertable objects to the presentation area. Left-click an R/3

System and place it in the desired position in the presentation area with a mouse-click. Then, define the transport paths between the systems by choosing Configuration ➤ Transport Path ➤ Create. (To remove incorrectly defined transport paths, select the menu path and choose Delete.) This function changes the mouse pointer in the presentation area into a pencil, with which you can draw a connecting line between the systems.

For each transport path that you draw, you must decide whether it is a consolidation, that is a transport from the integration system to the consolidation system with a corresponding transport layer, or whether it is a delivery from a consolidation system to a delivery system. In this way, a flow chart with the development data of the system landscape grows in the presentation area.

System Change Options

The last step is to define the *system change options* for each object within each R/3 System in the landscape. Objects in R/3 are, for example, programs, screens, menus, tables, or structures. The system change options are defined manually in each R/3 System. You must first consider whether the objects in an R/3 System should be changed at all. Change options cover both customer-specific objects created and developed, and objects delivered by SAP that can have customer-specific modifications. In a production system, it is a good idea to not permit any system change options. Changes permitted in a development system depend on the type and the scope of the software development, for example, whether SAP-specific objects are changed or not.

You set the system change options either directly by choosing Installation Follow-up, Transaction code SE06, or from the transport paths display of the TMS by choosing Environment ➤ System Change Options. To permit or prohibit changes, use the function

Global Settings. If you permit changes to the system, you can determine more precisely what changes. Within an R/3 System, you can set change options for the following:

Customer name area—All customer-specific software development with all the transportable tools available in R/3.

Local objects—All customer-specific, but not transportable (local), software development.

Objects in the SAP R/3 application components—Allows changes using the tools of the ABAP Workbench (Development Workbench) to all application components delivered by SAP.

SAP R/3 Basis components—Permits changes to all R/3 Basis components using all the available tools. All the components of the Development Workbench and ABAP Query, and the use of the Function Builder, are permitted. Changes to R/3 Basis components are not compared in an upgrade, that is, the old objects are overwritten with the new objects.

ABAP+GUI Tools—Permits only processing of SAP objects using the ABAP editor, the Screen Painter, and the Menu Painter. Changes to functions are not permitted.

Development Workbench—Comprises processing SAP objects using all the tools in the Development Workbench, that is, the ABAP Editor, the Screen Painter, and the Menu Painter, and changing Repository objects (see ABAP/4 Development Workbench). Changes to functions are not permitted.

Enqueue Function Groups—Comprises SAP functions for lock management with R/3.

ABAP/4 Query/SAP—Permits use of the ABAP Query tool to automatically generate reports.

Changing SAP-Specific Objects

All objects such as programs, screens, functions, tables, and structures that are delivered by SAP with the R/3 release are SAP-specific objects. Changes to these objects must be registered in the OSS system. The reason for this security mechanism is not just individual responsibility for the changes made. This mechanism also enables SAP to quickly localize and analyze customer-specific problems. If you need to change SAP original objects, you must consider the following:

- SAP cannot assume liability for any changes made to SAP-specific objects.

- If you upgrade your R/3 System, and this upgrade includes a new version of an object that was modified by you, you must decide whether to use the new SAP object or retain your modifications. SAP cannot assume liability for any resulting problems with SAP standard functionality or interfaces.

A logical consequence of this is that you must carefully consider any changes you make to SAP objects. Comprehensive changes to many SAP-specific objects increase the amount of follow-up work required during an upgrade, and you should therefore avoid these changes. If possible, you should use User Exits, the interfaces provided by SAP to integrate customer-specific function modules (see the SAP R/3 manuals). User exits are part of the extension concept offered by SAP for R/3. If you need to develop your own programs within the R/3 standard software, you should implement a system landscape that consists of, at minimum, a test system and a production system on separate computers.

RFC Connections

The role of RFC connections is not only within the Transport Management System between R/3 Systems. RFC allows you to execute function modules beyond computer and R/3 System boundaries. RFC connections can be used to execute functions and programs:

- On the application servers of the same R/3 System
- On different R/3 Systems
- In R/2 Systems
- From the external environment

To integrate a new R/3 System completely into an existing system landscape, you should define the planned RFC connections. These definitions are partly done automatically during the configuration of an R/3 System in the landscape. This includes the RFC connections needed for the TMS, as mentioned in this chapter. The RFC connections, *RFC destinations*, are also generated for all application servers in the R/3 System during installation. It may still be necessary to create additional destinations, for example, for copying clients from another system (see Chapter 7).

To define an RFC connection, all the data needed for communication with the partner system is stored under a logical name. The communication type is defined. A defined RFC connection can be used by each program, that is, it is not assigned permanently to one function module. The following is an example definition of an RFC destination to another R/3 System:

1. Choose Tools ➤ Administration ➤ Administration ➤ Network ➤ RFC Destinations, or use Transaction code SM59. An overview tree is displayed, showing all the RFC connections defined in the system.

2. Open the branch with the overview of R/3 connections.

3. Create new RFC connections by choosing Create, or adapt existing connections by choosing Change.

4. Specify the logical name of the connection in the field RFC Destination.

5. Select the connection type. Depending on the connection type, new entry fields will be displayed. Figure 5.14 shows

the screen for creating an RFC connection to another R/3 System. Figure 5.15 shows the possible connection types.

FIGURE 5.14:

Defining an RFC connection to another R/3 System

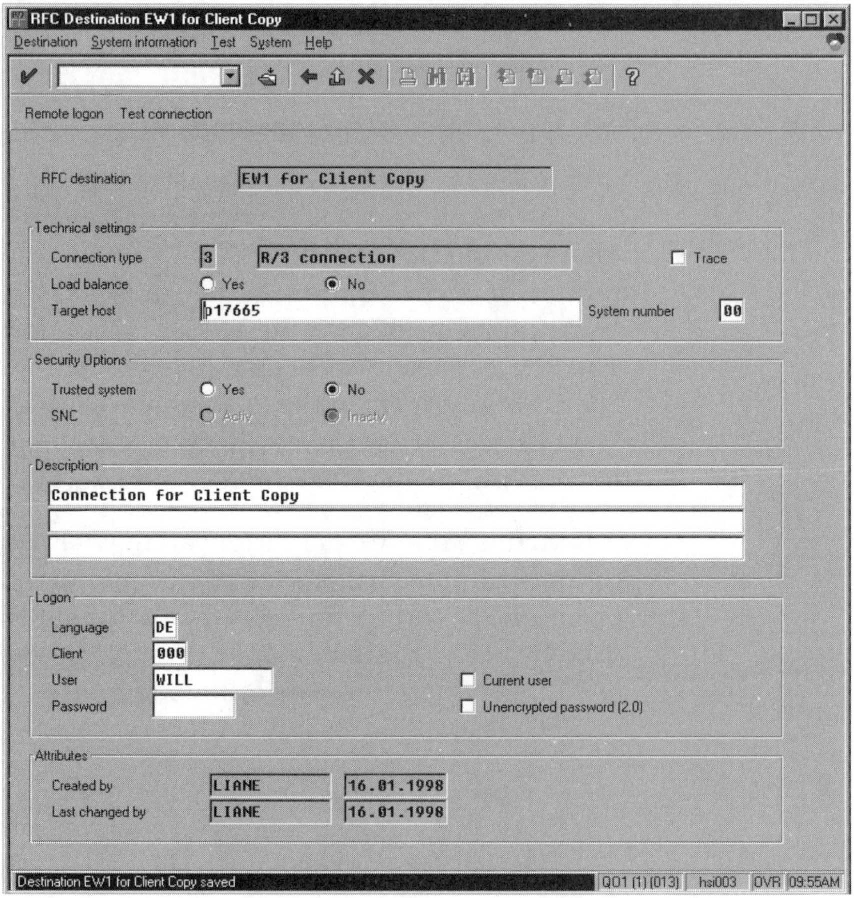

> **TIP** You can activate the Trace option in critical cases. A trace records all the processes that go through an RFC connection in a file on the operating system level. To evaluate logs from both the sending system and the receiving system, use report RSRFCTRC.

FIGURE 5.15:

Possible connection
types for RFC
destinations

Type of entry in RFCDES ☒

Type	Short text
I	Connection to application server with same database
3	Connection to R/3 System
2	Connection to R/2 System
T	Start an external program via TCP/IP
L	Reference entry (refers to another destination)
S	Start an external program via SNA or APPC
X	RFC via special ABAP/4 driver routines
M	CMC connection

6. Specify the target computer and the number of the instance on this computer.

7. For each RFC destination to another R/3 System, you must specify the logon language, the client, the user, and the password in the remote system. Alternatively, you can take over the data used when the RFC definition was created.

8. Test the connection by choosing Test Connection.

9. Save it. The R/3 System adds data about its creation and the date of the last change. The RFC connection is now defined.

The overview of the defined R/3 connections also shows you the entries generated during the configuration of the TMS. They always begin with TMSADM@ or TMSSUP@. Connection type 3 is used for these RFC connections between R/3 Systems.

The logon data for a connection are used to identify a user to the system when an RFC connection to a remote system is established. The assignment is static. For example, if the user password is changed in the remote system, the RFC connection definition must also be changed.

When you define RFC connections, you can use the name of a group of application servers instead of a single target computer. You must first enter the name of the group by choosing RFC ➤ RFC Groups. This method has the advantage that the computer with the lowest load is selected from the application server group to establish the connection, that is, an automatic logon load distribution takes place.

Other types of RFC connections are defined in the same way. Depending on the type, different information is required. To define an RFC destination to execute external programs, you must first select the target computers. These can be application servers, front-end workstations or an explicit host that is not being used by the current R/3 System. You must specify the computer name here for an explicit host. For front-end workstations and application computers in the same R/3 System, the computer names are already made known at logon. It is assumed that all computers can be reached through the network without the need to specify the user name and password again, that is, this data must not be entered explicitly. The external program to be started is assigned to the RFC connection to be defined.

It is also advisable to use entries of type "L." These are logical entries that reference another RFC destination. An RFC destination is defined first to determine only the physical part, that is the computer. Then, new connections of type "L" are created to reference this entry. The RFC connection of type "L" takes on the target computer and the connection type of the RFC destination it references. If necessary, the client, user, and password are added to the RFC connection of type "L." This allows greater independence when RFC destinations are defined. For example, if an R/3 System is moved from one computer to another, only the RFC destinations used as a reference for connection definitions of type "L" need to be modified.

Review Questions

1. For production purposes, it is recommended

    A. That at least two R/3 Systems on different computers for development/quality assurance and production are set up.

    B. That as powerful a computer as possible is set up on which a central R/3 System is available for all tasks.

    C. That multiple R/3 Systems run on a common, central database.

2. In a multi-system landscape, transport activities

    A. Can only be controlled from the system that the data is being imported into or exported from.

    B. Can be controlled centrally from the Domain Controller of the transport domain.

    C. Can only be controlled on the operating system level using the tp program.

    D. Can be controlled in a transport domain from each R/3 System in the domain.

3. What transport paths are there?

    A. Direct transport path

    B. Indirect transport path

    C. Consolidation path

    D. Delivery path

    E. Diversion

4. Which program on the operating level is used to perform transports?

    A. R3load

    B. R3INST

    C. tp

    D. dpmon

    E. sapdba

5. Which parameter file is used to control the transport control program?

    A. Default.pfl

    B. profile

    C. initparam

    D. TPPARAM

CHAPTER
SIX

6

Software Logistics

This chapter covers the topic of software logistics: the tools and methods for maintaining the R/3 software, distributing objects, and managing changes in the system landscape. First, there is a brief description of how a transport request is created and what is behind it. The chapter also covers the handling and the functions of the Customizing Organizer (CO), the Workbench Organizer (WBO), and the Transport Organizer (TO). You'll be shown how to transport the changes from one R/3 System to another and activate them.

Implementation Guide

R/3 contains standard solutions for almost all areas of a company's business processes. The term "standard solution" should be interpreted flexibly. The R/3 System frequently integrates multiple variants of processes. During the implementation of R/3 it is important to adapt the R/3 System to specific customer requirements by modifying the appropriate parameters and settings. This is known as *customizing*. During customizing, one of the available variants is chosen. The Implementation Guide (IMG) is particularly important for customizing. The IMG is required and is the basis both for customizing and other important tools such as the Profile Generator and the SAP Session Manager.

Creating an Enterprise IMG

With each R/3 System, SAP delivers a complete Implementation Guide for all R/3 application modules. One of the first tasks in a company planning to implement R/3 is to decide which are the relevant application areas for its specific purposes. This is known as creating the *Enterprise IMG*, the Implementation Guide specific to a company. The Enterprise IMG forms the framework for the subsequent Customizing activities. The following list is a short description, from a technical viewpoint, of how to generate the Enterprise IMG. The explanation of the business aspects is much more complex. (As this is not the task of the R/3 System administrator, the business aspects are not covered here.)

To generate the Enterprise IMG:

1. Choose Tools ➤ Business Engineer ➤ Customizing ➤ Basic Functions ➤ Enterprise IMG ➤ Generate, or use Transaction code SPRO.

2. Give the Enterprise IMG a distinctive name.

3. Choose the countries relevant for your company so that country-specific information can be used in the business tasks. The IMG can be generated for specific countries or for all countries.

4. Confirm your selection. A hierarchical tree of the complete Implementation Guide delivered by SAP is then displayed.

5. Click-select the R/3 components to be used by your company.

6. Generate your Enterprise IMG.

Once an Enterprise IMG has been generated, it can be extended while retaining the information already assigned. R/3 release upgrades make it necessary to regenerate the Enterprise IMG, as at least functional releases include new application components. All new nodes are highlighted in red. Nodes of components, which contain new modules, are highlighted in yellow in the IMG tree. You can only generate an Enterprise IMG if you chose explicitly to select or deselect all nodes that contain new nodes. The color highlighting is automatically removed when you select or deselect them.

Projects

From the Enterprise IMG, you can group tasks into projects, or you can separate them. Users implementing individual projects are supported by such integrated functions as project administration, including time scheduling, status maintenance, and documentation. For example, a project could be to implement Materials Management. From the Enterprise IMG, go to project maintenance by choosing Project administration. To create a new project, choose Create.

You can also change existing projects. Each project has a unique identification number. Project 001 is predefined as the SAP standard project. Figure 6.1 shows the header data for project 003, which comprises Materials Management (MM).

FIGURE 6.1:

Project 003-MM

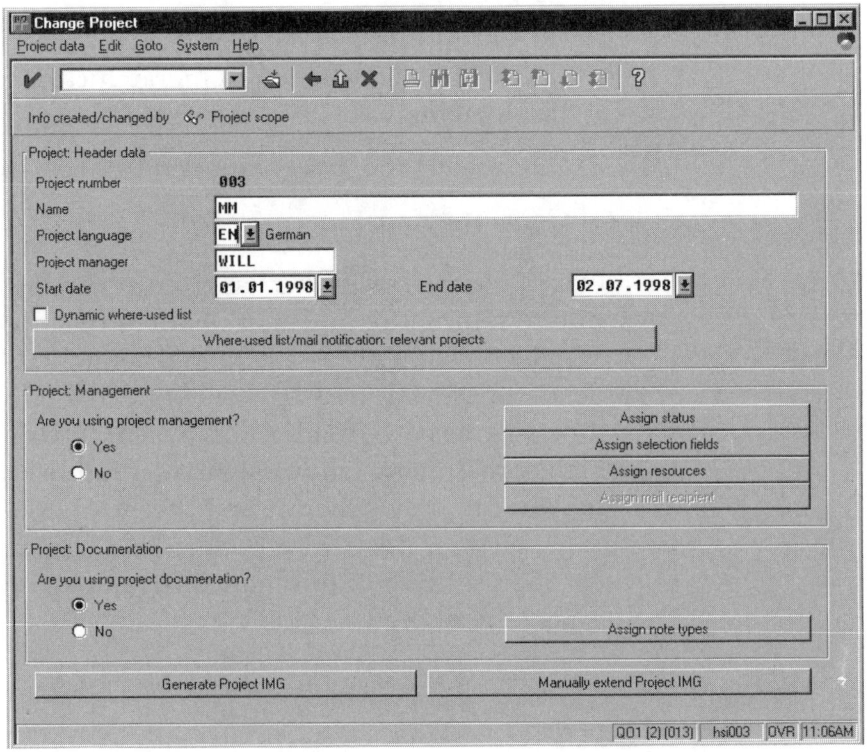

To select the subject areas relevant to this project, choose Generate Project IMG from the hierarchical module tree of the Enterprise IMG. In this case, only the subject area Materials Management is selected. All other subjects are explicitly deselected if they contain new nodes. R/3 automatically adds global subject areas. Generation can then begin.

You can also generate different views on the activities for the project. The project leader can create views on only the required, optional, critical, or uncritical actions in the project. These views assist you in evaluating the status of a project. The Implementation Guide is then used to perform the Customizing steps for the project.

Tasks and Change Requests

In the following sections you'll learn how you can make various modifications within R/3. The R/3 System provides different types of change requests for different types of changes.

Customizing Requests

As already mentioned, you need to make Customizing settings when you implement R/3. Customizing primarily concerns business processes and is therefore client-dependent, as a client represents a business unit. If a client has been set to automatically record changes (see Chapter 7), a task and a *Customizing request* are created automatically when a user in an R/3 System makes Customizing changes. If Customizing requests were created, you can explicitly control the assignment of tasks to the Customizing requests.

Transportable Change Requests

In addition to the changes within Customizing, it may also be necessary to develop your own new objects and modify objects delivered by SAP, so-called *SAP-owned objects.* This allows you to tailor the R/3 System to your requirements. Changes such as these are client-independent; that means they are in effect throughout the entire system. This change data is recorded immediately in a similar way to the Customizing actions, but in a task assigned to a transportable change request.

Local Change Request

In addition to the transportable changes, you can make local changes. For this type of change, there are tasks in local change requests. These changes cannot be transported to other systems.

When you assign a task in a change request to software development, security precautions are taken. The object is locked to users other than the owner of the task and the change request, unless the developer responsible explicitly transfers the authorizations for that task to another user. If a development project is completed, the tasks are released, followed by the change request. The object can only be changed again after the change request has been released. This mechanism prevents overlap of changes to the same object.

Request Number

All tasks and requests from customers have a unique ID, which is made up from the three-character R/3 System name, the ID *K9*, and a sequential five-figure number, for example, QO1K900005. Each change request has one owner, the project leader, who is responsible for administering the request. If necessary, the owner can be changed. A change request can be made up of multiple tasks, which are assigned to one user. A change request can be considered as a project, within which different users have separate tasks. A task can be transferred to another user.

The project can only be completed after all the tasks in a change request are completed and released, that is, after the change request is released. If the change request is transportable or a Customizing request, it is released automatically after it is transported. The change request becomes a transport request. The path taken by a transport request is defined when the system landscape is set up (see Chapter 4).

Customizing Organizer and Workbench Organizer

To administer change requests and their tasks, you can use the Customizing Organizer (CO) and the Workbench Organizer (WBO). You can use the CO to process all types of change requests. You can use the WBO to administer development work. The WBO and the CO provide views for different user requirements. The WBO is tailored to the requirements of developers in the area of the ABAP Workbench. Customizing requests are requests that they do not need, and indeed they reduce clarity. Change requests that result from this development work are frequently referred to as Workbench change requests.

The following example illustrates how to process change requests using the WBO and the CO.

You need to create purchasing groups in Materials Management in client 013. The table already contains three example entries of possible purchasers. Adapt these entries to your requirements. This is a typical change in Customizing. For the sake of simplicity, it is assumed that the user used to complete the task has the appropriate authorizations. This would be the case if, for example, the user were created by copying user SAP* (see Chapter 8.)

NOTE   You cannot use users SAP* and DDIC to administer change requests and to make changes in the system. These users perform the administration tasks that do not involve development activities.

Creating a Customizing Request

There are two ways to create a Customizing request:

- Make the change and then let the R/3 System generate the Customizing request and the task for the change

- Use the CO to create a Customizing request with a task. Then, make the change and assign the task explicitly.

The procedure you choose depends primarily on the user concept. By assigning authorizations, you can prevent users from creating their own change requests. This task can be reserved for a selected group of users. This procedure has the advantage that you retain control of Customizing requests and assignment. You can also withdraw the authorization from a developer to create any type of change requests, only allowing that developer to make changes if an authorized person, for example, the project leader, first creates and assigns the corresponding change requests. This allows you to coordinate development work in the R/3 System more effectively (see Figure 6.2).

Unclassified Change Requests

In addition to the types of change requests already described, you can use the CO to create unclassified change requests. Unclassified change requests are only assigned a type when a change is assigned. Depending on the type of change made, a Customizing or a client-independent change, the unclassified change request is converted to a Customizing request or a local or transportable change request.

FIGURE 6.2:

Managing a project

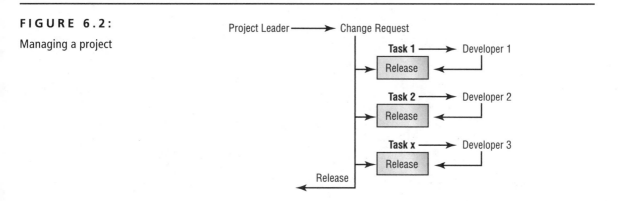

For this example, you could use the second way I mentioned earlier for creating a Customizing request:

1. Call the CO by choosing Tools ➤ Business Engineer ➤ Customizing ➤ Basic Functions ➤ Requests (Organizer) ➤ Create Requests/Tasks ➤ Customizing Request Management, or use Transaction code SE10. Figure 6.3 shows the initial screen of the CO.

2. Choose Request/Task ➤ Create or choose Display and then Request/Task ➤ Create.

3. As the type of change request, select Customizing Request.

4. You are prompted to enter a comment that describes the content and the people involved. A task is created in this Customizing request for each of the people you enter.

5. Save. The Customizing request is now created.

FIGURE 6.3:

The initial screen of the
Customizing Organizer

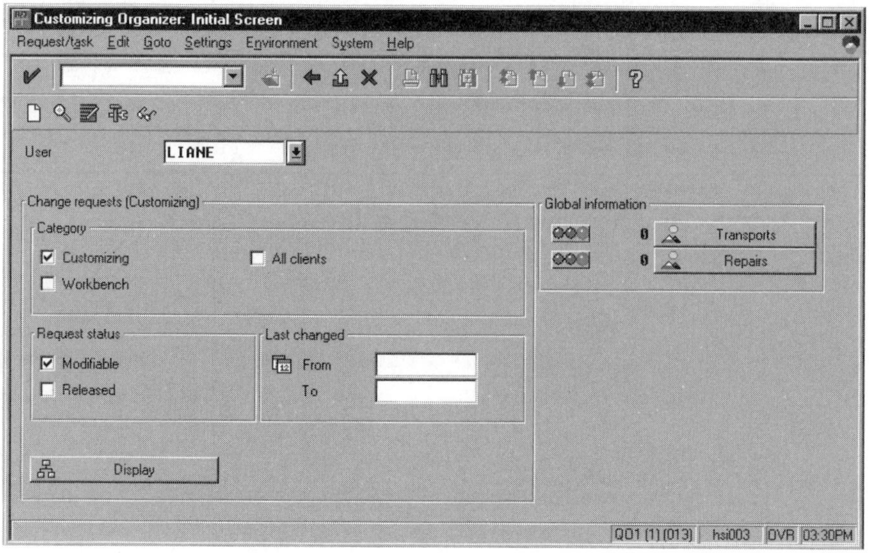

Figure 6.4 shows the screen for entering the data for a change request. The field Source client displays the client assigned to the Customizing request. The category CUST indicates that it is a Customizing request. The Target field contains the name of the R/3 System, to which the Customizing request will be transported when it is released. In this case, as shown in Figure 6.3, this would be the EXT system. This information is taken from the settings made when the system landscape is set up.

FIGURE 6.4:

Creating a Customizing
request

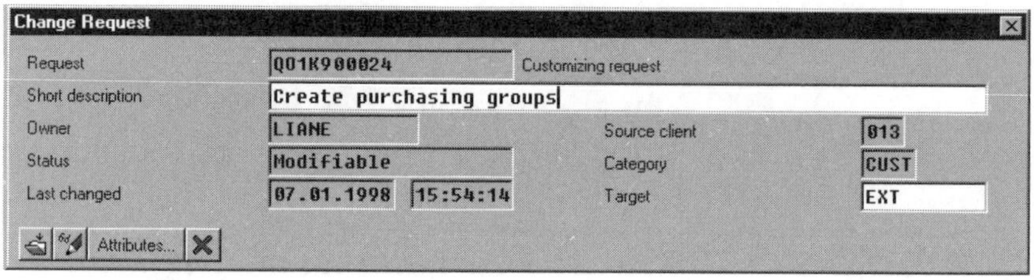

Figure 6.5 shows the hierarchical display mode of the CO. You can see the Customizing request QO1K900024 that has been created in client 013 with user WILL. The task QO1K90025 was assigned to the Customizing request. To change the owner of a request and/or task, choose Owner. To make further tasks available to a request, select the request and choose Request/Task ➤ Create.

FIGURE 6.5:

Displaying the change requests

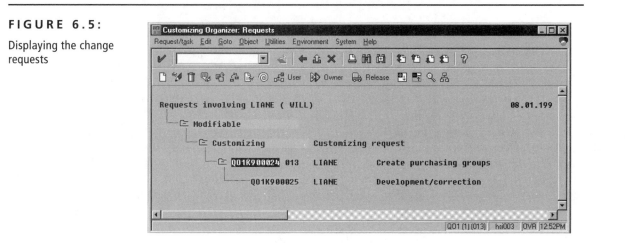

Assigning a Change to a Customizing Request

Now we'll look at how a Customizing change is assigned to a request.

In this example, we want to create purchasing groups in a company. To do so follow these steps:

1. From the maintenance screen for project IMG 003, open the structure up to Create Purchasing Groups and run this Customizing transaction (see Figure 6.6).

2. Make the desired entries.

FIGURE 6.6:

Creating purchasing
groups

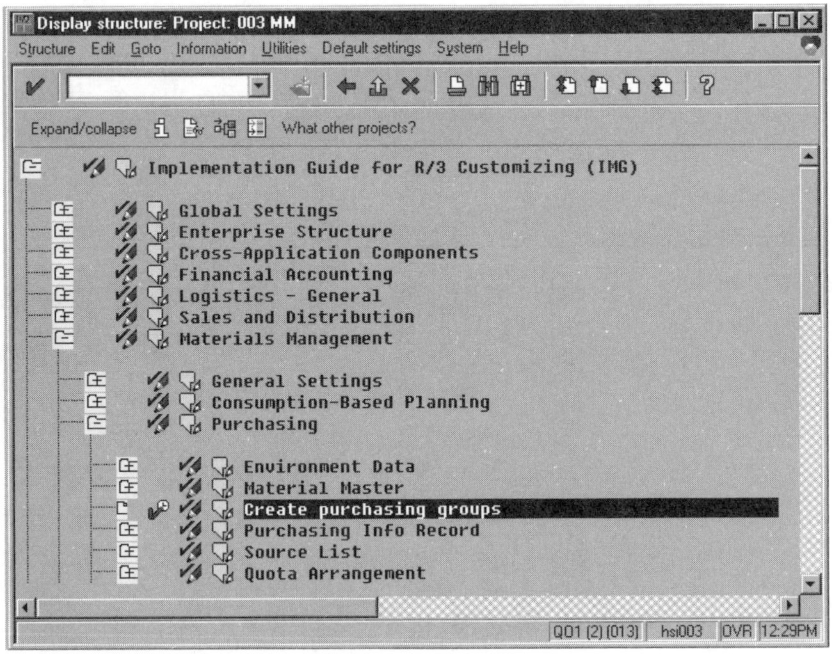

3. Save your entries. You are prompted to assign or create a new
   change request (see Figure 6.7).

4. Choose the request QO1K900024 and confirm. The change is
   now assigned to a Customizing request.

FIGURE 6.7:

Assigning a change
request

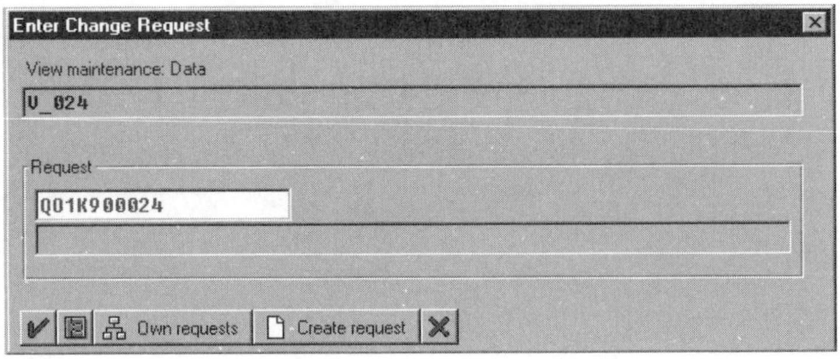

The changes are now saved physically. This means that changes to objects can only be made permanently if they are recorded in change requests.

Releasing a Customizing Request

The Customizing procedure has now been completed for this example. The Customizing request can be closed (released). To release a Customizing request that you are responsible for maintaining, follow these steps:

1. Start the CO (Transaction code SE10).

2. From the initial screen, select the desired category and status to display only the necessary requests.

3. Choose Display.

4. All the tasks in the Customizing request must be completed, that is, released by the owner. If a task has not been completed, as in this example, select the task (task QO1K900025 in this example) and choose Release.

5. You are prompted again to document the change made.

6. Save the final version of your documentation and exit the screen. All the changes in the task are passed to the assigned Customizing request. To get more information on the objects in the task, open the tree (see Figure 6.8). In this case, changes were made to object V_024.

7. If all the tasks are released, the Customizing request can be released in the same way. Select the Customizing request, choose Release, and document your actions.

The Customizing request is exported when it is released. A Customizing request can also be released to a transportable change request, which itself will only be released and transported later. This has the advantage that multiple Customizing requests can be collected and exported later as a group (see Figure 6.9).

FIGURE 6.8:

Released task
QO1K900023

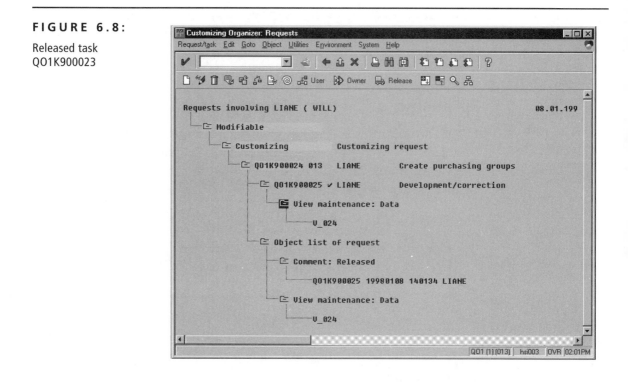

FIGURE 6.9:

Releasing a Customizing request

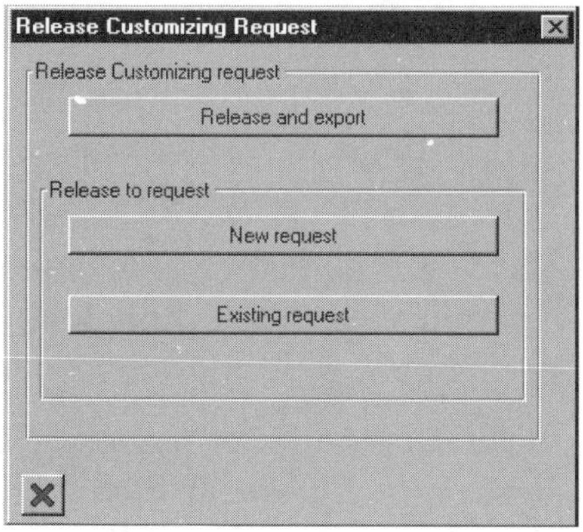

Technically, when data is exported, files are created in the transport directory tree on the operating system level. When these files are imported into another R/3 System, they cause the same changes to be made as were made manually in the original system. The export and import are performed by the `tp` program, but the export can be performed automatically when a change request is released. The import must be started explicitly.

Using the WBO

The Workbench Organizer is used for administering change requests that are generated from work with the ABAP Workbench. An important feature of these changes is the immediate systemwide—and client-independent—effect on the run-time environment. Depending on whether these changes are only local or whether they will be transported into other R/3 Systems, they are recorded using local or transportable change requests. The only difference between this type of request and a Customizing request is in the fact that it is client-independent. The changes assigned may be of a similar nature to Customizing changes. For this reason, it is often referred to as client-independent Customizing.

An example of this type of request is maintaining table USR40, which contains all the prohibited passwords in an R/3 System in generic form using * and ?. To maintain a table, choose Systems ➤ Services ➤ Table Maintenance.

You make changes to this table in the same way as you do for Customizing requests, except that if entries in this table are to be transported into other R/3 Systems, a transportable change request is necessary because the table is client-independent. You can use both the CO and the WBO for these types of change requests. These two tools are similar in usage, range of functions, and appearance. Unlike the CO, the WBO is used for administering development projects created using the ABAP Workbench. The ABAP Workbench offers the following tools for developers:

Repository Browser and Dictionary—To develop tables, structures, indexes, domains, matchcodes, etc.

ABAP Editor and Function Builder—To process programs and functions

Screen Painter—To develop screen masks

Menu Painter—To develop menu trees

Test tools

These tools are all used to develop or change R/3 functions. This separation of tasks between Customizing and new software development is the reason there are different administration tools: WBO and CO. The further development of R/3 functionality will only rarely be the direct responsibility of the R/3 System administrator, but the administrator will repeatedly come into contact with this area in the course of their systemwide administration tasks, such as performing R/3 upgrades (*Upgrades*) or sometimes importing corrections. The following example explains the most important procedures, focusing on administration tasks.

In this case, you want to create a new ABAP program and transport it to a different R/3 System.

Every user who wants to develop new objects in an R/3 System or to make modifications to objects delivered by SAP, the SAP-owned objects, must first be registered for that R/3 System using the OSS (see Figure 6.10). Either choose Registration from the menu and follow the menu path, or use Transaction code SSCR. SSCR stands for SAP Software Change Registration.

In this way, both the R/3 administrator and SAP have an overview of the degree to which customer-specific software is being developed in an R/3 System. Again, it is necessary to determine whether

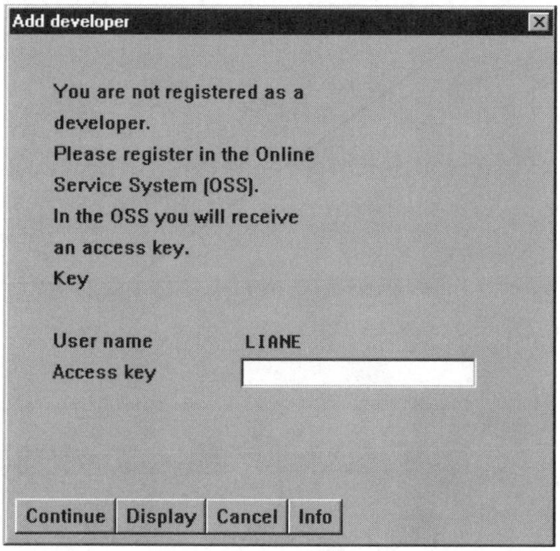

FIGURE 6.10:

Registering a developer

a change is to be made to an SAP-owned object or whether a new object is to be created.

Changing SAP-Owned Objects

Each change to a SAP-owned object involves registering the object using the OSS. When you change a SAP-owned object for the first time, you are prompted to enter the access key (see Figure 6.11).

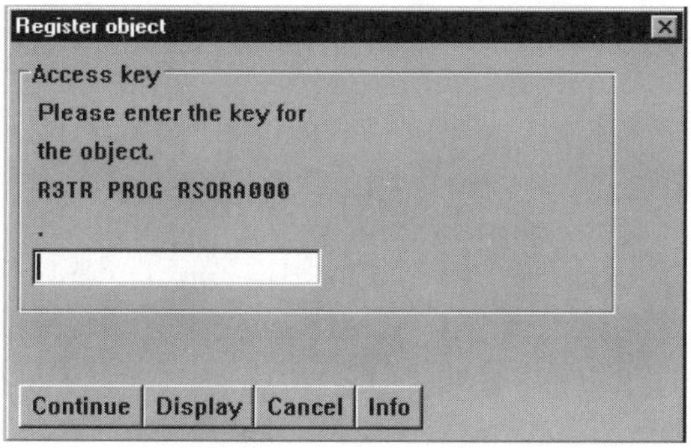

FIGURE 6.11:

Prompt for the access key

To obtain an access key, log on to the OSS and use Transaction SCCR to enter data on the desired object (see Figure 6.12) and copy the generated access key to the screen in Figure 6.11. Only then can the SAP-owned object be processed. These precautions are intended to restrict unauthorized changes to SAP-owned objects. The information about customer-specific modifications is also important for SAP customer service, which is then able to react more quickly and find solutions. Chapter 5 covers the possible consequences of these changes.

FIGURE 6.12:

Access key in OSS

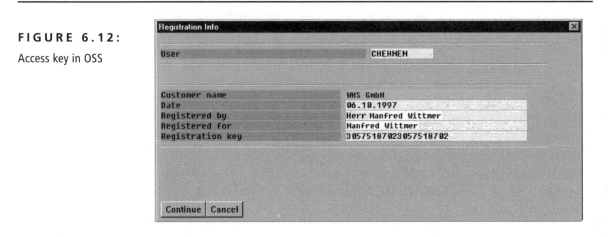

New Software Development

New software development in a system landscape (the task undertaken in this example) must be planned in detail in order to prevent conflicts with SAP-owned and customer-specific objects. New software should only be developed in a two- or, preferably, a three-system landscape. You must avoid mixing development and production work in the same system. We will assume that the system landscape is already completely configured as described in Chapter 5 and that the transport paths between the systems are defined.

Development Class

Before you can create new objects, you must create a *development class* in the integration system in which the software is being developed, and assign a transport layer. A development class is an object and must also be transported. Ideally, a development class contains independent or closely related objects grouped together in one logical unit. A development class is always assigned to an application area, for example, Basis (S) or Financial Accounting (F). Assigning a transport layer to a development class ensures that all objects in the development class are transported along the same path. Development classes can also be transported as one group with all the pertinent objects. Development class *$TMP* has a special role: it is used for all local (temporary), or non-transportable, objects.

Customer Name Range

SAP provides a separate *customer name range* to create objects, including, for example, a development class. This prevents name conflicts between SAP and customer objects. Beginning with R/3 release 4.0, the following rules apply for creating names of development classes and Workbench objects:

- Customers can use the name range beginning with "Y" or "Z," as in R/3 Releases before 4.0.

- Customers can apply for a separate name range for particularly large development projects. These name ranges have a minimum of five and a maximum of 10 characters. They begin and end with a slash (/). An SAP license key protects these name ranges from unauthorized access. Customer-specific name ranges are intended for complex customer-specific development projects or development projects by SAP partners.

> **NOTE**   Older R/3 releases have a name length limitation of eight characters. Customers can use the ranges Y-Z for their own objects, and T for a private test development class. Ranges A-S and U-X are reserved for SAP development work. For SAP-owned objects, the first letter of the development class refers to the application area.

To create a development class that is integrated into the ABAP Workbench, follow these steps:

1. Choose Repository Browser. Enter a new development class in the appropriate field and choose Display, and then you can create it. In this example, we will create the class ZZZZ (see Figure 6.13).

2. Display checks whether the object already exists. If the object does not exist, as is the case here, you are prompted to create it. Choose Yes.

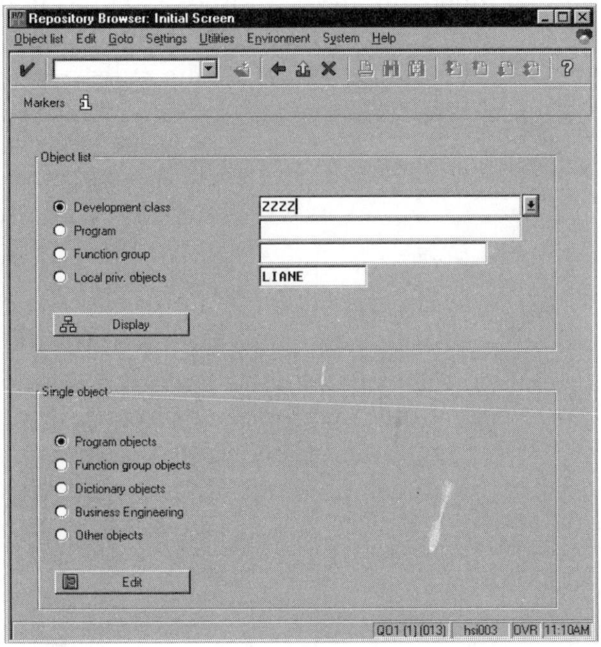

FIGURE 6.13:

The initial screen of the Repository Browser

3. Now we need to maintain the attributes of the development class. The transport layer is particularly important, as it defines the transport path for the changes. As only transport layer ZQO1 is defined in our system, the system proposes it (see Figure 6.14).

FIGURE 6.14:

Creating a development class

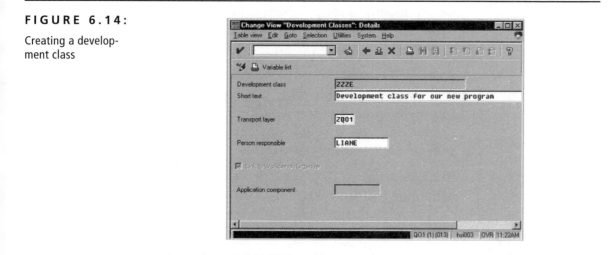

4. When you choose Save, you are prompted to assign a change request. Choose Create, which creates a new transportable change request for the change.

5. Confirm the generated request number, and the new development class is created.

The WBO provides a hierarchical overview of the change requests in the system. You can also restrict this overview to show the type and status of change requests. The more changes there are in the system, and the more change requests, the more important it becomes to remember the assigned request number.

The next step is to create the new program, as follows:

1. You can use the Repository Browser in the same way as before. This time, choose Program and enter the name: **ZWORLD**.

2. Choose Display to begin creating the new program. As it is a program, the ABAP editor is automatically called. You can also create a program by calling the ABAP editor directly from the ABAP Workbench.

3. Enter attributes for this object. These include a short text, an assigned application area, and the type of program to be created. Examples of program types are executable programs (1), function groups (F), or source texts (Includes I), which are inserted into other programs. In this case, the program is of type 1.

4. When you save this data, you are prompted to assign a development class. If you select Local Object instead of a development class, the object is automatically defined as a local object and is not transportable.

This information is used to create an object directory entry (see Figure 6.15).

FIGURE 6.15:

Creating an object
directory entry

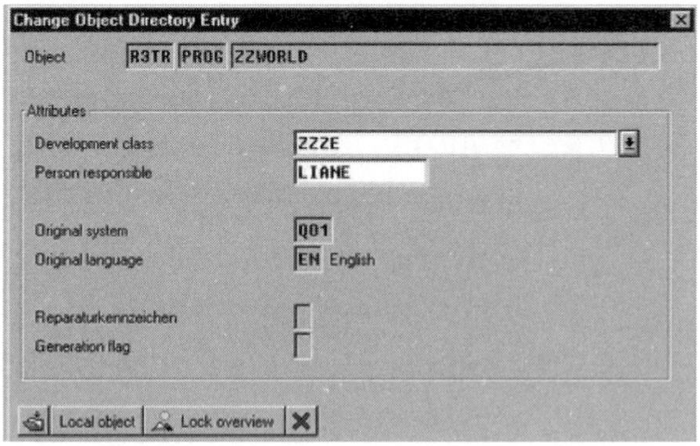

5. When you save the entries, change management is activated. You must now assign the entries to a change request in the same way as before. In this example, a request created for development class ZZZZ is proposed, and you only need to confirm it.

6. Only now can you create the source text by choosing Source Text. We will add the following line to the text that has already been generated:

```
Write 'Hello world!'.
```

When the program is executed, for example, by choosing Program ➤ Execute, a simple list with the words "Hello world!" would be generated.

7. Choosing Save completes the development activity in this example. Use the Repository Browser to display a hierarchy of the contents of the development class ZZZZ.

Object Catalog

There is an object catalog entry (also referred to as the object directory entry) for each object in the R/3 System (as we saw in Figure 6.15). The entry contains all the important information about the object. In addition to the development class of an object, the object catalog entry also records the maintenance language for that object. The maintenance language is important when documentation or text elements are created. The object's original system is important for the system landscape.

Original

An object is only an *original* in the system in which it was created. This attribute is linked to different protection mechanisms. In the system landscape, the objects in the integration system are original. This is where they are developed. Copies are transported into other systems for testing and ultimately for production use. Changes necessary to the object copies in these systems are known as *repairs*. If these changes are not also made to the original in the integration system, they can be overwritten with a new transport from the integration system.

Release and Export

The next task is to release and transport the changes. In this example, the contents of the transportable change request QO1K900035 will be transported into the system EW1. The procedure is similar to releasing and transporting Customizing requests.

1. Call the WBO from the ABAP Workbench by choosing Overview ➤ Workbench Organizer, or using Transaction code SE09.

2. Display all the relevant change requests for the user.

3. Open the change request, in this example, QO1K900035. Figure 6.16 shows the WBO display for this example.

FIGURE 6.16:

Overview of change requests for user WILL

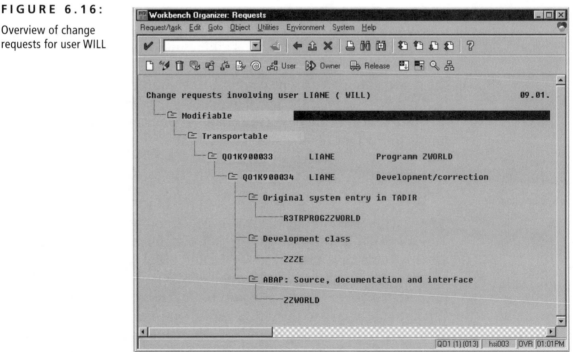

4. Release the assigned task, in this case QO1K900034, by selecting the task and choosing Release. When the task is released, you need to document it.

5. Release the transportable change, in this case QO1K900033, by selecting it and choosing Release. A transport request is automatically sent to program tp and the export of the data in the change request is started. The status bar displays information about the actions started, which indicates that the program tp is used for the export. You can now exit the WBO. Until the export is completed, the transport request will have an Open status. When the export is complete, the transport request is released.

6. Check the status of the export.

Logs

Transports (exports and imports) are performed in multiple steps. Each step is logged. When the transport is completed, the system sends a return code that gives an indication of success. You are advised to evaluate the logs and resolve any errors that occurred. If you do not, data imported into a system later may be incomplete.

Action Log

To display the logs, first select the transport request. Then choose Goto ➤ Action Log to display all the actions made for the transport request. Figure 6.17 shows this for the request QO1K900033. The log file is located in \usr\sap\trans\actlog\ QO1Z900033.QO1.

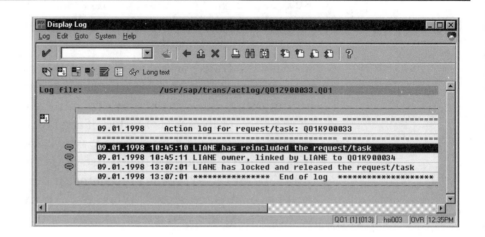

Transport Logs

In addition to the action log, separate log files are created in the subdirectory log of the transport directory for each transport. The log file name is made up as follows:

```
Log file name:= <SID of the source system><Step><Number of the
transport request>.<SID of the target system>
```

<Step> indicates the step performed in accordance with the following naming conventions:

A—Activate the Repository

C—Transport C source text

D—Import application-defined objects

E—Main export

G—Generate programs and screens

H—Repository import

I—Main import

L—Import command file

M—Activate enqueue modules

P—Test import

R—Compare versions after R/3 upgrade

T—Import table entries

V—Set version IDs for imported objects

X—Export application-defined objects

These logs are stored in a readable form on the operating system level and can be evaluated using operating system tools. The more common—and easier—way to view these logs is by choosing Goto ➤ Transport Logs. First the steps are shown in compressed form, and you can expand them in four stages. In this case, we are working with an export. A log file called Q01E900035.EW1 was created. The contents of this file have the highest expansion level for log files from the R/3 System. The log that follows shows an excerpt from this log file. Information of particular importance is shown in bold.

Report 6.1:

```
1 ETP199X#####################################
1 ETP150 MAIN EXPORT
1 ETP101 transport order     : "Q01K900035"
1 ETP102 system              : "Q01"
1 ETP108 tp path             : "/usr/sap/Q01/SYS/exe/run/tp"
1 ETP109 version and release : "251.09.01" "40A"
1 ETP198
4 ETW000 ===============================================
4 ETW000 control file: /usr/sap/trans/Q01K0035.Q01
4 ETW000 date&time    : 12.01.1998 - 10:05:16
```

```
4 ETW000 Connected to DBMS = ORACLE -- dbs_ora_tnsname = 'Q01'
- SYSTEM = 'Q01'.
4 ETW000
4 ETW000 =================== STEP 1 =====================
4 ETW000 date&time   : 12.01.1998 - 10:05:32
4 ETW000 function    : EXPORT
4 ETW000 data file   : /usr/sap/trans/data/R900035.Q01
4 ETW000 buffersync  : YES
4 ETW000 client      : 013
4 ETW000 Language    :
ABCDEFGHIJKLMNOPQRSTUVWXYZ0123456789abcdefghijklmnopqrstuvwxyz4
ETW000 Compression : C
4 ETW000 l.s.m.      : VECTOR
4 ETW000 commit      : 100000
4 ETW000 table cache : dynamic
4 ETW000 Use commandfile 'Q01K900035'.
3 ETW673XUse Commandfile "Q01K900035"
4 ETW000       /* Program ZWORLD */
4 ETW000       trfunction: 'K' (transport to consolidation system)
4 ETW000       trstatus  : 'R'
4 ETW000       tarsystem : EW1
4 ETW000       user      : WILL
4 ETW000       date      : 09.01.1998 - 15:11:26
4 ETW000 SELECT ADIR_BRACKET where name = 'R3TRDEVCZZZZ'
...
4 ETW678Xstart export of "R3TRDEVCZZZZ" ...
...
4 ETW000 SELECT * from TDEVC generic key = 'ZZZZ'
4 ETW000 SELECT * from TDEVCT generic key = 'ZZZZ*'
4 ETW000 SELECT ADIR_BRACKET where name = ''
4 ETW000 SELECT ADIR_BRACKET where name = 'R3TRPROGZWORLD'
4 ETW000 REPC_OR_DELETE from SMODILOG generic key = 'PROGZWORLD*'
...
4 ETW000   0 entries from SREPALOG exported (DEVCZZZZ*).
4 ETW000   1 entry from TDEVC exported (ZZZZ).
4 ETW000   1 entry from TDEVCT exported (ZZZZ*).
3 ETW679 end export of "R3TRDEVCZZZZ".
4 ETW678Xstart export of "R3TRPROGZWORLD"
...
4 ETW000   1 entry from TADIR exported (R3TRPROGZWORLD).
```

```
4 ETW000   0 entries from SMODISRC exported (CVPROGZWORLD*).
...
3 ETW679 end export of "R3TRPROGZWORLD".
4 ETW000 11508 bytes written.
4 ETW000 Transport overhead 79.9 %.
4 ETW000 Data compressed to 27.4 %.
4 ETW000 Duration: 21 sec (548 bytes/sec).
4 ETW000   0 tables in P-buffer synchronized.
4 ETW000   0 tables in R-buffer synchronized.
4 ETW000 COMMIT (11508).
4 ETW000 Summary:
4 ETW000   1 COMML exported
4 ETW000   1 COMMT exported
4 ETW000   1 DOCUT exported
4 ETW000   1 REPOS exported
4 ETW000   1 REPOT exported
4 ETW000 Totally 6 Objects exported
...
4 ETW000 Totally 3 tabentries exported
4 ETW000
4 ETW000 Disconnected from database.
4 ETW000 End of Transport (0000).
4 ETW000 date&time: 12.01.10000- 10:05:53
1 ETP150 MAIN EXPORT
1 ETP110 end date and time   : "19970112100554"
1 ETP111 exit code           : "0"
1 ETP199
#######################################
```

The return code is very important for the administrator. Return code 0, as shown in this example, indicates that no errors occurred during the export. Warnings are marked with a W as soon as they occur in the appropriate line of the log. Return code 4 is then returned. Serious errors, which may cause an incomplete transport, are marked with an E in the log. The return code in this case is greater than or equal to 8. The log files indicate where to look for the cause of the error. You must resolve the cause of the error and then repeat the export. Causes can be, for example, problems in the database. A canceled transport request would be displayed in the WBO with status Export Not Completed.

Cofile and Data File

In addition to the log files, the export generates a data file and a cofile containing metadata about the objects in the request. The data file and the cofile make up the actual data to be transported. They contain all the data necessary for an import. Cofiles are stored in the directory cofiles, and data files are stored in the directory data of the transport directory tree. The file names are made up as follows:

```
<File type><Number of the transport request>.<SID of the source
system>
```

File type K stands for cofiles, R and D stand for data files. In this example, the cofile K900035.Q01 and the data file R900035.Q01 were created.

Transport Organizer

The central starting point for evaluating logs is the Transport Organizer (TO), from which you can access the WBO and the CO. The Transport Organizer also provides the following functions:

Transporting copies and transferring originals—In addition to the change requests already described and the resulting transport requests, it may be necessary to move originals from one R/3 System to another. For example, this may be necessary if integration systems are added to the system landscape, as a result of which the development environment is moved to another system or divided between multiple systems. When a copy is transported, it really is only a copy of an object. The original remains in the original system.

Functions for evaluating client transports—See Chapter 7.

Object lists—Object lists are collections of objects that can be included in transport requests as templates. Object lists can be generated automatically, for example, through all the objects in a development class or other shared object attributes. You can also create object lists manually.

Administering deliveries from SAP or partners to customers— Corrections and preliminary releases delivered by SAP and its partners are administered separately, as they contain SAP-owned objects. You can recognize this type of transport request by its name, which is made up of SAPK<*Number*>.

We will not describe the TO in detail here, as it is beyond the scope of this book. The TO provides a number of functions for administering special transports between R/3 Systems, and mostly they do not represent the norm.

Importing Transport Requests

After releasing and exporting a transport request in R/3 releases prior to 4.0, you used to have to control the import phase manually on the operating system level by using the transport control tool `tp`. The TMS in Release 4.0 allows you to bypass this. The menu-driven administration of transport requests in the TMS replaces the direct `tp` call. When your system landscape is correctly configured, and the R/3 System is release 3.1H or later, you can perform all the necessary steps from each R/3 System in the transport domain.

Releasing an R/3 transport request in R/3 4.0 does not finish with the successful completion of the export. Instead, the transport request is automatically placed in the import queue of the target system if the target system is in the same transport group as the source system. A transport group has a common transport directory. If the source system and the target system have different transport groups, an interim step is needed to place the transport request into the import queue. First, we'll look at the import queue administration. To display the overview of the requests for the next import into the systems in a domain, from the TMS (Tools) ➤ Administration ➤ Transports ➤ Transport Management System, or Transaction code STMS), choose Overview ➤ Imports (see Figure 6.18).

FIGURE 6.18:

Import overview

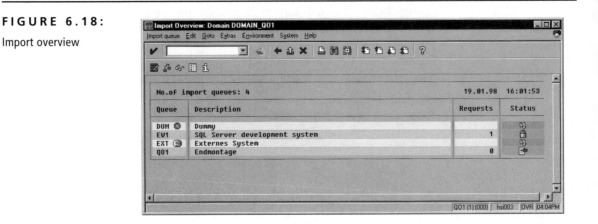

Figure 6.18 shows one transport request for system EW1 in the queue for the next import. For more detailed information about the type and scope of the requests, select the system. Figure 6.19 shows the import queue for this example EW1. From this display you can coordinate all the imports. The most important steps are described below.

Sequence of the Import Queue

The sequence of the requests in the import queue is determined at the time that the requests are exported from the source systems. The requests will be imported in this sequence. Released transport requests from the same transport group are automatically checked into the import queue of the target system. If the target system is assigned to a different transport group, you must first locate waiting requests by choosing Extras ➤ Further Requests ➤ In Other Groups ➤ In External Groups. If requests for the system are found, they are inserted into the import queue of the selected system.

FIGURE 6.19:

Import queue of system EW1

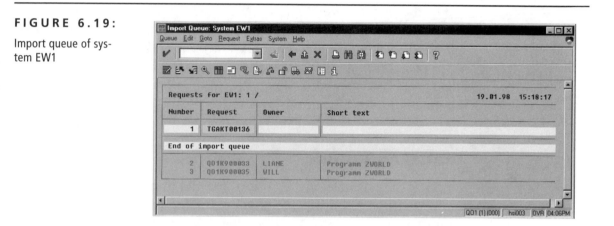

Opening and Closing the Import Queue

Completed development tasks should be imported in accordance with a schedule that is agreed on in advance with your developers. The imports are performed at fixed intervals. To prevent inconsistencies, and to achieve a defined intermediate R/3 System status, you can temporarily close the import queue at this time by setting an end marker. All requests that arrive after that time are retained for the next import. Figure 6.19 illustrates this situation. Request TGAKT00136 is waiting for the next import. Requests QO1K900033 and QO1K900035 are retained. These requests only arrived after the import queue was closed, and are therefore only relevant for the next import.

To insert an end marker into an import queue, choose Queue ➤ Close from this screen. To move the end marker in front of a request, choose Edit ➤ Move End Marker. To open a closed import queue, choose Queue ➤ Open.

Import

You can start an import into a system either for the entire queue up to the end marker (Queue ➤ Start Import) or for selected transports (Request ➤ Import). A request imported in this way is retained in the import queue. SAP recommends that you always import a complete import queue in order to prevent inconsistencies. You always need to select the target client if requests with client-dependent data are imported.

Status and Logs

To track the progress of the import, use the Import Monitor. Choose Goto ➤ Import Monitor. To display the log of the executing program tp, choose Goto ➤ TP System Log. In the import overview, the system into which data is being imported, is indicated by an icon:

To delete transport requests from the import queue or forward them to another R/3 System, choose Request. In the same way you do with the WBO or the CO, you can display the contents, logs, and sizes of selected transport requests.

Manual Use of the Transport Control Program

In exceptional cases, you will have to use tp manually on the operating system level with older R/3 Systems. Below is a brief description of tp calls that will be useful.

The transport control program tp is controlled by the parameter file TPPARAM in the subdirectory /bin of the transport directory, as described in Chapter 5. Before you use tp for the first time, it is useful to test whether a connection to the desired target system is possible. To do this, use the following command:

```
tp connect <target system> pf=/usr/sap/trans/bin/TPPARAM
```

The suffix pf= allows you to use a different parameter file. If you call the program tp directly from the subdirectory /bin of the transport directory, you do not need to explicitly assign the file TPPARAM. In the examples below, it is assumed that you are calling tp from the subdirectory /bin.

To append a request to the import queue of an R/3 System, use the command:

```
tp addtobuffer <request> <target system>
```

To run this command successfully, it is assumed that the data file of the request is in the subdirectory /data and the cofile is in the subdirectory /cofiles of the transport directory.

To import an individual request, use:

```
tp import <request> <target system>
```

To import the entire import queue, use the suffix all:

```
tp import all <target system>
```

To specify a particular client, use:

```
client=<number of the client>
```

If no client is specified, the data is copied into the client with the same number as the client from which the data was exported. If the client to be imported into does not exist in the target system, the import is canceled and an error message appears.

Review Questions

1. The R/3 transport system is

    A. Equivalent to copying a client.

    B. Used to exchange development and Customizing data between different R/3 Systems.

    C. Used to exchange data between different clients in one R/3 System.

2. A development class is

    A. A defined group of developers.

    B. Client-independent.

    C. Assigned to the object when an SAP original is changed.

    D. Assigned to a transport layer.

3. Modifications to SAP-owned objects

    A. Must be registered in the OSS.

    B. Are not permitted.

    C. Are strongly recommended to implement company-specific processes.

4. A repository object of an R/3 System

    A. Is automatically locked if a developer makes changes to an object. When the changes are saved, the lock is automatically removed.

    B. Can only be changed if a corresponding change request is assigned. The object is then automatically locked for changes by all users until the assigned task and the change request are released by the developer.

    C. Can only be changed if a corresponding change request is assigned. Changes to the object can only then be made by users named in the change request.

CHAPTER

SEVEN

7

Client Administration

The preceding chapters mentioned clients quite a bit. This chapter will summarize and explain their role in more detail. One important aspect of a system administrator's job is copying a client, either within an R/3 System or to another system.

Client Basics

The data in the R/3 database is divided into different classes. Some data is valid throughout the entire system. This data includes ABAP programs, the R/3 Repository, and the objects in it. Configurations in this area are also in effect throughout the system. This type of configuration is known as client-independent Customizing. (See Chapter 6 for more on Customizing.)

Other data is client-dependent, that is, it can only be viewed from one client. The client-dependent data includes Customizing, application, and user data. There are close connections between the client-dependent data classes. Application and user data is particularly affected by any client-dependent Customizing settings made. Application data is therefore usually only consistent in its own Customizing environment. Figure 7.1 illustrates the interaction between the different data classes. (The application data is embedded in the customizing data and the user data. It sits atop a base of client-independent data and data with system-wide validity.)

Understanding Clients

A client is an independently accountable business unit. This includes an independent balance sheet. Specific settings made as a result of business requirements are known as Customizing. Customizing can also be used to make system-wide settings, such as selecting the factory calendar. Almost all technical R/3 settings are client-independent. This means that clients in an R/3 System are suited, for example, for implementing relatively independent plant sections, but are less well suited for implementing business processes of completely independent companies. This is reflected in an Enterprise IMG that has systemwide validity and is client-independent.

FIGURE 7.1:

Data classes in the R/3 database

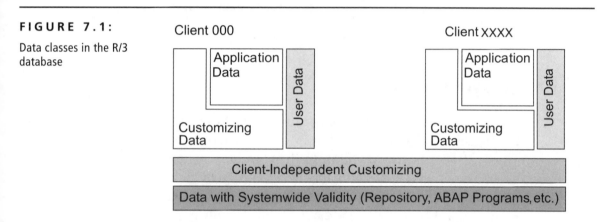

Technical Implementation

From a technical viewpoint, each client is identified by a three-figure number. This number is used as a key within tables that contain application data. Tables of this type are known as client-dependent. The first column is the field mandt. This is also the first field in the table's primary key. You can only access data that is assigned to the client that you select when you log on. In addition to the client-dependent tables, there are also client-independent tables. The data in client-independent tables are valid for all clients. These tables have no first column mandt. The content of these tables has an effect on the entire system.

Standard Clients

In the standard system, SAP delivers the following pre-configured clients:

- 000 for administration purposes and as a template for additional clients
- 001 for test purposes regarding the ECU (European Currency Unit) and as a template for additional clients
- 066 for SAP Remote Services

Standard Users

Users and their configurations, for example, their passwords, are client-dependent—that is, a user can only work in their configuration's assigned client. In the standard system, clients 000 and 001 are delivered with users SAP* and DDIC with passwords 06071992 and 19920706, and client 066 with user EARLYWATCH and password SUPPORT. (See also Table 1.1 in Chapter 1.) You can change the passwords of standard users.

Creating a Client

To be able to work with an R/3 System, you must create clients in which company-specific settings can be made. Normally, you copy an existing client, at first mostly client 000, or you copy a configured client from another R/3 System. You can copy clients within an R/3 System or from other R/3 Systems, or use a special transport request to transport a client from one system to another. Creating your own clients is one of the first steps in customizing a system, and is therefore one of the basic functions within the IMG (Implementation Guide). It is recommended that you create a separate client in an integration system for Customizing.

When you have completed the customization of this system, you can copy all the settings to the clients in the subordinate R/3 Systems—in particular the subsequent production system. You can then test the settings first in the consolidation system. This ensures the uniformity of the settings of R/3 Systems in the landscape, which is very important for subsequent test environments.

However, copying a client can only be seen as a first stage in initializing it. If, after completing the client copy, you make additional changes in the source client, which also need to be copied to the target client, you need to use the CTO (Change and Transport Organizing). Creating and copying clients is a typical task when you set up the system landscape in the R/3 implementation phase. Figure 7.2 illustrates the processes in chronological order for a two-system landscape. After a client is copied, a check phase follows, in the course of which additional maintenance or corrections may be necessary in the new client.

FIGURE 7.2:

Chronological development of a two-system landscape

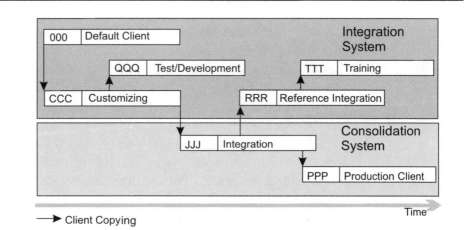

A client is created in two steps. The first step makes the new client known to the R/3 System, and makes important basic settings. The second step fills the client with data. Only then can a client function.

Client Role

The significance of each client in an R/3 System is determined by the tasks it is used for. When you create a client, this is reflected in the role assigned to the client. This role expresses the purpose served by the client and the attributes assigned to it. The possible attributes are:

- Production
- Testing
- Customizing
- Demonstration
- Training/Education
- SAP Reference

Change Options

Among the basic attributes of a client are the change options of its data and objects. These change options cannot override the change options defined for the R/3 System. The defined R/3 System change options have a higher priority than the change options defined for a client (see Chapter 5.) There are several change options for a client. It is advisable to protect clients used for production purposes against system changes. Even the use of the correction and transport system can be stopped in these clients (No Transports Allowed). This option deactivates the correction and transport system. For clients in which Customizing is performed, all changes must be recorded in case they are transported into other systems later (automatic recording of changes). Otherwise the CO will not be activated automatically when a setting is made. A configuration such as this (changes without automatic recording) is only suitable for demonstration or training clients.

Scope of the Changes

You can also limit the scope of the permitted changes using the following levels:

- Changes to the Repository and client-independent Customizing allowed

- No changes to client-independent Customizing objects allowed

- No changes to Repository objects allowed

- No changes to Repository and client-independent Customizing objects allowed

These levels define the application area of the client.

You can protect clients before they are copied or compared with other clients. The following levels are available:

Protection level 0—No limit

Protection level 1—No overwrite

Protection level 2—No overwrite, no external availability

The aim here is to prevent the client from being overwritten intentionally or unintentionally by copying additional client-dependent data from another client, particularly in a production client. A client with protection level 1 or 2 can no longer function as a target client. Protection level 2 also prevents external comparison access to the client. R/3 provides a special compare tool for clients. You can use this tool to check, for example, whether the Customizing in two clients is identical or what deviations there are. For example, this information is important for tests, in which the test environment must be identical to the production environment.

Protection level 2 prevents the compare tool from being used for the client concerned. This form of data protection prevents unauthorized access to a client's Customizing settings and to its customer data. If necessary, restrict the use of the new client to the following areas:

Starting CATT processes allowed—CATT stands for Computer Aided Test Tool. This comprises a set of special programs used by SAP to check how R/3 is functioning, especially new R/3 releases. When the CATTs are used, they generate test data that may be useful for demonstration purposes later.

Protect against SAP upgrade—If a client is protected against an SAP upgrade, the client-dependent data in that client cannot be modified. You should use this option if standard settings data delivered by SAP have been used in customer-specific Customizing without a separate copy being made. Otherwise new standard values delivered by SAP with an upgrade could have disastrous consequences for the client.

The attributes described above must be defined when a new client is being prepared, before it can be filled with data. To do this, follow these steps:

1. From the main R/3 menu, choose Tools ➤ Business Engineer ➤ Customizing ➤ Basic Functions ➤ Set Up Clients, or Tools ➤ Administration ➤ Administration ➤ Client Administration ➤ Client Maintenance. Transaction code SCC4 is assigned to this menu path. An overview of the clients available in the system is displayed (see Figure 7.3).

2. Choose Table View ➤ Change ➤ New Entries to define the attributes of the new client. The screen for maintaining the technical attributes is displayed (see Figure 7.4).

3. Assign a role to the client.

4. Select the client change options.

5. Define the scope of possible changes to client-independent objects in this client.

6. If necessary, protect the client against copies from—and comparisons with—other clients.

7. Save your changes.

All the settings for the new client have now been made. The steps described initially only cause an entry to be made in table T000, describing the attributes of the new client. The new client contains no client-specific data. Only user SAP* with password PASS is hard-coded in the R/3 System. When the copy is complete, you must change the password. To enable the client to function, you must then copy the appropriate data.

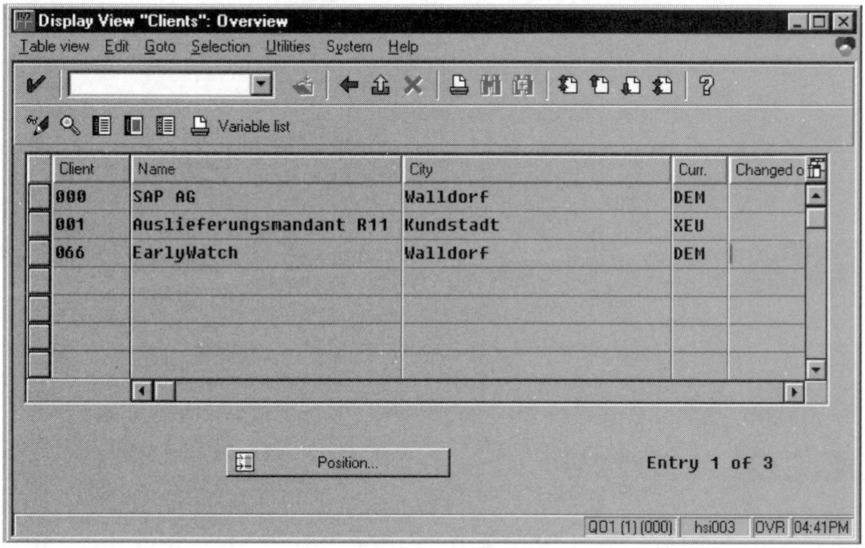

FIGURE 7.3:

Client maintenance

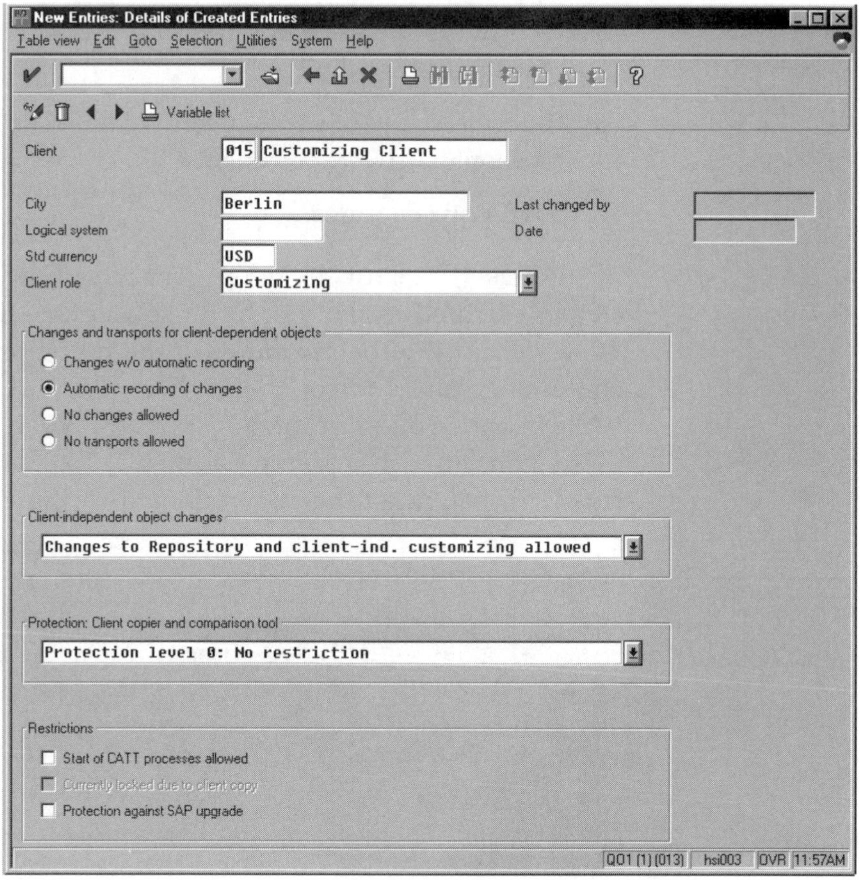

FIGURE 7.4:

Creating a client

Local Copy

As already mentioned, there are several methods for filling a newly created client with data. A client can:

- Be created in the same system by copying a client (local copy).

- Be created by copying a client in a remote system (remote copy).

- Be transported from one system to the target client by using a transport request (client transport).

The system landscape and the data volume in the client to be copied determine which method is chosen. The steps for the two methods are similar. To prevent inconsistencies, no work can be done in the source or target client while the copy is being made.

Data Profiles

In accordance with the data structures in the R/3 database, you can select data types for the copy. R/3 provides *data profiles* for this. Figure 7.5 shows the currently available profiles provided for copying clients.

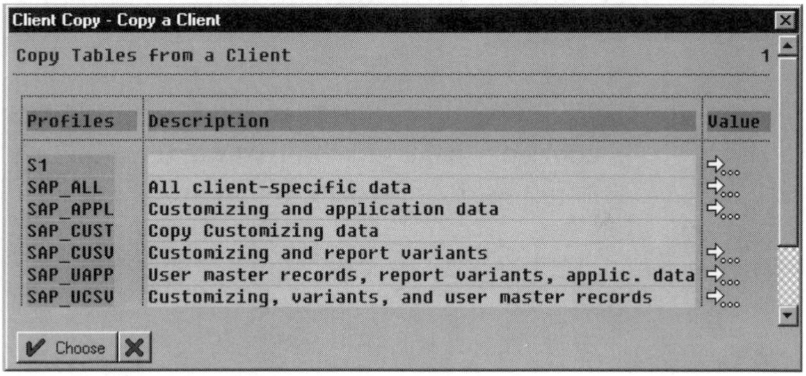

FIGURE 7.5:

Available data profiles

Profiles	Description	Value
S1		
SAP_ALL	All client-specific data	
SAP_APPL	Customizing and application data	
SAP_CUST	Copy Customizing data	
SAP_CUSV	Customizing and report variants	
SAP_UAPP	User master records, report variants, applic. data	
SAP_UCSV	Customizing, variants, and user master records	

Client Copy - Copy a Client

Copy Tables from a Client

Choose

You can also create your own profiles or change existing ones. To prevent confusion, it is advisable not to change existing profiles. You can also copy user master data and other application data from other clients. Figure 7.6 shows the screen for maintaining the data profile SAP_ALL, in which you can also find the exact scope of a data profile.

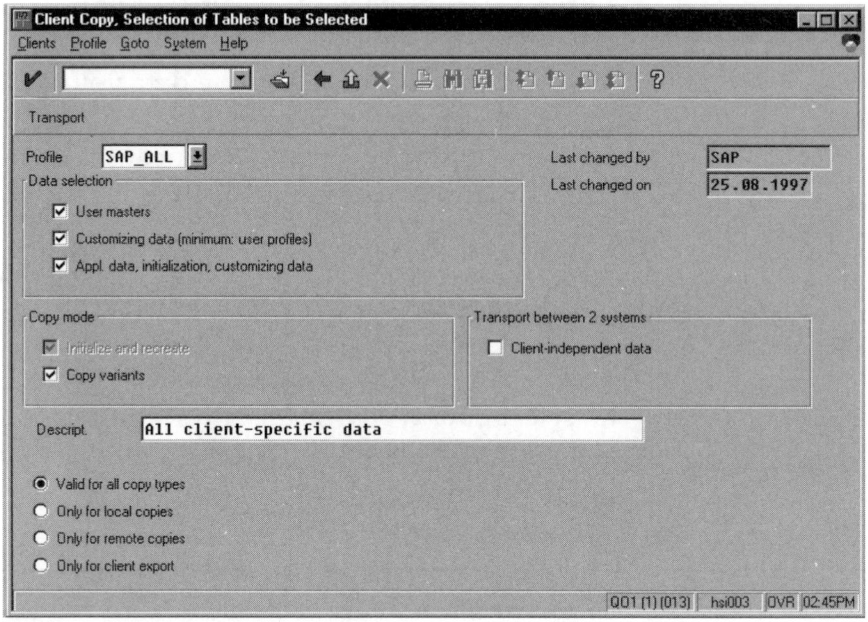

FIGURE 7.6:

Contents of the data
profile SAP_ALL

Let's first look at the procedure for making a local copy of a
client on the condition that the target client has already been prepared as described in the previous section. Follow these steps:

1. Log on to the newly defined client as user SAP* with password PASS.

2. Protect the source client against change activities by choosing Tools ➤ Business Engineer ➤ Customizing ➤ Basic
   Functions ➤ Set Up Client or, alternatively, Tools ➤ Administration ➤ Administration ➤ Client Administration ➤
   Client Maintenance.

   Select the source client and switch to change mode. Choose
   the option Currently Locked Due to Client Copy, and save
   your settings. When you create a client, this option is deactivated. It only becomes relevant if an existing client is used
   as a source client.

3. To access the client copier, choose Tools ➤ Business Engineer ➤ Customizing ➤ Basic Functions ➤ Set Up Clients ➤ Copy Source Clients, or Tools ➤ Administration ➤ Administration ➤ Client Administration ➤ Local Copy; or use Transaction code SCCL.

4. Use the profile to select the data to be copied from the source client (see Figure 7.7). If you are in doubt about the scope of the data selection of the available profiles, check the contents by choosing Goto ➤ Display Profile. To maintain profiles, choose Goto ➤ Change Profile, and Goto ➤ Create Profile.

FIGURE 7.7:

Copying a local client

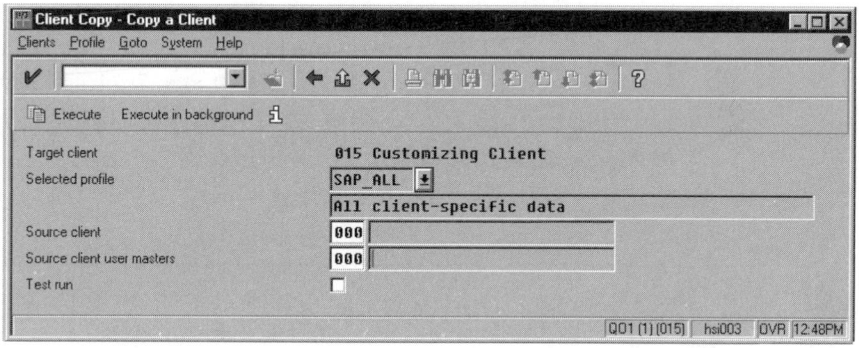

5. Copy the client in the background (Execute in Background).

6. To evaluate the copy procedure, choose Tools ➤ Administration ➤ Administration ➤ Client Administration ➤ Copy Logs; or use Transaction code SCC3. Detailed logs are generated for the copy procedure, and they can be accessed from every client in the system.

In theory, you can also copy a client in the foreground (Execute), but the copy process is automatically taken over by the current instance. In the background, you can select any instance, which provides the background service, in the R/3 System. Depending on the volume of data to be copied, and the capacity of the hardware, the process may take several hours.

If the copy were running in the foreground, a dialog process would be blocked for this time. The instance parameter rdisp/ max_wp_runtime limits the processing time for a dialog work process (see Chapter 2). If a transaction exceeds this time, it is canceled and rolled back. When a copy is executed in the background, you can choose the time at which it will start. When you execute a copy in the background, you can define the start time data by choosing Schedule Job.

If the copy is canceled due to certain problems, you can use the Restart Session option to create the copy. In this case, the copy procedure would be restarted at the point it was canceled, rather than beginning again from the start.

Use the Test Run option to first test the execution of the entire procedure. The results of a test run include an estimate of the data volume to be moved. This enables you to resolve any problems that occur, for example, with insufficient disk capacity, before the actual copy run.

NOTE   During the copy, the target client is automatically locked to users, but the administrator must make sure that users who were already logged on before the copy run log off from the target client.

TIP   To avoid unnecessary network load and performance reduction, it is best to perform the copy on the database server.

During the copy, you can check the logs from all other clients, for example, to track the progress of the copy. For an active copy run, you can also use the monitor, which graphically displays the progress of the copy based on the data volume still waiting to be copied.

The following are excerpts from the log file of a local client copy running in the foreground. The system is an initial system without its own customer data. Data was copied from client 000 to the newly created client 013. Important information is in bold type.

Report 7.1:

```
06.01.1998        Copy tables from client 1
---------------------------
Table                  No. of entries   Size    Time
              NS    DEL  Total Function  KBYTE    SEC
---------------------------
Client copy of 06.01.1998 15:22:13
SYSID...............................Q01
SAP Release.........................40A
Host................................hsi003
User................................SAP*
Parameter
Source client.......................000
Source client user masters..........000
Target client.......................013
Copy profile........................SAP_ALL
Table selection
Customizing data....................X
with application data...............X
Initialize and re-create............. X
06.01.1998 Copy tables from client 2
---------------------------
Table            No. of entries        Size
Time        INS    DEL  Total Function  KBYTE    SEC
---------------------------
ADDR_CLIENTCOPY_SELECT_TABLES executed  18(0)
entries copied
Runtime              1 seconds
Exit program ADDR_CLIENTCOPY_SELECT_TABLES executed successfully
RS_VARIANT_CLIENTCOPY executed  4( 2.868) entries copied
Runtime             321 seconds
Exit program RS_VARIANT_CLIENTCOPY executed
successfully
CLIENTCOPY_SELECT_TEXTID_ALL executed    0 entries found
Runtime              1 seconds
Exit program CLIENTCOPY_SELECT_TEXTID_ALL executed successfully
CLIENTCOPY_SELECT_TEXTID_STD executed    982 entries found
```

```
Runtime                   4 seconds
Exit program CLIENTCOPY_SELECT_TEXTID_STD executed successfully
CLIENTTRA_SELECT_TEXTID_FORM executed      0 entries found
Runtime                   0 seconds
Exit program CLIENTTTRA_SELECT_TEXTID_FORM executed successfully
CLIENTTTRA_SELECT_TEXTID_STYL executed      0 entries found
Runtime                   0 seconds
Exit program CLIENTTTRA_SELECT_TEXTID_STYL executed successfully
M_AKTEA       0       0      0 COPY        0       20
M_CFSTM       0       0      0 COPY        0        5
M_CFSTS       0       0      0 COPY        0        2
M_CKKAT       0       0      0 COPY        0        1

...
USGRPT        0       0      0 DEL.        0        0
USR21S        0       0      0 DEL.        0        0
USEG          0       0      0 COPY        0        1
Dev. Class      tables      entries           sec
Dev. Class:       119           54     00:04:10
Dev. Class: A     240       16.219     00:04:42
Dev. Class: B     260       15.932     00:02:57
Dev. Class: C   1.233       60.574     00:15:29
Dev. Class: D      53        8.256     00:00:20
Dev. Class: E       1            0     00:00:03

...
Exit program CLIENTCOPY_COPY_TEXT executed successfully
Exit program RCTXTCPY executed successfully
Exit program RGRSRS95 executed successfully
Exit program RPHGEN00 executed successfully
Exit program RPUMKX00 executed successfully
Exit program RPUPRR00 executed successfully
Exit program RS1ADRCL executed successfully
Exit program RSSOUSCO_FOR_CC executed successfully
SUSR_CLIENTCOPY_USERBUF_RESET executed 0(0) entries copied
Runtime                   4 seconds
Exit program SUSR_CLIENTCOPY_USERBUF_RESET executed successfully
Selected objects          :         11,892
Processed objects         :         11,231
Deleted tables            :            258
Memory requirements in KB :        201,620
Program run completed successfully.
Runtime in seconds        :         59,917
End of processing: 07:59:47
```

Using Remote Copy

Each R/3 System in a multisystem landscape has clearly defined tasks. For example, Customizing and production should be in separate R/3 Systems. To ensure that the settings made in the R/3 Systems are identical, you can copy clients beyond system borders. One way of doing this is with Remote Copy.

NOTE   A client can only be copied from one R/3 System to another if both R/3 Systems are the same release.

An RFC (Remote Function Call) is used to connect the R/3 Systems. For this reason, an RFC connection must be defined from the target system for the source system and the source client (see Chapter 5).

NEW!   In R/3 Releases prior to 4.0, the remote client copy is intended only for small data volumes. (The reason for this is the technical implementation of the RFC interface used for data transfer.) Small data volumes make it necessary to import all the data in the source client from a table into the R/3 System memory. The data is then transferred using RFC to the main memory area of the target system. There will at least be space in the R/3-specific main memory of both the source and the target client for the data volume of the largest R/3 table of the source client.

In R/3 release 4.0 the interface was improved considerably. Nevertheless, data transfer through the RFC interface is still slower than with a local copy or than a client transport between systems. This results in a considerable volume of data to be copied to the remote system and in a correspondingly long runtime. Due to the network connection alone, a remote copy is always slower than a local copy. During this time, neither source nor target client can be used.

With this method, the copy procedure should also run in the background to prevent a dialog process from being blocked. The long runtime causes the copy procedure to slightly exceed the run-time defined for dialog processes within the R/3 System. With this method, if the copy is canceled, you can also restart from the point of cancellation, if the corresponding restart option is activated.

The only difference between the procedures for a local copy and for a client copy from another R/3 System is that an RFC connection is needed for a client copy from another R/3 System. Follow these steps to make such a copy:

1. Create the new client in the target system, as described earlier in this chapter.

2. Log on to the target client of the target system with user SAP* and password PASS.

3. For the planned copy run, you must define the RFC connection between the R/3 Systems as the source client, if this has not already been done. Proceed as described in Chapter 5.

4. You should also protect the source client of the source system against changes during the copy. To do this, log on to the source system and lock the source client for the duration of the copy using the same procedure as for a local client copy.

5. Finally, you can start the copy in the target system. To access the appropriate client copier, choose Tools ➤ Administration ➤ Administration ➤ Client Administration ➤ Client Copy ➤ Remote Copy; or use Transaction code SCC9 (see Figure 7.8).

6. Using the profile, choose the data to be copied.

7. Choose the RFC connection. The source system and client are chosen automatically for the RFC connection.

8. Before the actual copy, test the RFC connection using RFC System check. In addition to testing the connection, the R/3 System releases are checked.

FIGURE 7.8:

Remote client copy

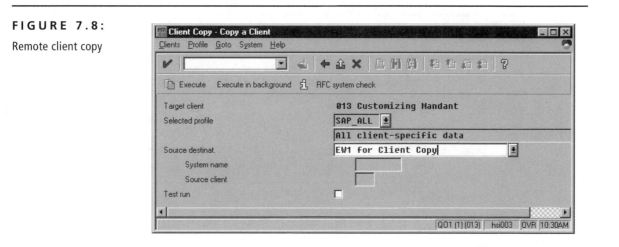

9. Start the copy in the background.

10. Check the status of the copy procedure from the target system. You can do this at any time by choosing Client Administration ➤ Copy Logs, or by using Transaction code SCC3.

The execution alternatives (background or foreground) and the options of a local copy are no different from those of a remote copy. For reasons already mentioned, background processing is preferable to foreground processing for both copy types.

You can test the copy procedure before you actually start the copy. Work in the source and target clients must be stopped before the copy is started. As with a local copy, locks are set by the system itself. When the copy run is started, you or another administrator must notify users who are already logged on—for example, using a system message (see Chapter 2). If necessary, you can cancel users' sessions from the process overview (Transaction code SM50) (see Chapter 2). If the copy procedure is canceled, it is possible to restart it, even for a remote copy.

NOTE   With a remote client copy, only table data is moved, not table definitions. If user-specific, client-dependent tables were created in the
source client, they are not automatically copied to the target client,
and an error may be caused. It is the responsibility of the user to create the necessary tables in the target client (manually using the
Repository maintenance tool, Transaction SE11, or a transport request
containing the table definitions). The automatically generated list of all
these tables will assist you in this. Only when these tables have been
created in the target system can the remote copy begin.

Client Transport

With a client transport, the data is not copied directly to the
remote target system. Instead, the transport control tool tp is first
used to create data and control files for the data to be exported
from a client and stored in the global transport directory. This
data can be imported into the target system later. A client transport can also be used to transport client-dependent data using an
external medium for a system outside the system landscape or to
create a backup of the client.

WARNING   For this method, it is imperative that the source and target systems are
using the same R/3 release. Unlike the remote client copy, the R/3
System itself cannot check the R/3 release, as no connection between
the systems is established. It is therefore the responsibility of the user
to check that the R/3 releases are the same!

Follow these steps to import a client:

1. Your first step should be to create the target client in the tar-
    get system. Unlike the local or remote copies, this step can
    also be made after the transport request has been made in the
    source system.

2. Then log on to the source client in the source system with a user with transport authorization (not SAP* or DDIC).

3. Using the client maintenance tool, lock the source client against changes.

4. Go to the client transport menu by choosing Tools ➤ Administration ➤ Administration ➤ Client Transport ➤ Client Export, or Transaction code SCC8.

   There are certain differences between the procedure for copying client-dependent data using a client export and the procedure for a local or remote copy.

   As with local and remote copies, you select the data to be copied using the data profile (see Figure 7.9). Unlike the local and remote copies, you can also use the client export to copy client-independent data. Profiles are available for this.

   The target system can be any system defined when the system landscape was defined, including virtual and external systems. The system only proposes R/3 Systems that have the same release as the source system.

FIGURE 7.9:

Selecting the data to be copied

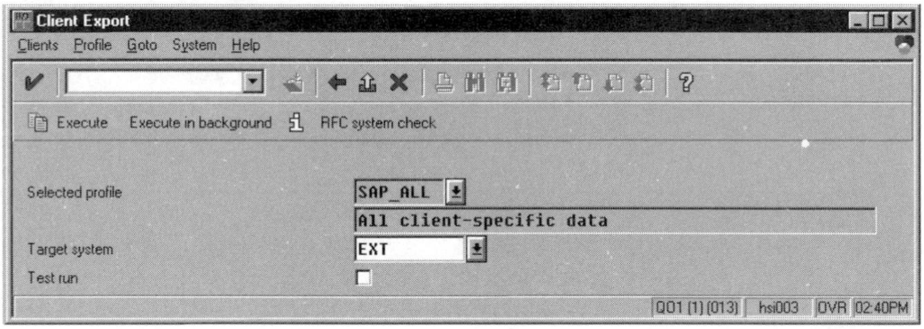

This method also supports both online and background execution with the already mentioned advantages and disadvantages.

When you confirm your selection, you are notified of which transport requests were created for this task (see Figure 7.10).

INFO client export

Client export

   Up to 3 requests are created, depending on the data selected and available:

   1. "Q01K000005" for transporting client-independent data, if you have selected this

   2. "Q01KT00005" for transporting client-specific data

   3. "Q01KX00005" for transporting client-specific texts, provided texts are available in this client

   When the transport requests have been created successfully, the data export is performed. This is carried out asynchronously by starting the transport program tp at operating system level, and can last several hours, depending on the data volume. The status of the export can be found using either transaction SCC3 or transaction SE01 and specifying the transport request.

5. Check the logs created for the copy run.

Logs are also created for this type of client data copy. The log file shown next is the copy log for the client export with profile SAP_CUST.

Report 7.2:

Source client	013
Source system	Q01
Copy type	Client export
Profile	SAP_CUST
- With Customizing data	X
- With application data	
- With user master records	

```
-  With variants
Status                          Completed successfully
User                            WILL
Last run on                     19.01.1998 / 13:49:16
Last entry on                               15:31:39
Release                         40A
Transport requests
- Client-independent            Q01K000004
- Client-dependent              Q01KT00004
- Texts                         Q01KX00004
Warnings about Dictionary errors
```

In addition to listing any errors that occurred, the log contains the names of the transport requests that were created for the client export. As well as tracking the status and progress of the client copy (Transaction code SCC3), in this case, you can also choose Client Transports in the Transport Organizer CO to evaluate the results. The Transport Organizer provides detailed information about the requests created.

NOTE   The operating system used with R/3 has a file size limit, for example, 2GB; the data files created for the transport request cannot grow beyond this limit. If a file is about to become larger than the limit, the transport will be canceled.

The data files created during the client export form the basis for the data import into another R/3 System. Table 7.1 shows the files created in the transport directory for a complete client export.

TABLE 7.1: Important Files for the Import

Subdirectory	File Name	Meaning
\data	RO<number of the request>.<SID>	Client-independent data
\data	RT<number of the request>.<SID>	Client-dependent data

TABLE 7.1: Important Files for the Import *(Continued)*

Subdirectory	File Name	Meaning
\data	SX<number of the request>.<SID>	ADO
\cofiles	KO<number of the request>.<SID>	Client-independent metadata
\cofiles	KT<number of the request>.<SID>	Client-dependent metadata

The file SX*<Number of the request>.<SID>* is special because it contains the Application Defined Objects (ADO) for the client. For example, if no client-independent data is exported during a client export, as is the case here using the profile SAP_CUST, a corresponding data file is not created. In this example, no file R000009.Q01 was generated.

To import this data into another R/3 System:

1. Copy the required files to the corresponding subdirectory of the local transport directory of the target system.

2. On the operating system level, from the subdirectory \bin of the local transport directory of the target system, execute the commands:

   ```
   tp addtobuffer <request> <target system>
   tp import <target system> client<target client>
   ```

   This runs the transport request with the client-independent data and then the transport request with the client-dependent data. These actions usually take a long time, as does the execution of the export.

3. The remaining file with the text elements requires a different procedure. Log on to the target client of the target system and access the client administration tool by selecting Tools ➤ Administration ➤ Client Admin. Choose Client Transport ➤ Post-Process Import. Select the request *<SID>*KT*<number of*

the request> and execute it online or in the background. This procedure copies and generates the client-dependent text elements.

The client import is now closed. In practice, the client import is questionable, especially if client-independent data are included. Client-independent data influence the entire R/3 System. This means that other clients in the target system are affected by the imported data. In the worst case, other clients will not be able to function after client-independent data has been imported from another R/3 System. On the other hand, if you do not copy the client-independent data from the source system, this can affect the imported client's capability to function if there are considerable differences between the source system and the target system. Therefore, when you export or import a client, you must pay particular attention to the differences between the source and target system.

In conclusion, a client copy is not suitable for merging data from multiple clients or copying the difference from one client to another. Copying clients should be considered the first step in developing a system landscape. When the copy procedure is completed, the data in the clients must be maintained using the CTO and, if necessary, transported.

Special Functions

The client administration tool offers some special functions:

Copying a Transport Request—This option lets you create a separate transport request containing only the client-dependent data from objects in the referenced transport request. This method is used when copying Customizing objects between clients in the same system.

Deleting a Client—Occasionally, you'll need to delete a client completely, for example, with R/3 Systems that were created from a copy of another system. Note that this function is critical. Almost as many changes are needed in the database as when a client is copied.

WARNING   Deleting a client can make it necessary to reorganize the entire database. You should therefore not perform this function without first considering the effects.

Table evaluations—This function lets you compare company and project-related data in different clients, even for clients in different systems, that can communicate through an RFC. This compare tool is complex and lets you compare data from all the IMG topic areas. For example, you can check whether the Customizing in two clients is identical. Differences are logged.

Tips for Making Client Copies

Client copies should be considered critical because of the data volumes that are moved when clients are copied. Probably the most frequent error is underestimating the data growth that occurs during a client copy. If the database proves to be too small, not only does the copy procedure stop, but it may be impossible to continue working with the system until the database is extended. Make a test run to find out the amount of data volume that will be added. Be sure to check whether there is sufficient space in the database!

Sometimes, indexes are missing from the database of the target system. When the client copy run is restarted, these missing indexes can cause duplicate records in tables, which would otherwise be prevented by the system. The copy procedure would be canceled.

Check the consistency of the database objects in the target system, in particular, the indexes. Use Transaction DB02 (see Chapter 15).

Review Questions

1. Which of the following statements about the R/3 client concept are correct?

    A. Customizing settings are always client-independent.

    B. A client is an independently accountable business unit within an R/3 System.

    C. Each client has its own application data.

    D. Each client has its own technical data, which is independent of other clients.

    E. Each client has its own application tables.

    F. The table field `mandt` is used to differentiate between client-dependent data within the tables with application data.

2. Which client copy methods does R/3 offer?

    A. Local copy

    B. Remote copy

    C. Data interchange procedure

    D. Client export

    E. Data backup

3. Which data can be copied in a remote client copy?

    A. Client-dependent application data

    B. Client-dependent table definitions

      C. Client-independent data

      D. All data in the R/3 System

4. What is the transaction code for checking the copy logs?

      A. SE38.

      B. There is none.

      C. SCC3.

      D. S000.

R/3 Users and Authorizations

There are different types of users in the R/3 System: users on an operating system level, database users, and R/3 users. The term *user* here does not refer to the individual human user, it is a technical system term like *client*. The users are fully independent of each other, and a user in one area is not necessarily a user in another area. This chapter deals only with R/3 users.

The user concept is one of the basic parts of R/3 security. To attain a high level of security, the R/3 System administrator must become familiar with the possibilities that the user concept offers and use them conscientiously. Those topics are covered in this chapter.

In addition to creating users and manually assigning authorizations and authorization profiles, you can also use the Profile Generator (available since R/3 Release 3.1G) to automatically generate authorization profiles for activity groups of users. This chapter describes the requirements that must be met and the best methods for doing this.

R/3 has its own user concept. After the R/3 System is installed and the system landscape is set up, one of the first steps is to create users in R/3. In the previous chapters, I've assumed that the R/3 users were created as a copy of the superuser SAP* and that they therefore have all the authorizations in R/3, in particular, authorization to perform the activities described. In the initial phase, the procedure can be done in this way, but it represents a gap in security, which we will now close.

User Master Records

Directly after installation, a number of standard clients and standard users are available in R/3, as described in the previous chapter. Users are always client-dependent, that is, they are only valid in the client assigned to them. A user also has a password, which you must enter when you log on, and which you can change at any time, including when you log on. When you log on, you can select the language you prefer to work in from the languages available in the R/3 installation. You can also select a logon language when you create a user. The user name and the user attributes comprise the *user master record*. A user master record consists of the following elements:

- User name
- Assigned client
- Password
- Company address
- User type
- Start menu
- Logon language
- Personal printer settings
- Time zone
- Activity group
- Authorizations
- Expiration date
- Default parameter settings

You do not have to make a selection for all these attributes, for example, you can choose not to set the expiration date (this setting limits the user's validity to a particular period). The complexity of the possible settings for a user allows you to adapt the R/3 System to a user's individual requirements, and also to restrict a user's authorizations to the assigned application areas.

Superusers

The superusers SAP* and DDIC have a special significance among R/3 users. By default, SAP* and DDIC are available in every client of the R/3 System. SAP* has all the authorizations in the R/3 System. User DDIC has all the authorizations for administering the R/3 Repository. They can only use the correction and transport system in display mode, which excludes them from developing any custom software.

One of the first tasks after installation is to secure these users by changing their default passwords to prevent unauthorized access to the system. It is also advisable to change the default password SUPPORT for user EARLYWATCH in client 066. The EARLY-WATCH user only has display authorization for performance monitoring functions, so this user represents only a minimal security risk. The passwords for SAP* and DDIC should be changed with great care, but they should also be kept so that they are available in an emergency.

To access the user maintenance tool from the main R/3 menu, choose Tools ➤ Administration ➤ User Maintenance. This menu contains all the functions for creating, changing, and deleting users, and for maintaining their attributes.

User Addresses

Let's take a look at user SAP*. Choose User, enter the user name in the appropriate field, and choose Change. If user SAP* has not already been changed, a screen similar to Figure 8.1 is displayed so you can enter user address data. You must at least enter the user's real name in this screen. This data will help to locate a user and contact them if necessary. You do not need to enter the same address for each user. Instead, you can create a company address (by choosing

Tools ➤ Administration ➤ User Maintenance ➤ Environment ➤ Maintain Company Address) and assign it to the user.

A user's attributes are grouped by subject areas like index cards. To change the subject area, select the tab for that subject area.

Logon Data

In the Logon Data tab, you must select a password and a type for each user. Figure 8.2 shows the settings for user SAP*, which have not been changed.

FIGURE 8.2:

Logon data for user SAP*

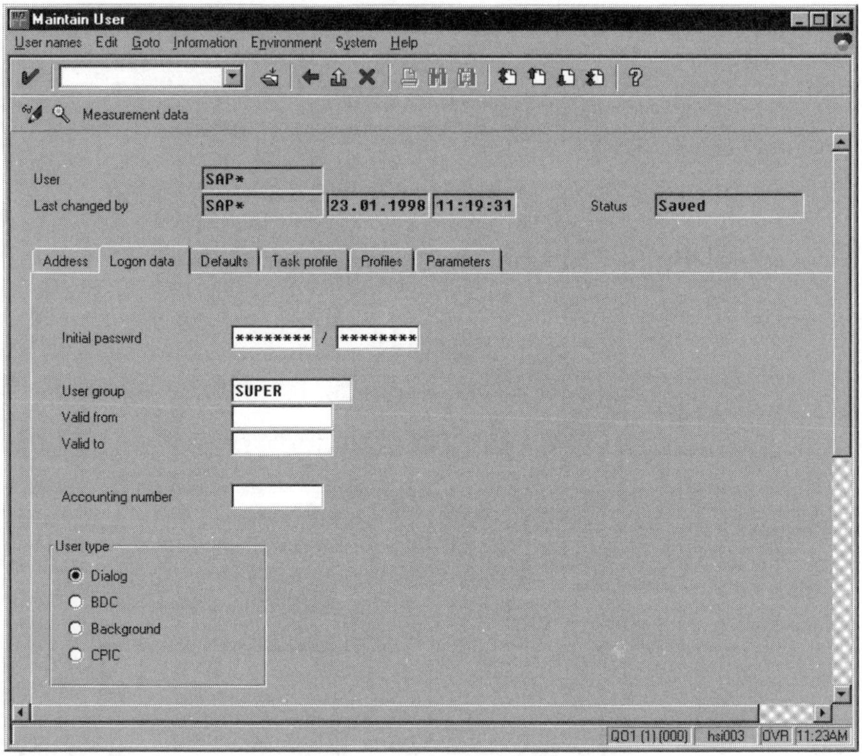

The password is displayed in encrypted form as you enter it. The user type determines which of the following ways the user can work in R/3:

Dialog—A dialog user can work with R/3 in any way. This includes background processing, batch input processing,

CPIC, and dialog (unless restricted explicitly by specific authorizations).

BDC—BDC reduces the range of functions to the use and execution of batch input sessions. This is explained in greater detail in Chapter 14.

Background—A background user can only be used to schedule and execute background jobs from other dialog users (see Chapter 9). A background user is not permitted to log onto the R/3 System and to work in dialog mode.

CPIC—CPIC users are also not able to work in dialog mode in R/3. They can only be used to exchange data through the CPIC interface. The CPIC user SAPCPIC is delivered by SAP in the standard system. This user has no authorizations and is only used for internal processes, such as executing external programs by users. You should not change the user data.

User SAP* is a dialog user. The user type does not impose any restrictions in the use of R/3.

User Group

SAP* is assigned to the user group SUPER. The user group serves documentation and technical information purposes and helps to coordinate the authorizations for maintaining the user data. A user in one user group can only maintain the data of a user in another group if the first user has been given explicit authorization.

The user group SUPER is the only user group defined in an R/3 System. This group should be used for all users who have a similar range of authorizations in the system. This is not mandatory, but it is advisable because logical assignment to a user group gives an indication of activity areas and authorizations. To create and maintain user groups from the user maintenance tool, choose

Environment ➤ User Group. For example, create a user group MM. This user group will be for users created later that work within Materials Management.

Authorizations

Creating a user is one of the tasks of an R/3 System administrator or a user administrator. The authorizations determine which activities a user of a particular user type and user group can perform. It should be the responsibility of another person, the authorization administrator, to assign authorizations. It is advisable to divide these task areas among at least two people to reduce security risks. If a user had authorization to set up new users and authorizations, that user could give himself or herself all authorizations for the R/3 System and have unrestricted access to data. This situation is prevented by dividing the task areas among more than one person. Authorization maintenance is either the sole responsibility of the user departments, or authorizations must be maintained in close cooperation with the user departments.

There are two distinct viewpoints concerning the assignment of authorizations. For user departments, the main priority is business activities that a user is permitted or denied. In contrast, for an R/3 System administrator, the main priority is the technical aspect of assigning and administering authorizations. The system administrator cannot decide which business authorization a user needs. The user departments must decide which authorizations to assign for which tasks.

NOTE   The sections that follow focus on the technical aspects and the handling of the authorization concept.

A user's authorizations are among the most important user attributes that need to be maintained. As with any software, assigning authorizations for R/3 has two sides. A user's permitted activity area should be restricted as closely as possible to that user's tasks. The security aspect is crucial here. On the other hand, a user should not be without the authorizations needed to perform required tasks. It is the task of the authorization administrator to harmonize these two sides. R/3's authorization concept is a complex system of individual authorizations that in turn form units, thus permitting a high level of fine tuning.

Authorizations and Authorization Objects

Each authorization in the R/3 System is based on an *authorization object*. From the technical viewpoint, an authorization object is a module that consists of a name, fields, and possible values that represent actions. The assignment of an authorization object to a process (for example, report, transaction, and update) is determined by SAP. To display an overview of the authorization objects available in the standard R/3 System, from the ABAP Workbench choose Development ➤ Other Tools ➤ Authorization Objects ➤ Objects.

The number of authorization objects in an R/3 System is considerable due to the functional range of R/3. To be able to distinguish between them more effectively, they are divided into areas known as object classes. For example, MM_E stands for the object class Materials Management-Purchasing. Select this area to display all the available authorization objects. A short explanation outlines the purpose of the authorization object. For example, choose M_BEST_EKG for die ordering. This authorization object comprises the authorization field ACTVT, which is in every authorization object by default, and the special field EKGRP (see Figure 8.3). The purpose of the fields and the values that they can accept is described in the R/3 documentation.

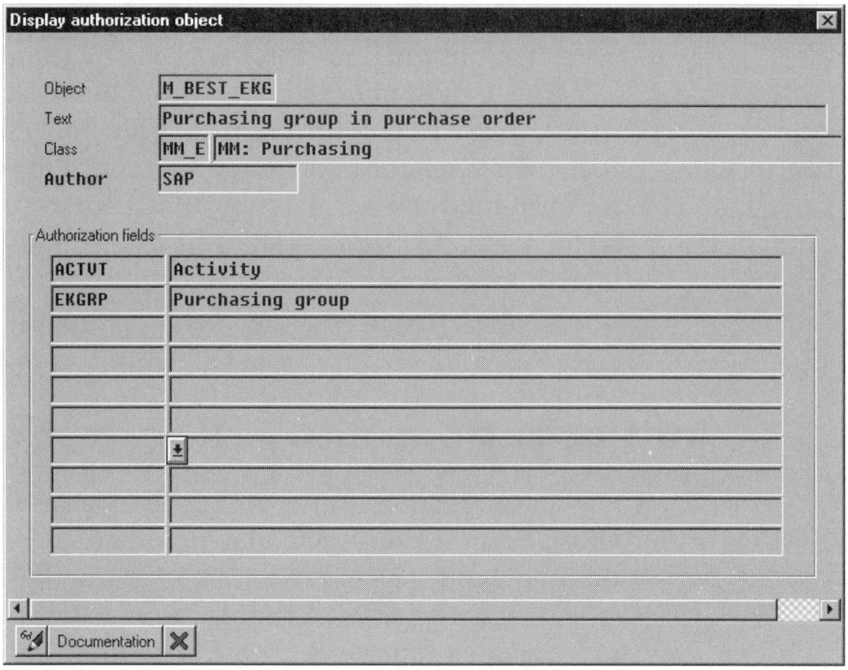

FIGURE 8.3:

Authorization object
M_BEST_EKG

In this example, you can assign a name or the name range of defined purchasing groups to the EKGRP field. Values 1–3 are permitted as activities. In the standard system, the values for the ACTVT field in Table 8.1 have the meanings that are listed.

TABLE 8.1: Possible Values for Field ACTVT

Value	Meaning
1	Create
2	Change
3	Display
...	Depending on the corresponding authorization object, you can define additional values for other special activities
*	All possible activities

To make an authorization into an authorization object, you assign values to it. The authorization is the smallest unit in SAP's authorization concept.

Most authorizations are already defined with the * value, so only company-specific values need to be entered. Let's assume that there is a purchasing group called XYZ. A user should be able to make changes concerning this purchasing group. To allow a user to make these changes, follow these steps:

1. From the user maintenance tool (Tools ➤ Administration ➤ User Maintenance), choose Authorization. A list of topic areas is displayed.

2. For this example, choose from the list Materials Management-Purchasing and from there, Purchasing group in purchase order.

3. All the predefined authorizations for this application area are displayed. To obtain more detailed information, choose Documentation.

4. You can now create new authorizations or modify existing authorizations. For this example, choose Create.

5. The name of the authorization consists of the authorization object (M_BEST_EKG) and two additional letters. When you create your own authorizations, you must use the customer-specific name range (see Chapter 6).

6. Create the authorization ZM_BEST_EKG to maintain the XYZ purchasing group (see Figure 8.4).

FIGURE 8.4:

Creating a new authorization

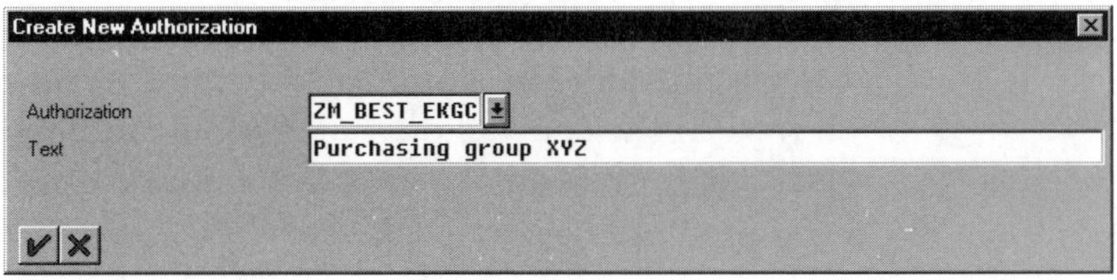

Create New Authorization	✕
Authorization	ZM_BEST_EKGC ±
Text	Purchasing group XYZ

✔ ✕

7. Choose the fields Activity and Purchasing group, and choose Maintain Values to enter the desired values. The exact authorization required for this example is created by assigning the value XYZ to the EKGRP field and XYZ to the ACTVT field, and by using the authorization object M_BEST_EKG.

8. Choose Save and Activate. The following screen with the new authorization is displayed (see Figure 8.5).

You could modify an existing authorization in the same way.

FIGURE 8.5:

Customer-specific authorization ZM_BEST_EKG

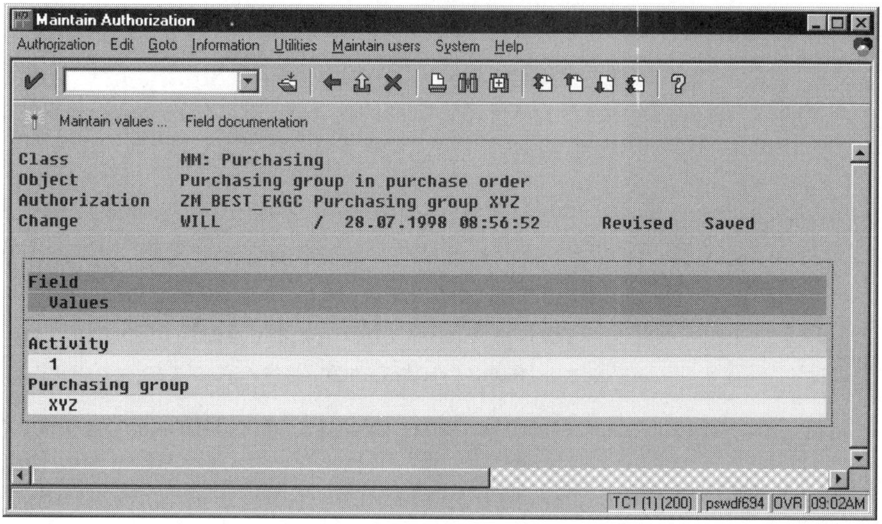

Authorization Profiles

If we consider the complexity of the R/3 System, we quickly arrive at the conclusion that creating and assigning all the necessary authorizations for each individual user is theoretically possible using this method, but it is not feasible in practice due to the effort involved. Authorizations can be grouped together into an authorization profile, and multiple authorization profiles can be grouped into a composite profile.

SAP provides a comprehensive set of predefined authorization profiles that are adequate for normal use. You can create your own authorizations at any time for programs that you have developed. These authorizations are based on new authorization objects of your own, which you can assign to existing profiles or to new profiles that you create.

To maintain authorization profiles, choose Profiles from the User Maintenance tool. Profiles in R/3 can have different states:

- Active and inactive
- Maintained (that is, adapted to current conditions or left unchanged)

In a system that is unchanged from the standard installation, all the profiles are *unmaintained*. If you create new profiles, they must be activated (made known throughout the entire system) before they are available in the system. The naming convention of the profiles is similar to that for authorizations; let's use the same example. Normally a user will not be permitted to change only one purchasing group, that user's responsibilities will probably encompass maintenance of the Purchasing area. For our purposes, we select all the active profiles from the area of MM (see Figure 8.6).

Of the profiles available, M_BEST_ALL corresponds most closely to our requirements (see Figure 8.7).

If you select this profile, the system displays the authorization objects used and the authorizations derived from them. You could now add further authorizations to the profile or swap already integrated authorizations, for example, adding ZM_BEST_EKG.

FIGURE 8.6:

Maintaining profiles

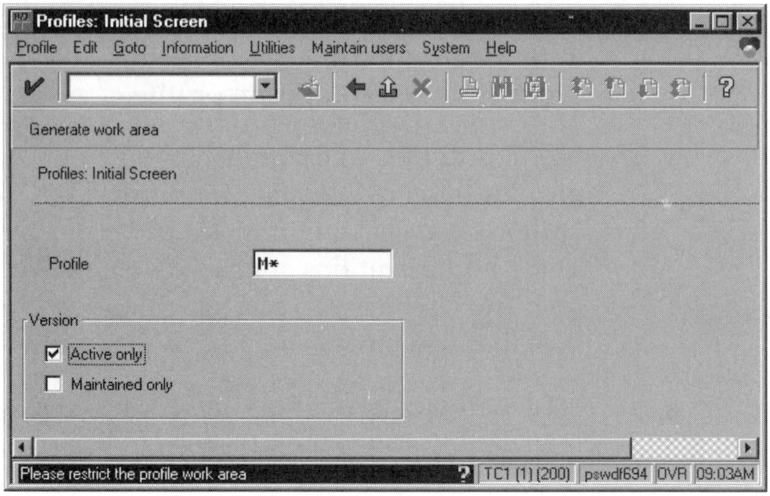

FIGURE 8.7:

Authorization profile
M_BEST_ALL

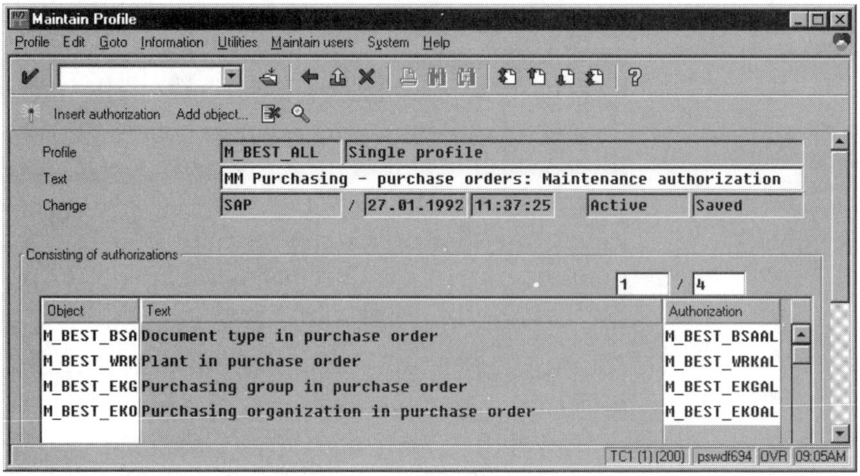

NOTE   It is advisable not to make any changes to existing profiles. Instead, make changes to your copies of these profiles.

You can also create new profiles by merging your own or standard authorizations and authorization profiles. These profiles are known as *composite profiles.* To manually assign the created profiles to a user, choose Profiles when you create a user. Figure 8.8 shows the profiles assigned to user SAP*. The profile SAP_ALL is assigned to that user, but this profile comprises all possible activities in an R/3 System.

FIGURE 8.8:

Authorization profile of user SAP*

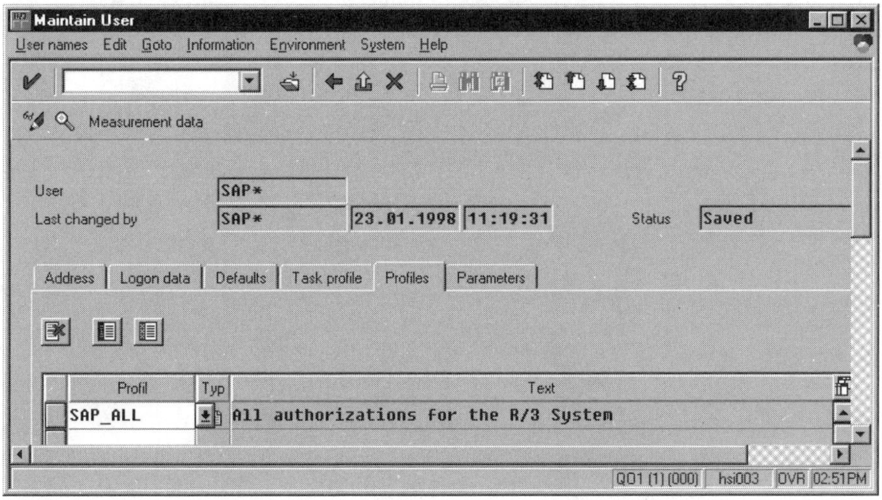

You are now able to create your own user. Let's call this user Hans. To permit this user to maintain purchasing groups using the authorization profile M_BEST_ALL, follow these steps:

1. Choose User Maintenance ➤ User.

2. Enter the user name **Hans**.

3. Choose Create.

4. Enter an initial password.

5. Enter the company address.

6. Choose Logon data.

7. Enter the user group **MM**.

8. Choose Profiles.

9. Enter **M_BEST_ALL** in the table.

10. Click Save.

Figure 8.9 shows the profiles of the new user Hans.

FIGURE 8.9:

Assigning profiles to
users

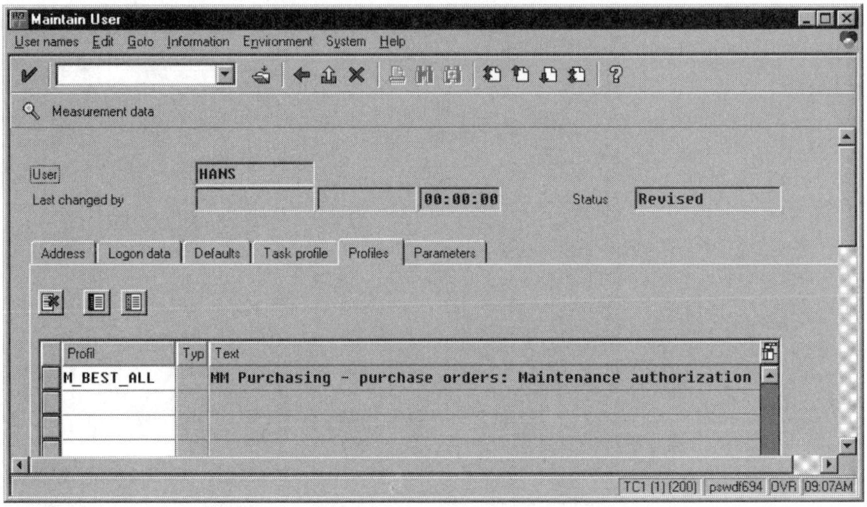

Important Profiles in System Administration

In large R/3 projects, system administration is usually divided
into multiple task areas and assigned to different people or
groups. User SAP* has the profile SAP_ALL, which comprises all
activities, including application-specific tasks. This user is therefore not suited for general work and should be protected against
unauthorized access. It is advisable to create special users with

their own individual authorization profiles. Table 8.2 shows the most important profiles.

TABLE 8.2: Important Authorization Profiles for Administration

Profile Name	Purpose
SAP_ALL	All authorizations in the R/3 System
SAP_NEW	All the authorization objects added in an R/3 upgrade for existing functions
S_A.ADMIN	Operator without configuration authorizations in the R/3 System
S_A.CUSTOMIZ	Customizing (for all system setting activities)
S_A.DEVELOP	Developers with all authorizations to work with the ABAP Workbench
S_A.DOKU	Technical writers
S_A.SHOW	Basis: Display authorizations only
S_A.SYSTEM	System administrators (Superuser)
S_A.USER	User (Basis authorization)
S_ABAP_ALL	All authorizations for ABAP
S_ADDR_ALL	All authorizations for central address administration
S_ADMI_SAP	Administration authorization (except spool configuration)
S_ADMI_SPO_A	Spool: All administration authorizations
S_ADMI_SPO_D	Spool: Device administration
S_ADMI_SPO_E	Spool: Extended administration
S_ADMI_SPO_J	Spool: Job administration for all clients
S_ADMI_SPO_T	Spool: Device type administration
S_LANG_ALL	All authorizations for language administration
S_SPOOL_ALL	Spool: All authorizations to administer spool requests, including reading inbound output requests
S_SPOOL_LOC	Spool: All authorizations except general read authorization
S_SPO_ATTR_A	Spool: Change all attributes
S_SPO_AUTH_A	Spool: Change all spool requests

T A B L E 8 . 2 : Important Authorization Profiles for Administration *(Continued)*

Profile Name	Purpose
S_SPO_BASE_A	Spool: Visibility and one-time printing
S_SPO_DELE_A	Spool: Delete spool requests
S_SPO_DEV_A	Spool: Administer all output devices
S_SPO_DISP_A	Spool: Display content of all spool requests
S_SPO_FEP	Spool: Front-end printing
S_SPO_PAG_AL	Spool: Unlimited number of pages on all devices
S_SPO_PRNT_A	Spool: One-time printing
S_SPO_REDI_A	Spool: Reroute all requests
S_SPO_REPR_A	Spool: Print all requests multiple times

In the initial stages of R/3 implementation, users frequently find that not all the authorizations they need are available. Immediately after a transaction is canceled due to missing authorizations, you can display a list of missing authorizations by choosing System ➤ Utilities ➤ Displ. Auth. Check, or by using Transaction code SU53. This Transaction shows you which authorizations you would need to perform an action.

The Profile Generator

The procedure described so far for assigning authorizations was the only method available up to and including R/3 Release 3.0F. In systems with a large or growing number of users, weaknesses in this approach become apparent:

- It is relatively difficult to distinguish between users. The greater the level of detail used to implement the authorization concept, the smaller the authorization units in the form of profiles and single authorizations that must be withdrawn or assigned.

- The system is relatively inflexible. If the authorizations in a user class are changed, the authorization profiles must be processed manually. If a change is made to an authorization profile, that may affect a large number of users. It is rarely possible to determine which users are affected.

- Authorizations are assigned on the basis of the names in the authorization profiles. However, the names are meaningless and only provide limited information about actions that are possibly connected.

Starting with R/3 Release 3.1G, the *Profile Generator* has been introduced gradually. The Profile Generator is based on the concept of authorization objects, authorizations, and authorization profiles. SAP delivers a large number of proposals for authorizations included with R/3. Use the Profile Generator to assign the authorizations to users.

NOTE Before you can use the Profile Generator, you must set the following parameter: `auth/no_check_in_some_cases` = Y. Then you must restart the R/3 System. To find out whether the parameter setting was successful, you can use report RSPARAM. To execute this report, use the ABAP Workbench editor.

Whereas previously you started from the authorization profile to select the permitted user activities, you can now select the permitted activities from the Enterprise IMG. A user's authorizations ultimately describe a configuration of a work center in an organization. The authorization profiles needed are generated automatically by R/3. It is less important which authorization profiles are used—you only need to define the range of activities of a user group. The comprehensive authorization profile generated in this way is no longer manually assigned to each user. Instead, users are assigned to one or more activity groups.

NOTE   An *activity group* is a subset of the actions from the set of actions defined in the Enterprise IMG.

Generating the Enterprise Menu

To be able to use the Profile Generator, the specific Enterprise IMG must be generated (see Chapter 6). The enterprise or company menu must be generated using the Enterprise IMG. The company menu represents a subset of the SAP standard menu, just as the Enterprise IMG is a subset of the SAP IMG.

NOTE   The SAP standard menu forms the basis for the SAP Session Manager, which was described in Chapter 1. It is the menu available in the Session Manager. The enterprise menu is also used by the SAP Session Manager. The SAP Session Manager can only be used fully after generation of the company menu.

To generate the menu views:

1. From the Enterprise IMG, choose Basis ➤ System Administration ➤ Users and Authorizations ➤ Maintain Authorizations and Profiles with the Profile Generator ➤ Maintain Enterprise Menu, or use Transaction code SSM1 (see Figure 8.10).

The window SAP Menu and Company Menu Generation is displayed. To complete the procedure in this window, do the following:

2. Select a language to work in.

FIGURE 8.10:

Generating the
SAP menu and
company menu

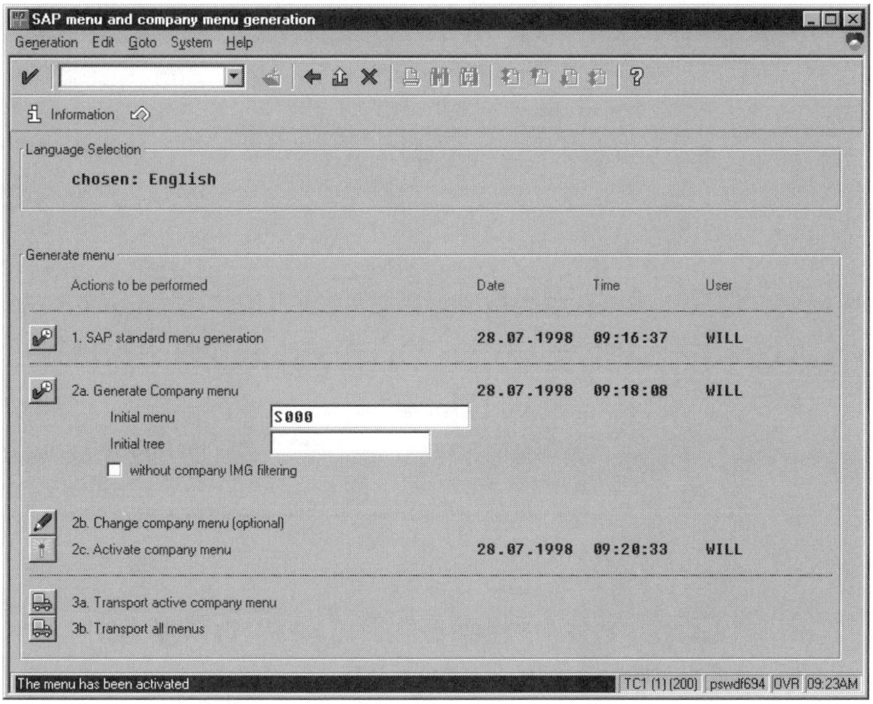

3. Generate the SAP standard menu by choosing the button in the row labeled "Generate SAP menu."

4. Generate the company menu using point "2a." You have multiple options. If you activate "without company IMG filtering," the SAP standard menu is also generated as the enterprise menu. With the default option, all the functions that are not contained in your company IMG, and as such are not relevant for your company, are removed from the SAP standard menu. You can also select an entry point other than the default Transaction code S000.

5. In point "2b," you can make additional manual changes to the company menu.

6. Activate the company menu.

To create settings that are as uniform as possible in a system land-scape, you can include the generated, active enterprise menu or all menus in a transport request and transport them into other systems. Use points "3a" or "3b."

It takes a few minutes to generate the enterprise menu, because all the menu options from the SAP standard menu must be compared with the restrictions in the Enterprise IMG.

If work is done in more than one language in your system, you must generate an enterprise menu for each language.

Copying the SAP Defaults to Customer Tables

The next step in preparing to use the Profile Generator is to copy the standard authorizations delivered by SAP (SAP defaults) into the customer tables. In the Enterprise IMG, choose Basis ➤ System Administration ➤ Users and Authorizations ➤ Maintain Authorizations and Profiles with the Profile Generator ➤ Edit SAP Check ID and Field Values ➤ Copy SAP Check ID and Field Values, or use Transaction code SU25 (see Figure 8.11).

During a new installation, all authorizations already defined by SAP, including all the default values, are first copied to customer-specific tables, where you can use the Profile Generator to change them.

After an upgrade, you only need to compare these values. Objects in the customer-specific name range are not changed.

After comparing the values, you can manually change authorization objects or composite profiles for individual transactions.

You can do this from the Enterprise IMG when you maintain the SAP Check IDs and Field Values by choosing Change Check IDs, or by using Transaction code SU24 (see Figure 8.12). This function lets you manually change the assignment of a transaction authorization. For example, from a full authorization to maintain all purchasing groups, you could create an authorization to maintain specific purchasing groups that begin with the letter *A*.

FIGURE 8.11:

Copying the SAP defaults

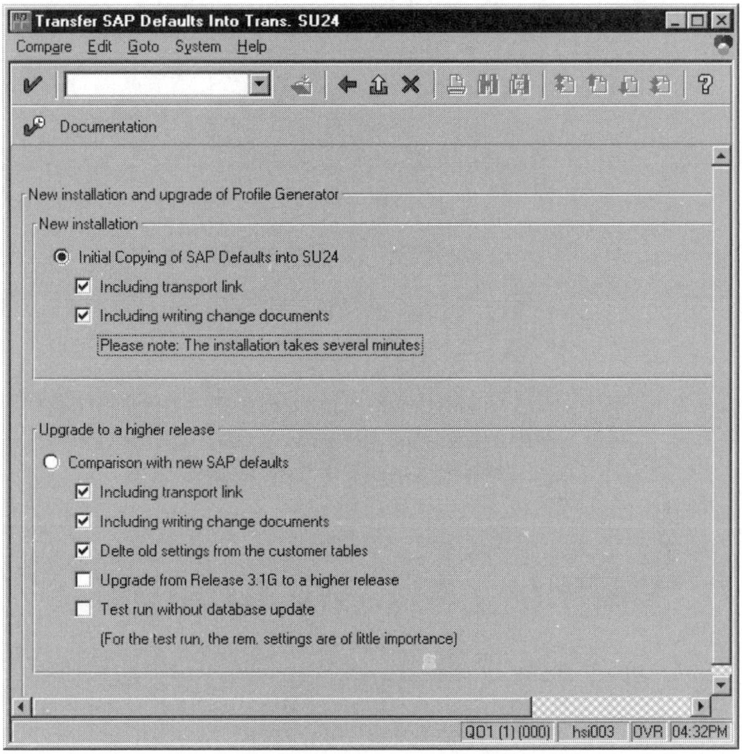

| NOTE | To allow these authorization changes to be transported, you must assign them to a customer-specific development class; that is, at least one customer-specific development class must have been created first. You can do this using either the Enterprise IMG or the Repository Browser, as described in Chapter 6. |

Figure 8.13 shows the check IDs for all authorization objects used by Transaction AL09.

In most cases, the defaults delivered by SAP will meet your requirements, so you will not need to make any changes to the authorizations and the check IDs.

Defining Activity Groups

The enterprise menu comprises all the activity fields in an enterprise. From this menu, the individual activity fields for the users are defined, for example, those for marketing people, accountants, or system administrators. You create activity groups that are authorized to use subtrees of the enterprise menu. The Profile Generator generates the necessary profiles for the defined activity groups. The user administrator need not be concerned about which profiles must be generated to permit specific activities. Instead, the main concern is which groups of users and which work centers there will be. One user can be assigned to multiple activity groups.

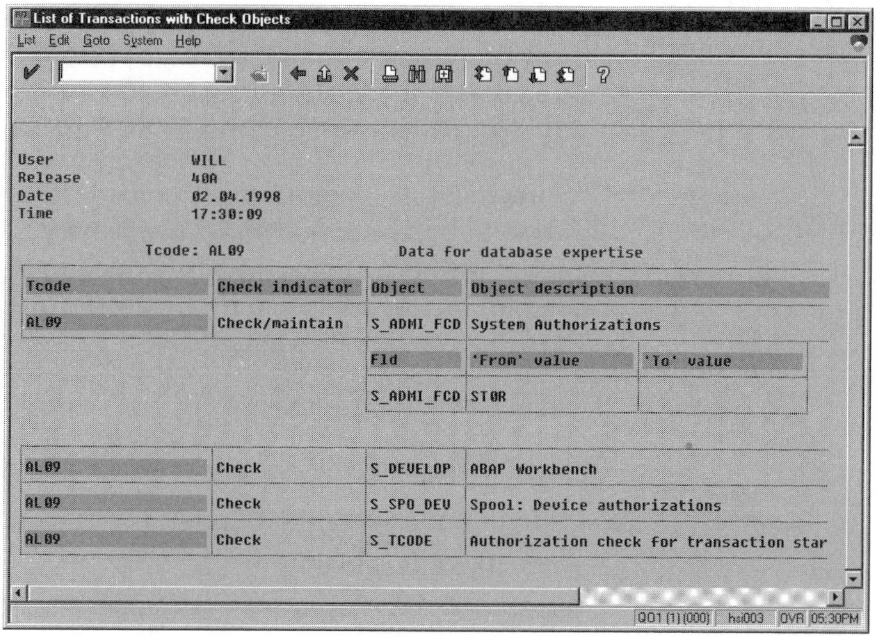

FIGURE 8.13:

Authorization objects
and check IDs for
Transaction AL09

Responsibilities

Within the activity groups, you can maintain responsibilities. There can be multiple responsibilities within an activity group. The activity group describes the activity, for example, maintaining purchasing groups. When you use responsibilities, the authorizations can be specified in greater detail, for example, to maintain purchasing group XYZ. You create a responsibility by assigning concrete values, such as a specific company code, to a defined activity group.

One way to use responsibilities within activity groups is to maintain organizational levels. Organizational levels are permanently defined fields in authorization objects, which reference the enterprise structure, for example, the company codes of an enterprise. The authorization profiles can, for example, be generated for different company codes. You can also attain this level of separation for the different responsibilities by manually maintaining the authorizations. Using responsibilities is optional. If you create an activity group without responsibilities, there is a 1:1 assignment between activity group and authorization profile; and activity group and responsibility are identical in this case.

Defining activity groups makes considerably less work for the user administrator. For example, if it is necessary to make changes to authorizations, you only need to change the activity groups. When they are generated, you can automatically activate the changes for all the assigned users.

Basically, activity groups are created in three steps:

1. Choose the activities from the enterprise menu.

2. Maintain the authorization fields in the authorization profiles, using responsibilities.

3. Assign the users or organizational units.

Let's consider this procedure with a relatively simple example. You need to create an activity group without responsibilities for the R/3 System administrators in the broadest sense. They need to have authorization to use all the tools in the CCMS (Computing Center Management System).

The first operation is performed with the following steps:

1. Choose Activity Groups from the user maintenance tool (Transaction PFCG) to create and maintain activity groups. Figure 8.14 shows the initial screen.

2. Enter the name of the activity group, for example *administrat.*

3. Select Basic Maintenance.

4. Choose Create.

5. Before you create the activity group, you must decide whether you want to generate responsibilities for the activity group.

In this example, you create an activity group without responsibilities.

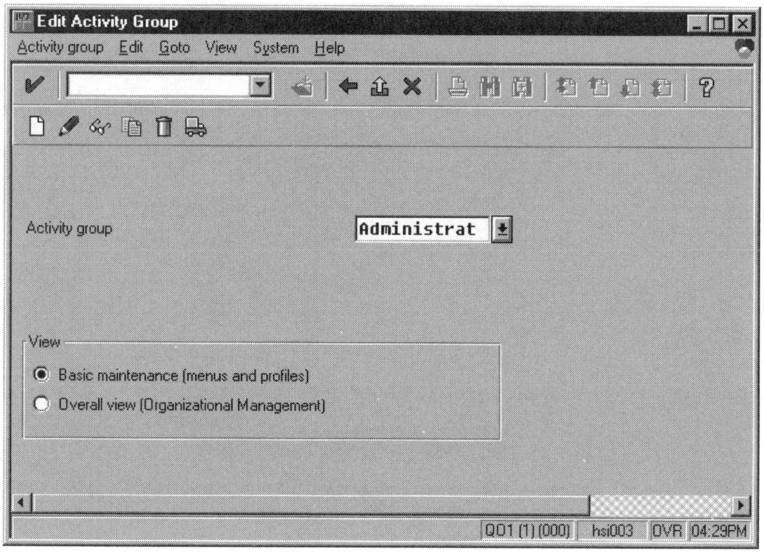

FIGURE 8.14:

Maintaining activity groups

NOTE	There are two levels of activity group maintenance. Basic maintenance is only for maintaining menus and profiles. The activity groups created are later assigned to actual R/3 users. The overall approach is more complex and is directly connected to organizational management. Instead of assigning real R/3 users by name, you assign positions, work centers, or organizational units are assigned, which provides considerably greater flexibility. It only makes sense to do this if you are using the organizational management within R/3. We will restrict this example to basic maintenance.

6. From the enterprise menu (Menu), choose the activities relevant for the activity group (see Figure 8.15). For this example, choose Tools ➤ CCMS (see Figure 8.16).

FIGURE 8.15:

Basic maintenance of
activity groups

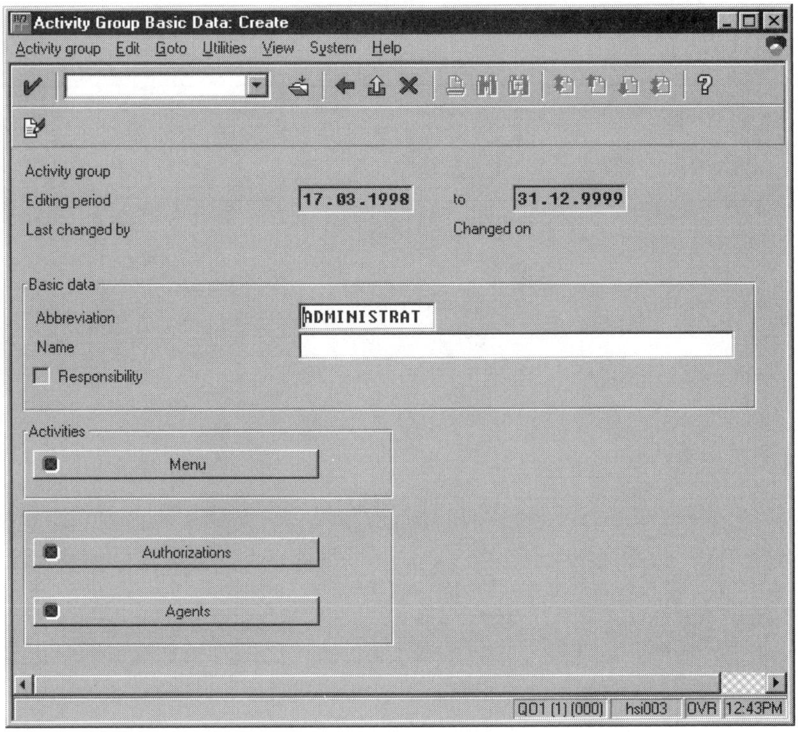

7. Save your selection.

8. Return to the basic maintenance dialog box. The status of the
    menu has changed to green now that maintenance is completed.

NOTE   When you are selecting the permitted activities, you can display the
Transaction codes for the activities. Choose Edit ➤ Technical Names ➤
Technical Names On.

User Menu

When you select the permitted activities for an activity group, a
menu tree consisting of these activities is automatically generated.

FIGURE 8.16:

Selecting activities

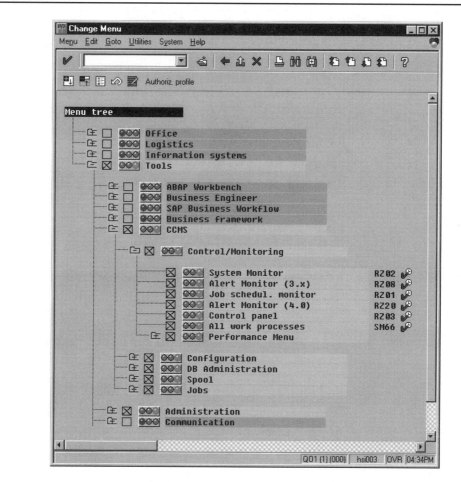

This menu is available as a *user menu*, in the SAP Session Manager, to all the users assigned to this activity group.

Next, you generate the authorization profile for the selected activities. Choose Authorizations when you are maintaining the activity group (see Figure 8.15). All the activities you selected before are displayed in a hierarchical list. A traffic light indicates the maintenance status of the node:

Green—The authorizations here all have values, but you should check these values.

Yellow—At least one field here requires values.

Red—There is a field here, for which no organizational levels have been maintained.

The status of an activity group, an object class, an object, an authorization, or a field can also be any of the following:

Standard—All the subordinate nodes do not have changes to the SAP standard.

Changes—At least one subordinate node was changed from the SAP standard.

Maintained—At least one subordinate field, which was delivered empty by SAP, was filled with custom values.

Manual—At least one authorization was added manually to the subordinate nodes.

Old—After an R/3 upgrade, existing and new objects and values are compared. If all the subordinate values are identical, that is, still current, the node is given the status of old.

New—The comparison found that new values were added.

You must make manual changes to the selection of authorizations, and you must assign values, if necessary. Figure 8.17 shows the authorizations selected for this example. The next steps are:

1. Choose a node and open it.

2. You can:

    - Deactivate undesired subtrees or individual authorizations by choosing

    - Add new full or individual authorizations by choosing Edit ➤ Insert Auth.

    - Create or change values for an authorization object by choosing the appropriate option in the row. For example, in Figure 8.17 it would be advisable to create values for the device authorizations in the spool system of R/3. These values describe device names, for which the authorization would be valid. For example, D* would be for all devices whose names begin with D.

- Manually remove or add individual Transaction codes, which point to actions. In this example no changes are necessary.

FIGURE 8.17:

Maintaining authorizations

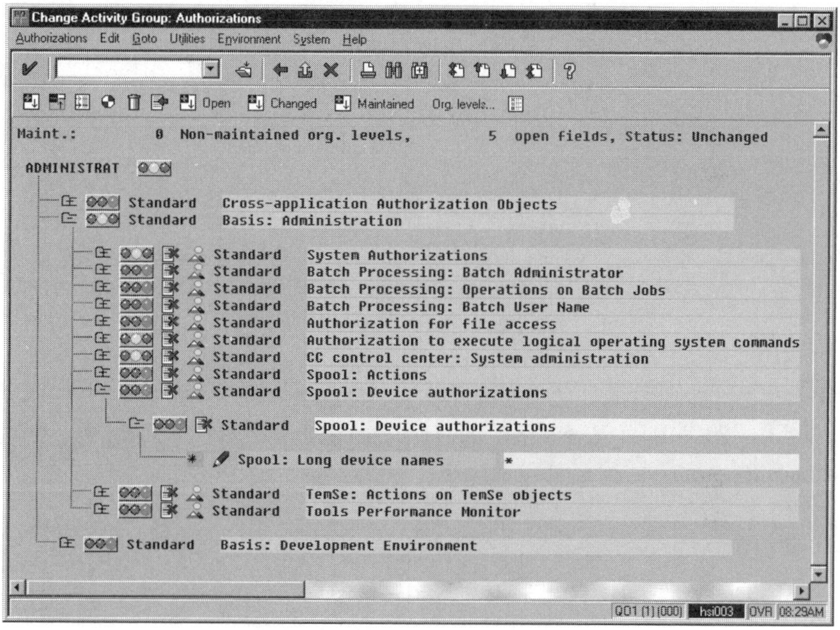

3. When you have made your changes, all the traffic lights should be green. Save your changes.

4. Choose Authorizations ➤ Generate.

5. You are prompted to specify a profile name. The system proposes a name, but this name is a combination of characters

and numbers for internal administration, and does not indicate the purpose of the profile (see Figure 8.18). For purposes of later identification, it is advisable to use a name of your own or enter a meaningful short text. In this example, we will use the name SYSADMIN.

Assign Profile Name for Generated Authorization Profile

You can change the default profile name here

Profile name | T-5000030 |

You will not be able to change this profile name later

Text | SYSADMIN |

6. Confirm your changes.

7. The system proposes that you generate the profile with all the necessary authorizations (see Figure 8.19). Click Generate to generate the profile now.

Exit Authorization Maintenance

Profile status: | Not generated |

Data status: | Saved |

☐ Flag for activation/generation

| 🌐 Generate | 🖱 Save | Exit | Continue |

8. Return to basic maintenance. The status of the authorization maintenance is green now that it is completed.

If you create an activity group with responsibilities, the Authorizations and User pushbuttons are replaced by Responsibilities. The essential difference is that the selected activities no longer have just one authorization profile. Instead, the activities are separated again through the different organizational levels or by manually maintaining authorizations. If the selected activities reference organizational levels, you can maintain organizational levels by choosing Org. levels. One authorization profile needs to be generated for each responsibility. The third and last operation, assigning users, is done for the individual responsibilities. In this example without responsibilities, assign a user to an activity group by choosing Agents when you are maintaining activity groups. Follow these steps:

1. Choose Agents.

2. To assign the users, choose User. (see Figure 8.20 for the example with user Hans).

FIGURE 8.20:

Assigning users

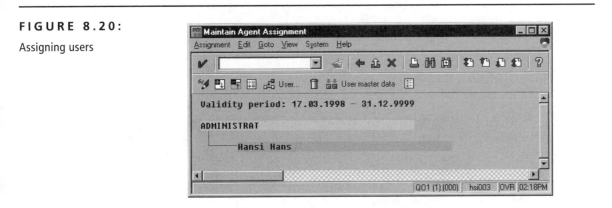

3. Choose User Master Data to assign the generated authorization profile to the selected users (see Figure 8.21). This is known as *updating the user master.*

4. Exit activity group maintenance.

This example is now complete. To check the success of what you've done, choose Profiles from the user maintenance tool. The generated profile was assigned to all the desired users. Figure 8.22 shows this for user Hans.

FIGURE 8.21:

Updating the user master

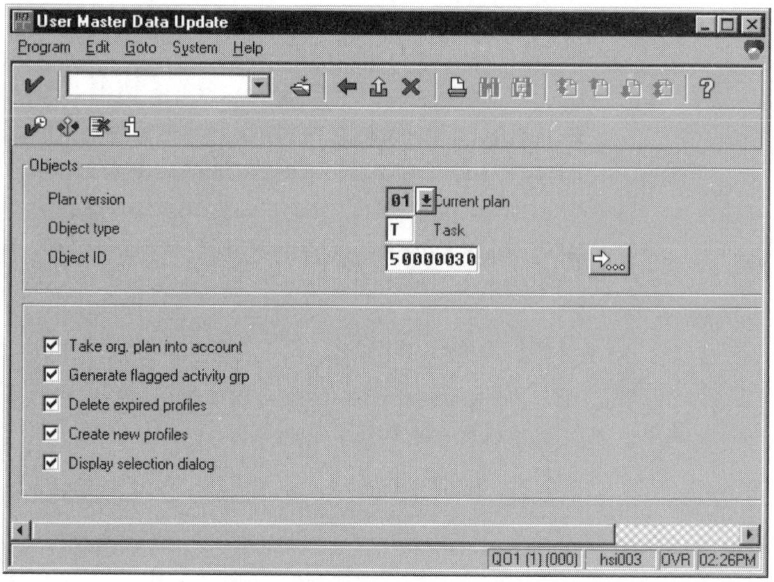

FIGURE 8.22:

Viewing user information after updating the user master

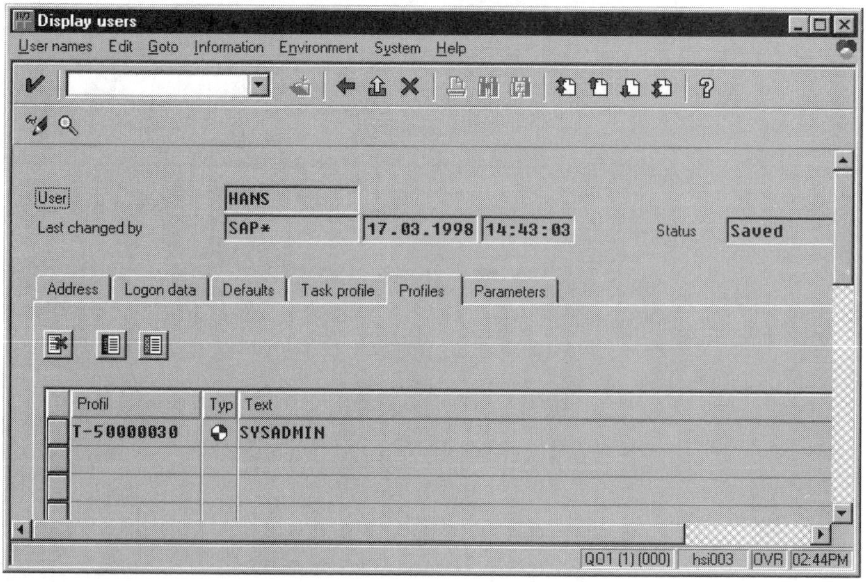

R/3 updates user master data using the report RHAUTUPD. To execute this report, choose User Master. This report finds all the changes to be made to the user master data, and you can apply different options. In addition to updating new or changed activity groups in the user master record, you can generate activity groups that are marked for generation. You can also assign authorizations for a limited time. The report automatically makes an update if you activate the option Delete Expired Profiles.

For security reasons, it is advisable to have at least two different people create and generate activity groups. In this way, the person generating the authorizations to assign can check them once again and prevent illegal authorizations from being assigned. This double verification principle means that, for example, the system administrator cannot assign any new authorizations to himself or herself.

Further Developments

As this relatively limited example shows, the Profile Generator is easy to use, but its use requires some practice. The procedure described and the screens shown come from a Release 4.0A system. (R/3 Release 4.5C will provide further enhancements to the layout and functionality of the Profile Generator.) The term *responsibility* is replaced by *derived activity groups*. The functions are displayed in index card form, similar to how the user maintenance tool appears. The basic idea behind central maintenance of authorizations and user assignment has been retained and will continue to be enhanced.

NOTE For a comprehensive description of how to use authorizations and the Profile Generator, please refer to *Authorizations Made Easy* by Sven Schwerin-Wenzel (SAP AG, 1998).

Additional Functionality

If you make changes to an existing activity group, you must regenerate the authorization profiles and, if necessary, update the user master record.

You do not need to generate the authorization profiles immediately, as you did in the previous example. Instead, they can be generated in a collective processing run. When the R/3 System is being implemented, multiple activity groups and responsibilities or authorizations are maintained at once. Frequently, multiple changes are required to already defined authorizations. It would make little sense to generate the objects after each individual change. You should therefore mark the definitions for generation later. Choose Flag for Activation/Generation (see Figure 8.19). To generate the definitions, use Transaction code PFUD for dialog and report RHAUTUP1 for generation in the background. In practice, it is helpful to schedule this report to run daily during a period of low system load, for example, at night. In addition, this report can be used to update the user master records. For information on how to schedule background jobs, see Chapter 9.

> **WARNING**   Avoid manually assigning generated authorization profiles to users. Doing this would cause you to lose the control and update functionality of the Profile Generator.

Switching to the Profile Generator

Some difficulties are connected with switching to using the Profile Generator in an R/3 System in which the authorization concept has been implemented without using the Profile Generator. There is currently no tool to convert the authorizations and authorization profiles used to the requirements of the Profile Generator. In existing—particularly older—R/3 Systems, the authorizations normally consist of many individual, even customer-specific, authorizations. These authorizations must be assigned individually within the menu tree with its activities. As there is no uniform structure, it is not possible to develop a tool to convert the authorizations. Switching to the Profile Generator is comparable to restarting the implementation of your company-specific authorization concept. This involves some effort, but afterwards it is much easier to structure subsequent routine maintenance work.

Validity Periods

In the full screen for maintaining activity groups, you can limit the time that activity groups and user assignments remain valid. For example, this allows you to plan periodically necessary or future authorizations. You can then use job RHAUTUPD to update the user master records.

Information System

The greater the number of people who work in an R/3 System, the more difficult and complex administration becomes. To help the system administrator retain an overview of the system, R/3 provides a special information system for authorizations. To access this information system, choose Tools ➤ Administration ➤ User Maintenance ➤ Info System. You can evaluate and compare the authorizations and user assignments in the system in a variety of ways. Figure 8.23 shows the initial screen of this tool. This information system is particularly useful when you switch to administering authorizations using the Profile Generator.

Personal Settings

The user administrator is largely responsible for maintaining the data in the user master record (described earlier in the chapter). Users from the application areas normally have no authorization to maintain this data themselves, apart from the company address.

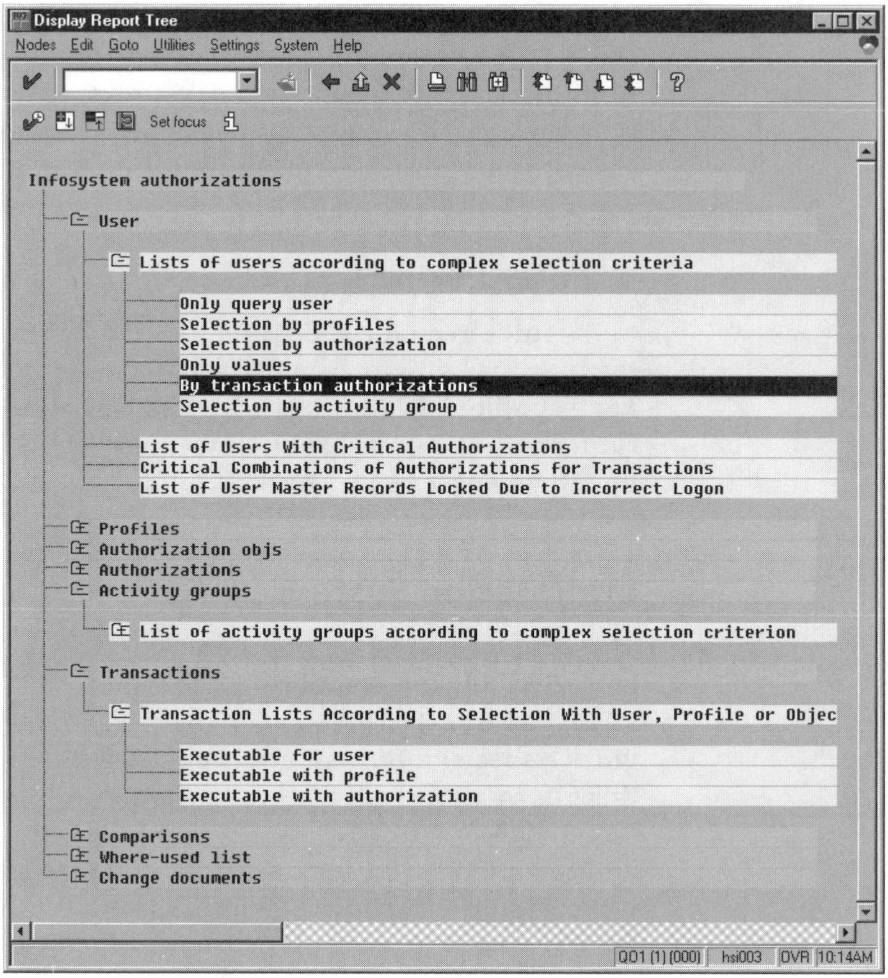

FIGURE 8.23:

The information system
for authorizations

In addition to this type of data in the user master record, all
users can define special settings for themselves to assist their work
with the R/3 System. For example, these settings specify a start
menu, a logon language, a default printer, and the data format or
default values for particular fields. To set your user defaults, choose
System ➤ User Profile ➤ Own Data. The system then displays the

window Maintain Own User Defaults, where you can select your company address, fixed values, and parameters. In the same way, all these parameters can also be administered by the system administrator using the general user maintenance tool, or by the user, provided that the user has sufficient authorizations. Figure 8.24 shows the maintenance screen for user defaults. This screen is opened in a new session so that you do not need to interrupt a work step to maintain the user defaults. The original session is unchanged.

FIGURE 8.24:

Maintaining user defaults

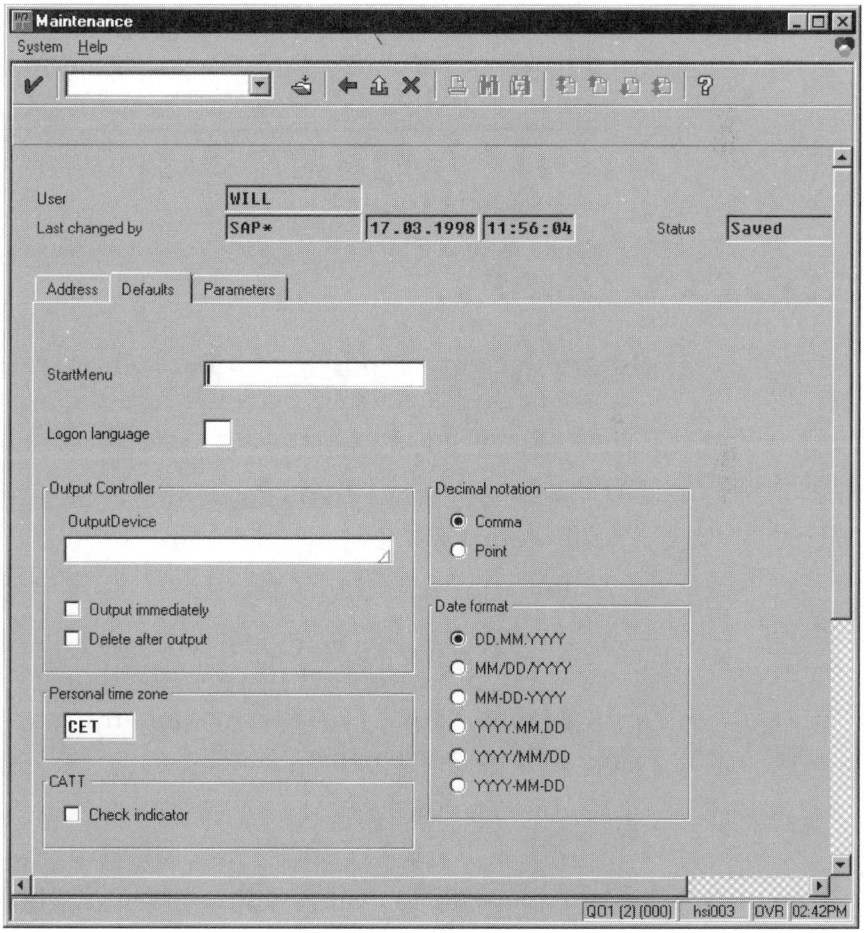

Maintaining parameters with user defaults allows you to set individual values for input fields. This does not mean that you no longer have to enter a value in a field explicitly. Instead, the field is filled with the default values you define. For example, you can define default values for the company code or a cost center. To display the technical information for an entry field, select the field and choose F1 ➤ Technical Info. The Parameter ID field contains the parameter name that you need for the default parameters. For example, BUK stands for the company code. You can use this abbreviation in your personal defaults.

NOTE　　Using R/3 3.1, you can set almost all of the personal user defaults available in R/3 Release 4.0 by choosing System ➤ User Profile ➤ User Defaults or ➤ User Address or ➤ User Parameters.

Internet Users

Beginning with R/3 Release 3.1G, you can execute more transactions using the Internet. Separate Internet users must be set up for these R/3 users. To set up an Internet user:

1. From the user maintenance tool, choose Internet User (see Figure 8.25).

2. Enter the user ID.

3. Specify the user type. The type essentially corresponds to an application area and restricts the user's authorizations. For example, KNA1 means that only the user can execute this Internet transaction.

4. Initialize the user.

5. The user is now active. The system automatically generates a password. To change your password, choose Password.

An Internet user can be locked and unlocked. As of this writing, no additional data is maintained for Internet users.

Review Questions

1. The Profile Generator:

   A. Is used to maintain and automatically generate R/3 profiles.

   B. Is used to create activity groups and corresponding authorization profiles, and to assign the users.

   C. Is an ABAP tool for generating authorization objects for programming.

2. Which statement is correct?

   A. A user can only belong to one activity group.

   B. A user can belong to multiple activity groups.

3. Which requirements for the use of the Profile Generator must be met?

   A. Parameter `auth/no_check_in_some_cases` must have the value Y in the instance profile.

   B. Only users DDIC and SAP* must be known in the R/3 System.

   C. The Enterprise IMG and the enterprise menu must already have been generated.

4. Which statement is correct?

   A. The term *responsibility* is used to mean the responsibility of the user administrator for maintaining authorizations.

   B. A responsibility groups together multiple activity groups.

   C. The terms *responsibility* and *activity group* are always identical.

   D. Responsibilities are used within an activity group to make a distinction between identical activities used for different organizational levels, such as company codes.

CHAPTER
NINE

9

Background Processing

In addition to online processing, R/3 also supports background job processing. This is particularly important for long-running programs that do not require any interactive input. This chapter focuses on managing background jobs. It shows you how to schedule background jobs to be triggered at particular times or by certain events, and how to analyze the processing logs.

Background Dialog Concepts

All non-dialog programs can be executed in the background. This is useful if processing is time-intensive. Online processing would block a dialog process for the entire duration of processing, and thus indirectly hinder other dialog users. For background processing, the R/3 System provides the background service with its background work processes, also referred to simply as background processes. Unlike dialog processing, during which each Logical Unit of Work (LUW) is assigned by the dispatcher to the next free dialog process, in background processing one process is assigned to a background job for the duration of processing. It is the system administrator or the normal user who sets the time at which the background job starts. You can select either a time or an event to trigger the job.

Background Scheduler

To trigger a job at a particular time, specify a start time when you schedule the job. A background scheduler is active within the instances of the R/3 System. At specified intervals, the background scheduler checks if there are any background jobs to be processed. The background scheduler is a program that is interpreted and processed within a specified dialog process. The background scheduler automatically selects the dialog process when the R/3 System is started. By default, the time interval for the background scheduler to become active is set to 60 seconds. The administrator can change this time in the instance profile by setting parameter `rdisp/btctime`.

A job start can be delayed as a result of the time interval between two background scheduler runs. If the delay is too long, you can decrease the time interval. If, on the other hand, the possibility of the job start being delayed is not important, you can increase the time interval. The reduced frequency of background scheduler runs affects the system load very little.

Event Scheduler

One event scheduler is active on the application layer of the R/3 System. You can select the instance for the event scheduler by setting parameter `rdisp/btcname` = `<computer name>` in the default profile of the R/3 System (DEFAULT.PFL). Unlike the background scheduler, which is time-driven, the event scheduler reacts to events and starts background jobs that were set to be triggered by a particular event defined in the R/3 System.

System Events

The standard R/3 System is delivered with a set of events. To display a list of these events, choose Tools ➤ CCMS ➤ Jobs ➤ Define Events ➤ System Event Names ➤ Display. The events delivered in the standard system are called system events. These events are frequently used for internal R/3 control, but can also be used by R/3 users for their own purposes.

User Events

Using the same menu path, you can also define new events of your own, *user events*. To define an event, you need to create an entry in a table.

Triggering Events

You can trigger an event in the following ways:

- From the menu, choose Tools ➤ CCMS ➤ Jobs ➤ Raise Event.
- Use the function module BP_EVENT_RAISE from an ABAP program in the R/3 System (for more information, see *ABAP/4 Development Workbench*, published by SAP AG, 1996).
- Use the external program sapevt.

sapevt

The program sapevt is in the directory \usr\sap\<*SID*>\ SYS\exe\run. You can use it as follows:

```
sapevt <event name> [-p <parameter>] [-t] [pf=<instance profile>
name=<SID> nr=<instance number>
```

Option –t writes a log file dev_evt to the calling directory of sapevt. Option –p can be used to pass a parameter that defines an R/3 module, for example FI. This allows you to assign events to application areas, for example:

```
sapevt SAP_TRIGGER_RDDIMPDP name=Q01 nr=00
```

This call triggers event SAP_TRIGGER_RDDIMPDP in the R/3 System QO1.

Within the R/3 System, event control is used, for example, to transport objects between R/3 Systems. Transports performed using the transport control program tp run in multiple phases. In addition to the actual data import, the individual objects frequently need to be generated or activated. The tp program therefore triggers the event SAP_TRIGGER_RDDIMPDP when the data import is complete. In an R/3 System, the job RDDIMPDP is always scheduled to be dependent on this event. If the event SAP_TRIGGER_RDDIMPDP occurs, the job RDDIMPDP is automatically executed in the background. This method allows you greater flexibility. You cannot always predict when actions will be completed, which means that you cannot establish a dependency between background jobs. Event control provides additional possibilities.

To obtain information about the configuration of the schedulers and the location of the event-driven scheduler in particular, choose Jobs ➤ Background Objects. This allows you to make changes to the settings.

Defining Jobs

There is an R/3 Transaction for defining background jobs. It is available as part of the Computing Center Management System (CCMS), which you call by choosing Tools ➤ CCMS. To define the job, choose Jobs ➤ Definition, or use Transaction code SM36 (see Figure 9.1).

Frequently, scheduling background jobs is also directly integrated into the applications, for example, when you copy a client or update a user master record.

NOTE   Depending on the application, the appearance of the job's data entry screens may differ or particular job attributes may be preset. The principles and possibilities of background processing described in this section are still valid and can be applied in these special cases.

A background job definition covers three main areas:

- General information, such as job name, job class, and target computer
- Information about the start time or a triggering event
- Processing steps

General Information

The general information forms the basis for the definition of a
background job (see Figure 9.1). You should choose a job name that
indicates the purpose of the job, as all the logs and overviews
that will need to be analyzed later will be based on this job name.

Job Class

The job execution priority is determined by the job class assigned to the job. There are the following job classes:

A: Highest priority—Jobs that ensure the functioning of R/3 and are time-critical.

B: Medium priority—Periodic jobs that ensure the functioning of R/3.

C: Normal priority—Job class C is the normal job class for R/3 users.

The job class is used to assign system resources. If a large number of class C jobs frequently wait to be processed, causing class A jobs to wait for the background process to be released, the system administrator can explicitly reserve background processes for processing class A jobs. These background processes are then only used to process jobs of these classes. To learn how to do this, refer to Chapter 13.

Target Computer

In a distributed R/3 System, you can also designate an R/3 instance with a background service to process a job. If you do not specify an instance, R/3 selects the first available background process in any instance at the time of execution. If a log is generated at the end of a job run, you can use Spool List Recipient to send it to a user. In this way, different people can administer and analyze the results of a background job.

Start Time

The next step is to select the parameters that determine the start time. Choose Start Date from the initial job definition screen (as shown back in Figure 9.1). You can define that the job start at a particular time or to be triggered by an event (see Figure 9.2). You can also set a job to be processed depending on another job that is already defined. Then, the background job is started when the first job is completed. If you only want to start the second job if the first job is processed successfully, use the option Start Status-Depend. If the first job is interrupted, the dependent second job is given the status of canceled and is not processed.

You can also make processing of a job dependent on an operating mode switch in the R/3 System. (Operation modes in an R/3 System are discussed in Chapter 14.) The time-driven scheduling of jobs allows you to process jobs periodically. For example, this can be useful for data backups.

You can set the time interval to be every minute, every hour, daily, weekly, etc. To set time intervals that are different from the usual periods, choose Restrictions. This option is useful, for example, for working around public holidays in the factory calendar. For time-sensitive jobs, you can set a time after which the job will not be started. When you have finished defining the start time, save your data.

Processing Steps

To complete the definition of a background job, describe the processing steps that make up the job. A processing step is the execution of an independent program, for example, an ABAP program or an external program. A background job can consist of one or more such processing steps. To define the steps, choose Steps from the job definition tool (see Figure 9.1).

Each processing step can be executed by a user different from the user assigned by the scheduler. Authorization checks are always based on the user assigned. In this way, you can give different groups of users the authorization and responsibility for scheduling a job and for analyzing the job results. For example, using explicitly assigned users can make it easier to analyze the results of a background job later, because generated lists can be assigned uniquely to a particular user. For this purpose, you can define background users (see Chapter 8).

Processing steps can consist of ABAP programs, external commands, or external programs (see Figure 9.3).

ABAP Program

As already mentioned, you can execute all non-dialog ABAP programs in the background. To do this, choose ABAP Program (see Figure 9.3). Enter the name of the ABAP program and, if necessary, a language in which to generate a log. Many ABAP programs are controlled by variables, for example, the program RSPFPAR. This program generates a list of all the set instance parameters. Before you execute the program, you can restrict the name range of the instance parameters to display.

To execute this type of program in the background, you need to create variants of a program. Behind this is a variant name, under which fixed values for a program's variables are stored. To define a variant, use the ABAP Workbench (Tools ➤ ABAP Workbench, or Transaction code S001) with the editor by choosing Goto ➤ Variants ➤ Create. You must enter the variant name and the parameter values. You schedule an ABAP program variant defined in this way for background execution. Figure 9.3 shows the scheduling of the ABAP program RSPFPAR, for which a variant called ALL was created to generate a list of the currently defined instance parameters. To control printing of this list, choose Print Specifications.

External Commands

An external command consists of a logical name and an assigned external program with selected parameter values, which can vary depending on the operating system. Before you use external commands in background processing, you must define them in the CCMS by choosing Configuration ➤ External Commands ➤ Change ➤ Command ➤ Create.

The standard R/3 System already contains many external commands. Taking into account the customer name range, you can also create additional external commands. Figure 9.4 shows the example of command ZLIST, behind which lies the command ls with the parameters -lisa to display the contents of the current directory on UNIX systems. For Windows NT systems, you could set up an external command of the same name that conceals the corresponding command dir. A command defined in this way can be used both when you define background jobs and from the CCMS. Choose Jobs ➤ External Commands, or use Transaction code SM49, select a command, and then choose Command ➤ Execute.

When you define a step of a background job, the external command to be executed is determined by its name, for example, ZLIST, and by the operating system, for example, UNIX. You can also define the target computer and additional parameters.

As you define each step of a background job, you must save it. A table shows all the defined steps. A background job must consist of at least one step.

When you have entered the general information, the start time, and a definition of the steps of the background job, the definition of the background job is complete. You must then save the data.

In addition to the menu method, R/3 provides an interface
(*Application Programming Interface,* or *API*) to schedule background
jobs. You can use the API in your own ABAP programs (see *ABAP/4
Development Workbench*, SAP AG, 1996), or *Documentation of the
SAP R/3 System*, SAP AG, 1998.

External Program

You can use the External Program function to execute external
programs, that is, programs outside of R/3. You can also select a
target computer and which parameters to pass.

Analyzing Jobs

To analyze and monitor background jobs, choose CCMS ➤ Jobs ➤ Maintenance, or use Transaction code SM37. You can select the jobs using various criteria, such as user, time period, or event and job status (see Figure 9.5). You can restrict the selection criteria using the authorization concept. The user here is the user under whose name a job step was executed. The user can also be a special background user. To analyze your own jobs, choose System ➤ Own Jobs.

Based on the selection made, a list of background jobs is generated (see Figure 9.6).

FIGURE 9.5:

Choosing job runs to analyze

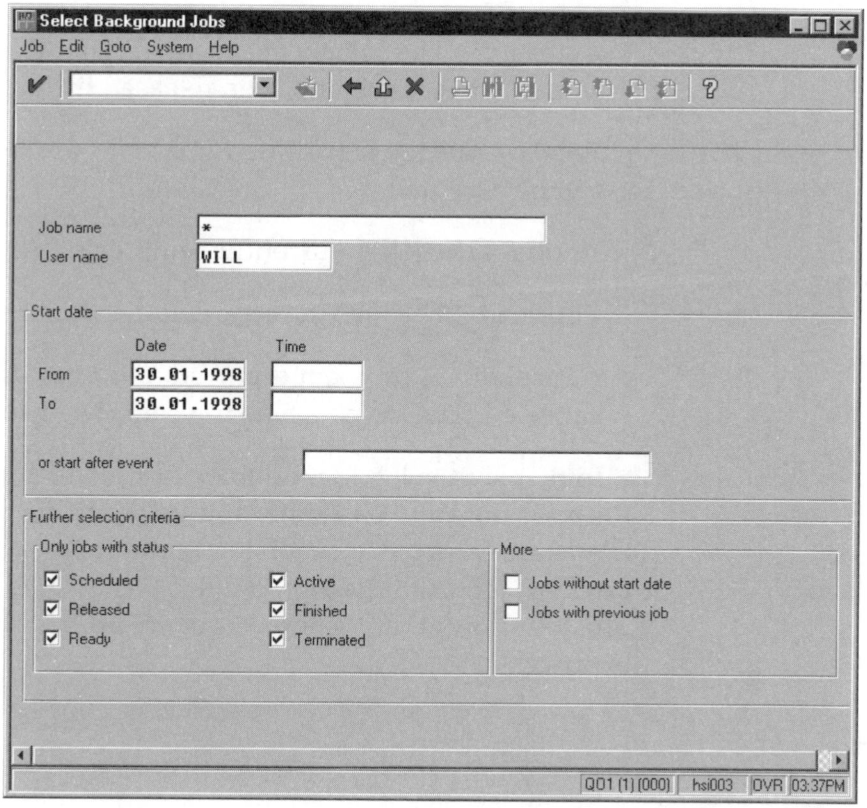

FIGURE 9.6:

The job overview shows the list of background jobs.

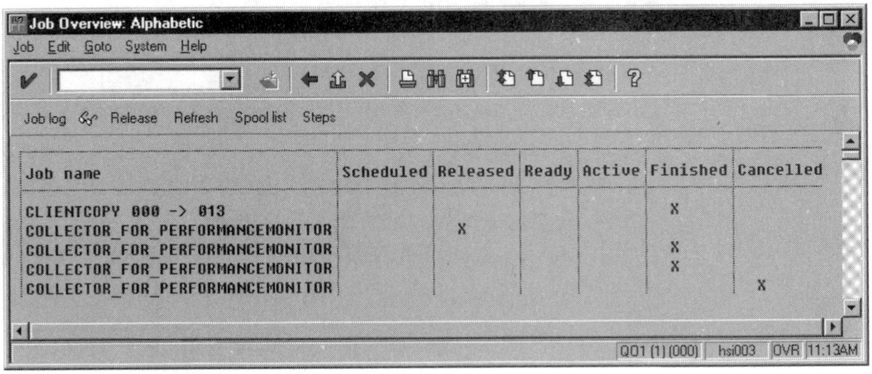

The status of each job is one of the following:

Scheduled—All job data was saved.

Released—The system checked whether the job definition could be executed, and then released it.

Ready—The job is waiting for system resources so that it can be executed.

Active—The job is currently being processed.

Finished—The job was completed successfully.

Canceled—A problem occurred and processing had to be canceled. The job could not be completed successfully.

To display the job log, double-click on a job. The job log records the start time and end time, and valuable information about why jobs were canceled. The job log that follows was generated for the canceled job COLLECTOR_FOR_PERFORMANCEMONITOR. The log shows that the job was canceled because the R/3 license expired.

Report 9.1:

```
------------------------------------
|Date     |Time    |MsgId/No. | Message          |
------------------------------------
|23.03.1998 |13:00:34 |00     |516 |Job was started  |
|23.03.1998 |13:00:35 |00     |175 |Logon denied
                   (License expired) |
|23.03.1998 |13:00:35 |00     |564 |Job was cancelled
          after system exception ERROR_MESSAGE.
```

The job overview contains information about all the important operations that concern background jobs. These include displaying and changing scheduling data; canceling, deleting, and moving the execution to other computers; and checking the generated spool lists. In addition to the list overview, you can also use a graphical overview with similar functions. To call the graphical monitor, choose CCMS ➤ Control/Monitoring ➤ Job Scheduling Monitor (see Figure 9.7). The status of the jobs is highlighted.

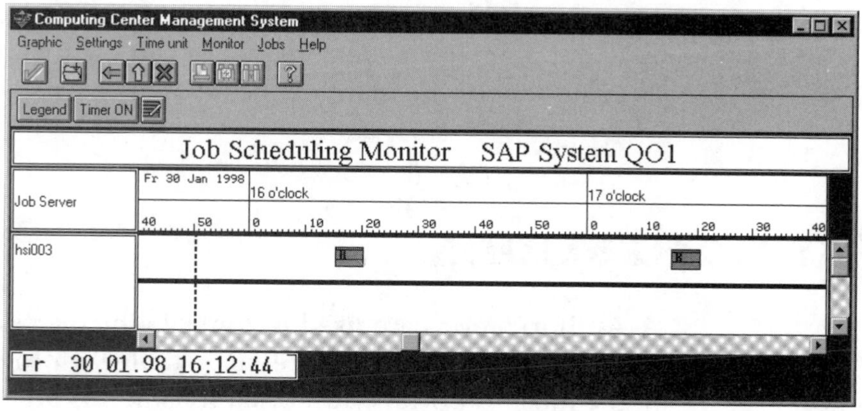

FIGURE 9.7:

The graphical job overview in the CCMS

Analysis Functions

Unlike dialog processing, in background processing, problems concerning a user are not immediately apparent to that user. CCMS (Tools ➤ CCMS) provides additional special functions.

When you have made changes to the profiles in R/3, it is advisable to check the settings for background processing by choosing Jobs ➤ Check Environment. You can also check whether the authorizations needed for processing have been assigned and whether the database tables are consistent for background processing. Choose Goto ➤ Additional Tests.

To obtain a summary of the selected background jobs showing their planned and actual start times and run times, choose Jobs ➤ Performance Analysis. Large discrepancies between planned and actual start times indicate a bottleneck in the available background processes, because this means that a long time elapsed between when the job was released and when a background process could be made available for processing. If you know that there were no performance bottlenecks during the execution of the scheduled background jobs, you should check the resources and consider increasing the number of background processes with parameter `rdisp/wp_no_btc` in the instance profiles or by using the profile maintenance tool. (See Chapter 13).

Authorizations

Authorizations are used to control which actions a user can perform in background processing. Table 9.1 provides an overview of the most important authorizations in this area. If you use the Profile Generator, the authorizations are assigned automatically when you select the actions.

TABLE 9.1: Authorizations for Background Processing

Authorization	Meaning
S_BTCH_ADM	Administrator for background processing, client-independent.
S_BTCH_JOB	Operations with background jobs, client-dependent.
Possible values:	
DELE	Delete jobs of other users.
LIST	Display spool lists of other users.
PROT	Display logs of other users.
RELE	Schedule your own jobs and release them for execution.
SHOW	Display job details of other users.
	Use the field Job Group to restrict the authorization to specific job names.
S_BTCH_NAM	Use a background user explicitly.
S_RZL_ADM	CCMS system administration.

Maintenance Jobs

For an R/3 System to continue to function, it is necessary for specific jobs to be executed at more or less regular intervals. For example, these jobs might delete tables that are no longer needed or collect statistical data for performance analysis. It is the responsibility of the system administrator to schedule and monitor these jobs. Table 9.2 lists the most important programs. Depending on the applications used, or whether or not you are using your own custom applications, additional jobs may be necessary.

TABLE 9.2: Important Maintenance Jobs

Program	Meaning	Time
RSCOLL00	Collects the general statistical data for R/3 System performance analysis. Schedule in client 000 as DDIC. Normally scheduled at delivery under the name. COLLECTOR_FOR_PERFORMANCEMONITOR.	Hourly
RSBPCOLL	Collects the statistical data to analyze the average run time of periodically executed jobs.	Daily
RSBTCDEL	Deletes all logs for successfully completed jobs. The system administrator can use variants to define the number of days after which a log is deleted. Client-dependent.	Daily
RSBPSTDE	Cleans up the run-time statistics of the background jobs. All objects older than the specified date are deleted.	Monthly
RSBDCREO	Deletes the logs of background input processes. (See Chapter 13.) Log BI<*SID*><`instance name`> in directory \usr\sap\<*SID*>\SYS\global is minimized by deleting processed entries. Client-dependent.	When needed
RSPO0041	Deletes obsolete spool objects. Client-dependent.	Daily, depending on the print activities
RSPO0043	Deletes spool lists, which are the remnants of canceled background programs. Checks the consistency of the spool tables.	Daily
RSSNAPDL	If the maximum number of entries is exceeded, deletes run-time errors entries (short dumps) that are older than six days.	Daily
RDDIMPDP	Converts transport requests.	Event-driven
SAPRSLOG	Administration job that updates the object lists and navigation indexes, normally active under the name EU_PUT.	Daily
SAPRSEUT	Administration job that updates the object lists after a transport, normally active under the name EU_REORG.	Daily

To obtain further information on the attributes and parameters of these jobs, refer to the documentation for each program. Use the ABAP Workbench editor (Transaction code SE38). Specify the program name, then choose Documentation ➤ Display.

Review Questions

1. Which transaction is used to analyze the job logs?

    A. SE38

    B. SM37

    C. S000

2. Which external program is used to trigger events in the R/3 System?

    A. sapevt

    B. sapxpg

    C. sapstart

    D. spmon

3. What does the status of Ready mean for a background job?

    A. Scheduling of the job was completed and saved.

    B. The job was executed and the log is ready to be printed.

    C. The job is waiting for system resources so that it can start.

CHAPTER

TEN

Update Service

10

Update is a particularly important service in the R/3 System. Update services should not be considered in isolation, because they work in close collaboration with other R/3 System services, such as dialog or background. Update requests are not generated directly by users. Instead, they are generated by users' dialog or background activities.

Update problems have a negative effect on the efficiency of the entire R/3 System. Therefore, resolving update problems should be a high priority. This chapter introduces the fundamental concepts and explains how to use the integrated R/3 tools to monitor update.

Like background processing, update is also performed outside of dialog. This chapter outlines the tasks of the system administrator.

Update Concepts

In the R/3 environment the term *update* means to make asynchronous changes to the R/3 database after data has been entered in dialog. For example, if a user enters data, this data is first passed to the dialog process. The changes to the database are not made by the dialog process itself. Instead, special update processes make the changes; the changes are made asynchronously.

Users will notice greater system performance with asynchronous changes when compared with synchronous data changes; changes made immediately by the dialog process itself. A user can enter, change, and delete data in quick succession without having to wait for these requests to be executed when asynchronous changes are made. The update process processes these requests in the background.

Asynchronous updating is particularly beneficial for making comprehensive data changes, for example, changing business data or creating orders. Asynchronous updating increases R/3's scalability. Users normally do not have any influence on whether their database changes are made asynchronously or synchronously. That depends on the ABAP program used.

V1 and V2 Updates

Asynchronous updating has an additional advantage in the way it implements R/3 Logical Units of Work (LUW) compared with database transactions. R/3 LUWs are converted to independent LUWs, which in turn consist of multiple database transactions. Data entry and updating can be administered separately, and update operations can be bundled.

An update consists of V1 and V2 updates. The steps that make up a V1 update are basic and time critical. They are used for business operations, such as changes to the material in stock. Changes to these objects must always be made as quickly as possible. V2 updates are mainly used for statistical purposes and are subordinate to V1 updates. You must therefore handle V1 updates with higher priority than V2 updates. This is done by making available separate update work processes, those in classes UPD and UPD2. For example, you can use the work process overview in Transaction SM50 to check the distribution of work processes (see Chapter 2). In this way, the update operation can be split and the individual parts can be updated independently of each other.

The user does not have any influence on how the update for an operation is split. This is determined during the programming stage by the function module CALL FUNCTION *<function name>* IN UPDATE TASK (see ABAP/4 Development Workbench, SAP AG, 1996).

From the viewpoint of the system administrator, it is not important to know which operations a user is performing (which transactions are generating update records). By the same token, it is not important for the user to know how the update operation is performed internally in R/3. For the user, throughput and results are what count. It is the task of the system administrator to ensure that this actually happens. The following sections explain the tools and methods available.

Configuration of the Update

The application server that coordinates the update processes in an R/3 System is defined for the entire system in the default profile, DEFAULT.PFL, by parameter rdisp/vbname. The number of V1 and V2 update processes is determined for a particular instance by the parameters rdisp/wp_no_vb and rdisp/wp_no_vb2 in the instance profile. The simplest way to maintain the parameters is by using the Profile Parameter Maintenance Tool integrated into the R/3 System (see Chapter 13). The decisive factor that determines the number and distribution of the update processes is the number of update records waiting to be processed in a reasonable time. The upper limit is set by the capacity of the hardware—the resources available to the R/3 System. This means it is necessary to monitor the work of the update processes.

Monitoring the Update Service

The importance of the update depends on the role of the R/3 System in the landscape. In a development system, the update is less important, but if the update fails in a production system, work comes to a halt as a result. Normally, the update process in an R/3 System works without errors occurring and does not require further attention. If, for example, database problems occur, they are exceptional situations that must be resolved as quickly as possible.

To monitor and analyze problems during the update, choose Tools ➤ Administration ➤ Monitoring ➤ Update, or use Transaction code SM13 (see Figure 10.1).

FIGURE 10.1:

Update service monitoring

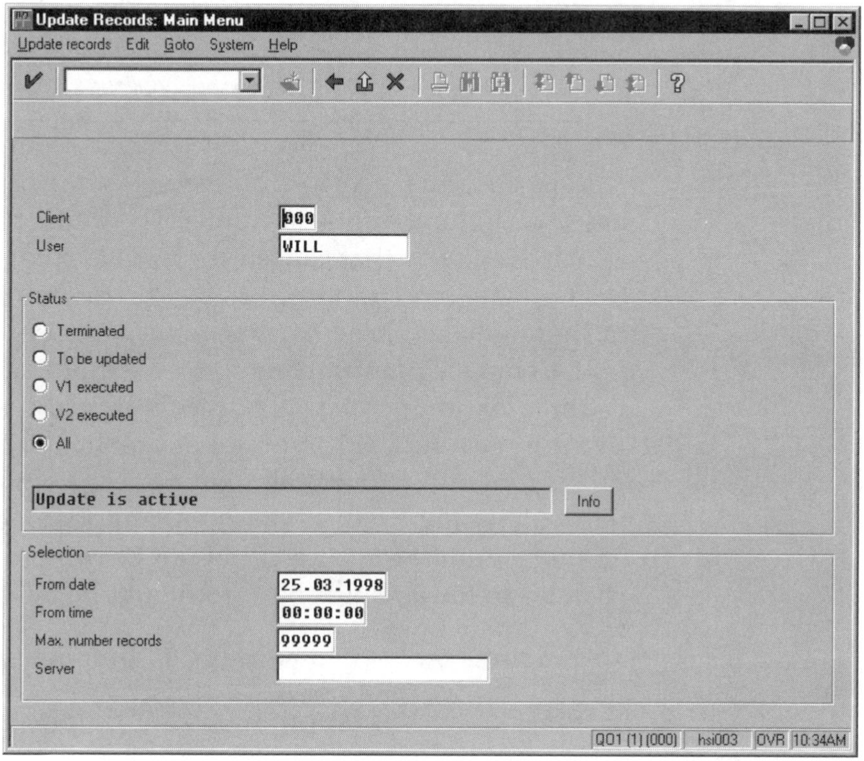

Checking the Update Status

It is important to know the current status of an update. In serious error situations, such as with serious space problems in the database, the update is automatically deactivated. This is known as an *update termination*. A message in the status bar notifies you that the update was stopped and requests that you wait. The session remains blocked until the update is restarted. If this happens, the

R/3 System administrator must be notified immediately so that the problem can be resolved.

TIP

If errors occur throughout the system, you can deactivate the update service manually by choosing Update Records ➤ Update ➤ Deactivate. After the problems are resolved, choose Activate to activate the update again. Update terminations and problems are recorded in the R/3 System log (see Chapter 15).

From the initial screen, you can select the update processes based on a number of conditions. The time of arrival, status, and Transaction code that caused the update record are displayed for each update record to be posted. The volume of data waiting to be updated at a particular time gives you a picture of whether the update capacity is sufficient for the requirements. The time spent waiting for an update work process should not be longer than five minutes. As a rule, you set approximately one update work process for every four dialog processes. Terminated updates are particularly important. A terminated update means that the operations to update a record could not be completed, that is, the changes to the R/3 database could not be made.

An update record can have one of four statuses:

Init—The record is waiting for the update.

Auto—If the update is active, the record is automatically updated.

Run—The record is being processed.

Err—An error occurred, causing the update to be terminated.

Analyzing the Cause of a Termination

You should always analyze the cause of terminations. You must resolve what is causing update records to be terminated and make a decision about what procedure to use in the future. Business considerations are decisive here, so you can only make the analysis in close collaboration with the user department. To perform an analysis, do the following:

1. From the Update Record Administration menu (Tools ➤ Administration ➤ Monitoring ➤ Update, or using Transaction code SM13), choose Terminated, specify the client, the user, and the time period.

2. Choose Execute.

3. The system displays a list of terminated updates, as in Figure 10.2. For each record, you see the client, the user, a timestamp, the Transaction code that created the update, and the status.

FIGURE 10.2:

Analyzing update termination

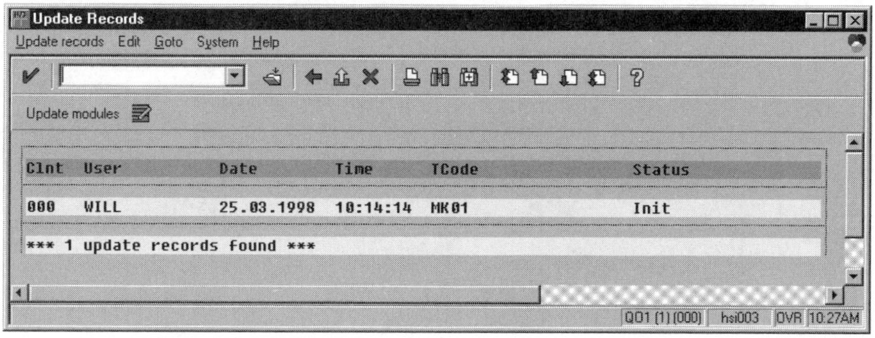

Figure 10.2 shows a record with status *init*. The record is waiting for the update, which was either terminated or could not be completed because there is insufficient capacity.

4. Analyze the update termination, together with someone from the user department responsible.

You can select individual update records and test them by choosing Update Records ➤ Test. To execute an update in debug mode, choose Update Records ➤ Debugging. Before you use this function, consider that it places a heavy load on system resources.

If this does not provide a result, check the record's update header. The update header contains all the administration data of the update record. Choose Goto ➤ Update Header (see Figure 10.3).

FIGURE 10.3:

The update header displays administrative data.

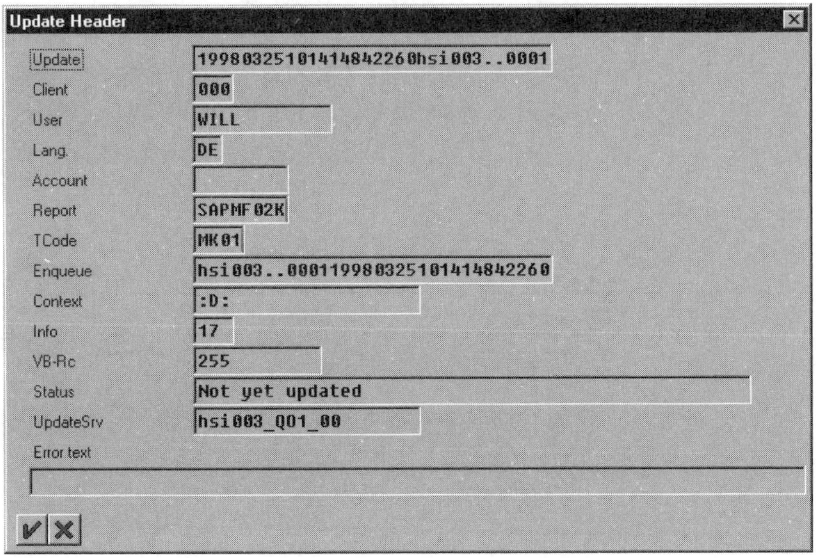

Update Header		✕
Update	199803251014148422260hsi003..0001	
Client	000	
User	WILL	
Lang.	DE	
Account		
Report	SAPMF02K	
TCode	MK01	
Enqueue	hsi003..00011998032510141484226 0	
Context	:D:	
Info	17	
VB-Rc	255	
Status	Not yet updated	
UpdateSrv	hsi003_Q01_00	
Error text		

Updating Specific Records

To find out which function modules need to be executed to update a record (update modules), choose Update Modules from the list of the terminated update records. Figure 10.4 shows this for the record from Figure 10.3. Here, the non-updated record consists of two V1 components.

To check the actual data in an update record, choose Update Records ➤ Data.

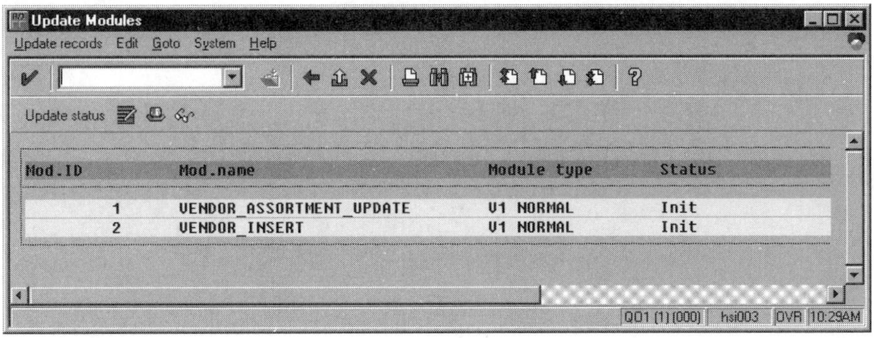

FIGURE 10.4:

Update Modules shows which function modules need to be executed to update a record.

Analyzing Errors

You should check the R/3 System log for indications of errors. From the main R/3 screen, choose Tools ➤ Administration ➤ Monitoring ➤ System Log, or use Transaction code SM21.

There are two types of problems. The first type, systemwide problems, can be caused by database problems and frequently cause the update to be terminated. For example, this could happen if the maximum size of a table was reached in an Oracle system. If this problem is resolved, you can assume that the update will restart automatically and no further problems will occur.

The other type of update problems are of a more isolated, local character. They are often caused by programming errors in customer-specific objects. To resolve this type of problem, you should involve the developers and the user departments. Working together, you must decide what to do about the terminated update records. To delete, repeat, update, or reset individual or all update records from the list of update records, choose Updated Records, then Delete, Repeat Update, Update, or Reset. *Repeat Update* means that the update is continued. *Update* means that the update record is still in its unprocessed state (status init), as shown in the example in Figure 10.2. If repeating an update or updating it does not have the desired effect, the records must be deleted or reset—or processed again.

If the problems cannot be resolved, use the OSS (for more on the OSS, see Chapter 3). If the problems are of a general nature, you will find many Notes that offer relevant information. If you do not find a solution, open a problem message in OSS to be processed by the SAP Hotline.

Please pay attention to the following when trying to solve a problem:

- V2 updates can only be executed after V1 updates are complete. When a V1 component is processed, the system automatically attempts to process the related V2 component.

- The R/3 System can be configured so that the user whose update request caused an error can be automatically notified. To do this, use parameter `rdisp/vbmail` = 1. The value 0 deactivates automatic user notification. By default, this parameter is set to 1 when the R/3 System is installed.

- The parameter `rdisp/vbdelete` specifies a period in days after which incomplete update requests are deleted when the R/3 System or the instance is restarted. Depending on whether the parameter was set in the default profile or in the instance profile, it takes effect throughout the entire system or in just one instance. When the R/3 System is delivered, this parameter is set to the default value of 50 days. To never delete incomplete update records, set the parameter to 0.

- The parameter `rdisp/vbreorg` determines whether incomplete update requests are deleted when the R/3 System or an instance is restarted. The value 0 suppresses this reorganization value 1 activates it. You can also delete incomplete update requests using report RSM13002. Incomplete update requests are caused by terminations (rollbacks) explicitly triggered by a user for requests that were already partly written to the database.

During normal R/3 operation, the R/3 System administrator is concerned with three main questions regarding an update:

- Is the update service active?

- Are there update terminations?

- How big is the queue of waiting update requests?

Monitoring the update activities is one of the daily tasks of the system administrator.

Review Questions

1. Which components make up an update?

    A. V1 and V2

    B. Pre- and post-update

    C. Test and main update

2. Which status does an update record have if it is waiting for an update?

    A. Active

    B. Released

    C. Init

    D. Start

3. Which R/3 profile parameter is used to send a message to a user whose update request was canceled?

    A. `rdisp/vbmail`.

    B. A message is always sent to the user.

    C. `rdisp/vbdelete`.

CHAPTER
ELEVEN

11

Output Configuration and Administration

When users work with the R/3 System, they generate many output requests with a varying level of importance, such as invoices, documents, patient status reports, or audit trails. The spool system provides an essential part of R/3 Basis functionality. R/3 System administrators must work with operating system administrators to configure the output devices within the R/3 System and monitor and ensure that these devices are functioning correctly. This chapter focuses on these tasks and provides you with practical information.

Output Basics

Output requests are created from, for example, the requests from dialog and background processing. A user chooses a device configured in the R/3 System (see Figure 11.1) for the data to be output. A user then creates a *spool request.*

Inbound data must either be formatted for the selected output device and (possibly) stored until the output device is ready to receive the data. The *output request* that was created from the spool request is then sent to the output device. These tasks must be performed by the R/3 spool service. There are three main task areas:

Data storage—The data in a spool request is stored unformatted in temporary sequential objects (*TemSe*). Physically, TemSe is either a table in the database or a file outside the database in the file system of the application server. This is controlled by the instance parameter `rspo/store_location`. The default value is `db`, to store data in the database. The value `G` stores the data in the R/3 directory `/usr/sap/<SID>` `SYS/global`. If the data is stored in the database, it is automatically subject to the administration and security procedures of the RDBMS, such as transaction and log management. At the same time, this places a certain load on the

RDBMS. If the TemSe is stored in the R/3 directory, there is less load on the RDBMS, but you forego the benefits provided by the RDBMS.

FIGURE 11.1:

A user creating a spool request

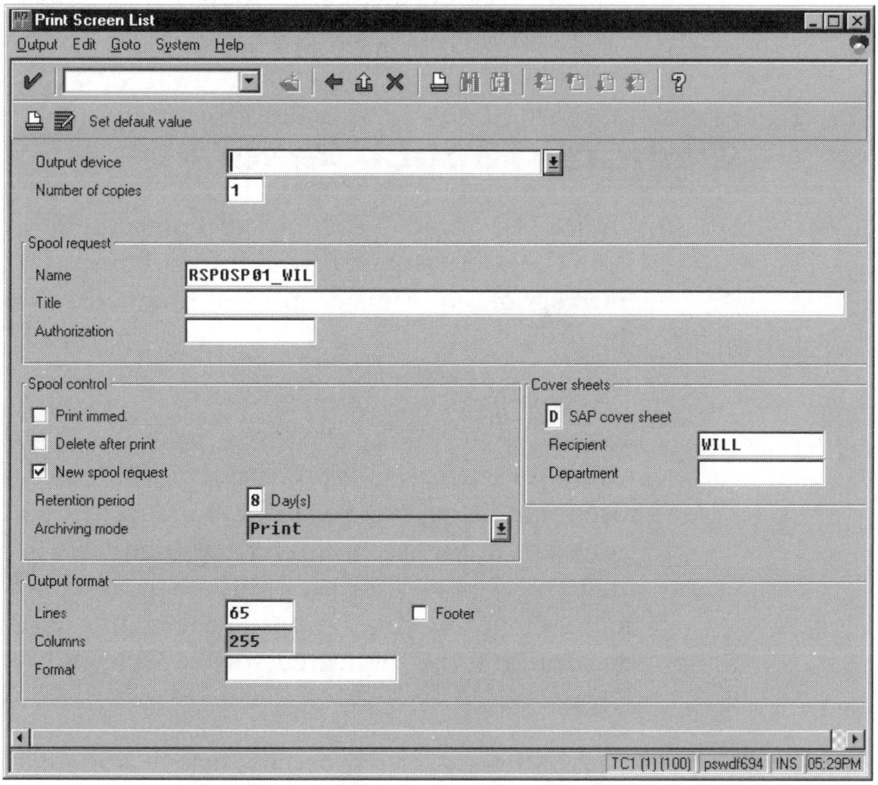

Device management—All devices used for output must be defined within the R/3 System. For this, the devices must already be configured and available on the operating system level of the computer. When a device is configured within the R/3 System, a device driver is assigned to the device and a connection is defined. This indirectly determines how R/3 formats the spool request data stored in the TemSe to generate the desired output for the device.

Output management (Output Management System, OMS)—
Output management consists of formatting, coordinating, executing, and monitoring the output requests. The spool work processes are used for this. Printers and output devices can also be connected using a third-party Output Management System certified by SAP. This enables you to integrate R/3 output processes into an existing OMS infrastructure.

Dedicated Spool Servers

Figure 11.2 shows a simplified representation of the processes from the user request through to the output request to a device. Each spool request is addressed to an output device selected by the user.

Normally, you cannot assume that this output device can be accessed by every application server in the R/3 System through the spool service. Therefore, the definition of an output device also includes an assignment to an application server, which functions as a *dedicated spool server*. All requests to this output device are processed by the spool service of the spool server and passed to the device. If you define an alternative server, you can prevent disruption if the dedicated spool server fails.

NOTE   In R/3 releases before 4.0, the output device definitions included a fixed assignment between a device and one instance. The spool service could only be implemented by one spool work process per instance. In periods of high system load, this sometimes caused serious bottlenecks. For example, if the single spool work process for an instance was not able to process all the waiting requests in an acceptable time, an instance failed and caused all its assigned printers to fail too. Each spool service had its own request management, which forced each spool service to perform the same tasks, which was in effect task redundancy.

FIGURE 11.2:

Spool administration
in R/3

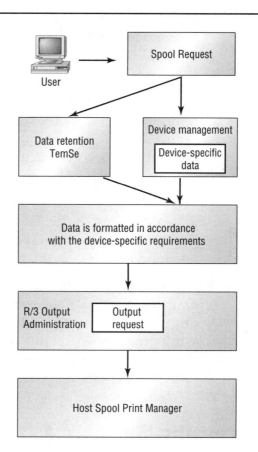

The centralization of administration tasks in R/3 Release 4.0 reduces considerably the load on the database. All spool work processes in the instances form a unit, and any number of spool work processes can run on one instance. The number of spool work processes is limited only by the main memory of the application servers.

The procedure for administering requests has changed as follows:

- Each instance with a spool service administers its inbound output requests in its own spool request queue. The request queues are objects in the main memory area of the instance.

- If excessive load situations occur, causing the spool request queue to overflow, a dispatcher queue is used to collect the inbound requests.

- If space becomes available again in the spool request queue after it has overflowed, the spool work processes transfer requests again from the dispatcher queue to their own spool request queue. Spool request processing is only continued when the dispatcher queue is empty or when the spool request queue is full.

- The entire request queue is administered in the main memory area and stored in the database. If the dispatcher queue overflows, requests are removed from the main memory area, meaning that data in the main memory area is lost.

- At intervals of about 20 minutes, the spool work processes in an instance check the database to find out whether there are any of this type of "forgotten" requests. If multiple spool work processes are active on an instance, an internal procedure ensures that only one spool work process processes the "forgotten" requests.

Processing Sequence

Adherence to the processing sequence, that is, processing the requests in the sequence that they arrive, can only be ensured when there is only one spool work process in the instance. When multiple spool work processes are active in an instance, some requests may be processed before others that arrived before them. When you define a device, there is a special option to ensure the processing sequence of a specific output device.

A spool work process always processes all the requests for a device in the spool queue before it accepts subsequent requests. This means full parallelism between multiple spool work processes is restricted.

Configuring the Landscape of Output Devices

When you configure a landscape, you should first use the following technical criteria to determine which class each output device belongs in:

Production printers (time-critical printers)—Requests processed by these printers are used immediately for production operation. These requests should be processed locally on application servers to avoid network problems. Mass printing requests should not be sent to these printers, as they will cause other requests to wait. You must ensure that the computer to which the output device is connected is active.

Mass printers—There are large volumes of requests to be output, which are inevitably time-intensive. These printers should therefore be fast and accessible locally from an application server.

Work center printers—A work center printer is situated locally at a user's work center and is used for relatively low-volume printing without urgent time requirements.

Test printers—You can assign a separate printer class to new printers or changes in the output configuration.

From the application viewpoint, there can be another class of output devices in addition to the technical criteria:

Printers for requests that are subject to particular security requirements—This type of output request is, for example, generated in the Human Resources Management area. From a technical viewpoint, these requests can be both time-critical and large. The output devices should therefore be accessible locally from an application server. To meet the increased security requirements, it is advisable to run the output devices and application servers in a separate network.

These logical groups of output devices must now be assigned to the available spool instances, the *spool servers.* To make the definitions more flexible and less system-dependent, R/3 Release 4.0 lets you define logical servers.

Logical Servers

Logical server is a name for a real physical application server or another logical server. It defines a mapping between a logical name and another logical name or a real application server. For a logical server, you can also define an alternative server. If the logical server were to fail, all the waiting tasks would be redirected to the alternative server. The alternative server could in turn be a logical server or a real application server.

Figure 11.3 shows an example of the use of this method. The logical server LOG1 is assigned to the printer group I; logical server LOG2 is assigned to printer group II. LOG1 is a mapping to the real application server APPL1; LOG2 points to the application server APPL2. LOG2 also acts as an alternative server for LOG1.

If the application server APPL1 fails (and with it the logical server LOG1), the logical server LOG2 would automatically process the requests, which would then be processed by application server APPL2. It would be conceivable to transport this configuration into another R/3 System that has only one application server, Test1. In this case, the mapping of the logical servers LOG1 and LOG2 would have to be changed to assign them to the application server Test1 (see Figure 11.4).

Using logical servers reduces dependency on the definition of the output device landscape. The definitions you make can even be transported into a different R/3 System and adapted to that system with relatively little work.

FIGURE 11.3:

An example of the use of a logical server

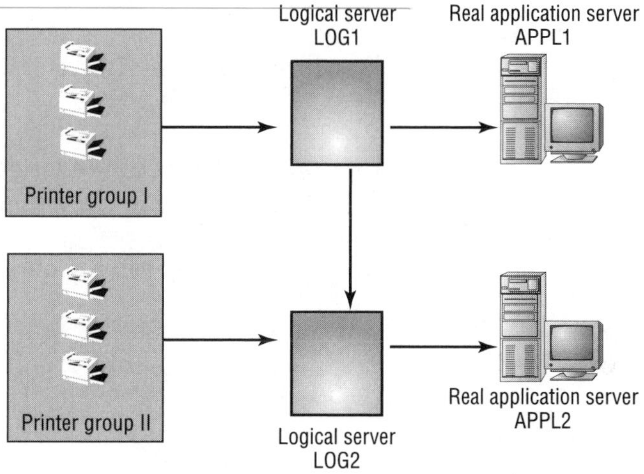

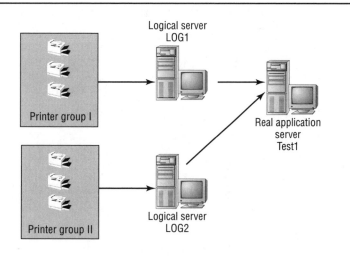

FIGURE 11.4:

Changing the configuration

Classification

The spool servers, real or logical servers, can be classified in accordance with the classifications of the available output devices:

V—High volume printing (mass printing), for example, cost center lists

P—Production printing (time-critical printing), for example, documents, accompanying documents

D—Desktop printing, for example, SAP documents

T—Test server or test printing

– —Unclassified

Configuring Output Devices

After the available output devices are classified, they are assigned to the spool servers. You must set the following attributes for each output device:

- Full logical name of the device in the R/3 System
- A short four-character name
- Device type in accordance with the device drivers available in R/3
- Device class:

  (blank)—Normal printer

  A—Archiver

  F—Fax machine

  T—Telex

- Spool server, which can be a real application server in the R/3 System with a spool service or a logical server

- Host printer that represents the name of the computer that is administering the output device or to which the device is connected

- Access type to the host spool

You should choose printer names whose first letter reflects the device classification, for example, V_xxxx for mass printing. This makes it easier to later assign authorizations for the printer classes.

For each device, you can set the following processing options:

Monitoring through monitoring infrastructure—You can use the analysis tools to analyze how the device is processing the requests.

Do not send output status from host system—The R/3 spool work process does not wait for confirmation from the operating system spool.

Send each copy as own print request—A separate spool request is created for each copy to be output.

Sequential request processing—The sequence for this device is kept.

Access Methods

The *access method* describes in the broadest sense the method or the protocol that is used to transfer data for the output request from the spool server to the host printer. Data can be transferred from the spool service of the assigned spool server directly to a host spool system, to an Output Management System, to a network printer, or to the program SAPLPD. SAPLPD is a program between a spool server, the R/3 spool service, and a Windows print manager. SAPLPD is started on the Windows computer and is available for Windows 3.1, Windows for Workgroups, Windows 95, and Windows NT PC in a 16- and 32-bit version.

Local Access Methods

The output device can be accessed directly from the spool service of the spool server, that is, the spool service passes the data directly to the spool or print manager of the host. The following are the options for access methods:

Access method L—The spool service stores the data to be printed as a file on the host. From there, the data is printed using the appropriate host spool command, for example `print` for Windows NT or `lpr` for UNIX systems. You can use *command groups* to specify which command is used. If you do not specify a command, the default values are used for the instance parameters `rspo/host_spool/print` and `rspo/host_spool/query` for printing and status request.

For Windows NT systems, the default setting would be

`rspo/host_spool/print = print /d:&P &F`

/d stands for the printer connection option, &P is the macro for the port to be used (LPT1, COM1...), and &F is the file to print.

Access method C—In contrast to access method L, the data is not stored temporarily in the host file system; it is passed directly to the system print manager using the programming interface. This access method can only be used for Windows NT and AS/400 systems.

Access method E—This access method can be used when you use an OMS. The OMS must be suited for connecting to the R/3 spool system (see the section later in the chapter on "Output Management Systems").

Access method P—Access method P is used to print simultaneously to multiple printers. Printers of the same type are grouped together into the same device pool. A device pool can comprise a maximum of 15 devices defined in the R/3 System. Device pools can in turn contain other device pools. Up to 5 levels can be nested.

Access method F—This access method is used for *front-end printing*. The output device is connected to the user's front end. When the user submits an output request, it is processed by the user's dialog work process, not by the spool service of the assigned application server, as in the access methods listed previously. The dialog work process passes the generated output requests directly to the SAPLPD program or the spool system of the UNIX workstation. This access method generates additional load on the dialog service. The spool service of the R/3 System is not used.

Remote Access Methods

For the access methods that follow, the data is transferred from the spool service of the spool server through the network to the spool or the print manager of the printer host. These access methods are therefore quite sensitive to network problems. If problems occur when a connection is being established, the spool service of the spool computer must wait, possibly until a timeout is reported.

WARNING These methods should not be used for production printing or large print volumes. If the receiving printer does not have sufficient memory for the inbound request, the spool service can only send the data at the speed at which the printer can output it. Likewise, you should avoid mixing remote and local access methods on the same spool server, in order to prevent the log from changing frequently.

You can choose the following remote access methods:

Access method S—This access method is used for printers that function as work center printers for a Windows system. Data is compressed and sent through the network to the SAPLPD program that is started on the front end.

Access method U—Access method U can be used as a protocol to the spool system from UNIX or OS/2 systems. It is possible to use access method U together with the SAPLPD program on Windows systems, although access method S would be more appropriate. Access method U is based on the Berkeley protocol (RFC 1179).

Special Access Methods

For output devices other than printers, there are special access methods:

Access method X—This access method can be used to output SAPcomm requests by fax. Spool requests of this type are subject to special processing. A spool server is not assigned directly. SAPcomm is specified instead of the spool server.

Access method I—This access method is used with SAP ArchiveLink. The spool system is only used as temporary storage for documents to be archived. SAP ArchiveLink handles further processing.

Output Management Systems

Beginning with R/3 Release 4.0, you can connect external Output Management Systems (OMSs) to the R/3 spool system. The application programming interface XOM-API is used for this. This interface will undergo further development in future R/3 releases.

OMSs are mainly used in complex IT landscapes. A connection from R/3 to an OMS allows you to take advantage of an OMS from within the R/3 System. The information provided by OMSs regarding the status of an output request is more precise and direct than that provided by the R/3 System and is particularly useful.

NOTE   To use an OMS with R/3, the OMS must be certified by SAP. For more information, visit the SAP site on the Internet at `http://www.sap.com` and choose Partners ➤ Complementary Software. A non-certified OMS may require some manual modifications.

ROMS and LOMS

Within R/3, a distinction is made between a *real* OMS (ROMS) and a *logical* OMS (LOMS). The definition of a ROMS describes the concrete OMS in the IT environment—the interface between the spool service and the external OMS. The LOMS is a subset of the ROMS. It describes how the output devices assigned to it use the ROMS.

When you define a ROMS, you use a command interface (command prompt) or the RFC interface XOM-API to determine how the OMS is to receive instructions. XOM-API enables you to use RFC Callback, explicit status query, or cyclical status query (polling) to query the status of a job to report to an R/3 instance. You can obtain information about the device status using an explicit query (a queue query) or using RFC Callback, for which the OMS passes the information through RFC to an R/3 instance. In addition, you can delete requests from the OMS request queue. If you want the ROMS to support fax as well as printing, you can choose this function.

When you use the RFC Callback interface, you need to define an initialization instance within the R/3 System with an initialization command. The OMS documentation describes which initialization command to specify, or you can find the command by viewing the OMS configuration file. The reconfiguration query in the R/3 System is used by the callback client to check and modify the configuration. The suggested time between two requests is 300 seconds.

Administration Procedure

To call the spool administration and analysis tool from the main R/3 menu, choose Tools ➤ CCMS ➤ Spool. To administer the R/3 spool, choose Spool Administration or use Transaction code SPAD. You can choose between three views for simple, extended, and full administration (see Figure 11.5).

Defining the Spool Servers

In the first step, you define the logical and real server as follows:

1. Choose Spool Server ➤ Change, then Spool Server ➤ Create. The screen labeled Spool Admin.: Server (Change) is displayed (see Figure 11.6).

2. Maintain the attributes of the server. If you activate the Logical Server option, you can press Enter to display an additional entry field for the resultant mapping. By deactivating the Non-exclusive spool server option, the sequence of the output requests is set for this device.

3. Save and exit the screen.

The servers and their status are highlighted in color (see Figure 11.7).

Select a server and choose Mapping from the screen to define a logical or real server to display the assignment for the servers (see

Figure 11.8). Horizontal lines indicate the mapping of a logical server to another logical server or to a real server. Vertical lines indicate alternative server relationships.

FIGURE 11.5:

A full view of the spool administration menu

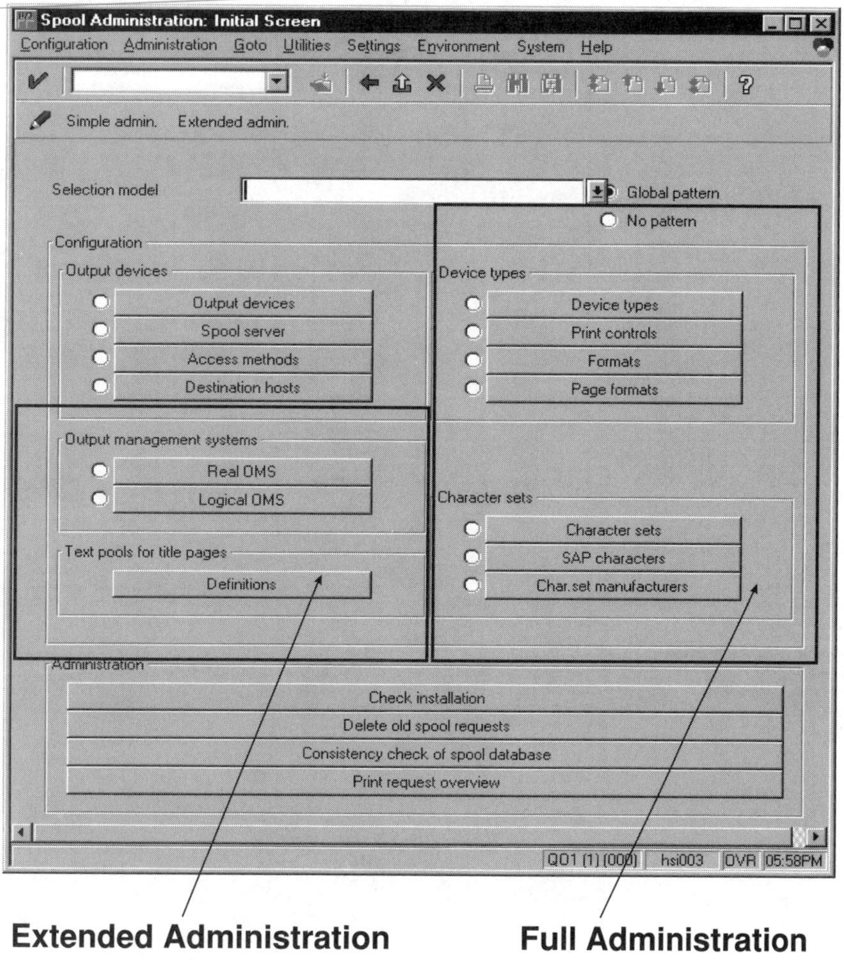

Extended Administration   Full Administration

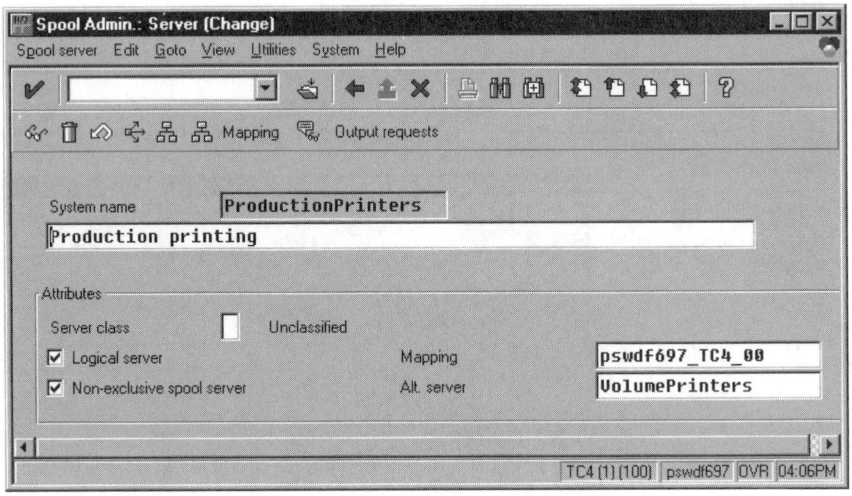

FIGURE 11.6:

Defining a logical or real server

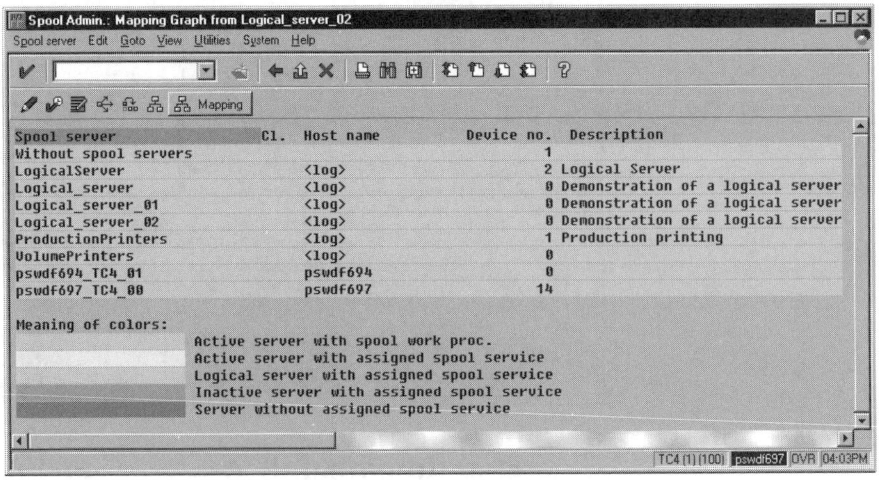

FIGURE 11.7:

An overview of the servers defined

FIGURE 11.8:

Mapping the servers

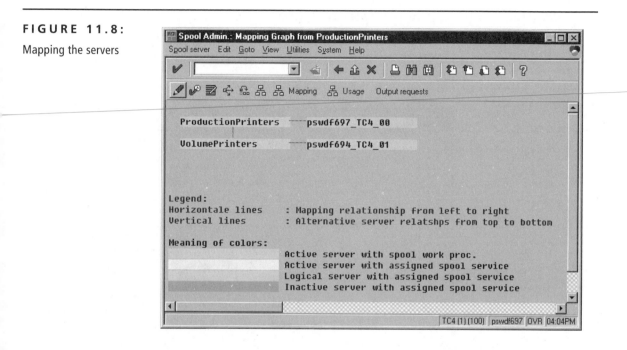

Defining the External OMS

To use an external OMS, you must define in the next step an ROMS and, if necessary, an LOMS. This is part of the extended spool administration. Defining external OMSs requires a precise knowledge of the spool system on the server. Study the OMS documentation to find out the attributes of your ROMS. Figure 11.9 shows the screen for this. To access this screen, choose Real OMS from the extended spool administration menu as shown in Figure 11.2.

The output devices are only defined and assigned to the servers when these two steps are completed: defining the spool servers and the external OMS. To define output devices follow these steps:

1. From the spool administration tool, choose Tools ➤ CCMS ➤ Spool ➤ Spool Administration, then Output Devices. The

system displays an overview of the defined output devices and their assignment. This overview includes a series of device-specific analysis functions.

2. Choose Change. To create a device, you must be in Change mode.

3. Choose Output Device ➤ Create. Figure 11.10 shows the screen for creating the device function. The possible OMS attributes were described earlier in this chapter.

4. Choose F5 to go to the next screen, where you can set processing rules for output requests. Figure 11.11 shows an example of a printer for which the original sequence of the output requests' arrival was activated.

5. Choose Paper Tray Info to create settings for the paper feed.

6. To classify a device, choose Edit ➤ Classification.

7. For each device, you can explicitly define where the data to be printed is stored temporarily: in the database or in the file system. Choose Edit ➤ Data Storage.

8. Save and exit the screen. The overview of the defined output devices is displayed.

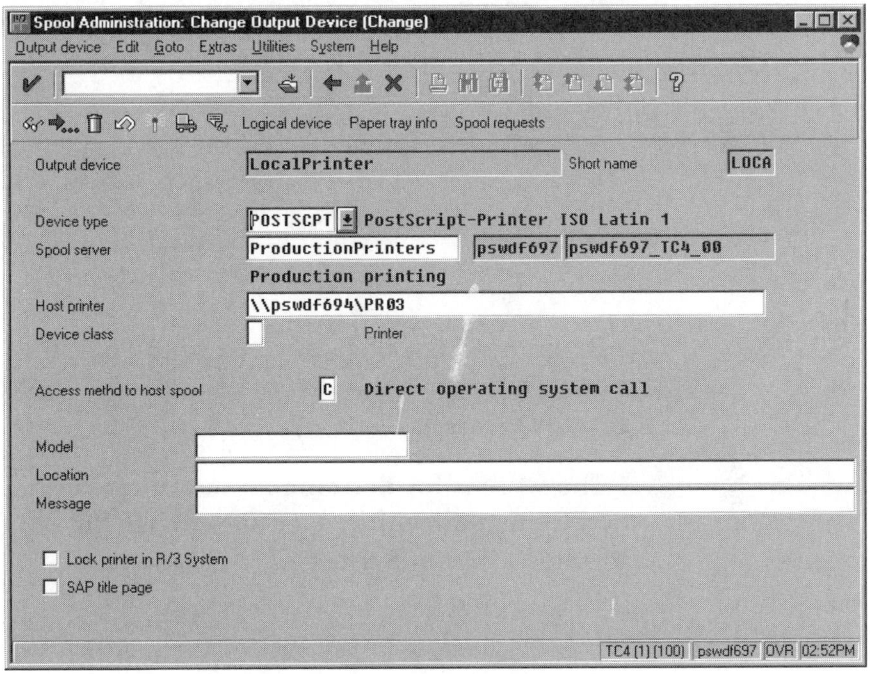

FIGURE 11.10:

Defining the output device (Display mode)

TIP   It is advisable to set up all the devices that are assigned to the same spool server in the same way.

To assign the device definitions to a transport request and transport them into other R/3 Systems, press Ctrl+F3.

If you need to take a device out of operation for a short period, press Ctrl+F2. This deactivates a device; you can activate it in the same way.

The screens for defining an output device also provide a function to display waiting spool requests for a defined device. To do so, choose Spool Requests.

Analyzing and Resolving Errors

There are two ways to track the operation of the R/3 spool:

- In the CCMS, choose Spool, then Output Management (Transaction code SP01). If you have the appropriate authorization, you can also access the Transaction by choosing System ➤ Services ➤ Output Control.

- For statistical purposes, choose Spool Administration, then Overview of Print Requests.

You can use Transaction SP01 to display the output requests for selected users and a selected date (see Figure 11.12). Authorizations are used to determine whether a user can view the requests of other users. Authorizations also determine which actions are permitted on waiting requests. For example, requests can be output again, redirected to another printer, or their content can be viewed.

FIGURE 11.12:

An overview of print requests in the system, Transaction SP01

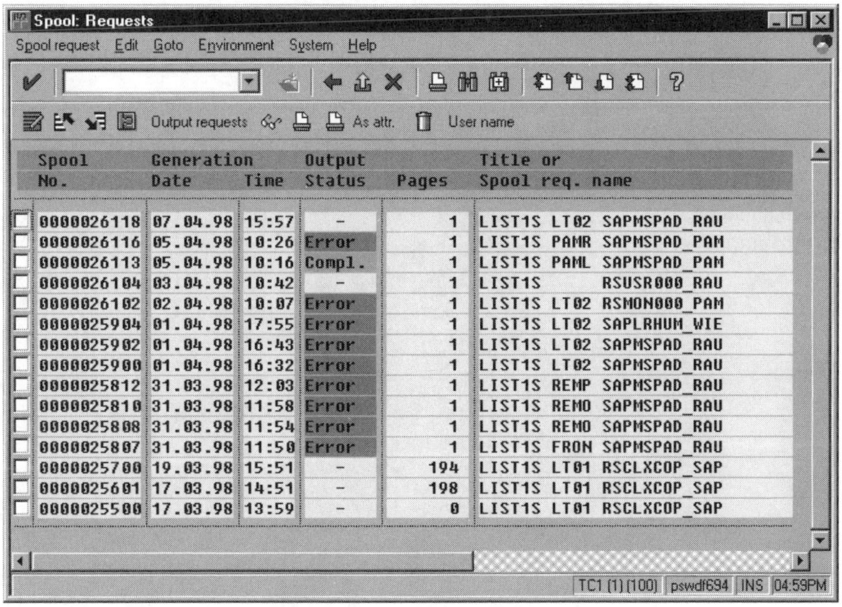

Problems or errors in output control are indicated by missing or corrupt output. With the appropriate authorizations, the administrator can view the output log, which will contain indications of the cause of the error.

To display an overview of your own spool requests, choose System ➤ Own Spool Requests.

> **NOTE**
> If printing problems occur, you should first check whether the device is functioning properly on the operating system level. Use the operating-system-specific commands, such as `1pr` or `print`. A device that cannot be accessed from operating system level cannot be accessed from the R/3 System.

The overview of the output requests within the spool administration (Transaction SPAD) comprises both the configuration functions of the spool system and statistical information such as the number of print requests per device, per server, per user, etc. (see Figure 11.13).

FIGURE 11.13:

A statistical overview of distribution and number of output requests

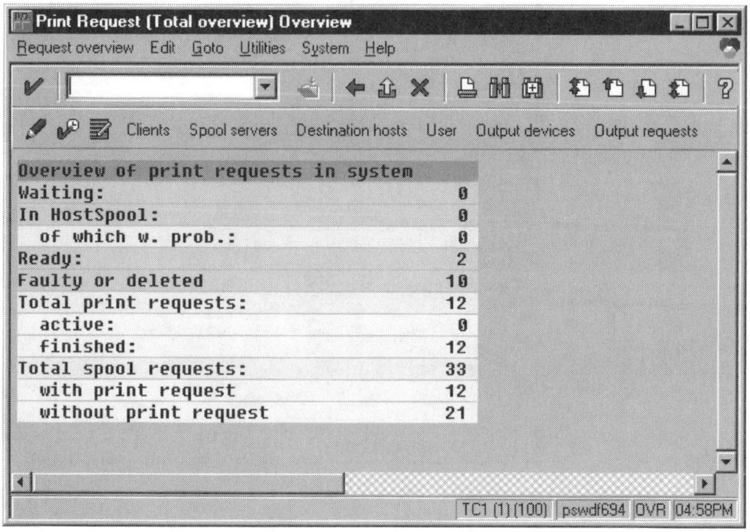

This information is useful for assessing the overall configuration of the landscape of the output devices. The load should be distributed evenly over the R/3 instances.

Maintaining TemSe

To display statistics on the fill level and content of TemSe, from the spool administration tool, choose Environment ➤ TemSe Administration (Transaction SPAD). To display a detailed list of the data for each user and client, and their space requirements in TemSe, choose TemSe Database ➤ Memory Allocation.

When its data is stored in the R/3 database, the size of the TemSe database is limited by the size of the tablespace or the database. If the TemSe data is kept in the file system, the size of the file system is the upper limit. For performance reasons, you should keep the TemSe database as small as possible. The administrator must ensure that obsolete spool requests are deleted from the TemSe, especially if automatic deletion of processed spool requests is inactive. To do this, schedule report RSPO0041 to run regularly (see Chapter 9) or choose TemSe Database ➤ Reorganization.

To be able to respond to problems in good time, you should check the consistency of the TemSe database daily. From the TemSe administration menu, choose TemSe Database ➤ Consistency Check or execute Report RSPO0043 (see Chapter 15).

Using Authorizations

As with all activities in R/3, the activities in this area (configuring, printing, analyzing, etc.) are restricted by special authorizations. The following is a list of authorization areas:

Device authorizations—S_SPO_DEV

Display authorizations for spool requests—S_ADMI_FCD

Authorizations for operations on spool requests—S_SPO_ACT

Authorizations for limiting the maximum number of pages to print (starting with R/3 Release 4.0B)—S_SPO_PAGE

Authorizations for administering the TemSe—T_TMS_ACT

Normally these authorizations are assigned from R/3 Release 4.0 using the Profile Generator. Figure 11.14 shows the authorization tree.

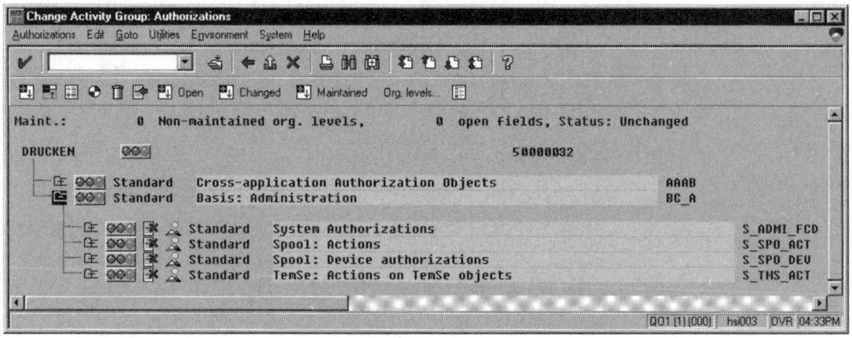

FIGURE 11.14:

The Profile Generator: authorizations for spool administration

Device Authorizations

The device authorizations define the output devices for which a user can generate requests. The name, or generic name, of one or more output devices is assigned to the authorization object. It is a good idea to apply certain naming conventions when the output devices are defined. If the first character of the printer name reflects a group assignment, for example, D* for all desktop printers, it is easier to define authorizations for particular output groups.

Display Authorizations

The authorization object S_ADMI_FCD determines which output requests a user can display. All users can display information about their own spool requests by choosing System ➤ Own Spool Requests. To display spool requests, use Transaction code SP01. The authorization value SPOR extends the authorization to display spool requests to all users in the same client. To authorize a user to display all the spool requests of all the users in all the clients, assign the authorization value SP01.

Action Authorizations

The authorization object S_SPO_ACT determines which actions a user can perform on the spool requests visible to that user. Table 11.1 shows the available authorization values.

TABLE 11.1 Authorization Values for Object S_SPO_ACT

Authorization Value	Authorization To
BASE	Display all spool requests.
ATTR	Change request attributes.
AUTH	Change the authorization value.
DISP	Display the content of a spool request.
DELE	Delete spool requests.
PRNT	First output.
REDI	Redirect a spool request to another device.
REPR	Repeat output of a request.

Review Questions

1. Which access methods are there?

    A. Local access methods

    B. Remote access methods

    C. Special access methods

    D. Access methods with formatting

    E. Access methods without formatting

    F. Internal access methods

    G. External access methods

2. For which authorizations does R/3 provide authorization objects?

    A. Device authorizations

    B. Display authorizations

    C. TemSe administration authorizations

    D. Authorizations for operations with spool requests

3. Which access methods are recommended for mass printing?

    A. Local access method L for transferring to the host spool using the appropriate command interface

    B. Local access method C for direct transfer to the Print Manager of the host spool using the appropriate command interface

    C. Local access method F for front-end printing

    D. Remote access method S for work center printers through SAPLPD

    E. Remote access method U based on the Berkeley protocol

4. Which three areas are there in the R/3 spool system?

    A. User administration

    B. Authorization administration

    C. Output administration

    D. Device administration

    E. Access methods

    F. Data storage (TemSe)

5. What is a dedicated spool server?

    A. A selected application server in the R/3 System that is used for central spool administration.

    B. The application server assigned to an output device defined in the R/3 System. The spool service of the dedicated spool server handles the processing and administration of the spool requests passed to this device.

    C. The front-end computer (desktop) that is currently used for front-end printing.

    D. The application server in an R/3 System that is explicitly assigned to a user as a spool server for that user's spool requests.

CHAPTER

TWELVE

Data Archiving

This chapter focuses on archiving data that has been deleted from the database and discusses the tool used for archiving, the *Archive Development Kit* (ADK). This chapter describes the basic handling and background of archived data.

What Is Archiving?

Depending on your viewpoint, the term *archiving* in the R/3 environment can refer to any of three areas. First, in the area of database administration, the term *data archiving* refers to backing up the archive log.

Second, from the viewpoint of the application, archiving refers to the use of the SAP ArchiveLink interface to archive inbound and outbound documents. The applications are already prepared to be connected to the archive system and must be configured (as discussed later in the section on "Customizing") so that, for example, invoices, receipts, bills, and other application-specific documents can be stored in the archive.

Third, from the viewpoint of the R/3 administrator, archiving is primarily removing obsolete data from the database and storing it in an archive. That's why this chapter focuses on that activity.

Reasons for Archiving

An R/3 database normally grows continually over the years. After a period of time, which is determined by legal requirements and company-specific factors, a lot of the data becomes meaningless and represents unnecessary ballast for daily work. The bigger a table is, the more time-intensive and expensive it is to search. Larger data volumes also require more resources, such as main memory, hard disks, and backup devices. The administration cost grows with the size of the database. For those reasons, it is necessary to remove data from the database.

Archiving Requirements

For legal reasons, data must be retained and must be readable if required. Frequently, you must guarantee that the data has remained unchanged. Archives saved using WORM (Write Once, Read Multiple) or CD-ROM media are appropriate for this.

Archive Development Kit

The ADK is the interface between the archiving programs of the application (for example, the data archiving) and the archiving files. The ADK provides function modules with the functions needed to allow the archiving programs to write prepared archive data to directories outside of the database (see Figure 12.1).

Database records are archived in three phases.

FIGURE 12.1:

Basic principles of the Archive Development Kit (ADK)

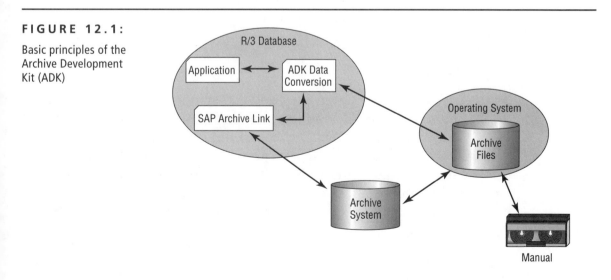

Phase 1

The first step is to determine which data can be archived. This must be decided by the departments involved, as the R/3 System administrator is not in a position to judge the relevance of business data. The administrator is responsible for the technical implementation of the archiving process. Archiving objects are defined within the R/3 System. An *archiving object* comprises the logical unit of physical data that belong together, for example, financial accounting documents, bank master data, purchase requisitions, travel data, or payroll accounting results. Also included are all the programs needed to archive this data, for example, editing programs, as well as read, write, and delete programs.

Data can only be archived for one archiving object at a time, in order to retain the logical consistency of the database. The data volume to be archived is determined by the defined archiving period. All the data that was generated in that period is archived. The data defined by the archiving object and the chosen time period is then prepared and copied to a directory on a hard disk outside of the database. To prepare the data, the data is extracted from the database in an RDBMS, hardware-independent format, which involves font-independent code pages, record structure, and number format. The data is also compressed.

Phase 2

After the data has been extracted and stored in files, the extracted data can be deleted from the database. Before the data is deleted, the system automatically checks whether the files generated in phase 1 can be read. A special program is generated to do this. Data is only deleted if it is in the files generated in phase 1. Depending on the configuration, the checks can be performed automatically after the data has been extracted, or they can be done manually.

Phase 3

In phase 3, the files generated in phase 2 are transferred to the actual archive.

Hierarchical Storage Management

There are multiple archiving systems that you can use to create the archive. You can use *Hierarchical Storage Management (HSM)* to automate the process. ArchiveLink and HSM support the use of optical storage media and document management systems. To ensure that the archiving systems function and are compatible with the R/3 ArchiveLink interface, SAP offers a certification procedure for archive vendors. For information on the certified vendors on the Internet, visit **www.sap.com** and choose Partners ➤ Complementary Software.

In addition to using an archiving system, you should also manually back up the archive files generated in phase 1 to another medium, such as tapes (see Figure 12.2).

WARNING Data can be archived during normal R/3 operation. However, the increase in read and write activities can negatively affect performance. You should therefore archive the data at times of low system load.

FIGURE 12.2:

Data archiving procedure

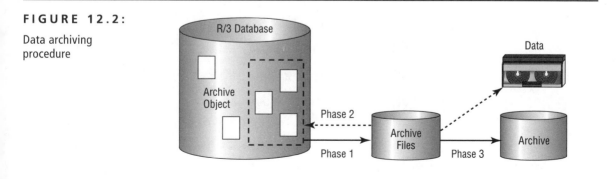

Customizing

Data from an R/3 System may need to be archived because of the increased cost of maintaining a growing database and because some of the data is no longer needed.

Which Data?

The R/3 System administrator or the database administrator cannot decide which application-specific data can be archived. As I mentioned earlier, this is the responsibility of the user department, with which the R/3 System administrator will need to cooperate during the archiving.

The first task is to convert the application view into the technical R/3 database view. You must address the question of which archiving object best meets the requirements. Archiving objects are sometimes connected logically and chronologically to each other. To display a network graphic from the main R/3 menu, choose Tools ➤ CCMS ➤ DB Administration ➤ Data Archiving ➤ Table/Object ➤ Archive Admin. ➤ Goto ➤ Network Graphic.

To obtain more details, follow these steps:

1. Go to the start of the ADK. Choose Tools ➤ CCMS ➤ DB Administration ➤ Data Archiving, or use Transaction DB15. The screen Tables and Archiving Objects is displayed.

2. You have two options:

    • Select a table and display all its archiving objects.

    • Select an archiving object and display all its tables.

To switch between these two areas, press Shift + 5.

In Figure 12.3, all the archiving objects for Table RFBLG were sought. The Financial Accounting Table RFBLG was in the archiving object FI_DOCUMNT. All the related tables for the archiving object were then found.

How Much Data?

Once you've made a decision about the archiving object, you must determine the volume of data to be archived. To determine whether archiving will be beneficial, you'll need information about the current physical and logical size of the tables in an archiving object in the database. The *physical size* is the actual space occupied in the database. The *logical size* is the number of records in the table. There are two methods of analyzing the size, both of which are highly database-dependent.

The first method is to find out the current size of a table, select a table and choose Online Space Info. This may take a few minutes, depending on the RDBMS you are using and the size of the table.

The second method for analyzing size is to choose Statistics Space Info if the statistics used by the SQL optimizer are sufficient for your needs. The sizes specified based on the statistics provide only the situation—or even only an estimate based on a sample at the time that the optimizer statistics were last updated. If this update took place a long time in the past, the table may have changed greatly in the meantime. You must consider this when you estimate the size of the tables. All the RDBMSs used with R/3 work with cost-based optimizers from R/3 Release 4.0. Therefore, the database administrator must regularly update the statistical data, which in turn forms the basis for the cost estimates by the optimizer. For more information, please refer to the RDBMS documentation.

Where?

When you've collected the necessary information for the archiving object and the relevant tables, you must configure the archive. Switch to the archive administration tool by choosing Table/ Object ➤ Archive Admin. or by using Transaction code SARA.

Figure 12.4 shows the initial screen before an archiving object has been selected. When you specify the name of an archiving object, the executable actions are automatically extended.

FIGURE 12.4:

The initial screen
of the archive
administration tool

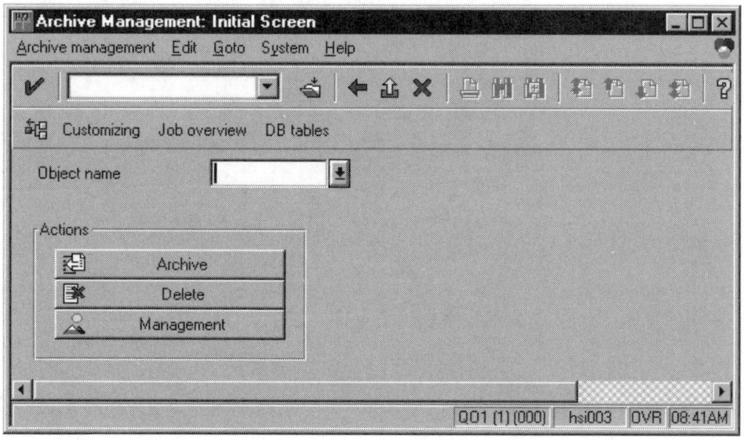

Choosing DB Tables again shows all the tables in an archiving object. The necessary archive data must be defined for the selected object. You must first decide where to write the data to be archived. Use Customizing, a complex topic covered in the following sections.

Archiving Object-Specific Customizing

This area concerns the technical settings, such as the size of the archive to be generated and the configuration of the delete program that is run subsequently.

Figure 12.5 shows the possible technical settings for the archiving object FI_DOCUMNT. The logical file name ARCHIVE_DATA_FILE has been assigned.

The size of an archive is limited by technical hardware factors. There must be sufficient space in the chosen disk area and in the archive. In the first phase of archiving, the data to be archived is copied to files outside the database. The second phase, deleting the successfully copied data, can be configured to automatically start when the first phase is complete.

When the data has been deleted, you can create a new index by choosing Make Index. A new index will make it easier to locate data in the archive file. From a technical database viewpoint, deleting is a change transaction that—unlike copying—is recorded in the RDBMS log. The database administrator must ensure that the log area (for example, the rollback segment for Oracle) is configured to be sufficiently large. Choose the parameter Commit `counter` to limit the "size" of a database transaction. You can determine how many records are deleted before a commit is executed. You can use the variants to make the following settings for the test and production run:

- Test run
- Detailed log
- Restart after cancellation
- Delete your own matchcode

You can define further technical application settings, such as which records to delete, by choosing Setting for Post-processing Program and Variant. These settings are client-dependent, which means they must be defined separately for each client.

You'll need to use the client-independent settings in Basis Customizing to modify the physical file name behind the logical file name ARCHIVE_DATA_FILE in Figure 12.5. A default value is already assigned to all logical file names.

Basis Customizing

A distinction is made between client-dependent and client-independent settings. It is here that the archive system is actually connected. The assignments are made between logical and physical client-dependent and client-independent file names. Figure 12.6 shows client-independent Customizing (Transaction FILE). A physical, client-dependent file name can be assigned to any logical file name. You can use the client-dependent Basis Customizing (Transaction SF01) to define a client-dependent assignment between the logical and physical file name. The client-dependent settings overwrite the client-independent settings.

Application-Specific Customizing

For some archiving objects, you may also need to make application-specific settings, which are client-dependent. The application

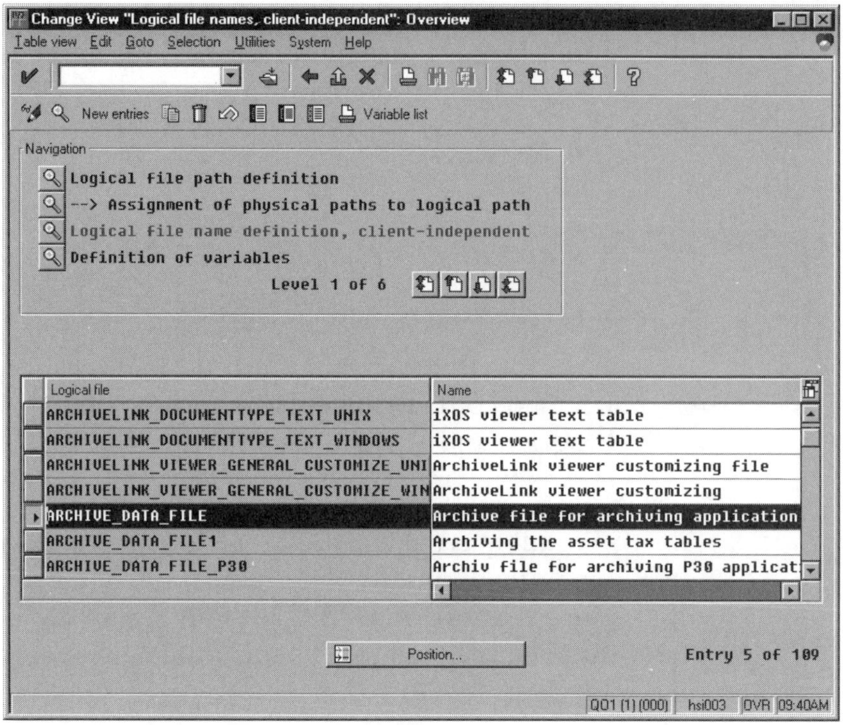

FIGURE 12.6:

Client-independent
Customizing for
archive data

manager is responsible for making these changes. The system administrator is responsible for making the technical settings.

A Customizing Summary

Before getting involved in the specifics, there are a few things you should keep in mind when Customizing. When you customize an archiving run, you need to:

- Make sufficient disk space available.

- Set the database parameters, in particular the log areas, to sufficient sizes.

- Customize the archiving parameters for the application.

An archiving run needs at least two background processes. Additional background processes can speed up the archiving run.

Controlling and Analysis

You can control and analyze an archiving run from the initial screen of the archive administration tool (Transaction SARA). You can perform the actions suggested by the transaction for the archiving object (see Figure 12.7).

FIGURE 12.7:

The archive administration Initial Screen

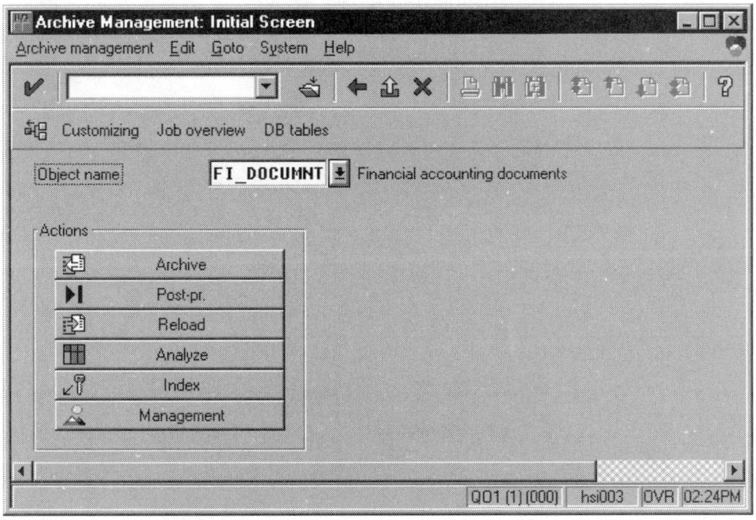

The actions and the sequence in which they are carried out depend on the archiving object, so I can only make general comments here. For more details, please refer to the appropriate R/3 documentation.

A complete archiving run is made up of the following actions:

Archiving—You determine the start time of the archiving run and the possible parameters for output control (see Figure 12.8). Use the variant maintenance tool to define the application-specific data selection. Figure 12.9 shows the background job that is automatically scheduled based on this data (Job overview, Transaction SM37).

FIGURE 12.8:

Generating the archive files

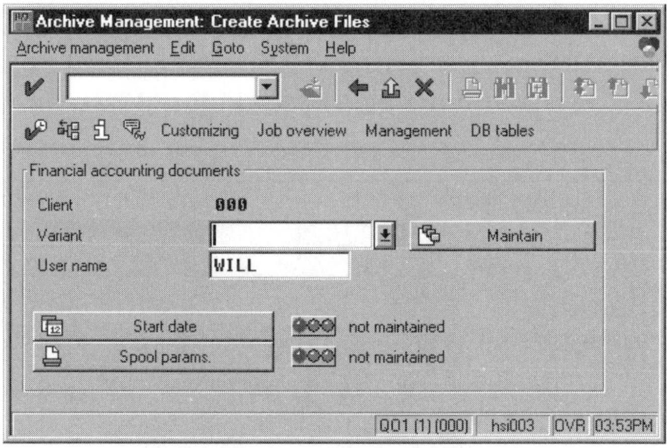

FIGURE 12.9:

The background job scheduled for archiving

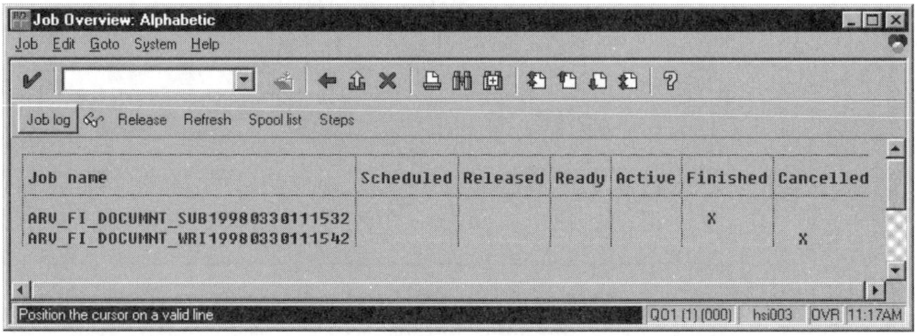

Post-Processing—Follow-up processing comprises deleting data from the database after it has been archived. If you do not want to have the data automatically deleted immediately after it is archived, you can explicitly define a start time, the output parameters, and a variant.

Reload—When you reload data, it is imported from the archives back into the database. To make this possible, SAP ensures that the delivered archiving objects are release-independent, meaning that the structures and definitions of archivable data remain compatible.

Analysis—Application-specific analysis programs are available by choosing this option in the initial screen of the Archive administration, depending on the archiving object selected. For example, for the archiving object FI_DOCUMNT these programs are the compact document journal or a line item journal.

Administration—The archive administration tool contains all the detailed logs that exist for this archiving object. The files generated and their size are displayed for each archiving run. This information is important for the administrator, especially if these files are saved manually (not by using an archive system). These logs are also the starting point for an error analysis. If an archiving run is terminated, the run can be restarted from the point of termination when the cause of the error has been found. The most common causes of errors are:

- Insufficient disk space

- Files larger than 2GB (these still cause problems with some operating systems)

- Terminated processes

- Database log areas that are too small or transaction size that is configured as too large (parameter `Commit counter`)

WARNING If data is deleted manually without first being transferred to the archive, that data will be lost. Before data is deleted from the database, the generated archive files must be backed up in an archive system or on a separate medium.

Review Questions

1. What is an archiving object?

    A. CD-ROM or WORM

    B. The archiving files created by the archiving run

    C. The logical unit of physically related data and the programs needed for archiving

2. What is meant by data archiving?

    A. Saving the archive logs

    B. Archiving documents such as inbound and outbound print lists, and invoices or documents from application components

    C. Removing data from the database and storing it in an archive system or on separate media

3. Which tool is used in R/3 data archiving to transfer data to an archive?

    A. SAP ArchiveLink

    B. HSM (Hierarchical Storage Management)

    C. ADK (Archive Development Kit)

    D. RFC

4. Which statement is correct?

    A. The entire archiving process can take place during normal R/3 operation.

    B. The entire archiving process must take place while the R/3 System is stopped.

    C. When the archive files are generated, no work can be done in the R/3 System.

CHAPTER

THIRTEEN

13

Data Distribution and Transfer

Data distribution and transfer are important parts of the business framework in R/3. Data distribution means the exchange of data between an R/3 System and at least one other R/3 System or external systems. Data is being distributed constantly between at least two active systems. Data transfer is more important, for example, when you are migrating from another system, such as R/2. The data in the other system is prepared and transferred to an R/3 System.

Due to their complexity, these task areas are not the sole responsibility of the system administrator, who will need to cooperate closely with specific departments, developers, and technicians to implement these scenarios. The task of the R/3 System administrator consists of monitoring configured processes and coordinating the resolution of problems. This chapter explains the technical background and provides information to help run the processes efficiently. Less emphasis is placed on business aspects than on the technical side in this chapter. The system administrator must be in a position to recognize problems and address their causes.

Application Link Enabling

The business processes in a company frequently cannot be mapped with a single central system. This is due primarily to a distributed information flow, for example, between the relatively independent subsidiaries of a company. It can also be due to technical bottlenecks caused by the size of just one central system.

Security aspects are also important factors. It may be necessary to communicate with external systems, for example, a warehouse management system. Because Application Link Enabling (ALE) is such a complex subject, this chapter covers only the fundamental business and technical aspects of this technology. The chapter focuses on the most important aspects of ALE processing from the viewpoint of the system administrator.

Technical Basics

Application Link Enabling is the technology used by R/3 to support distributed business processes. ALE contains the business scenarios and function modules that allow you to transfer data from or to an R/3 System without developing customer-specific programs. ALE is closely connected with Workflow Management within R/3, that is, the data is not only transferred between the systems, but also triggers follow-up actions in the R/3 System. From the R/3 viewpoint, the following data can be exchanged:

Transaction data—data from applications

Master data—such as customer or material master data

Customizing data—used for an overall ALE view

Data can be exchanged between R/3 Systems, between R/3 and R/2 Systems, and between R/3 and external systems. The implemented scenarios focus on the distribution between R/3 Systems. The distribution of data between R/3 Systems is largely independent of the R/3 release being used. This means that all the R/3 Systems in the system landscape do not need to be upgraded at the same time. When data exchange with external systems is implemented, an R/3 System can only receive or make data available. The external system prepares the data in accordance with the interfaces defined by R/3, or the external system processes the data made available by R/3. The systems are integrated through non-permanent synchronous or asynchronous communication.

The following functions and interfaces form the basis of communication with ALE:

- *Electronic Data Interchange (EDI)* with all its components such as monitoring, archiving, and *Intermediate Document (IDoc).* (IDoc is defined in detail in the sections that follow.)

- RFC, mostly as transactional RFC (tRFC)

- CPI-C

- TCP/IP

The advantage of transactional RFCs over synchronous and asynchronous RFCs is that the calls are buffered, even if the recipient partner is not active. When the partner is available again, a new attempt can be made to transfer the data. If an R/3 System is receiving the data, the requests are handled as transactions.

In addition to data being distributed using transactional RFCs, data can also be distributed using CPI-C functions, for example, to R/2 Systems, and also using the Internet. In rare cases, the data distribution is based on sequential files.

Methods

When IDocs are generated, one of three methods is used, depending on the application (see Figure 13.1). Normally, the IDocs are generated directly from within the application. The second method is to generate the IDocs from *change pointer*. For each change to an object (for example, to a master record) a change pointer is set in Table BDCP. The Report RBDMIDOC is used to generate an IDoc from these change pointers. The third method uses R/3 message control to generate the IDocs. Here, the application makes message entries of type ALE in Table NAST. Depending on the configuration, these entries can be analyzed either immediately by R/3 message control or periodically using Report RSNAST00 to generate IDocs. The method chosen depends on the application, that is, it cannot be chosen by the user.

FIGURE 13.1:

A method of generating IDocs

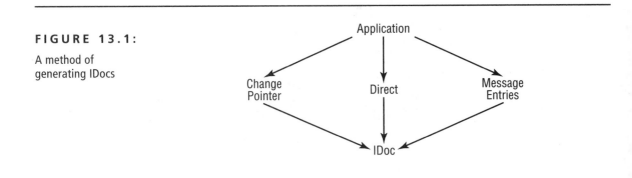

IDoc

IDoc types form the container for the data to be exchanged. There is a special IDoc type for each application area that provides data to be exchanged. The data sent, including the tables and fields, is defined based on IDoc types. An IDoc type represents a structure description. An IDoc type that is filled with data in accordance with the structure rules is known as an *IDoc*. The ALE technology is integrated into both the applications and Customizing. ALE provides a number of distribution services. The sender can receive information about the progress of processing.

The IDoc type can be seen as a type of container that matches a particular type of data. Each IDoc type is identified by its name. The name indicates how an R/3 System will process an IDoc type. *IDoc* and *IDoc type* are frequently used as synonyms.

An IDoc consists of multiple segments. For each segment there is a structure description and documentation. On the database level, multiple tables are used to store this data. An IDoc is organized hierarchically (see Figure 13.2).

Each IDoc contains a control record that consists of technical information needed for transfer, such as the sender, recipient, message type, and status. The control record is administered in Table EDIDC. The control record determines which processing steps are necessary for the transferred data. The control record is followed by the actual data of the ALE message. This data is stored in different segments in accordance with the hierarchy. A cluster table describes the structure of the segments and contains the data to be distributed in one of the fields. However, the structure and the name of this table are dependent on the R/3 release. In R/3 Release 4.0, it is Table EDID4 that contains the data to be distributed in EDID4-SDATA. The processing status is recorded in Table EDIDS.

FIGURE 13.2:

IDoc structure

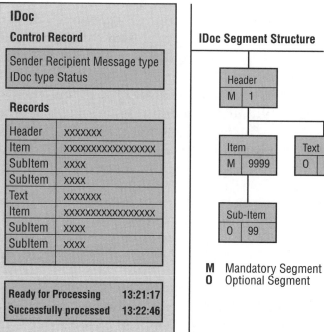

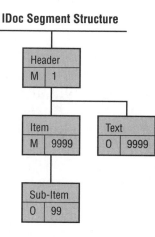

Which table contains which data is only of interest if the distribution definitions and the data to be distributed are checked during the implementation period. You can use the R/3 table maintenance tools to check the data. During normal operation, the storage methods on the database level have a subordinate role.

You determine during Customizing which data will be exchanged between systems. It is not the responsibility of the R/3 System administrator to define the ALE connections. The application managers or consultants are responsible for this. The R/3 System administrator is, however, responsible for the technical implementation, and must ensure that the ALE interface is functioning correctly. For this, the R/3 System administrator needs to have an idea of the application requirements and how they are implemented technically.

ALE Configuration

This section uses a simple example to illustrate the configuration procedure for ALE distribution between two R/3 Systems. Instead of using two separate R/3 Systems, the example uses clients 200 and 100 linked using ALE in the same R/3 System TC1. The exchange of material master data should be defined. This section focuses on the technical aspects and the tasks of the system administrator rather than the application.

First Steps

To start ALE Customizing from the Enterprise IMG, choose Tools ➤ Business Engineer ➤ Customizing. The steps can be accessed in the Enterprise IMG from the menu option Cross-Application Components, Transaction code SALE (see Figure 13.3).

FIGURE 13.3:

ALE Customizing

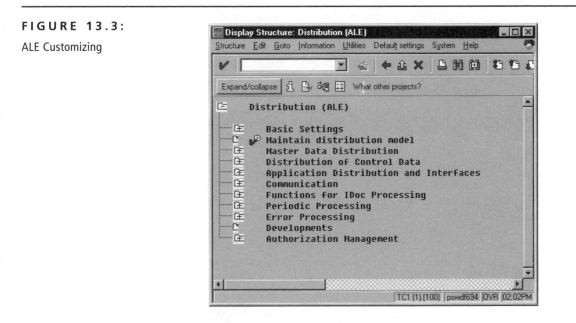

The order of the tasks is the order in which they are to be processed. The settings described below all start from the ALE Customizing screen.

Basic Settings

The basic settings comprise preparatory definitions for the Customizing of distribution that follows. These settings include:

- The definition of logical systems
- The definition of number ranges
- The definition of the ISO codes
- Basic Workflow settings

Logical Systems

A *logical system* is the name of a partner in the distribution. In this example, these are clients 100 and 200 of the R/3 System TC1. Figure 13.4 shows how to define the logical systems, which you access by choosing the Execute icon from the Customizing tree.

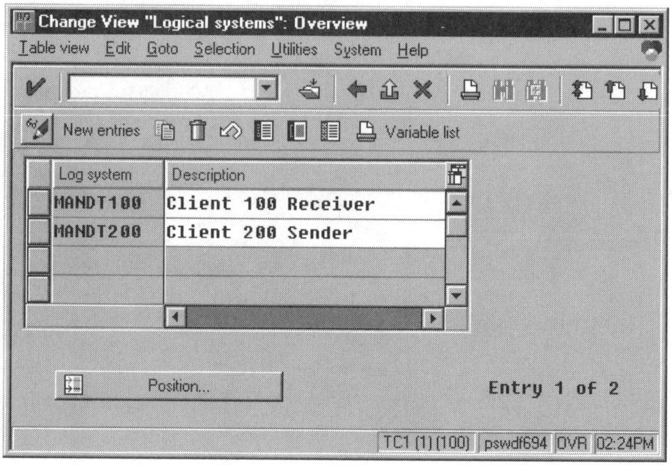

FIGURE 13.4:

Defining the logical systems

If the option Automatic Recording of Changes is set for the client, changes are automatically recorded in a Customizing request assigned by the user (see Chapter 7). You can use this request to transport tested basic settings into other systems. In this example, both clients are in the same R/3 System, so the definition of the logical systems will be automatically available in both clients.

Next, the logical system names are assigned to the selected clients of the R/3 System. You branch from the Enterprise IMG or Transaction SALE to the client maintenance tool. The name of the logical system is entered and saved in the Logical System field. Figure 13.5 shows the relevant part of the client maintenance tool.

FIGURE 13.5:

Assigning the logical system to a client

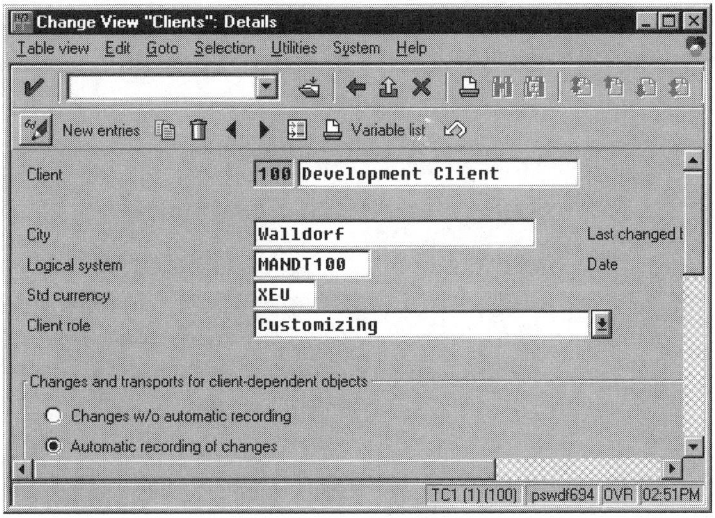

Number Ranges

Maintaining the number ranges is of greater importance for the applications than for the technical basis of the R/3 System. *Number ranges* are used to assign unique numbers to business documents in the R/3 System. If data is exchanged with another R/3

System, it is advisable to assign numbers by restricting the number range uniquely for both systems, that is, the external and internal number ranges must be defined to not overlap. In the case of IDocs, the number ranges are also used to determine their sequence. From the technical viewpoint, the assigned numbers are used as keys within the cluster Table EDID4.

ISO Code

The ISO codes setting defines the conversion between the ISO code and units of measure. When the data in an IDoc is transferred, the ISO code assigned in that particular R/3 System is always used instead of the direct unit of measure. The default assignments delivered by SAP are stored in a table, which can be changed in the customer system. You must therefore ensure that the ISO code is defined in the same way in both the sending and the receiving system.

Basic Workflow Settings

As the use of ALE is directly connected to R/3 Workflow Management, you must also make basic settings for workflow. In this example, you do not need to set the number ranges, ISO codes, and the basic Workflow settings.

Maintaining the Distribution Model

The distribution model uses the logical system names to describe the data flow in the system landscape. You can only create and maintain the distribution model in one system. This ensures that only one active version of the model exists in all the systems. In the ALE Customizing screen, choose Maintain Distribution Model, then Edit ➤ Model View ➤ Create, and specify a name for the distribution model. Choose Create Message Type to define the logical sending and receiving system and the type of data to be distributed. At this stage, your application consultant must know which message type meets the application needs. For example, choose MATMAS to distribute material master data (see Figure 13.6).

FIGURE 13.6:

Defining the message
type for distribution

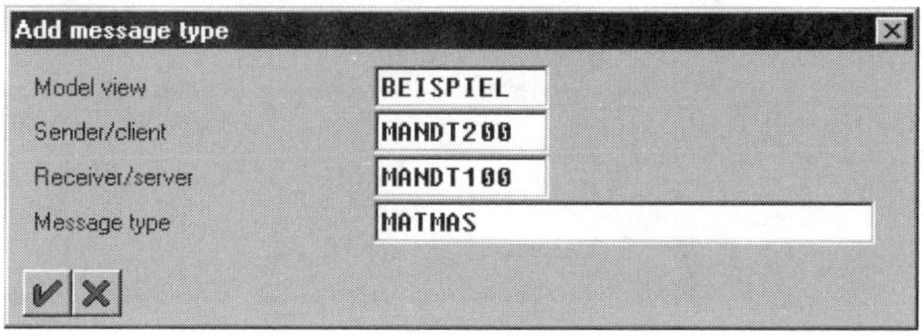

In Figure 13.6 you define that all changes to the material master record in the logical system MANDT200 are distributed using ALE to the logical system MANDT100. Your application consultant can restrict this to particular materials by defining filter conditions (Create filter) and, for example, only distributing materials in one group. Filters can also be used to distribute only particular data for an object (views). For example, it may be useful to transfer the Material master data to another system without the information on inventory levels.

You can also define data conversions if the Customizing settings differ between the systems in the distribution model. To define this, you generally use the basic ALE distribution menu (Transaction code SALE): Choose Functions for IDoc Processing ➤ Settings for Filtering. Figure 13.7 shows the simple distribution model for this example.

Data-Specific Settings

The menu options Master Data Distribution, Control Data Distribution, and Application Distribution, and the interfaces in ALE

FIGURE 13.7:

Defining the
distribution model

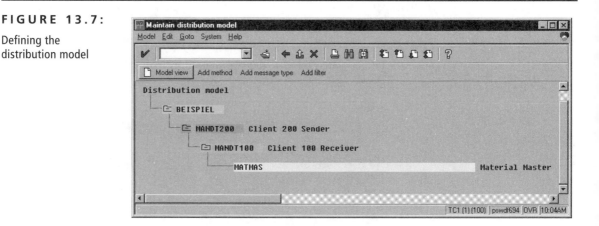

Customizing allow you to make a more precise distinction between the data to be distributed and the use of further ALE functionality. To change the settings for the distribution of Material master data, choose Master Data Distribution. For this, the generation of change indicators is activated. A change indicator marks changes made to a master record and allows you to generate an IDoc from those changes.

You can generate the IDocs manually or periodically by running the program RBDMIDOC in the background. In this example, the generation of change indicators for message type MATMAS is activated.

NOTE	For more information, refer to the R/3 documentation; these settings are relevant for the technical side of the application.

Communication

The distribution model was first used to determine which data is distributed. To specify the technical settings regarding how the data is distributed, choose Communication in the ALE Customizing tool. Independent of the technical application settings, communication must be defined between the partners in the distribution model.

RFC Connection

Communication between the systems is based on RFC technology. You must therefore specify the RFC connection data. (This topic is discussed in detail in Chapter 5.) In connection with ALE, an RFC connection must be defined from the sender to the recipient. The name of the RFC connection should, if possible, be the same as the logical system to be assigned.

When you define the RFC connection, it is important to assign a user with the authorizations needed to process the data. If possible, the R/3 user should be a CPI-C user in the receiving system so that the user cannot be used to log on from the sending system to the receiving system for dialog processing. For a planned tRFC connection, to determine the number of failed attempts after which the send attempt is canceled, choose Destination ➤ TRFC Options from the screen to define RFC connections (Transaction SM59) (see Figure 13.8).

FIGURE 13.8:

tRFC Options

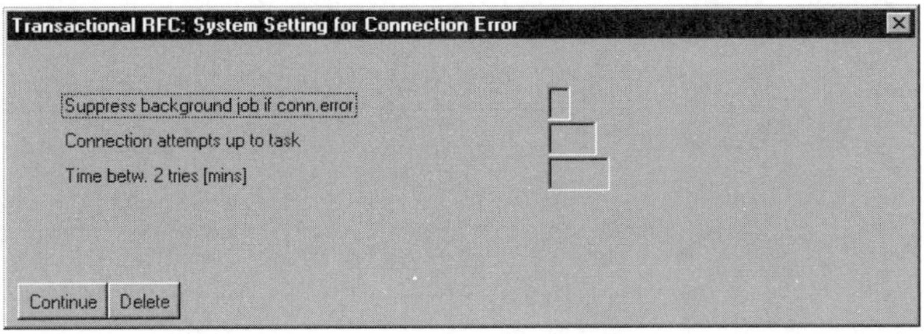

The tRFC connection can be configured so that for every transmission error, the system schedules a background job that attempts to repeat the transmission 15 minutes later. If many transmission attempts are canceled, a corresponding number of background jobs is generated, and they can be processed in parallel. This can cause an overload in background processing in the sending system and with processing in the receiving system. It is better to deactivate automatic repetition of transmission attempts and generation of background jobs. Instead, you can schedule report RSARFCEX to run periodically and process terminated requests. This procedure is recommended especially for transferring data to an external system that only has one receiving interface.

For performance reasons, you should use groups of application servers when you define the RFC connection if the receiving system is an R/3 System. This allows the load to be distributed over the application servers of the receiving system (see Chapter 5).

Next, the defined RFC connection to the recipient is assigned to the receiving logical system.

Partner Agreements

The inbound and outbound parameters for the communicating systems are described in the partner agreements (Communication ➤ Generate Partner Agreements) of the ALE Customizing tool (see Figure 13.9). The partner system is the other system in each distribution. In this example, the settings are made by the sending system, MANDT200. The partner system is MANDT100.

NOTE   The Version option determines whether your R/3 System is Release 4.0 or 3.0/3.1.

You can configure the connection between the systems in such a way that, if an error occurs, the receiving system notifies the sending system of the result of the ALE request. If the user departments wish, an RFC connection from the sending system to the

FIGURE 13.9:

Defining the partner
agreements

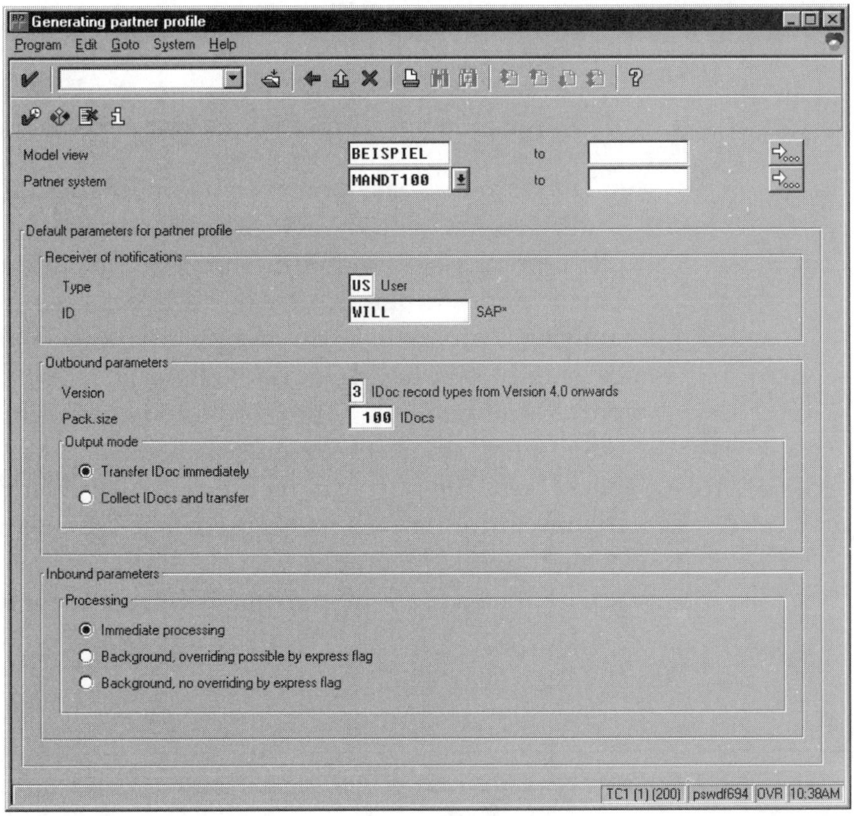

receiving system must be defined. Use parameters Type and ID
to define which user, and which organizational unit or location,
receives the message.

The packet size and the output mode are defined for the outbound parameters. You can send each generated IDoc to its recipient immediately, or collect multiple IDocs and send them together.
The disadvantage of sending multiple small packets is that the
connection to the target system must be opened and a logon executed for each packet. This causes a relatively high reduction in
performance. If you collect IDocs and then send them, there are

temporary differences between the data in the sending and the receiving systems. When a large number of IDocs is sent, load peaks are caused in the receiving system. A compromise must be found between these two situations. SAP generally recommends that you collect multiple IDocs and send them as one packet.

The inbound parameters to be maintained in the receiving system affect the way the IDocs are controlled in that system. IDocs can be processed immediately or in the background. Normally, performance is better if inbound IDocs are not processed immediately, and are instead processed during periods of low load. Processing of inbound IDoc packets can thus be performed in parallel. When you have completed the definition, save and generate the partner agreements. When the partner agreements are generated, the port and resulting details concerning IDoc processing are automatically generated. The partner agreements determine how the messages from ALE processing are handled. They are dependent on the partner type and the message types to be sent. Figure 13.10 shows the communication data flow between the logical systems.

FIGURE 13.10:

Technical settings

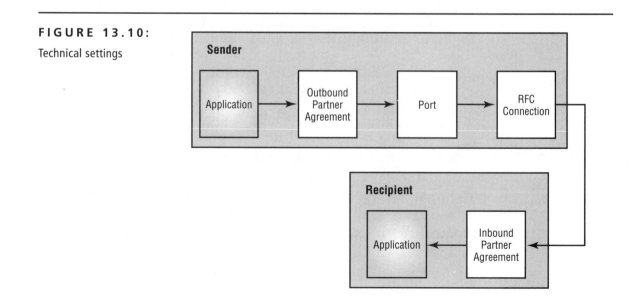

Port

A *port* defines the type of connection with the partner. Data can be sent either through tRFC, sequential files, CPI-C to an R/2 System, or the Internet. A unique port number is assigned for each port.

NOTE The partner agreements can only be generated successfully if the names of the RFC connections match the names of the logical systems. If the names do not match, the partner agreements must be maintained manually.

To ensure that the settings that were made and generated function correctly, choose Check Partner Agreements and Model Settings.

Distributing Model Settings

All the settings for distribution must be known to both partner systems. For this reason, the last step is to distribute the model settings. From the distribution model maintenance tool, choose Edit ➤ Model View ➤ Distribute.

The definition of the ALE connection is now complete. In this example, an IDoc is generated from every change to the material master data, and this IDoc is sent to the partner system. With the previous settings, generation, sending, and processing must be activated manually. In practice, background jobs are normally scheduled using the ALE Customizing tool. Choose Periodic Work.

It should be emphasized that the above description of data distribution is only related to the technical aspects of the definition of an ALE connection. The technical application possibilities have been kept in the background, as they are not the responsibility of the R/3 System administrator. In practice, the definition of an ALE connection will be far more comprehensive and complex.

Monitoring and Analysis

If the ALE connection was configured so that a message is sent about execution from the recipient to the sender, you can quickly check on the sender's side whether the transmission was successful. The advantage of this procedure is that, if an error occurs, the messages can be sent directly to the organizational unit responsible, and resolved and processed again there. This is known as *auditing*. The message type AUDIT is available for this, and is used to send messages about the receiving IDocs and how they were processed. However, this procedure is relatively performance-intensive; you may sometimes not be able to use it, or you may only be able to use this message type during periods of low load.

In addition to cross-system monitoring, R/3 offers many local analysis tools. To access the monitoring tools, follow these steps:

1. Choose Logistics ➤ Central Functions ➤ SCP Interfaces ➤ Environment ➤ Monitoring ➤ ALE Administration or Tools ➤ Business Framework ➤ ALE ➤ Administration. The Transaction code is BALE.

2. Use the overview of the IDocs in a system (Monitoring ➤ IDoc Overview) to display all the IDocs of a particular message type for a specified period.

Figure 13.11 shows the overview from the sending system. The status tells you about the result of the send operation.

Conversely, the overview in the receiving system shows the status with which processing ended (see Figure 13.12). All the IDocs sent by client 200 were processed successfully (Status 53). In addition to the distribution in the example of the message type MATMAS, this system also sends messages of type MATFET. Error 29 occurred when this IDoc was sent.

FIGURE 13.11:

IDoc overview in the sending system

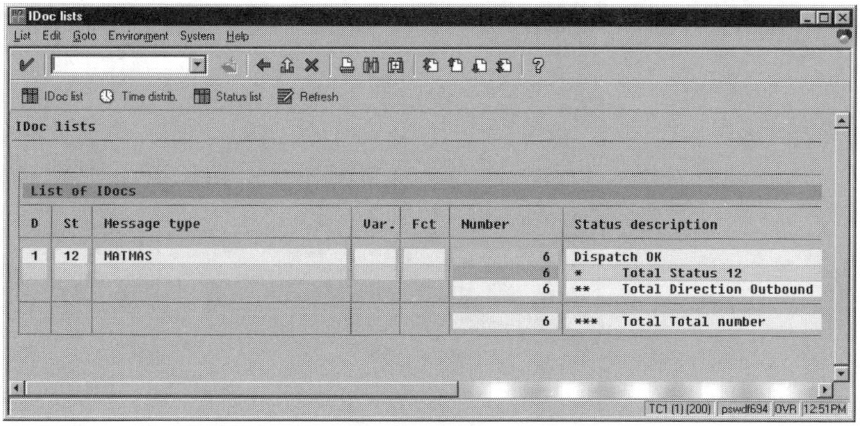

FIGURE 13.12:

IDoc overview in the receiving system

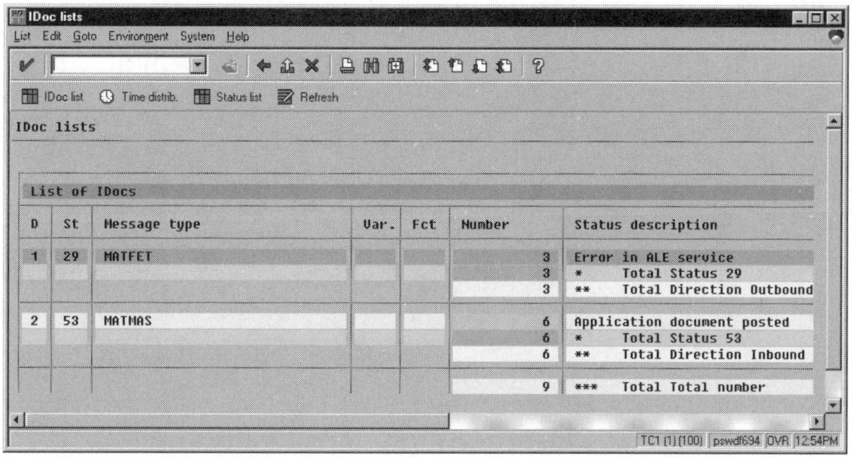

To obtain more detailed information about an IDoc, select and double-click the IDoc. Figure 13.13 shows the messages for an IDoc in status 29.

FIGURE 13.13:

Error log

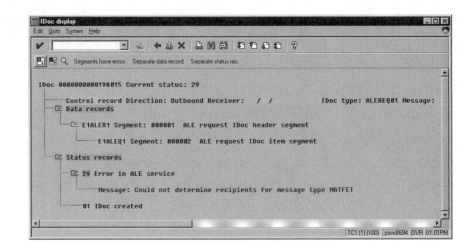

According to the messages in Figure 13.13, no recipient could be found for the generated IDoc. There was a configuration error in the ALE service. In other cases, you may need to analyze the data in the IDoc. Functions are available for this. Terminated transmissions can be repeated.

TIP

This operation can be automated, but for performance reasons it is better to repeat the operation manually once any errors have been resolved.

The described IDoc overview and additional analysis functions are integrated into the monitors for ALE administration. To access the ALE administration tools, choose Monitoring ➤ ALE Administration, or use Transaction code BALE. Table 13.1 gives an overview of the functions for ALE administration.

TABLE 13.1: ALE Administration

Menu	Functions
Monitoring	Provide overviews of type and number of sent or received IDocs
	IDoc tracking
	Audit analysis (send confirmations)
	Inbound processing
Periodic processing	Analyze change indicator
	Process inbound and outbound IDocs
	Reorganize the change indicator table
	Inbound processing
	Outbound processing
Control data	Request administration
	Request distribution
	Workbench Organizer
Goto	Process data from:
	ALE application
	ALE master data
	ALE development

Checking the processing of IDocs also includes checking the work of the scheduled background jobs that process the IDocs. Table 13.2 shows the programs.

TABLE 13.2: Background Jobs for Distribution

Program	Function
RSEOUT00	ALE outbound processing.
RSDAPP01	ALE inbound processing.
RSNAST00	Send messages.
RBDMIDOC	Generate IDocs from change indicators.
RBDMOIND	Change status after tRFC transmission.
RBDCPCLR	Reorganize the change indicator table.
RSARFCEX	Process terminated IDoc send procedures.

If the IDoc processing analysis indicates no problems, you should still check the performance of the ALE connection. To do so, in the sending system (from the monitoring tools), choose IDoc tracking (see Figure 13.14). The number of IDocs that have been sent and their average, maximum, and minimum transfer time are displayed for the period specified. If the maximum and minimum deviate greatly from each other, this indicates that there are temporary bottlenecks. To check the transmission times for each IDoc, choose SendIDoc ➤ RecvdIDoc.

The received IDocs are processed using dialog work processes. To process IDocs in the target system, processes are also reserved for the ALE functionality in addition to the usual dialog work processes for the dialog user. You can configure the system to process received IDocs in parallel or sequentially. For parallel processing, you must reserve approximately the same number of additional dialog work processes as there are IDocs arriving in parallel. Sequential processing requires fewer dialog work processes, but only one IDoc can be processed at a time, which can easily cause a queue to form and can negatively affect performance of the receiving system.

IDocs cannot overtake other IDocs while they are being processed. The technical team must discuss the advantages and disadvantages

FIGURE 13.14:

IDoc tracking

FIGURE 13.14:

IDoc tracking

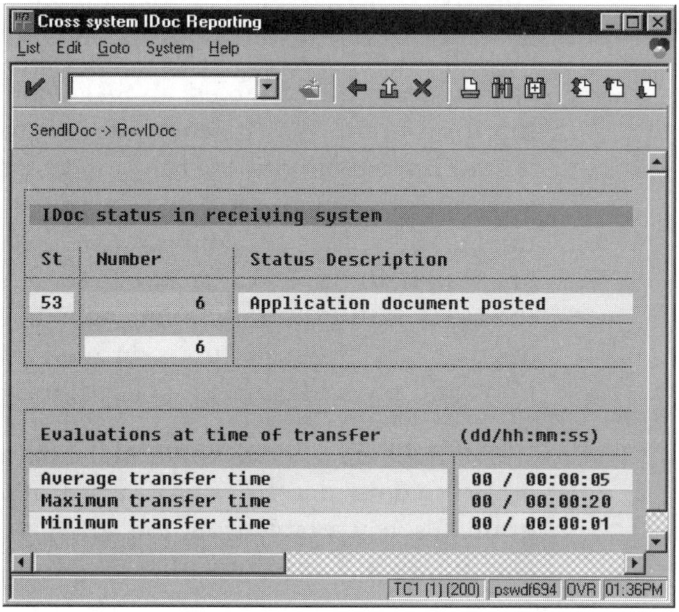

of the processing methods with the user department and implement appropriate technical measures. In addition to the load distribution between R/3 instances using groups for the definition of the RFC connection, it may be an advantage to run a separate R/3 instance especially for processing IDocs. The critical factors here are performance and technical resources. The technical administrator of the R/3 System and its hardware is responsible for making this decision.

Data Transfer with Batch Input

Batch Input is the method by which data can be imported from sequential files in the shortest time into an R/3 System. Batch Input is frequently used when importing legacy data, for example, data from R/2 Systems.

Batch Input Sessions

To prepare the data from the sequential files and import it into corresponding R/3 tables, an SAP customer must develop a batch input program. This batch input program reads the data, prepares it, and imports it into the *batch input session.* A batch input session simulates the entering of Transaction codes and data in dialog mode. The values are actually read from the sequential file and are assigned to the Transaction's screen fields. The structure of the batch input session defines which screen fields they are assigned to. The structure is derived from the assigned Transactions and the SAP structures used in those Transactions.

SAP delivers a series of standard batch input programs. To generate the data structures used (for use in Cobol, PL/1, or C programs), select a table from the ABAP Workbench, then choose Dictionary ➤ Environment ➤ Generate Table Desc.

This batch input procedure allows you to import data for each R/3 dialog screen, while still ensuring the necessary data integrity. This applies both to standard R/3 programs and to customer-specific programs within the R/3 System.

Automatic Logging

Automatic logging of Transactions is particularly helpful. The corresponding batch input session structures and a batch input program can be generated automatically from these Transaction logs. To start automatic logging, follow these steps:

1. Choose System ➤ Services ➤ Batch Input ➤ Edit ➤ Recording, or use Transaction code SHDB.

2. Execute the Transactions from which data will be imported using the batch input procedure. These logs can be used to generate and modify the sessions.

3. Next, the ABAP program can be generated and modified, if necessary. (Manual programming changes are thus reduced to a minimum.)

If the screen fields of the Transactions assigned to a batch input session were filled with values, the batch input session is imported into the batch input queue. From this point, the session can be processed, that is, the Transactions are executed in the background and the data is processed. From the database viewpoint, Table APQD is used to store the sessions, and also for the batch input queue.

There are two ways to process batch input sessions:

- In dialog mode. Choose System ➤ Services ➤ Batch Input.

- Automatically, by scheduling the ABAP program RSDBLSUB.

Figure 13.15 shows the basic batch input procedure.

FIGURE 13.15:

Basic principles of batch input

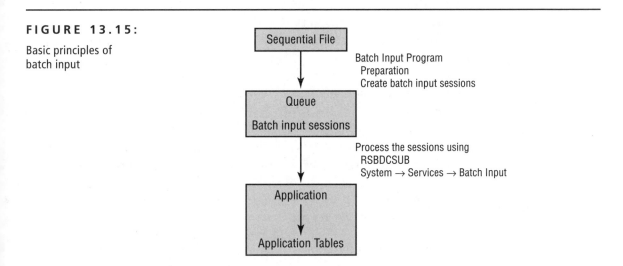

From the system administrator's viewpoint, monitoring batch input operations is of primary importance. Batch Input imports large volumes of data into the R/3 database in a relatively short time. The system administrator must give particular consideration to the space requirements in the database, the increased write activity, and the subsequent increase in data in the database logs. The system administrator should be notified of planned batch input runs and of the estimated data volume before the run starts.

When you develop a batch input program, you must consider the length of the transactions. Since a batch input program runs in the background, no screen changes take place, which means that no commit is made from the database viewpoint. You must therefore control the length of a transaction using explicit commits in the program. If transactions are too long, problems may arise (for example, with the size of the rollback segment for Oracle or with the size of the transaction log in other RDBMSs).

To analyze the batch input runs, choose System ➤ Services ➤ Batch Input ➤ Edit, or use Transaction code SM35 (see Figure 13.16). Views showing different aspects are available for your analysis. Technical program or factual errors cannot be resolved by the system administrator; this must be done in close collaboration with the user departments.

To save space, successfully processed sessions should occasionally be deleted from the database. Use the background report RSBDCREO for this. This report also reorganizes the log files stored in the directory \usr\sap\<*SID*>\SYS\global. All the logs for which there are no longer batch input sessions are deleted.

WARNING To reorganize the log file, you once more need to have about as much disk space in the directory on the operating system level as the log file itself uses. By default, the file is reorganized in directory \temp of the application server. To explicitly define the directory, use the instance parameter bdc/altlogfile.

In addition to this procedure for importing data into an R/3
System, there are three other methods, which are more important
from the developer's viewpoint than from the system administrator's viewpoint. Data imports using these methods normally only
affect the system administrator in as much as he or she must
ensure that there is sufficient space in the R/3 database. For the
sake of the completeness of our discussion, I'll briefly discuss
these three methods.

Direct Input

Strictly speaking, direct input is a continuation of the development of the Batch Input procedure. Whereas with Batch Input the

data is first imported into a session (assigned to the corresponding screen fields), this step is not performed in direct input. Instead, the function modules delivered by SAP are used to import the data. It is the responsibility of the developer to call the appropriate function module. While with Batch Input all the data consistency checks are performed automatically through the use of R/3 screen (Dynpro) technology, with direct input these checks are performed by the function modules. Currently, SAP provides function modules for data import for the areas of material master, investments, sales orders, and planned independent requirements. Logging, as done in Batch Input, is not available with direct input. The R/3 System administrator cannot monitor processing using Transaction SM35. The developer is responsible for logging. Direct input is faster, but, unlike Batch Input, it cannot be restarted automatically, and it is more difficult to handle if an error occurs.

Fast Input

With fast input, the step of importing data into a session is also replaced with a different procedure. The data to be imported is first written to an internal table and from there processed by executing a Transaction using the ABAP statement CALL TRANSACTION. The structure of the internal table must correspond to the data structure required for this Transaction. With fast input, the developer is also responsible for logging processing. Fast input is also faster than Batch Input because there is no logging, but it is normally slower than direct input.

LSM Workbench

R/3 Release 4.0 includes a new tool for data import, *Legacy System Migration Workbench (LSM Workbench)*. This tool is based on the *data mapping* method. The structure of the data to be imported is mapped to the new structure of the data in R/3. For more information, please refer to the OSS.

Review Questions

1. Which statement is correct? For data distribution based on ALE:

   A. A permanent connection between the partner systems is established.

   B. The partner systems are not permanently connected during data transfer.

   C. Functions of the RDBMS, for example SAPDBA, are used to exchange data.

2. Which methods can be used to exchange data?

   A. CPI-C

   B. Sequential files

   C. tRFC

   D. Internet

   E. telnet

3. What Transaction code is used for ALE monitoring?

   A. SM51

   B. STUN

   C. MM01

   D. BALE

4. How can tRFCs terminated due to communication errors be processed?

   A. Automatically by activating the automatic repeat option when you define the tRFC connection

   B. By scheduling the job RSARFCEX

    C. By scheduling the job RSEOUT00

    D. By resolving the error and executing the application transaction again

5. Which options exist to send IDocs?

    A. Event-driven, for example, operation mode switching

    B. Delayed, by scheduling the jobs

    C. Immediately

    D. Send individually after the IDocs are generated

    E. Collect IDocs and send them as a packet

6. What is the Batch Input procedure used for?

    A. To import data from sequential files into the R/3 database

    B. To process mass data in the background

    C. To import data using the transport control program tp

Maintaining Instances

Throughout this book there have been frequent references to instance parameters, which play an important role in the configuration of the R/3 System and the processing of user requests by R/3. The assumption has been that if the profile needed to be adapted, an operating system editor would be used. This procedure is practical, but it has drawbacks, as the user must ensure that the changes are correct. The integrated R/3 profile administration and parameter maintenance tool is much easier and safer to use. This chapter describes their handling and instance characteristics, such as *operation modes* and automatic operation mode switching.

Maintaining Profiles

The R/3 profile maintenance tool provides the following significant benefits for users:

Central administration—You can administer and maintain profiles for all the instances centrally.

Version management—You can save each saved change to a profile as a version in the R/3 database.

Consistency checks—After changes are made, the consistency of the profile is checked, that is, the logical relationships and rules for the parameter settings are checked.

Comparison between active and saved profiles in the database—You can analyze deviations between the currently used profile and the profile saved in the database.

Immediate activation of selected parameters—You can activate selected parameters immediately, without having to restart the R/3 System.

Profile maintenance within R/3 is mandatory when the administrator uses system monitoring tools, such as the *Control Panel,* and operation modes.

Importing Profiles

You can use the profile maintenance tool in R/3 to centrally maintain the default system profile DEFAULT.PFL, and the start profiles Start_*<instance name>_<computer name>* and the instance profiles *<SID>_<instance name>_<computer name>* for all instances. The significance and contents of these profiles were described in Chapter 2. To maintain these profiles with R/3 tools, the profiles must first be imported from the file system into the R/3 database. To do so, follow these steps:

1. Choose Tools ➤ CCMS ➤ Configuration ➤ Profile Maintenance. The screen Edit Profiles is displayed (see Figure 14.1).

FIGURE 14.1:

The dialog box for maintaining profiles

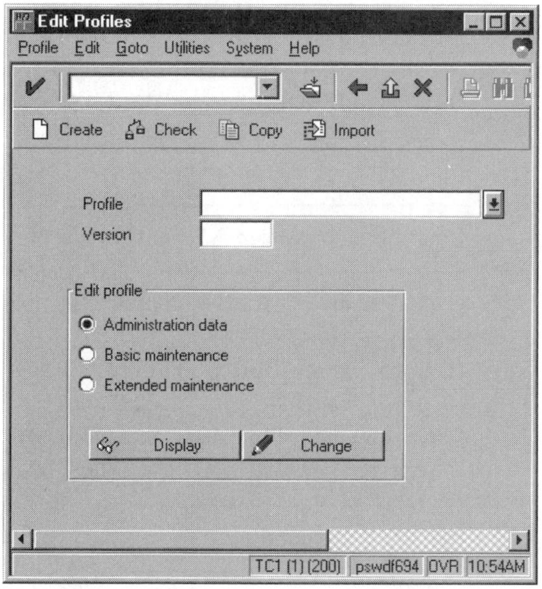

2. Choose Utilities ➤ Import Profiles ➤ Of Active Servers.

The central directory structure of the R/3 System allows the profiles for all instances to be imported and saved in the database. The following report shows the import log for the central system QO1 (along with the subsequent consistency check). During the import, a consistency check is performed for all the parameters in the profiles.

Report 14.1:

```
-------------------------------------
|Importing start and instance profiles for all active servers  |
-------------------------------------
|Following default profile imported:                           |
-------------------------------------
|hsi003_Q01_00:/usr/sap/Q01/SYS/profile/DEFAULT.PFL            |
-------------------------------------
|Following instance profiles imported:                         |
-------------------------------------
|hsi003_Q01_00:/usr/sap/Q01/SYS/profile/Q01_DVEBMGS00_hsi003   |
-------------------------------------
|Following start profiles imported:                            |
-------------------------------------
|hsi003_Q01_00:/usr/sap/Q01/SYS/profile/START_DVEBMGS00_hsi003 |
-------------------------------------
|Log of profile import.                                        |
-------------------------------------
|Profiles imported without error.                              |
-------------------------------------
|Full check of instance profiles and a default profile         |
-------------------------------------
|Log for the default profile, individual check                 |
|Profile name        : DEFAULT                                 |
|Physical profile name: usr/sap/Q01/SYS/profile/DEFAULT.PFL    |
|Check on server      : hsi003_Q01_00                          |
-------------------------------------
|No errors found                                               |
-------------------------------------
```

```
|Log for the instance profile, individual check    |
|Profile name           : QO1_DVEBMGS00_HSI003     |
|Physical profile name:                            |
|/usr/sap/QO1/SYS/profile/QO1_DVEBMGS00_hsi003|
_____

|No errors found                                   |
_____

|Log for instance profiles, full check             |
|Profile name           : QO1_DVEBMGS00_HSI003     |
|Physical profile name     :                       |
|/usr/sap/QO1/SYS/profile/QO1_DVEBMGS00_hsi003|
|Log for full check                                |
_____

|No errors found                                   |
_____

|Full check of start profiles                      |
_____

|Log for the start profiles, individual check      |
|Profile name           : START_DVEBMGS00_HSI003   |
|Physical profile name     :                       |
|/usr/sap/QO1/SYS/profile/START_DVEBMGS00_hsi003   |
_____

| No errors found                                  |
_____

|Log for the start profiles, full check            |
|Profile name           : START_DVEBMGS00_HSI003   |
|Physical profile name     :                       |
|/usr/sap/QO1/SYS/profile/START_DVEBMGS00_hsi003|
|Log for start profile list                        |
_____

|No errors found                                   |
_____
```

The preceding log shows the individual phases of the import consistency check. The log begins with the import of the default, instance, and start profile. (As this is a central R/3 System, there is only one start profile and one instance profile.) After that, the relationships of the parameters of each profile are checked. In this example log, no problems were diagnosed. After the individual check, a full system-wide check is performed for each profile class. Here, the system checks whether the basic rules for configuring an R/3 System are fulfilled. For example, these rules include the conditions described in Table 1.3 in Chapter 1. In the case of the central R/3 System in the preceding example, this check ran without finding any problems.

Copying Profiles

The imported profiles form the basis of the changes to the parameters. To load individual profiles into the database, specify the profile name and choose Import. You particularly need to do this if you are adding new R/3 instances to an existing R/3 System. Before you make changes to the active profiles that were generated during system installation, copy the profiles to new names or at least generate a new version of the profiles. By doing this, you can return to the old profile state if problems occur. You can save the profiles under a new logical name (administration name) in the database. The physical assignment of the profile is retained. You can choose any name as the administration name of the profile in the database.

The advantage of making a distinction between user-defined administration names and actual profile names on the file level in the operating system is that it makes administration easier. In this way, you can maintain different variants of the same profile for different purposes under different administration names. For example, you could reserve and maintain special profiles for specific actions such as settlement runs or even upgrades. Follow these steps to copy an existing profile:

1. From the profile maintenance tool (Tools ➤ CCMS ➤ Configuration ➤ Profile Maintenance, or Transaction code RZ10), choose Copy. A window opens in which you are prompted to enter the source and the target. The system proposes the

source that you specified at the start of profile maintenance. You can change the source.

2. Enter the name of the target. You can use the same profile name as the target if you want to generate a new version of the profile, or you can enter a new profile name (see Figure 14.2).

Copy Profile

From
    Profile   `DEFAULT`
    Version   `000001`

To
    Profile   `DEFAULT_NEW`

Copy ✕

3. Choose Copy. Version 1 of the new profile is generated. If you have used the same name, the system simply generates a new version of the profile.

Maintaining Profiles

You maintain the profiles in three stages:

Administration data—The administration data includes a comment that indicates the nature and purpose of the profile, the profile type (instance profile, default profile, or start profile), the time the profile was activated, and the name of the user that activated the profile. The related operating system file and the application server are also included. Figure 14.3 illustrates this for the profile DEFAULT_NEW, which was generated from a copy of the default profile.

FIGURE 14.3:

Maintaining the
administration data for
a profile

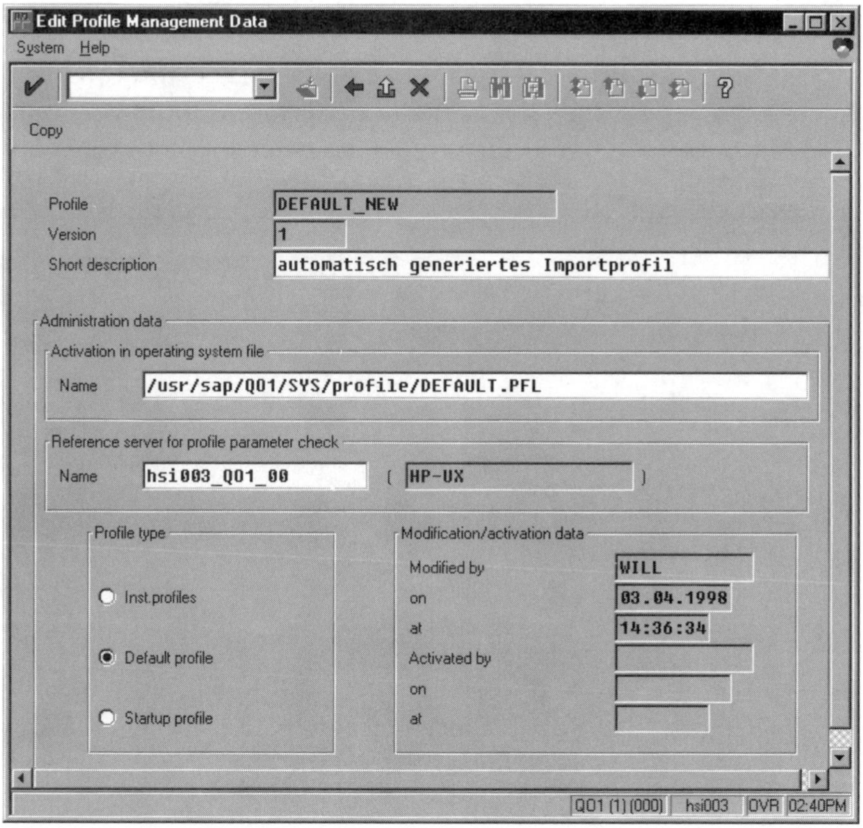

Basic maintenance—Basic maintenance mode comprises
maintenance of the parameters of a selected profile. The
appearance of the basic profile maintenance tool depends
on the profile type, as different profiles have a different significance and different content. Basic maintenance simply
allows you to modify the most important parameters and
provides the user with logical names for the parameters.
Figure 14.4 shows the basic maintenance menu for a default
profile.

Extended maintenance—Extended maintenance mode
shows the content of a profile in unformatted form, that is,

the real parameter name is displayed. This mode is designed for use by experts. You can use it to change parameters that are already in the profile and to create new parameters by choosing Parameter ➤ Create. To delete a parameter, choose Parameter ➤ Delete.

If you want changes to a profile to be permanent, the changes must first be made temporarily. Choose Copy. If you do not use this function, you are prompted to confirm that you do not want to make the change permanent when you exit the screen. If you do not save when this prompt is displayed, your changes are lost when you exit the profile maintenance mode you are using. The profiles are only saved permanently in the database when you choose Save.

However, before you save, you should first choose Check in order to check that the profile is logically correct. When you save, your changes are still not copied to the profiles on the operating system level. The changes are only saved in files on the operating system level when you choose Profile ➤ Activate. Your changes are still not in effect for the instance. The instance must be restarted for the parameters to take effect.

Maintaining an Instance Profile

Only some of the parameters in the instance profile can be changed while the system is still running. To find out which parameters these are for a profile, from the profile maintenance tool (Transaction code RZ10), choose Profile ➤ Dyn. Switching ➤ Display Parameters. To have these particular settings take effect immediately, choose Profile ➤ Dyn. Switching ➤ Execute. All the other changes can only be activated by restarting the instance.

To maintain an instance profile:

1. Copy the profile with a new name, using the profile maintenance tool (Transaction code RZ10).

2. To change the assignment to the file on the operating system level or to an application server, choose Administration data.

3. Choose Basic Maintenance. You can now modify the parameters for the type and number of work processes and their buffer (see Figure 14.5). You can also maintain the following settings:

   • Choose Directories to maintain the R/3 directories.

   • Choose Language to define your preferred logon languages and character set combinations for an application server. By default, English and German are always available in an R/3 System. You can perform language imports to make additional languages available (see Chapter 4).

- To configure the settings for the main memory areas of the instance, choose Memory Management.

FIGURE 14.5:

Basic maintenance of an instance profile

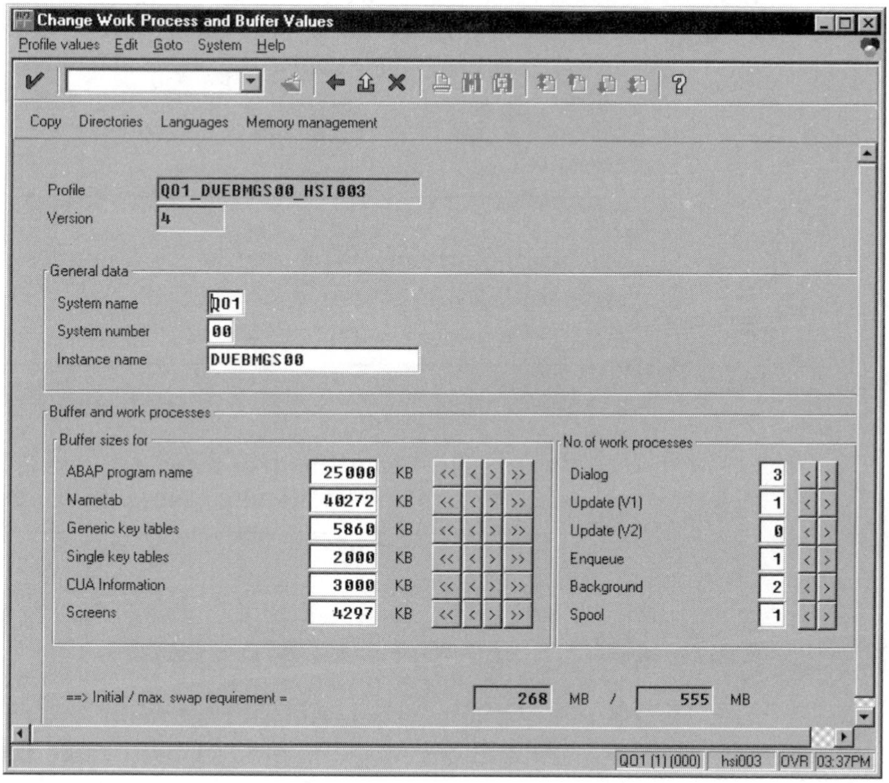

4. When you have made your changes, choose Copy.

5. If you need to maintain further parameters that were not in the basic maintenance menu, choose Further Maintenance.

6. Exit extended maintenance by choosing Copy.

7. Check your changes, and correct any discrepancies if necessary.

8. If the check was successful, choose Save. R/3 automatically creates a new version of the profile.

9. To activate the changes, choose Profile ➤ Activate. R/3 automatically creates a backup of the profile on the operating system level.

NOTE   The changes to the profiles take effect only when the instance is restarted, except for selected parameters for the configuration of main memory areas, which can be changed dynamically. Changes to the default profile of the R/3 System take effect only when the entire R/3 System is restarted.

The initial screen of the profile maintenance tool displays the status: not saved, saved, activated.

NOTE   In basic maintenance mode the required initial and maximum swap requirement of the instance is displayed for the changes made to an instance profile. Please note that the initial value should not be more than 150 percent of the total main memory of the computer.

Checking Up on Parameters

Previous chapters covered working with the integrated R/3 profile maintenance tool. They described which parameters are available to configure the different areas of R/3. However, there are many more parameters than previously discussed. From the customer viewpoint, not all parameters are relevant. You should therefore consult SAP before you change them. Short descriptions of the most important parameters in the R/3 System can be found in the glossary. The sizes of the main memory areas of an instance are particularly important for performance.

To find out which parameters are currently active in your R/3 System, execute the RSPARAM report. Each R/3 parameter has a default setting, which is implemented in the R/3 kernel. Your own personal settings in the profiles overwrite these values. The

RSPARAM report generates a list that displays both values for each parameter. You can also select additional parameters and read the available documentation.

sappfpar

On the operating system level, user *<sid>*adm can use the sappfpar program to obtain information about the parameter settings and the main memory area for an instance. The sappfpar help call gives you a brief overview of the program's options:

```
sappfpar <parameter name>
```

displays the current value of the parameter.

```
sappfpar all
```

lists all the defined parameters.

```
sappfpar check
```

checks the set parameters including the configuration of the R/3 main memory areas. The resulting main memory requirements are also calculated.

To pass an instance profile with the command, use pf=*<instance profile>*. To pass an instance number, use nr=*<instance number>*. To pass the R/3 System name, use name=*<SID>*.

memlimits

The program memlimits on the operating system level is also useful. This program is also available for user *<sid>*adm. It compares the main memory requirements of the R/3 System, calculated from the parameter settings, with the defined kernel parameters of the operating system. If the R/3 requirements exceed the limits defined in the operating system, problems may occur, or you may even not be able to start the R/3 System.

Operation Modes

An *operation mode* of one or more instances is created by defining by the type and number of work processes assigned for a specific period. Operation modes are intended to cope with users' fluctuating requirements of the R/3 System in the course of a day. Many dialog users work with the system during the day, while at night the amount of background processing normally increases. It is usually helpful to define one operation mode for day operation and one for night operation. A specific number of work processes of specified types are assigned to an operation mode. The R/3 System can switch the operation mode automatically in accordance with a defined schedule.

NOTE   Operation modes can only be created if the profiles of the instances were first imported using the R/3 profile maintenance tool.

Creating an Operation Mode

To create an operation mode:

1. From the CCMS, choose Configuration ➤ OP Modes/Servers ➤ Operation Mode ➤ Create.

2. Enter a name for the operation mode and a short description. Be sure to use uppercase and lowercase letters properly.

3. Decide whether the operation mode is for production or test purposes. You can only switch to a test operation mode manually in exceptional situations. Figure 14.6 shows how to define an operation mode for day operation (Transaction code RZ04).

4. Save your definition.

FIGURE 14.6:

Creating an operation mode

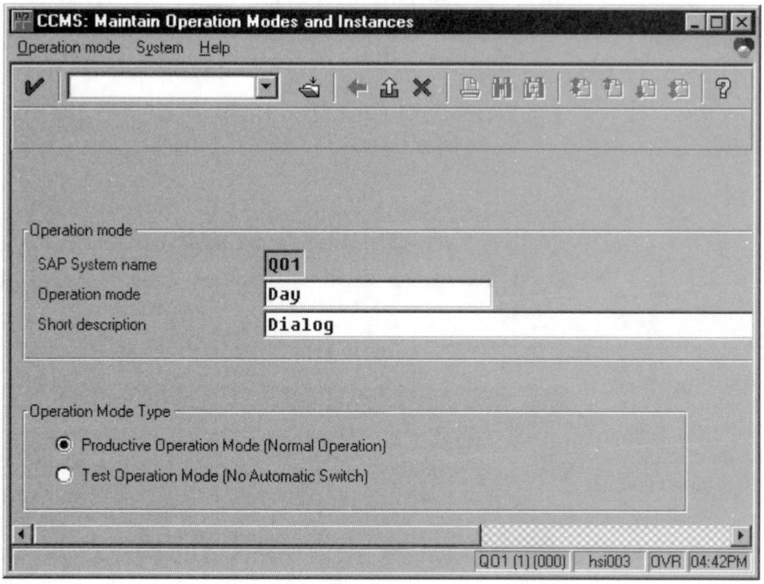

The defined operation modes are displayed in the overview (see Figure 14.7).

FIGURE 14.7:

Overview of operation modes

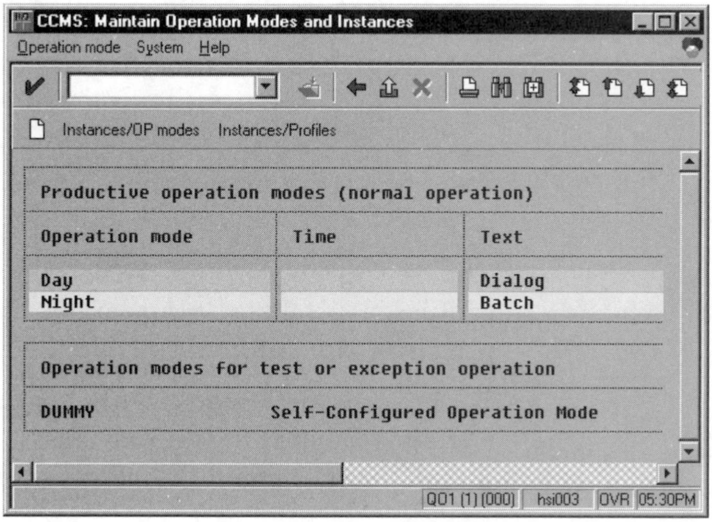

Registering Instances

Now register all the instances in your system:

1. From the CCMS, choose Configuration ➤ OP Modes/ Servers.

2. Choose Instances/Profiles. You see the currently active default profile. In unmaintained status, you see no application servers or instances (see Figure 14.8).

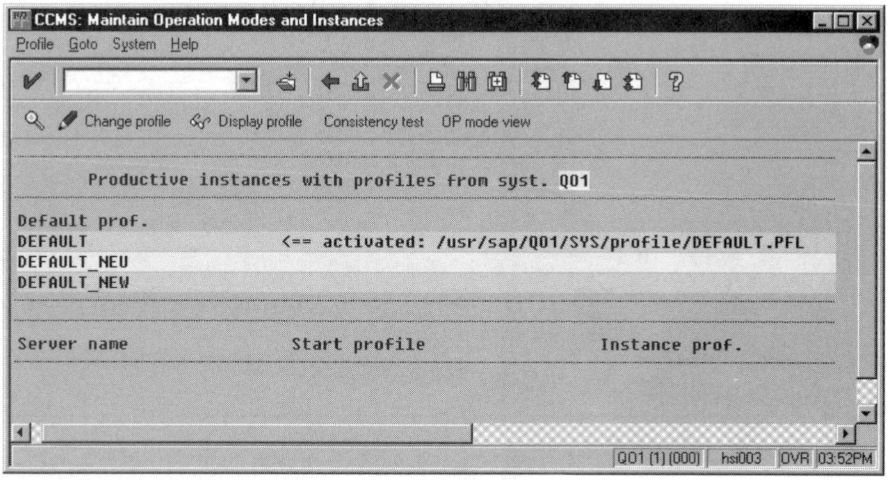

FIGURE 14.8:

An overview of initial operation modes and instances: Profile view

3. Choose Profile ➤ Create new instance (see Figure 14.9).

4. Enter the name of the application server and the instance number.

5. Choose Current settings. The currently active settings for the profiles, as well as the type and number of the active work processes, are automatically applied (see Figure 14.10).

6. To enter an operating system user who is authorized to start and stop the instance and the password, choose Maintain Start User. By default, the start user is <*sid*>adm.

7. To make changes to profiles, select the profile and choose Change. The profile maintenance tool opens automatically.

8. In a separate window, you can now set up an operation mode by maintaining the distribution of work processes within the total number taken from the instance profile (see Figure 14.11).

9. Save your changes.

You assign further instances of an R/3 System to the defined instance profiles in the same way.

FIGURE 14.9:

Maintaining instance data

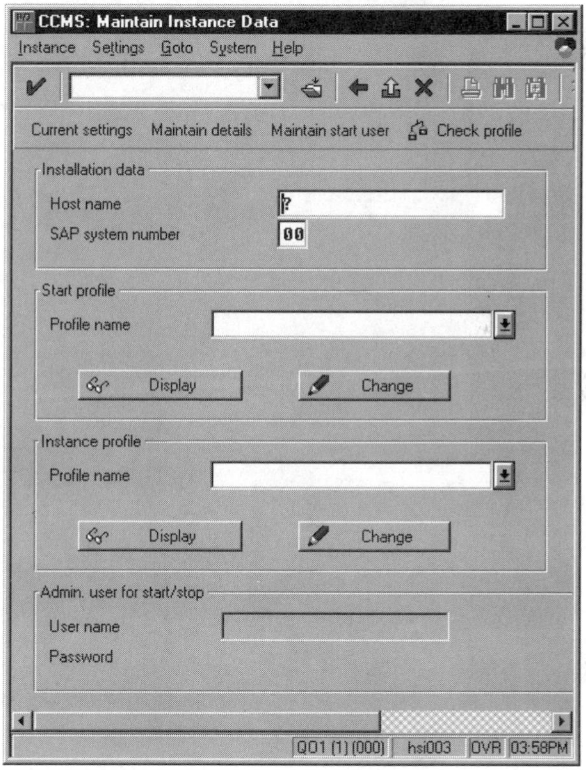

> **WARNING** If the total number of background processes is the same as the number of background work processes for job class A, only class A jobs can be executed from that instance.

FIGURE 14.10:

Applying the current settings

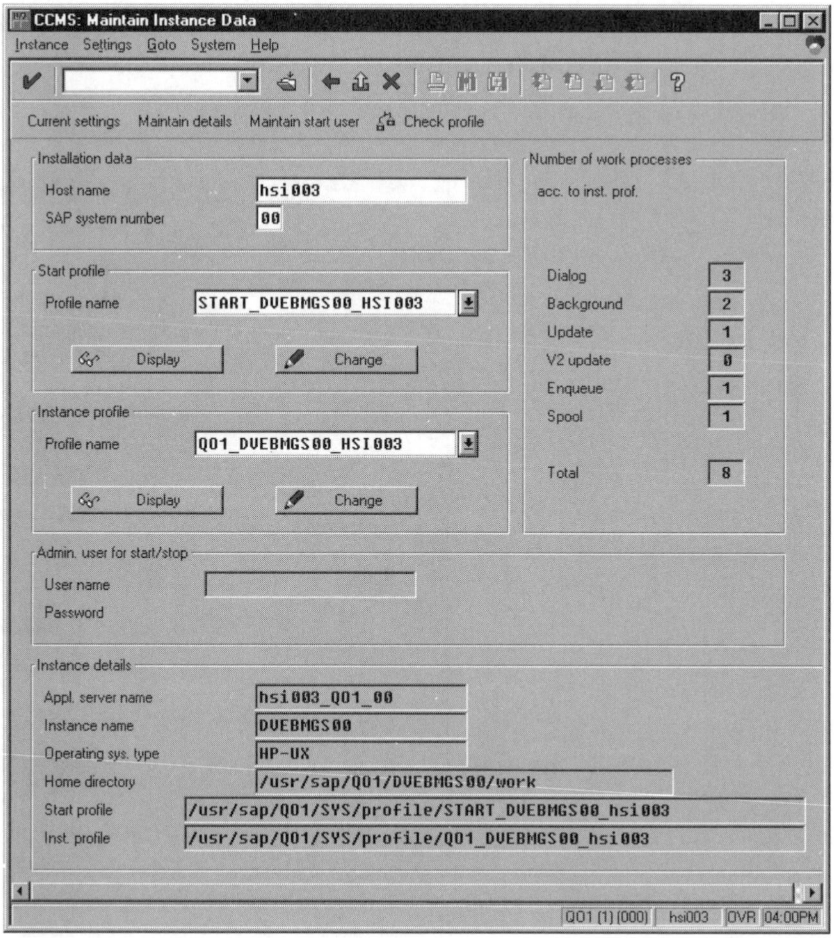

To display the assignments made between operation mode and instance characteristics, from the operation mode overview, choose

Instances/OP Modes or, from the profile view, choose OP Mode View (see Figure 14.12).

FIGURE 14.11:

Maintaining the distribution of work processes

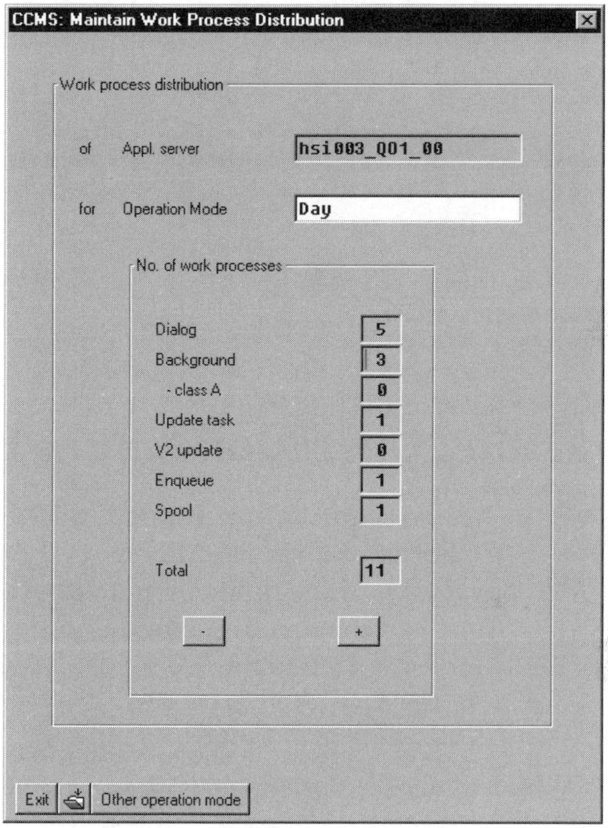

To make changes, double-click the operation mode to select it. The screen for distributing work processes is displayed. To change the operation mode assignment, choose Other OP Mode. Save your settings. From the menu, you can also access the profile and instance maintenance tool.

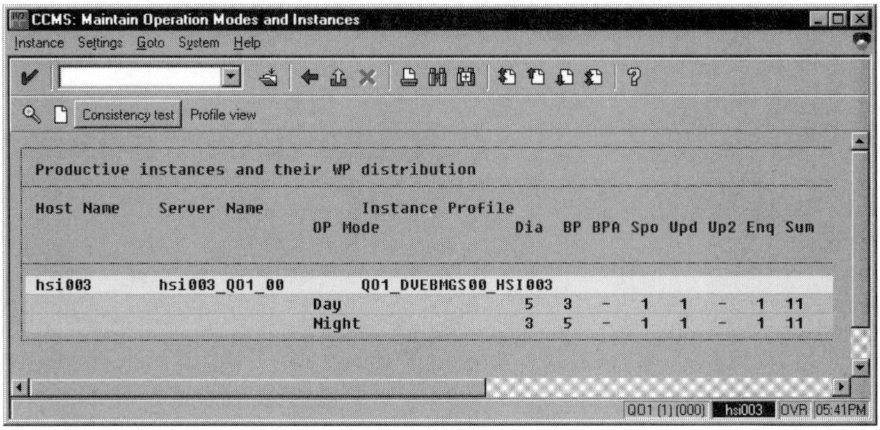

FIGURE 14.12:

Maintaining operation modes and instances: Operation mode view

Setting Operation Modes in the Timetable

Finally, set up the operation modes in the timetable. From the CCMS screen, choose Maintain OP Modes/Instances to display an overview of the defined operation (as shown back in Figure 14.7). To set up the operation modes in the timetable, choose Operation Modes ➤ Timetable (see Figure 14.13).

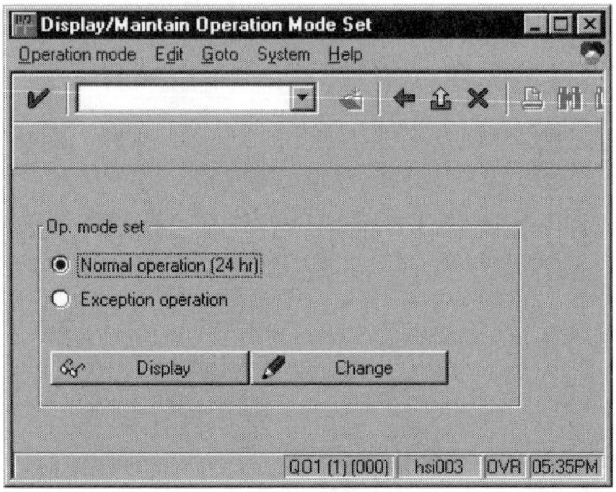

FIGURE 14.13:

Maintaining the timetable for operation modes

To maintain the timetable:

1. Choose Normal Operation ➤ Change.

2. To select the time interval, choose Edit ➤ Time Period ➤ 15 Minutes, 30 Minutes, or 60 Minutes.

3. To mark the start and the end of the desired time interval, click the start of the interval and choose Operation Mode ➤ Mark Interval, or press F2. Click the end of the desired time interval, and choose Operation Mode ➤ Mark Interval, or press F2.

4. To assign an operation mode, choose Assign and enter its name.

5. Repeat points 3 and 4 until there are no more gaps in the timetable.

6. Save (see Figure 14.14).

To delete assignments, choose Delete assignment. An arrow in the timetable marks the current time.

Exception Rules

You can also define an exception operation that differs from the normally valid timetable for specific days and times. Choose Display/Maintain Operation Mode Sets (Transaction code SM63). For example, this can be useful for occasional maintenance work or special settlement runs. When you have completed this work, you can display the assignments made by choosing from the CCMS overview: Maintain OP Modes/Instances (see Figure 14.15).

The steps for automatically switching operation modes are now complete. When the times that have been defined arrive, the R/3 System automatically redistributes the work processes. Transactions that have started are completed first, which means that a delay may occur.

FIGURE 14.14:

A timetable for operation modes

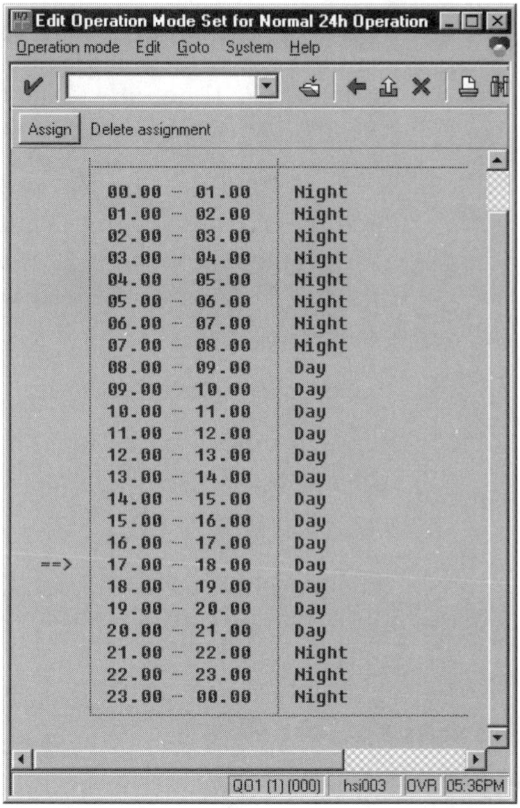
Edit Operation Mode Set for Normal 24h Operation
Operation mode Edit Goto System Help
Assign
Delete assignment
00.00 – 01.00 Night
01.00 – 02.00 Night
02.00 – 03.00 Night
03.00 – 04.00 Night
04.00 – 05.00 Night
05.00 – 06.00 Night
06.00 – 07.00 Night
07.00 – 08.00 Night
08.00 – 09.00 Day
09.00 – 10.00 Day
10.00 – 11.00 Day
11.00 – 12.00 Day
12.00 – 13.00 Day
13.00 – 14.00 Day
14.00 – 15.00 Day
15.00 – 16.00 Day
16.00 – 17.00 Day
==>
17.00 – 18.00 Day
18.00 – 19.00 Day
19.00 – 20.00 Day
20.00 – 21.00 Day
21.00 – 22.00 Night
22.00 – 23.00 Night
23.00 – 00.00 Night
Q01 (1) (000)
hsi003
OVR
05:36PM

NOTE

Defining different operation modes does not automatically produce different R/3 profiles. When an instance is restarted, the profile content is always used. In the case where an instance is restarted, the operation mode must be switched manually.

WARNING

In R/3 Systems in which instances are run on a mix of Windows NT and UNIX systems, problems may occur when operation modes are switched automatically.

FIGURE 14.15:

An overview of assignments

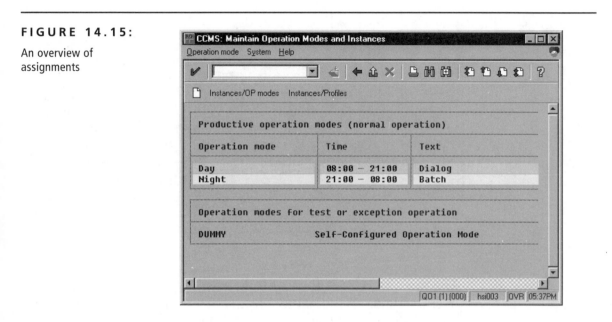

The Control Panel

To monitor the instances and the operation modes of an R/3 System, use the Control Panel. To access the Control Panel, choose Tools ➤ CCMS ➤ Control/Monitoring ➤ Control Panel, or use Transaction code RZ03 (see Figure 14.16).

You can use the Control Panel to:

- Check the status of all instances in the R/3 System, including the operation modes

- Start and stop the instances, and manually change the operation mode

- Display overviews, for example, of the type and number of the work processes

- Access the Alert Monitors

FIGURE 14.16:

The Control Panel

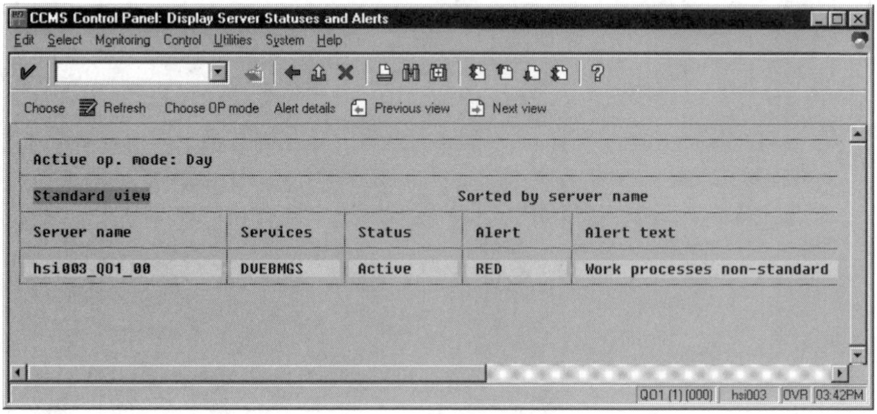

The initial screen of the Control Panel displays an alert on the current state of each instance. To display more information about components of the alert, choose Alert Details or press Shift+F4. Critical alerts are displayed with a red background; warnings are in yellow. To define when an alert is critical, you use threshold values (see "System Monitoring" in Chapter 15).

When R/3 is installed, default threshold values already exist for all the Alert Monitors. These defaults need to be modified for the specific situation in your company. When you have analyzed the alerts, you can reset some or all of them (Alert Details ➤ Reset or Monitor ➤ Alerts of a Server ➤ Reset All) or acknowledge them (Alert Details ➤ Acknowledge or Monitor ➤ Alerts of a Server ➤ Acknowledge All).

The Control Panel is one of the most important and comprehensive R/3 System monitoring tools. You can use the Control Panel to display all the important information about the status of the individual instances. Analyzing this information is one of the daily tasks of the system administrator.

Logon Groups

In R/3 Systems with multiple application servers, it is important to distribute the load as evenly as possible over all the computers. You can set up *logon groups*. A logon group is a subset of all the available application servers in an R/3 System. When users log on to the R/3 System, they choose their assigned logon group. From this group, the R/3 System assigns users an application server, which has the least load with respect to the response time. This is known as *logon load balancing* between instances.

When you set up logon groups, to know which user groups exist for each of the application areas is critical. Each instance has its own main memory area.

Defining a Logon Group

Ideally, all the programs used by the users in an instance and a large part of the data would already be available in main memory. The closest we can get to this ideal situation is if the tasks of the users in an instance are as similar as possible. You define a logon group for this user group. To define a logon group:

1. Choose Tools ➤ CCMS ➤ Configuration ➤ Logon Groups, or use Transaction code SMLG.

2. Choose Create Entry.

3. Enter the name for the logon group, and assign the instances that you want.

4. To save the data choose Copy.

Figure 14.17 shows the screen to define and display an overview of logon groups. This example has the logon groups Public and Test; each has one assigned instance.

You can also specify a maximum load for each instance in the form of an upper limit for the average response time and a maximum number of users. If one of the load limits for an instance is reached, new users who log on are logged on to the remaining instances in the logon group. If the explicitly defined load limits are reached for all the instances in a logon group, R/3 ignores the load limits and logs new users onto the instance with the lowest load in the logon group. Load limits defined for an instance are valid in all logon groups that include that instance.

FIGURE 14.17:

Maintaining logon groups

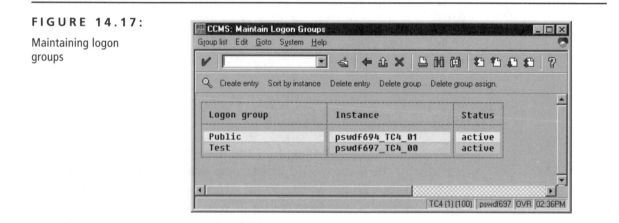

Assigning an IP Address to the Application Server

You can also assign a special IP address to an instance for logon from front ends. You need to do this if you are using separate local networks within the R/3 System. A particularly fast network is frequently used between the application servers and the database server because the volume of data makes a higher transfer rate between these computers desirable. The computers on the presentation layer are normally integrated into the general network.

In this case, the application servers have two network cards and thus two IP addresses. You must define which IP address is valid for the front ends.

To define the load limits for an instance in logon groups and the IP address, follow these steps:

1. From the logon group maintenance tool, (Tools ➤ CCMS ➤ Configuration ➤ Logon Groups, or Transaction code SMLG), choose an instance.

2. Select the instance by choosing Edit ➤ Select or pressing F2.

3. Press F8 to access the extended maintenance tool. Figure 14.18 shows the screen for maintaining the load limits for an instance.

4. Enter your data.

5. To save, choose Copy.

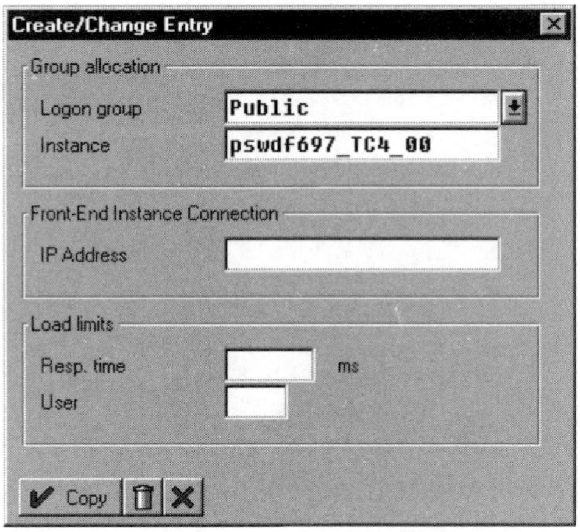

FIGURE 14.18:

Maintaining the load limits and the IP address of an instance

SAPLOGON

The defined logon groups can only be used when you are working with the SAPLOGON program or the SAP Session Manager. A SAPGUI must always be called directly to an instance in an R/3 System. Automatic logon load balancing among the instances in a logon group cannot be used in this case.

The SAPLOGON program and the SAP Session Manager each use a different method. First, these programs contact the Message Server of the desired R/3 System. The Message Server transfers data about the available logon groups, and a user can then select a logon group. The information about how to connect to the Message Server must be either defined and saved by the user (see Figure 14.19) or stored by the system administrator in the sapmsg.ini file in the Windows system directory. This file could also be administered using TCP/IP. the sapmsg.ini file contains entries in the following form:

<SID>=<application server>

FIGURE 14.19:

Specifying the Message Server of R/3 System TG2 in SAPLOGON

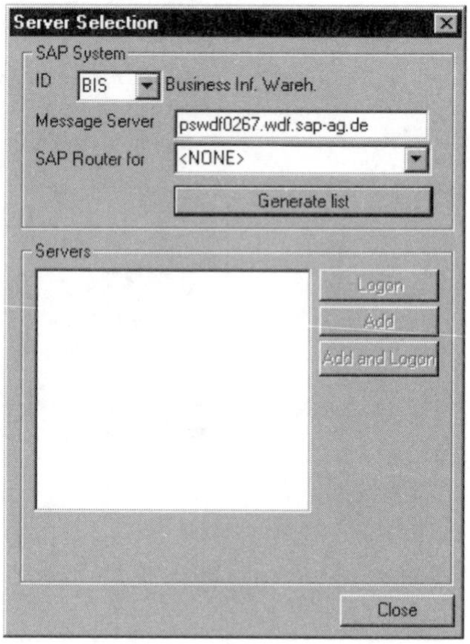

The TCP/IP port used for the SAPLOGON program to communicate with the Message Server of the R/3 System is stored in the local file called `services`. The file entry is in the following form:

```
sapms<SID>    <port number>
```

Review Questions

1. What is meant by an operation mode?

    A. An operation mode describes the number and type of work processes in one or more instances.

    B. An operation mode additionally comprises all the settings for the R/3 main memory areas.

    C. An operation mode denotes the status of the R/3 System: *active* means ready for operation; *DB active* means that only the R/3 database is available, and the R/3 System is stopped.

2. What is a logon group?

    A. All users that are assigned to the same user group comprise a logon group.

    B. A logon group is a logical unit of a subset of all application servers in an R/3 System.

    C. All users with the same tasks comprise a logon group.

3. Which R/3 parameters can be changed and activated while R/3 is running?

    A. None

    B. Selected parameters to assign the R/3 main memory areas

    C. Type and number of work processes

    D. All parameters

4. How do you find out the initial and the maximum swap requirements of an instance for the current configuration?

   A. Add up the appropriate parameter values in the instance profile.

   B. Perform basic maintenance for the instance profile.

   C. sappfpar check pf=<*instance profile name*>.

System Monitoring

Monitoring individual R/3 Systems is one of the important routine activities of the system administrator. This task is no less important than assigning system settings, and it is an important contribution to error-free system operation. System monitoring should be preventive in nature. This chapter focuses on the tools for system monitoring and how to use them. It includes a list of administration tasks that should be performed regularly. First, let's take a look at the different ways that an R/3 System can be monitored.

The Alert Monitor

The Alert Monitor was developed for use in global monitoring of one or more R/3 Systems, with an emphasis on the most important components and processes and their performance. If problems develop, the administrator can be notified in a number of ways. In addition, a color change always highlights the source of the problem. The advantage of the Alert Monitor is in the way it relays information to the system administrator without the administrator having to explicitly request the information.

The R/3 System provides a series of tools for analyzing its different components, but the administrator must perform the analysis. With R/3 Release 4.0A, this has changed with the completely rewritten Alert Monitor, which uses selected parameters and threshold values to analyze the different areas in the R/3 System landscape and, if necessary, to issue warnings. On the basis of the information in the Alert Monitor, the system administrator can perform a detailed analysis with a special integrated R/3 tool.

R/3 Releases before 4.0A had separate Alert Monitors, each for the different areas, such as operating systems, R/3 buffers, or RDBMS. The new alert architecture is considerably more flexible. The architecture covers all the important system, database, and operating system administration areas for R/3.

SAP delivers a Basic Alert Monitor (called *Basic Monitor* for short) with default settings. Using this monitor, customers can create their own monitors with special views of selected areas, add additional alerts, and change the default settings. Third-party tools can also be integrated into the monitor. The extent to which changes to the Basic Monitor are necessary or desirable depends on the requirements of the customer. In smaller R/3 Systems and in the system implementation phase, the Basic Monitor with only a few customer-specific modifications is normally enough.

The Alert Monitor is relatively self-explanatory and easy to understand. However, it is more complicated to define your own Alert Monitors or integrate your own alerts. Because of the level of complexity, this chapter can only lay the foundation. It introduces you to the terms used in the Alert Monitor concept, which forms the basis for possible changes. In the second part of the chapter, you learn how to customize the Basic Monitor for the customer-specific requirements of an R/3 System.

Monitor Terminology

To call the Alert Monitor from the CCMS (Tools ➤ CCMS), choose Control/Monitoring ➤ Alert Monitor (4.0), or use Transaction code RZ20.

Basic Monitor

As mentioned earlier, SAP delivers a Basic Monitor, as shown in Figure 15.1. This Basic Monitor consists of a choice of monitors that form a tree hierarchy for the following areas of the individual servers:

- Operating system
- Database
- R/3 services

- R/3 basis

- System log

Areas that are not relevant for an application server, such as the database, are not included. The Basic Monitor, and all the customer-specific Alert Monitors derived from the Basic Monitor, make up a collection of additional monitors that is known as a *monitor collection*.

FIGURE 15.1:

The Basic Monitor

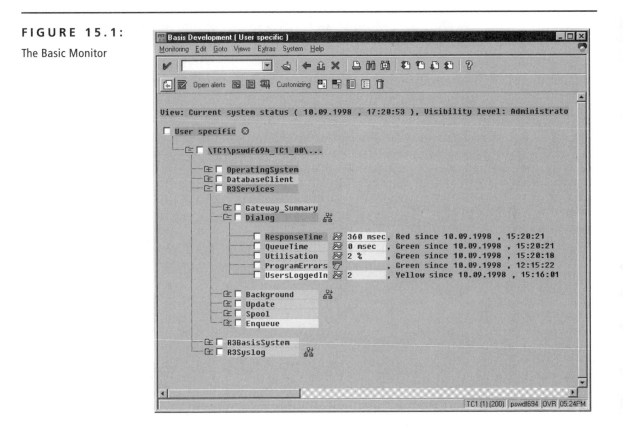

Monitoring Tree Elements

The nodes in the branches of the Alert Monitor monitoring tree are known as *Monitoring Tree Elements (MTE)*. An MTE logically groups the subordinate leaves or the subordinate MTEs. This is also known as a *Monitoring Summary Node*.

Monitor Attributes

The leaves of the Monitoring Tree are made up of the *monitoring attributes*. The monitoring attributes describe the information type of individual R/3 System elements to be monitored. Each of them relates to a single characteristic of a monitoring object. There are the following types of monitoring attributes:

Counters—Represent such values as the unit of measurement or the frequency of an event. If the defined threshold values are exceeded, its color changes. This monitoring attribute is used, for example, for performance alerts.

Individual messages—When a single defined message is issued, an alert is triggered.

Collecting messages—The messages in a log file, for example, are monitored. Character strings previously defined as critical trigger an alert.

Heart beat—These monitoring attributes are used for monitoring whether elements in the system are still active (alive), for example, R/3 Services. If the monitored element fails, an alert is triggered.

Text attributes—Unlike the monitoring attributes already described, text attributes are simply used to collect the description of a Monitoring Tree Element. They cannot themselves trigger alerts.

Monitoring Object

All the monitoring attributes that relate to a monitored object or situation are grouped into a logical unit, the *monitoring object*. The data gathered for a monitoring object is physically stored in a *monitoring segment*. Examples of monitoring objects are:

- The dialog that consists of the monitoring attributes Answer Time, Program Errors, and Users Logged In

- The R/3 System log, which consists of the Syslog ID and the Syslog Freq

- The CPU with the monitoring attributes CPU Utilization and 5min Load Average

At the same time, a monitoring object is an MTE and, in fact, the smallest monitoring summary node. Multiple MTEs can be grouped into one MTE. An MTE of a superordinate node always assumes the highest value of the assigned MTE. Table 15.1 shows which values an MTE can assume. The red highlighting of an MTE indicates the highest alert level. A summary MTE is always assigned the value with the highest priority; that is, if a value of an assigned MTE is red, the monitoring summary node is also red.

TABLE 15.1: Possible Values of an MTE

Value	Meaning
Red	Problem or error
Yellow	Warning
Green	No problems
White	No information available

If the data for an MTE is stored in a separate monitoring segment, the MTE is known as *real*. MTEs that simply help provide an overview and do not have their own monitoring segment are known as *virtual.* They are indicated by ⊗ . The following icons indicate the monitoring attribute type:

⊠ Counter

▨ Other

A monitoring object is represented by ⬚.

Customizing

The Alert Monitor provides a visual cue to critical situations. The point at which the color changes is based on the settings defined. SAP delivers default settings for the Basic Monitor, but you need to modify these settings so that the Alert Monitor can provide meaningful information on your particular R/3 System. This is known as *Customizing* and must be done in every R/3 System. (Customizing is a complex and important aspect of R/3. For more on this topic see Chapter 6.)

Monitor Tree Class

Let's take a closer look at an MTE (like the one shown in Figure 15.1). Apart from the virtual MTEs, which are simply used to make a logical structure, each MTE is described by the *Monitor Tree Class.* For example, to display or change the Monitor Tree Class of an MTE, select MTE R3Services, and then choose Customizing (see Figure 15.2).

The Monitor Tree Class is made up of the following:

Descriptive text—Consisting of a message, message number, and text that appears if a critical situation occurs.

Visibility for user groups depending on a user's authorizations—Different views are permitted for monitoring, detailed analysis, and developer.

FIGURE 15.2:

Description of an MTE by the Monitor Tree Class

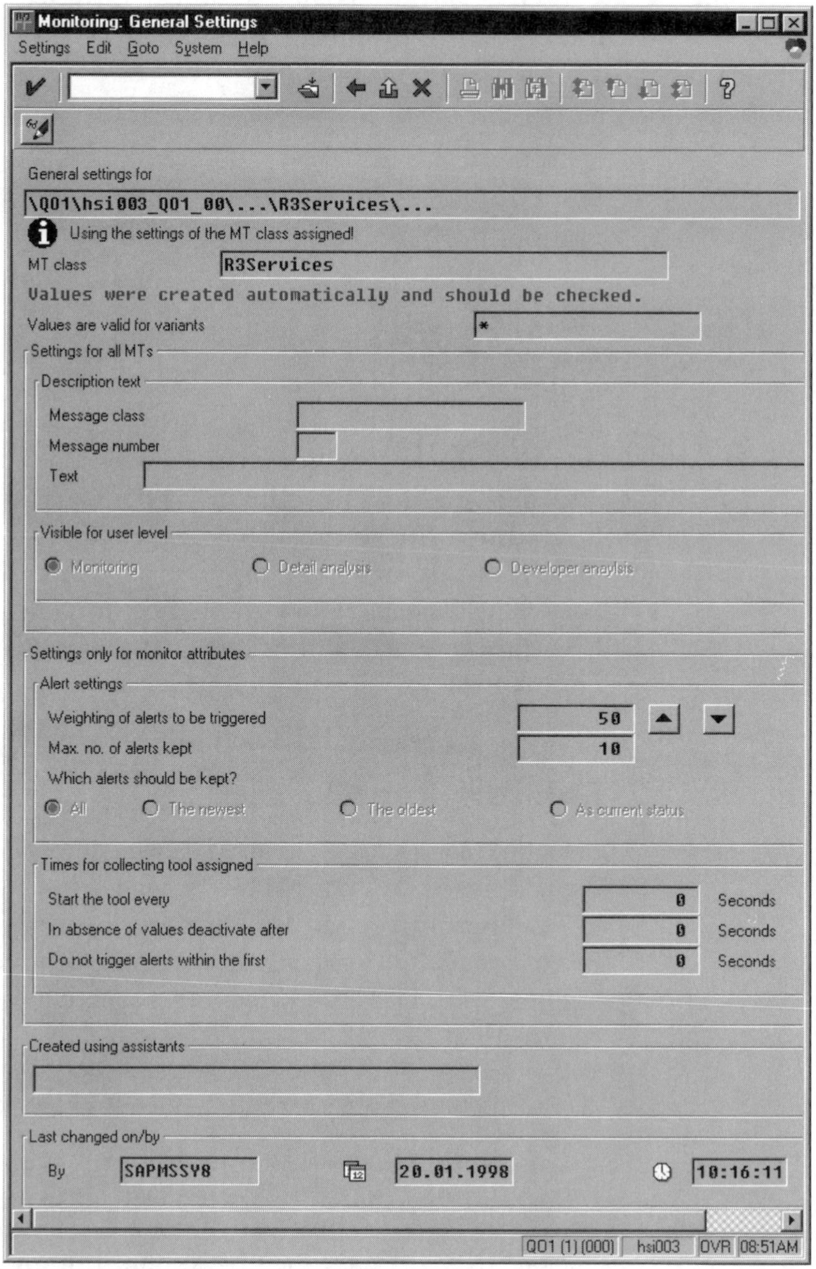

Settings for monitoring attributes—The weighting, the maximum number of alerts to be retained, and which alerts to retain: all, the last alert, the oldest alert, the most recent alert.

Collecting Tool—The *Collecting Tool* is the tool that determines the values and supplies those values to the assigned monitoring attributes. In the superordinate Monitor Tree Class, you define how frequently to get new values. In the example for the R/3 Services, this value is 0, which means that the data called is current.

Each MTE has a unique name and a number (*Unique Identifier, UID*). You can assign each MTE up to three types of tools for data retrieval and alert handling. The following tools can be used:

Collecting Tool—Used to retrieve data for analysis, for example, performance measurements. All MTEs are already assigned Collecting Tools by default in the Basic Monitor.

Analysis tool—Analyzes the inbound data, for example, filters messages. Only some analysis tools are assigned in the Basic Monitor, which is released with the standard R/3 System Release 4.0A.

OnAlert Tools—If a problem is analyzed, these tools react, for example, by sending a message. The OnAlert tools can be defined by the administrator or by a user with these authorizations, they are not assigned by SAP in the Basic Monitor.

To display an overview of the assigned tools in the Alert Monitor, choose Extras ➤ Tool Configuration ➤ Tool Assignment ➤ To MTE class.

For example, the Collecting Tool CCMS_Kernel_Function is assigned to the MTE R3EnqueueQueueLength. To find out how this logical name of the tool is defined—what type of program lies behind it—choose Extras ➤ Tool Configuration ➤ Tool Definition. Figure 15.3 shows the tools currently available in R/3 4.0A and which object is actually executed.

FIGURE 15.3:

Defining tools

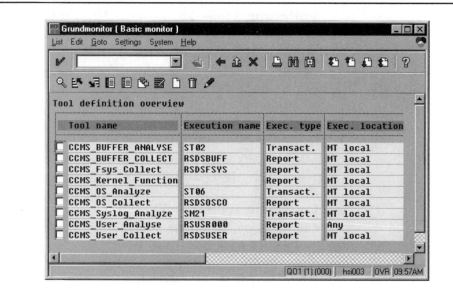

The system administrator can create new tools and integrate them into R/3. For example, you could create an ABAP program that sends a defined message to a particular user in the system if a problem occurs.

Customizing Group

In addition to the Monitor Tree Class, you can also define the monitoring attribute Customizing Group. For a monitoring attribute, choose Customizing from the Alert Monitor screen. Depending on the type of monitoring attribute being defined, the Customizing Groups are divided into:

Threshold values—An alert is triggered when the value exceeds or falls below the defined threshold value. Threshold values are, for example, used for performance measurements, such as AnswerTime in the MTE Dialog (see Figure 15.4).

Message-sensitive values—Often used for error analysis, for example, for ProgramErrors (see Figure 15.5). You can define a reaction to a specific message.

To access the Customizing screen, choose Tools ➤ CCMS ➤ Configuration ➤ Alert Monitor ➤ Sett./Thresh. (4.0) (Transaction code RZ21). This screen summarizes the Customizing details described earlier for all the MTEs.

You must pay particular attention to the threshold value settings. If threshold values are set too low and are already being exceeded in normal R/3 System operation, red alerts will be triggered constantly. An alert would be triggered for a situation that is actually normal.

Threshold values that are set too high, and are never exceeded, distort the signals given by the Alert Monitor. Even if the situation reaches a critical area, the color would not change, and you would not be warned of the problem. Therefore, it is necessary to set the threshold values so that all the alerts are normally green. Warnings only need to be issued for situations that deviate from normal. In the initial phase of R/3 System implementation, it is difficult to set appropriate threshold values. It is sensible to begin by working with the default values delivered by SAP or with your own estimated values. You need to improve these values iteratively as you gain experience.

Defining Your Own Monitor

From the Basic Monitor, you can define your own monitors. The advantage of defining your own monitors is that you can focus on user-specific areas. To define your own monitor:

1. From the Alert Monitor display (Tools ➤ CCMS ➤ Control/ Monitoring ➤ Alert Monitor (4.0) ➤ Edit ➤ Load Monitor, or

FIGURE 15.4:

Defining threshold values

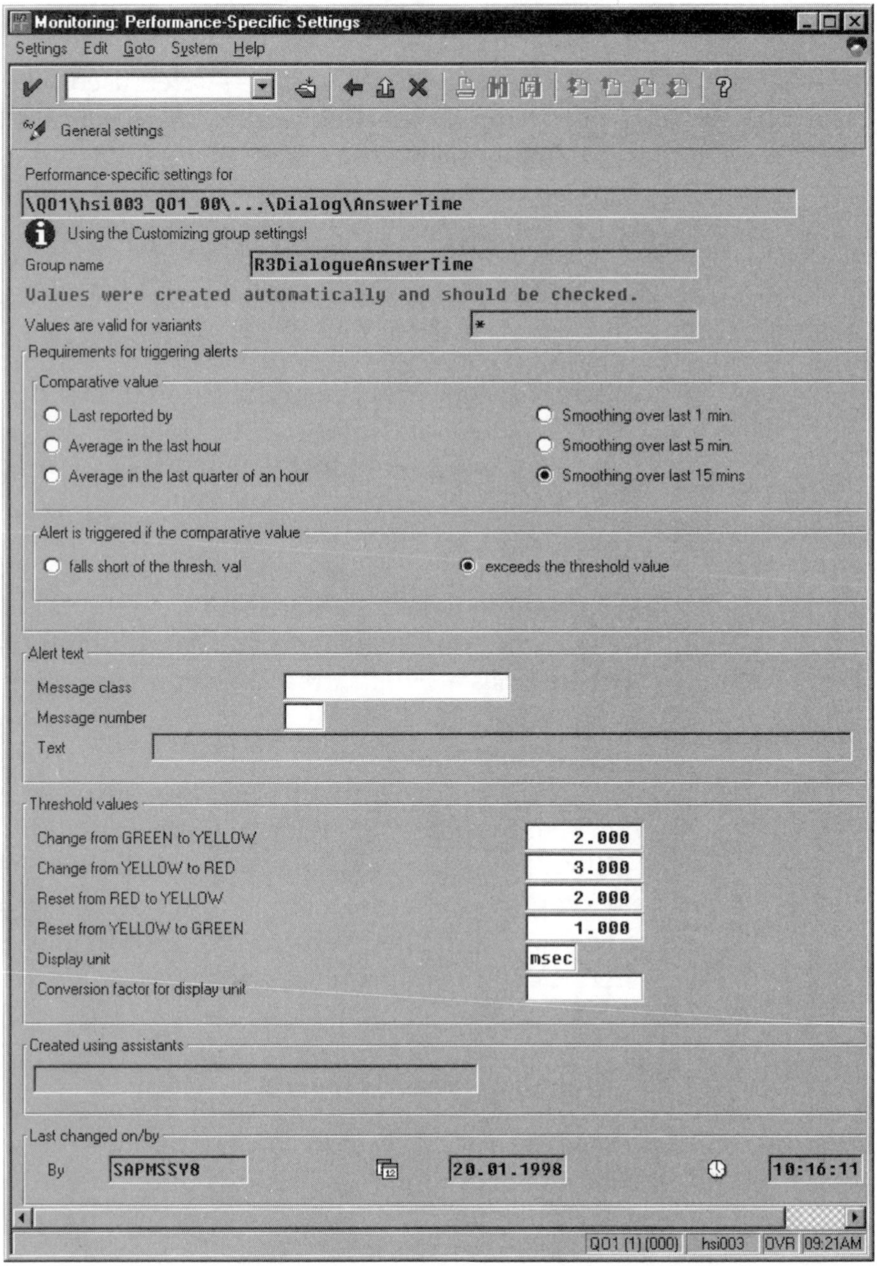

FIGURE 15.5:

Defining a message-sensitive Customizing Group

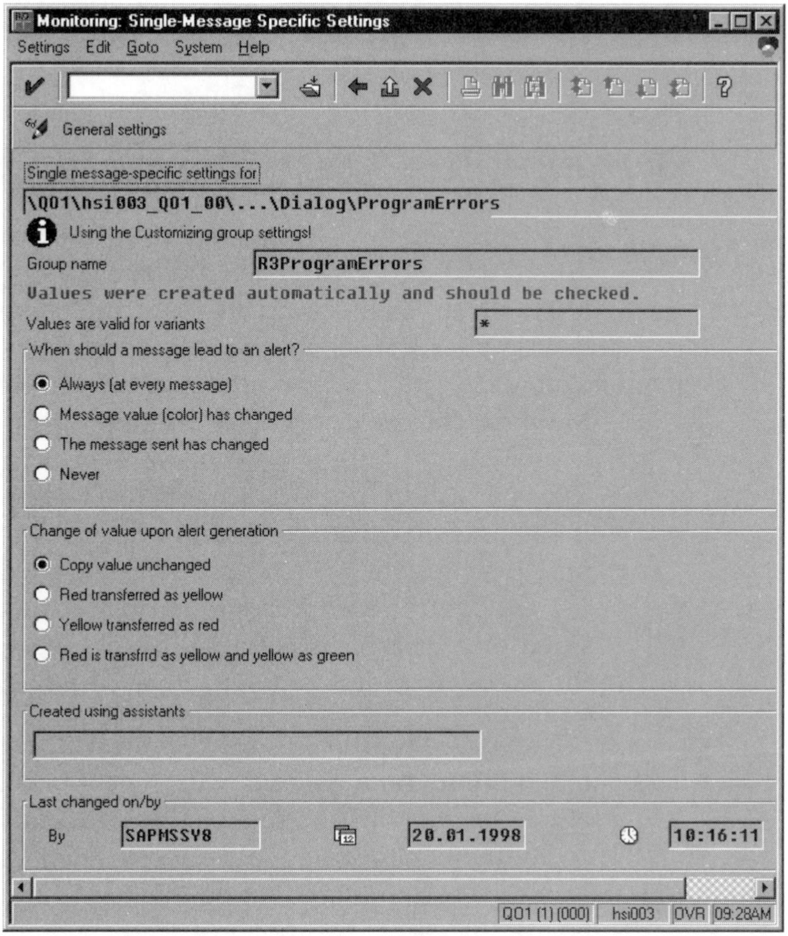

Transaction code RZ20), choose Monitor ➤ Create. The Basic Monitor is displayed in change mode.

2. From the generated Basic Monitor, select all the MTEs that are important for you.

3. Save.

4. Specify a name for the new monitor. You use this name to access your new Alert Monitor.

In future R/3 releases the Alert Monitor will be expanded to comprise many more areas and tools, thus providing considerably more information.

Handling the Alert Monitors

To ensure that R/3 System functions are available permanently, you must analyze the relevant alerts. To display the data for an alert, select a monitoring attribute and choose Display Alerts. The data in the Alert Monitor are updated. To suppress known alerts, choose Complete Alerts in this display or directly from the Alert Monitor. The selected values are then not used by the analysis tool to analyze the situation. New values are only analyzed when they are determined. You should only use this function after an analysis if you have resolved the source of a problem or were able to diagnose the cause of a message with certainty. To find and analyze the current data, choose Current State. You can evaluate the current situation in comparison with other situations. To display details for a selected monitoring attribute, choose Detailed Data.

The Alert Monitor groups together all the aspects of an R/3 System, giving you a general overview. If problems occur, the system administrator can use special detailed analysis tools. You cannot currently access these tools directly from the Alert Monitor. The way the tools are handled by the user is not uniform across the board; instead, it is problem-specific. Some of these tools were described in previous chapters, so this chapter only mentions them briefly and focuses on other special tools.

Server and Process Overview

To display a detailed overview of the status of the instances of an R/3 System and the R/3 work processes, use the Control Panel (Transaction code RZ03), which is described in Chapter 12. The server overview is described in Chapter 2. This section provides some additional details on this topic that are important for the system administrator.

Server Overview

To display the server overview, choose Tools ➤ Administration ➤ Monitoring ➤ System Monitoring ➤ Server, or use Transaction code SM51. The server overview shows all the available instances in an R/3 System (see Figure 15.6). For each instance, you can display the active processes (Processes) and all the logged on R/3 users (Users) and their sessions. To start a SAPGUI to another instance in the R/3 System, choose Remote Login. This function is useful if activities are only available locally on an application server, for example, the local system log in Windows NT environments.

FIGURE 15.6:

Server overview

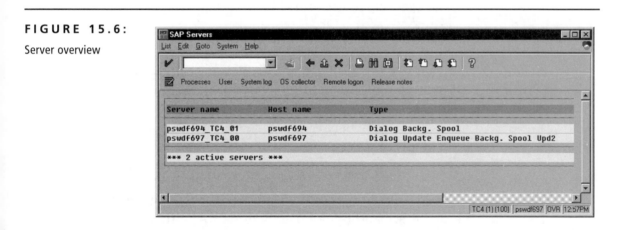

Process Overview

You can display the process overview for an instance from the server overview, or by choosing Tools ➤ Administration ➤ Monitoring ➤ System Monitoring ➤ Processes, or by using Transaction code SM50. The process overview displays tables with the following information:

- Process type:

    DIA—Dialog work process

    UPD—Update

    UPD2—V2 update

    ENQ—Enqueue work process

    BTC—Background work process

    SPO—Spool work process

- Process number
- Process status, for example:

    active—currently working

    waiting—waiting for new requests

    stopped—waiting for confirmation from another component, for example, CPIC

- Currently assigned users, including client
- The program currently being executed
- The action and table currently being processed

To add information to the process overview on CPU usage by the processes and by the user actions currently being performed, choose CPU. Figure 15.7 shows a section of the process overview. The Developer user is currently performing an action that has caused a table to be read directly.

For example, the process overview allows you to identify long-running LUWs. To obtain detailed information on the processing step, choose Detail Info. The system displays the currently processed table and the resources required. For experts, the

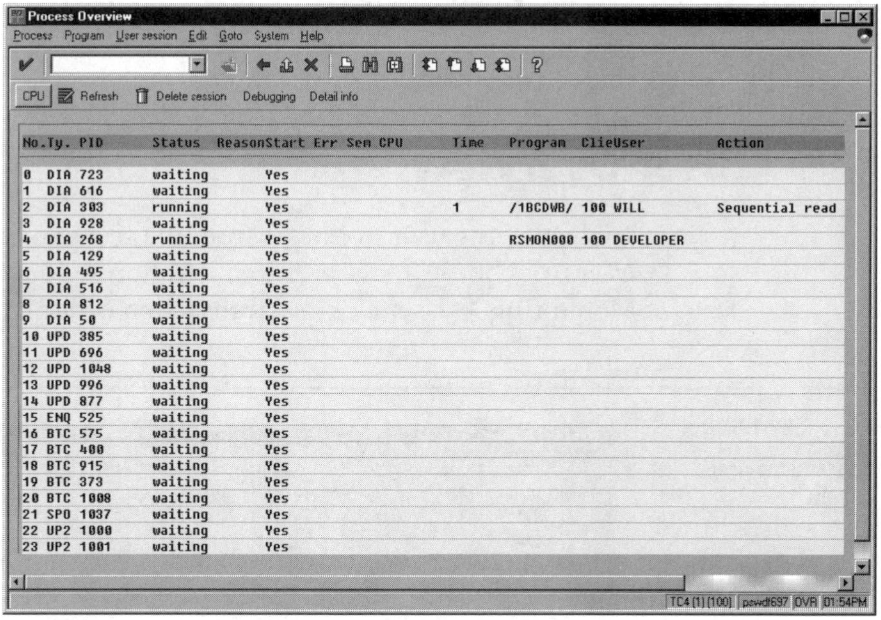
Process Overview
Process Program User session Edit Goto System Help
CPU Refresh Delete session Debugging Detail info
No.Ty. PID Status ReasonStart Err Sem CPU Time Program ClieUser Action
0 DIA 723 waiting Yes
1 DIA 616 waiting Yes
2 DIA 303 running Yes 1 /1BCDWB/ 100 WILL Sequential read
3 DIA 928 waiting Yes
4 DIA 268 running Yes RSMON000 100 DEVELOPER
5 DIA 129 waiting Yes
6 DIA 495 waiting Yes
7 DIA 516 waiting Yes
8 DIA 812 waiting Yes
9 DIA 50 waiting Yes
10 UPD 385 waiting Yes
11 UPD 696 waiting Yes
12 UPD 1048 waiting Yes
13 UPD 996 waiting Yes
14 UPD 877 waiting Yes
15 ENQ 525 waiting Yes
16 BTC 575 waiting Yes
17 BTC 400 waiting Yes
18 BTC 915 waiting Yes
19 BTC 373 waiting Yes
20 BTC 1008 waiting Yes
21 SPO 1037 waiting Yes
22 UP2 1000 waiting Yes
23 UP2 1001 waiting Yes

FIGURE 15.7:
The process overview for an instance

debugging mode may be interesting and informative when executing an ABAP program. To activate this mode for a selected process, choose Debugging. The program statements are then executed step by step. The user is automatically given control of the program flow.

Executing a program in Debugging mode is very resource-intensive and can therefore only be done in a test or development system. If serious problems occur, you can cancel or restart a work process (Process ➤ Cancel with Core, Process ➤ Cancel without Core, Restart after Error ➤ Yes). The affected Transaction is rolled back. The user is normally sent a message saying that the dialog work process was canceled by the system administrator.

WARNING Canceling an update or enqueue process is more critical than canceling a dialog work process. Manually canceling these work processes has consequences throughout the system and should be avoided, particularly in a production system.

If a work process fails, the dispatcher of the instance attempts to replace the lost work process by restarting a corresponding work process.

User Overview

To display the user overview from the server overview, choose Users, or choose Tools ➤ Administration ➤ Monitoring ➤ System Monitoring ➤ Users, or use Transaction code SM04 (see Figure 15.8).

FIGURE 15.8:

Displaying the user overview

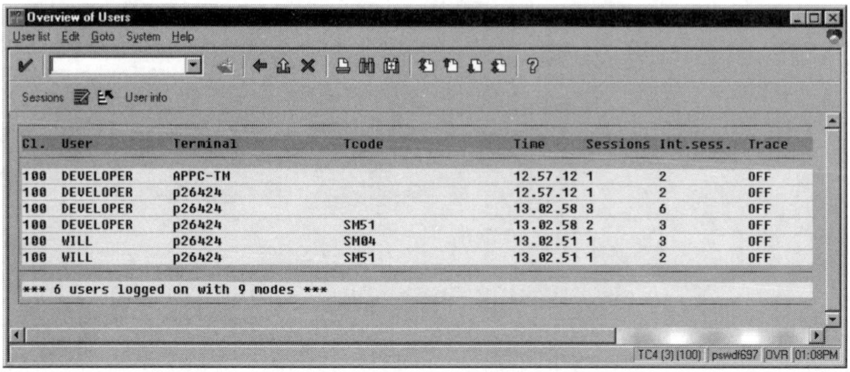

The user overview gives you a picture of the current user activities. For each logged-on user, the overview shows the terminal from which that user logged on, the Transaction that user is currently using, the number of open sessions, and the logon time. You can activate a user trace for selected users by choosing Edit ➤ Trace ➤ Trace On. This trace records all the actions of the user. In the same way, the user trace can be deactivated and analyzed. To demonstrate a procedure to another user, choose Edit ➤ Copy Session. The session of the selected user is taken over. All actions that you make in your session are shown in the other session. The user can follow your actions.

Global Process Overview

In addition to the process overview described earlier, there is another global process overview in R/3. To display the global process overview, choose Tools ➤ CCMS ➤ Control/Monitoring ➤ All Work Processes, or use Transaction code SM66. The two overviews provide almost identical information. The global process overview differs from the process overview mainly in the method used to obtain the information about work process activity. This method allows you to obtain information about the work processes without having to use the processing services of the work processes in an instance.

The global process overview functions even if the work processes of a particular instance in the R/3 System are in full use. The global user overview, which you access from the process overview, works in accordance with the same method. To display the global user overview, choose Goto ➤ Global User Overview, or use Transaction code SM04.

The server overview is the point at which to start analyzing activity in the overall R/3 System. It provides information on all the actions from the viewpoint of users and processes.

> **NOTE** Only the most important integrated overview functions are described here. Additional functions and analysis features are described in the R/3 documentation.

System Log

Checking the system log is one of the daily tasks of a system administrator. To display the system log, choose Tools ➤ Administration ➤ Monitoring ➤ System Log, or use Transaction code SM21. The system log is written locally for each application server to file SLOG00.log in directory \usr\sap\<*SID*>\<*instance*>\ log. (See Chapter 2 for details on using the system log.) By default, the file can grow to a size of 500KB. The data is then stored in a backup file and SLOG00.log is filled again. To change the size of the file, use parameter rslg/max_diskspace/local.

TIP   In UNIX systems, there is also a global system log. The file in directory /usr/sap/<SID>/SYS/global/SLOGJ is filled to a size of 2MB by default. To change the size, use parameter rslg/max_diskspace/global.

A wide range of selection criteria is available to analyze the system log. Figure 15.9 shows an excerpt from a system log for system TC4. The system log indicates an operation mode switch and the related actions. At 12:38, there was a further transaction rollback. The cause of a runtime error was a timeout; in other words, a dialog process exceeded its runtime. The TA column shows that the work process was W0.

The system log is the most important log for normal R/3 operation and is the starting point of problem analysis. For further information on the system log, see the SAP R/3-System manuals published by SAP.

Optimizing Performance

Optimizing R/3 performance is of fundamental importance. Poor response times are reflected directly in increased costs. R/3 therefore has a large number of integrated tools for performance analysis, working on the basis of continuously collected statistics. Analyzing this data requires a high level of skill and experience with the R/3 System. (It is not the goal of this book to cover analysis in all

FIGURE 15.9:

An excerpt from a system log

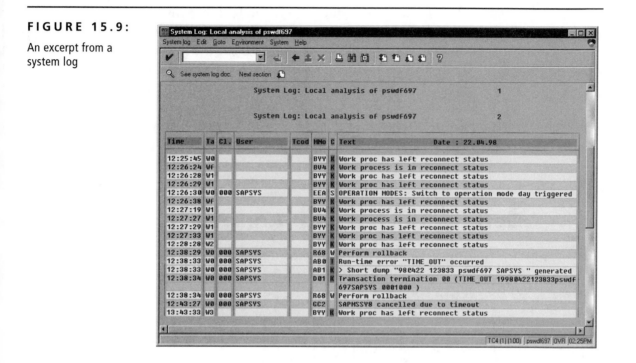

its complexity.) SAP and its partners offer all R/3 customers the EarlyWatch and GoingLive services. As part of these services, SAP analyzes the performance of the customer system and recommends ways to optimize its performance.

Performance Analysis Basics

All performance analyses in an R/3 System are based on the data collected by collectors over time. On the operating system level, the saposcol program collects important data on the performance of the components outside R/3. Within R/3, the background job COLLECTOR_FOR_PERFORMANCEMONITOR collects this data and the performance data for the other R/3 components, such as the database and the R/3 buffers. This background job is the ABAP program RSCOLL00, which is executed every hour.

The summarized data is written to Table MONI, the *performance database*. The system administrator must reorganize this table periodically to delete obsolete data. To set the parameters for reorganizing the performance database, that is, Table MONI, from the CCMS, choose Control/Monitoring ➤ Performance Menu ➤ Workload ➤ Analysis ➤ Goto ➤ Parameters ➤ Performance Database. Part of the work of the background job COLLECTOR_ FOR_PERFORMANCEMONITOR is to automatically reorganize the performance data on the basis of these settings.

Getting Started with Analysis

You can access all the performance analysis tools from the CCMS. Choose Control/Monitoring ➤ Performance Menu, or use Transaction code STUN. From the performance monitoring menu, you can monitor:

- The R/3 buffers

- The operating system

- The database

- The workload

Under normal circumstances, you start with the monitor for global workload analysis (Workload ➤ Analysis), which you can also generate for selected instances and time periods. Figure 15.10 shows the workload analysis screen for the current day for the entire R/3-System QO1.

The average response time of an R/3 System is of particular interest. The R/3 response time displayed is measured from the time the user request reaches the Dispatcher to the time of the confirmation of the result by the dialog process. This time should be less than 2 seconds. Figure 15.10 therefore shows a system that

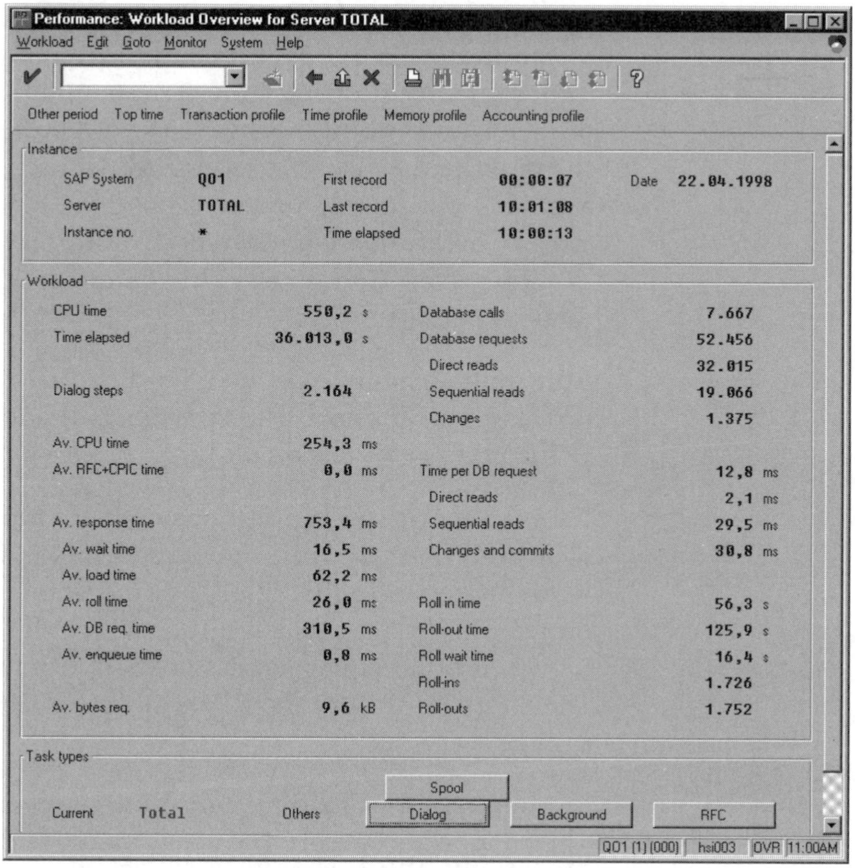

FIGURE 15.10:

Workload analysis

had a low load, and an average response time of 254 ms. The following parameters are especially important:

Wait time—The time that the Dispatcher needs to assign a dialog work process to a user request. A high wait time indicates that there are too few work processes or too many long work steps that are blocking dialog work processes. The wait time should make up about 1 percent of the average total response time of the R/3 System.

Load+Gen time—An intermediate code is first generated for all the ABAP programs to be executed. This code is stored in the reserved tables and loaded into the ABAP buffer for execution. In an R/3 System that has been running for long enough to attain a stable buffer fill level, all the intermediate codes used for ABAP programs should be available in generated form, if possible. Ideally, they will already be available in the ABAP buffer in the main memory. The Load+Gen time should be under 10 percent of the total response time.

Roll time—The time needed to unload and reload user contexts, such as authorizations, when a dialog work process is switched.

DB request time—The response time of the database is measured from the time the request is sent from the dialog work processes to the RDBMS to the time that the confirmation is sent by the database. It also includes the time needed to transfer the request across the network to the database. The DB request time should be about 40 percent of the average request time.

Enqueue time—The time needed to process lock requests.

Processing time—The processing time is not shown directly in the workload analysis. Processing time is calculated by the formula:

Processing time = Response time – Wait time – Load+Gen time – Roll time – DB request time – Enqueue time

CPU time—The time during which the CPU is occupied by work processes. If the processing time is many times longer than the CPU time, there could be an input/output problem. Normally, the CPU time should be about 40 percent of the total response time.

From this monitor, you can perform a detailed analysis using the special monitors.

Database Administration

The database administrator is responsible for administering the RDBMS and the database. The tasks involved are RDBMS-specific and can only be described here generally. For more details, see any of a number of books on the subject of RDBMS, for example, *High Performance Oracle 8* by Pete Cassidy (published by Coriolis Group, 1998), and *Microsoft SQL Server: Planning and Building a High Performance Database* by Robert D. Schneider (Prentice Hall, 1997).

The same administration tools are available for each RDBMS used with R/3. However, their appearance and the names used for the administration tools may differ.

Weekly Planning

The database is central to R/3; it is the central storage repository for data. For that reason, it is important to regularly back up the data so that you can restore it if an error occurs. A weekly plan is integrated into R/3 for tasks that need to be performed regularly. To access it from the CCMS, choose DB Administration ➤ DBA Scheduling, or use Transaction code DB13.

The most important database administration tasks can be scheduled for background processing (see Figure 15.11 for an example using Oracle). These tasks are:

- Saving the database while the system is running (online) or stopped (offline)

- Performing incremental data backup

- Saving the log area

- Saving individual data areas (tablespaces, DB spaces)

- Updating the optimization statistics

- Analyzing the database structure

FIGURE 15.11:

Weekly planning with an Oracle database

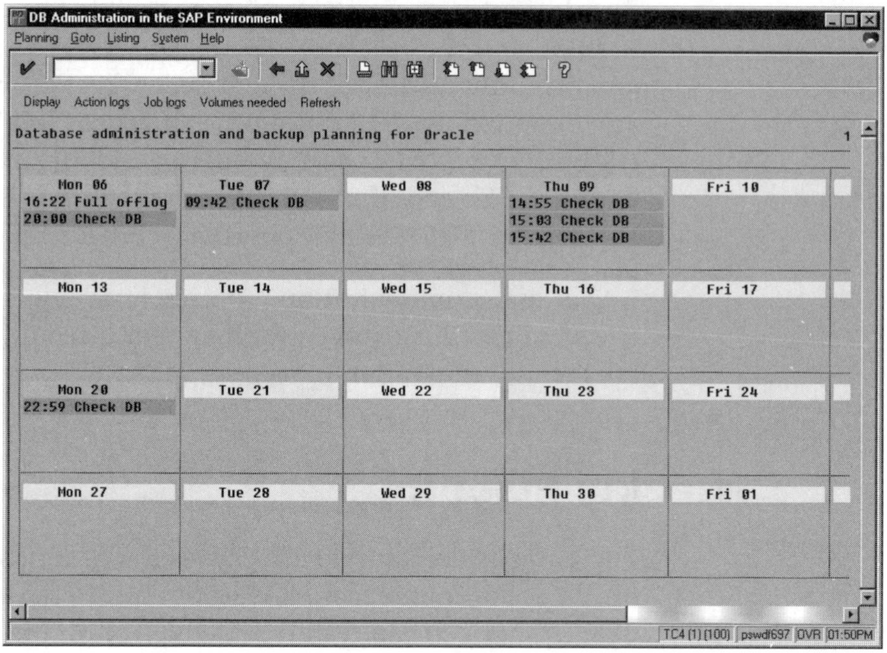

Using the Cost-Based Optimizer

All of the RDBMSs used with R/3 4.0 use a *cost-based optimizer* to determine the execution strategy of the SQL commands. If there are multiple execution plans, the cost-based optimizer determines the least expensive strategy. The volume of records to be read is used to measure the cost. The strategy for executing commands is determined on the basis of statistics on the data within a table, for example, the number of records in a table or the number of different values in an indexed column that represent the *selectivity* of an index. (The more different values a column contains, the more selective the index is.)

In addition, the optimizer uses information about the distribution of values within a table and its columns. The statistics used by the optimizers are not updated automatically. The database administrator must do this every week. To display information about the optimizer statistics to be used, choose from the CCMS (Tools ➤ CCMS) Cost-based Optimizer.

The only safe method of excluding corrupt blocks in the database that are caused by hardware errors is to analyze and verify the entire database. However, this is very time-consuming and causes increases in input/output activity on the hard disks. In R/3 Systems with very large databases, it is difficult to perform a full analysis. If hardware problems occur, you need to perform a full analysis, at least of the affected areas.

Scheduling Backups

You should back up the entire database at least once a week. For information on which backups are performed when, refer to the weekly plan in the CCMS. Choose the desired function in the weekly plan, then Goto ➤ Backup Logs, or use Transaction code DB12. If an error occurs, you'll also need the log data to restore the database and recover the data changes made since the last full backup. All the data must be available in the log areas.

Each RDBMS only overwrites data in the log if that data has been backed up. If the data was not backed up, there is the danger that the log area may be filled, and that data may be lost if a hardware error occurs. If this happened, you would not be able to operate the database or R/3. Outside R/3, there is the SAP tool SAPDBA for database-specific administration for Oracle and

Informix. To administer SQL Server, use the Enterprise Manager, which is part of the SQL Server product.

Monitoring Database Fill Level and Objects

The database administrator must continuously monitor database growth. If the database does not have sufficient space to store the data, the R/3 System may not be able to continue its work. You must therefore regularly check the database fill level and expand the database if necessary. To obtain information about the database size and the objects in it, from the CCMS choose Control/ Monitoring ➤ Performance Menu ➤ Database ➤ Tables/Indexes, or use Transaction code DB02. This monitor provides information about the current database fill level and its history, and the size of individual objects such as tablespaces or tables and indexes. Figure 15.12 is a graphic representation of the history of the database fill level. A prognosis is generated to allow the administrator to locate the time of a potential bottleneck.

In addition to checking the space required by individual objects, the R/3 System regularly checks the objects defined in the R/3 Data Dictionary and in the database. The system administrator must ensure that there are no differences between R/3 and the database. Missing indexes can seriously impede performance. You should use this monitor to check the consistency of the objects and use the R/3 Data Dictionary (ABAP Workbench ➤ Dictionary) to create missing objects, especially after an R/3 upgrade.

Lock Entries

As described in Chapter 1, the R/3 System provides its own lock management using the Enqueue work processes. Normally the

FIGURE 15.12:

History of the database
fill level

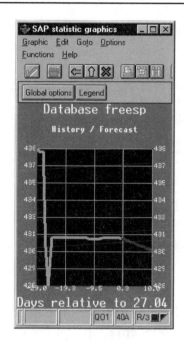

lock entries are created and deleted automatically. If problems do occur in the R/3 System, for example, if the Dispatcher for an instance or entire instances suddenly fails, obsolete lock entries may sometimes remain in the system. Lock entries can also remain in the system if users switch off their computers without first logging off the R/3 System. This is the most frequent cause of obsolete lock entries. You must therefore check the lock entries daily and, if necessary, delete them manually:

1. Choose Tools ➤ Administration ➤ Monitoring ➤ Lock Entries, or use Transaction code SM12. In the screen displayed, you can select which lock entries to display. You can set restrictions for the table name, the lock argument, the client, or the user.

2. Choose List. The system displays a list of the currently held locks (see Figure 15.13).

FIGURE 15.13:

A list of the lock entries in an R/3 System

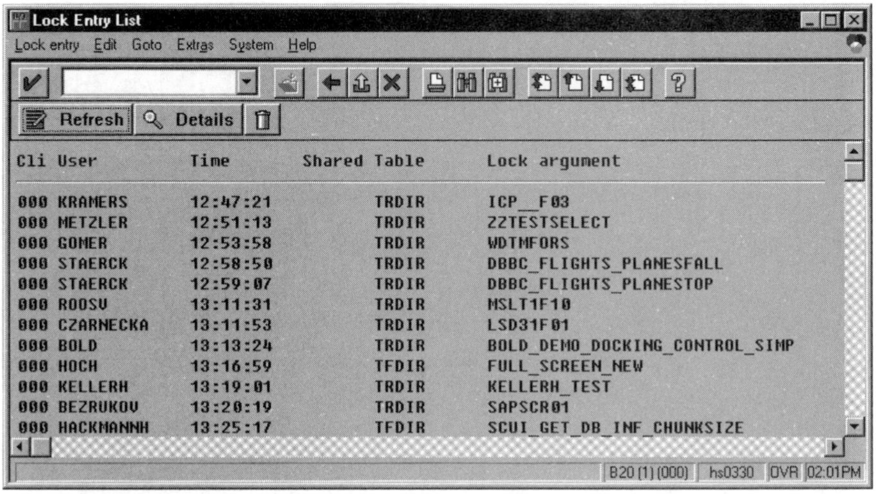

3. In addition to the user and the client that hold the lock, the system displays the generation time of the lock and the table. The lock argument (lock key) is particularly important. The Shared column tells you whether the lock is being used by multiple users. To sort the list, choose Edit ➤ Sort.

4. Check the times that the lock entries were created. You should analyze lock entries that are kept for a particularly long time. To display more information about an entry, such as the Transaction code that created the lock entry, double-click the entry.

5. If the lock entries were caused by an update, check the update transactions.

6. Check whether the user for a lock entry is still logged on.

7. Lock management problems are very likely to be a result of other problems. If you find obsolete lock entries, you must investigate the application area. To delete an obsolete lock entry, select the lock entry and choose Delete. Deletion of lock entries is recorded in the R/3 system log or the instance log.

> **NOTE** Do not delete locks unless you are absolutely certain about what you are doing! A lock entry should only be deleted if your analysis shows without doubt that the lock entry really is obsolete.

Runtime Errors

If an ABAP program is executed and canceled, a *dump* is generated and saved for the error. In a development system, a dump is an important programming tool. It is primarily the responsibility of the developers to analyze and resolve the error. Runtime errors cannot occur in production systems in which no software development work is done. Nevertheless, the system administrator must check daily whether any programs were canceled, and if so, why. From the CCMS, choose Control/Monitoring ➤ Performance Menu ➤ Exceptions/Users ➤ Dump Analysis, or choose Tools ➤ Administration ➤ Monitoring ➤ Dump Analysis.

In addition to the cancellation location and the error type, all the important peripheral information is saved for each program cancellation. This information includes, for example, the time of the cancellation, the R/3 release, the RDBMS, the operating system, and the variable values. Analyzed and obsolete runtime error records should be deleted from the database to save space. Use report RSNAPDL (see Chapter 9 for details).

Developer Traces

A developer trace is written for the processes of each R/3 instance. The trace is written to the files **dev_<xx>** in the directory **\usr\sap\<SID>\<instance>\work**.

<xx> stands for:

w<n>—Work process and its number

rfc<n>—RFC process and its number

ms—Message server

rd—Gateway reader

dev_disp—Dispatcher

The number of the work process is the same as the number displayed in the process overview. To take a look, choose Tools ➤ Administration ➤ Monitoring ➤ System Monitoring ➤ Process Overview (Transaction code SM50). To analyze the log files from R/3, choose Monitoring ➤ Traces ➤ Developer Traces.

These files are particularly important if an instance cannot be started or processes are canceled while the system is running. You can determine how much is logged for each instance by using parameter rdisp/TRACE. If this parameter is not specified, the default value 1 is assumed and only error situations are logged with basic details. The value 0 deactivates the developer traces. The parameter accepts values up to 3. However, you should only raise the parameter value selectively to analyze a specific error, as increasing the logging level also increases the write load of the files. In a production system, you should set a logging level of no higher than 1 for normal operation.

SAP System Trace

To log processes within the R/3 System, use the SAP system trace (Tools ➤ Administration ➤ Monitoring ➤ Traces ➤ SAP System Trace). You should only use the SAP system trace if you have a specific goal and are working in cooperation with SAP, as the logged information is not simple to interpret and is very comprehensive. The SAP system trace is not suited for use with production operation.

SQL Trace

To analyze problems—in particular to analyze the performance of individual R/3 Transactions—you can activate a selective SQL trace. Choose Utilities ➤ SQL Trace ➤ Trace On, and specify the R/3 user to be monitored. All SQL commands generated by that user are recorded together with duration, result, and data. The SQL trace can be activated for all the work processes except the Enqueue service, for only for the Enqueue service, or for both (see Figure 15.14).

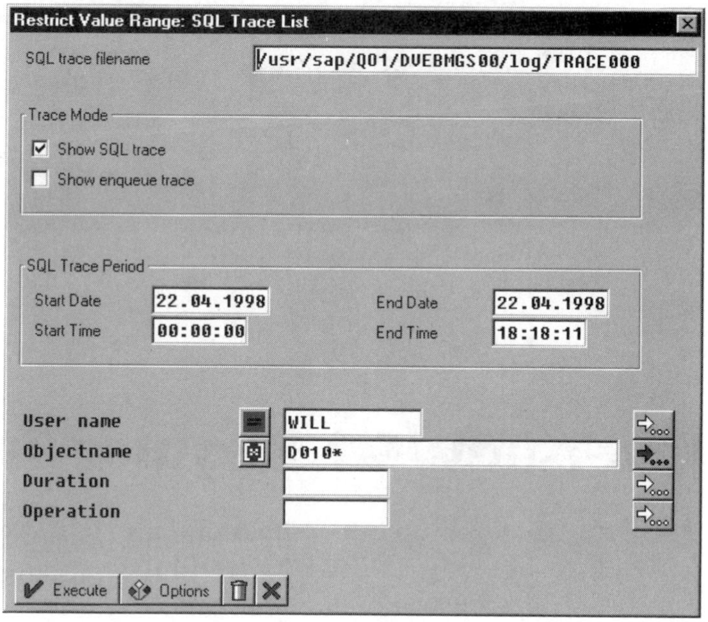

FIGURE 15.14:

Activating the SQL trace

Figure 15.15 shows an excerpt from a SQL trace, for example, the DB Request time for the command `Select where tabname= 'RSTRNTR'` was `174 ms`. The duration of an operation is always specified in milliseconds. Commands that exceed a specific run-time—and can thus be critical—are highlighted in red. The column Object displays the name of the object (table, view) that the command references. To call the execution plan determined by the optimizer for this command, choose Explain SQL. To go to the ABAP program, from which the SQL statement was generated, choose ABAP/4 Display.

FIGURE 15.15:

Excerpt from a SQL trace

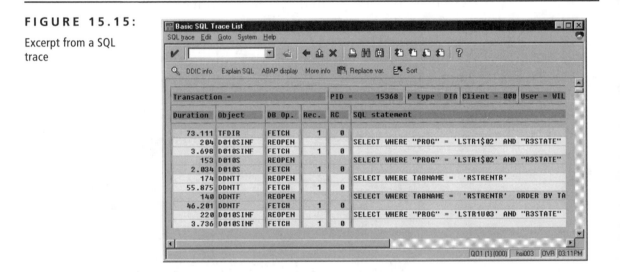

An Overview of Regular Tasks

To wrap up our discussion of how best to keep things running smoothly, Table 15.2 lists all the regularly recurring tasks that an administrator should schedule for a production R/3 System. You can modify system monitoring tasks in development systems and consolidation systems, where the level of failover security does not normally need to be very high. There is frequently no update in development systems. There is consequently no need to monitor updates.

TABLE 15.2: Regular Administration Tasks

Activity	Menu Path	Transaction	Schedule
Check the Alert Monitor	Tools ➤ CCMS ➤ Control/Monitoring ➤ Alert Monitor (4.0)	RZ20	More than once a day
Check the system log	Tools ➤ Administration ➤ Monitor ➤ System Log	SM21	Daily
Check the status of the instances and operation modes	Tools ➤ CCMS ➤ Control/Monitoring ➤ Control Panel	RZ03	Daily
Check the status of the application server and work processes	Tools ➤ Administration ➤ Monitor ➤ System Monitoring ➤ Servers	SM51, SM04, SM66, SM55	Daily
Check the update service	Tools ➤ Administration ➤ Monitoring ➤ Update	SM13	Daily
Check the spool service	Tools ➤ CCMS ➤ Spool ➤ Output Management	SP01	Daily
Check the lock entries	Tools ➤ Administration ➤ Monitoring ➤ Lock Entries	SM12	Daily
Check for runtime errors	Tools ➤ Administration ➤ Monitoring ➤ Dump Analysis	ST22	Daily
Check the logs for background jobs	Tools ➤ CCMS ➤ Jobs ➤ Maintenance	SM37	Daily
Check the maintenance jobs to be executed regularly	Tools ➤ CCMS ➤ Jobs ➤ Maintenance	SM37	Daily
Check the optimizer statistics	Tools ➤ CCMS ➤ DB Administration ➤ DBA Scheduling	DB13	Weekly

TABLE 15.2: Regular Administration Tasks *(continued)*

Activity	Menu Path	Transaction	Schedule
Perform and check the backups	Tools ➤ CCMS ➤ DB Administration ➤ DBA Scheduling	DB13	Daily
Check the database administration logs	Tools ➤ CCMS ➤ DB Administration ➤ Backup Logs Tools ➤ CCMS ➤ DB Administration ➤ DBA Logs	DB12 DB14	Daily
Check the database consistency	Tools ➤ CCMS ➤ DB Administration ➤ DBA Scheduling	DB13	Weekly, if possible
Check the database fill level	Tools ➤ CCMS ➤ Control/Monitoring ➤ Database ➤ Tables/Indexes	DB02	Monthly
Check the consistency of the database objects	Tools ➤ CCMS ➤ Control/Monitoring ➤ Database ➤ Tables/Indexes	DB02	At a minimum, after upgrades
Performance analysis	Tools ➤ CCMS ➤ Control/Monitoring ➤ Workload Analysis	ST02	When necessary
Check Batch Input	System ➤ Services ➤ Batch Input ➤ Edit	SM35	Regularly, when Batch Input is used
Check the ALE transactions on sender and recipient sides	Logistics ➤ Central Functions ➤ SCP Interfaces ➤ Environment ➤ Monitoring ➤ ALE Administration	BALE	Daily. when ALE is used

Review Questions

1. To which directory are the developer traces written?

   A. \users\<*sid*>adm

   B. \usr\sap\<*SID*>\<*instance*>\work

   C. \usr\sap\<*SID*>\SYS\global

2. Your R/3 System cannot be started. Where will you find information on the cause of this problem?

   A. startdb.log

   B. startsap_<*computer name*>_<*instance number*>.log

   C. R/3 log

   D. Developer traces

   E. System log

   F. SQL trace

3. A user informs you that his or her session was terminated with an error. Unfortunately, the user has no details about what happened. Where would be the best place to start your analysis?

   A. Do not start an analysis. Without any details, you cannot find the cause of a cancellation.

   B. Check all the runtime errors that occurred in your R/3 System.

   C. Check the system log.

   D. Check the backup logs.

APPENDIX A

A

Transaction Codes

The most important R/3 Transaction codes for R/3 System administration are listed in Table A.1. R/3 Transaction codes are entered in the command field of the SAPGUI. You can use the following switches:

Switch	What It Does
/n<*Transaction code*>	Exits the currently active R/3 Transaction and starts the new Transaction in the same window (session).
/o<*Transaction code*>	Starts the new Transaction in a new window (session).
/h<*Transaction code*>	Starts the new Transaction in debugging mode.

If you type **/h** without a Transaction code in the command field and then press Enter, the current Transaction is processed in debugging mode.

TABLE A.1:   Commonly Used Transaction Codes

Transaction Code	What It Means
AL01	Global Alert Monitor 3.X
AL02	Database Alert Monitor
AL03	Operating System Alert Monitor
AL05	Workload Alert Monitor
AL11	Display operating system files from the CCMS
AL12	Buffer synchronization
BALE	ALE administration and monitoring
DB02	Missing database objects and space requirements

TABLE A.1: Commonly Used Transaction Codes *(Continued)*

Transaction Code	What It Means
DB12	SAPDBA protocols
DB13	Weekly planning
FILE	Archiving: Assignments between logical and physical file names—client-independent
OSS1	OSS Logon
PFCG	Profile Generator: Maintain activity groups
RZ01	Graphical background job scheduling monitor
RZ02	Network graphics of the instances
RZ03	Control Panel: Operation modes and server statuses
RZ04	Maintain instances
RZ06	Maintain threshold values for Alert Monitors
RZ08	R/3 Alert Monitor
RZ10	Maintain the profile parameters
RZ20	Alert Monitor 4.0
RZ21	Customizing the Alert Monitor 4.0
S00	Short message
SA38	ABAP reporting
SAD0	Address management
SADC	Addresses: Maintain communication types
SALE	IMG Application Link Enabling
SAR	Maintain Transaction codes
SAR0	Display the standard reporting tree
SAR1	Structure of an Archiving object
SAR2	Define Archiving objects

TABLE A.1: Commonly Used Transaction Codes *(Continued)*

Transaction Code	What It Means
SAR3	Customizing archiving
SAR4	Define archiving classes
SAR5	Assign archiving classes
SAR6	Archiving Time Generator
SARA	Archive administration
SARL	ArchiveLink Monitor
SC38	Start report remotely
SC80	CATT utilities
SCAM	CATT management
SCAT	Computer Aided Test Tool
SCC1	Client copy with help of a transport request
SCC3	Client copy log
SCC4	Client copy administration
SCC5	Delete clients
SCC6	Client import
SCC7	Client import—post-processing
SCC8	Client export
SCC9	Remote client copy
SCCL	Local client copy
SCMP	View/Table Comparison
SCPF	Generate IMG
SCPR1	Customizing Profiles: Maintenance Tool
SCPR2	Compare Customizing profiles
SCU0	Customizing comparison

TABLE A.1: Commonly Used Transaction Codes *(Continued)*

Transaction Code	What It Means
SDBE	Explain a SQL statement
SDW0	Start ABAP Workbench
SE01	Transport Organizer
SE03	Workbench Organizer: Tools
SE06	Set up the Workbench Organizer
SE07	Display Transport System status
SE09	Workbench Organizer
SE10	Customizing Organizer
SE11	R/3 Data Dictionary maintenance
SE12	R/3 Data Dictionary display
SE14	Convert Data Dictionary tables on database level
SE15	Repository Info System
SE16	Display table content
SE17	General table display
SE93	Maintain Transaction codes
SEU	Repository Browser
SF01	Archiving: Assignment between logical and physical file names—client-independent
SFT2	Maintain public holiday calendar
SFT3	Maintain factory calendar
SHDB	Record batch input
SICK	Installation check
SM01	Lock Transactions
SM02	System messages

TABLE A.1: Commonly Used Transaction Codes *(Continued)*

Transaction Code	What It Means
SM04	User list
SM12	Display and delete locks
SM13	Display Update records
SM21	System log
SM28	Installation check
SM30	Maintain views
SM31	Maintain tables
SM35	Batch input monitoring
SM36	Schedule background jobs
SM37	Overview of background jobs
SM39	Job analysis
SM49	Execute external commands
SM50	Work process overview
SM51	Instance overview
SM56	Number range buffer
SM58	Error log for asynchronous RFC
SM59	RFC connections (display and maintain)
SM63	Display and maintain operation modes
SM64	Trigger an event
SM65	Analysis tool for background processing
SM66	Global work process overview
SM69	Maintain external operating system commands
SMEN	Session manager menus
SMLG	Maintain assignments of logon groups to instances
SMLI	Language import

TABLE A.1: Commonly Used Transaction Codes *(Continued)*

Transaction Code	What It Means
SMLT	Language Administration
SO00	SAPoffice Short Message
SO01	SAPoffice Inbox
SO02	SAPoffice Outbox
SO03	SAPoffice Private Folders
SO04	SAPoffice Public Folders
SO21	Maintain PC work directory
SO99	Upgrade information system
SOA0	ArchiveLink workflow document types
SOA1	ArchiveLink early archiving
SOA2	ArchiveLink late archiving
SOA3	ArchiveLink settings for early archiving
SOA4	ArchiveLink settings for late archiving
SOA5	ArchiveLink simultaneous archiving
SOA6	ArchiveLink settings for simultaneous archiving
SP00	Spool and related areas
SP01	Spool control
SP02	Display output requests
SP11	TemSe contents
SP12	TemSe administration
SPAD	Spool administration
SPAM	SAP Patch Manager (SPAM)
SPAU	Display modified objects in the runtime environment
SPCC	Spool consistency check
SPDD	Display modified DDIC objects
SPIC	Spool: Installation check

TABLE A.1: Commonly Used Transaction Codes *(Continued)*

Transaction Code	What It Means
SPRO	Start Customizing
SPRP	Start project administration
SSM1	Session Manager generation call
SSM5	Create activity groups
ST01	SAP system trace
ST02	Statistics of the R/3 buffer
ST03	Workload analysis
ST04	Statistics on RDBMS activities
ST05	SQL trace
ST06	Operating System Monitor
ST07	Application Monitor
ST08	Network Monitor
ST09	Network Alert Monitor
ST10	Table call statistics
ST11	Display developer traces
ST12	Application Monitor
ST14	Application analysis
ST22	ABAP runtime error analysis
ST4A	Oracle: Analyze the shared cursor cache
STAT	Local Transaction statistics
STMS	Transport Management System
STUN	R/3 performance menu
SU01	User maintenance
SU01D	Display users
SU02	Maintain authorization profiles

TABLE A.1: Commonly Used Transaction Codes *(Continued)*

Transaction Code	What It Means
SU03	Maintain authorizations
SU05	Maintain Internet users
SU10	Mass changes to user master records
SU12	Delete all R/3 users, also SAPoffice
SU2	Maintain user parameters
SU20	Maintain authorization fields
SU21	Maintain authorization objects
SU22	Authorization object usage in Transactions
SU24	Modify SAP check ID
SU25	Apply the SAP defaults to customer tables
SU26	Adjust authorization checks
SU3	Maintain own user data
SU30	Full authorization check
SU52	Maintain own user parameters
SU53	Display check values
SU54	Display menu for the SAP Session Manager
SU55	Display menu for the SAP Session Manager
SU56	Analyze user buffer
SUPC	Profiles for activity groups
SUPF	Integrated user maintenance
SUPO	Maintain organization levels
SUSE	Maintain self-upgrading software
SWDC	Workflow definition: Administration
SWUE	Trigger an event
TU02	Display active parameters

Profile Parameters

R/3 has a wide range of profile parameters. It is delivered with default settings already implemented for all profile parameters. Customers can change all the parameters, but they are warned not to change parameters in a random fashion. Relatively few of the parameters need to be adjusted by customers. All of the other parameters should be changed only after you have consulted SAP, or if SAP has recommended that they be changed. Individual settings made by customers overwrite the default values.

The tables in this appendix list the most important R/3 parameters. Table B.1 shows parameters that are set only in the R/3 default profile DEFAULT.PFL and that affect the whole system.

TABLE B.1: Parameters in the Default Profile

Parameter	Meaning
SAPSYSTEMNAME	3-character identifier (SID) of an R/3 System
SAPDBHOST	Name of the database server
sna_gateway	Name of the computer on which the SNA Gateway is running
sna_gwservice	Port of the SNA Gateway
rdisp/mshost	Name of the computer on which the message server is running
rdisp/vbname	Instance whose update service functions as a dispatcher for updates
rdisp/enqname	Instance that provides the Enqueue service
rdisp/btcname	Instance that provides the Event Scheduler
rdisp/bufrefmode	Parameter for synchronizing the buffers in distributed systems For a central instance: sendoff/exeauto For a distributed system: sendon/exeauto
rdisp/bufreftime	Time between two buffer synchronizations in seconds Default: 60
auth/no_check_in_ some_cases	Activate the Profile Generator N: inactive (default) Y: active

TABLE B.1: Parameters in the Default Profile *(Continued)*

Parameter	Meaning
dbs/ora/tnsname	Logical name of an Oracle database Is used with Oracle SQL*Net V2 to identify the Oracle database. The name must be specified in the configuration file `tnsname.ora`. Default: `$(SAPSYSTEMNAME)`

The parameters listed in Tables B.2 and B.3 are typical parameters in the instance profile. The parameters can also be used in the default profile `DEFAULT.PFL`. If other values are not assigned in an instance profile, parameter values in the default profile are valid throughout the entire R/3 System.

TABLE B.2: Parameters in the Instance Profiles and Their Default Values

Area	Parameter	Meaning
Dialog	rdisp/wp_no_dia	Number of dialog work processes
Spool	rdisp/wp_no_spo	Number of spool work processes

	rspo/store_location	db in the database
		G in the global directory of R/3
		    /usr/sap/<*SID*>/SYS/global
		L in the local file on the instance
		    /usr/sap/<*SID*>/<*instance*>/data
		T locally in the directory /tmp (Unix) or \TEMP
		    (Windows NT)

	rspo/host_spool/print	Operating system command for printing, including options
	rspo/tcp/retries	Number of attempts to establish a connection to a remote output device (access method U) Default: 3
	rspo/tcp/retrytime	Time in seconds between two attempts to establish a connection to a remote output device Default: 300

TABLE B.2: Parameters in the Instance Profiles and Their Default Values *(Continued)*

Area	Parameter	Meaning
	`rspo/tcp/timeout/connect`	Permissible wait time in seconds to establish a connection to a remote printer Default: 10
Update	`rdisp/wp_no_vb`	Number of update work processes
	`rdisp/wp_no_vb2`	Number of update work processes for V2 updates
	`rdisp/vbreorg`	Delete incomplete update requests when restarting the instance: 1: active (default) 0: inactive
	`rdisp/vbmail`	Notify a user if an update is terminated 1: active (default) 0: inactive
	`rdisp/vbdelete`	Number of days after which terminated update requests are deleted Default: 50
Background	`rdisp/wp_no_btc`	Number of background work processes
	`rdisp/btctime`	Time in seconds between two background scheduler runs Default: 60
Enqueue	`rdisp/wp_no_enq`	Number of enqueue work processes
R/3 Memory	`rsdb/ntab/entrycount`	Maximum number of buffer entries in the TTAB buffer Recommended: 30,000
	`rsdb/ntab/ftabsize`	Size of the FTAB buffer (in KB) Recommended: 30,000
	`rsdb/ntab/irbdsize`	Size of the IRDB buffer (in KB) Recommended: 4,000
	`rsdb/ntab/sntabsize`	Size of the STAB buffer (in KB) Recommended: 2,500
	`rsdb/cua/buffersize`	Size of the FTAB buffer (in KB) Recommended: 5,000

TABLE B.2: Parameters in the Instance Profiles and Their Default Values *(Continued)*

Area	Parameter	Meaning
R/3 Memory	zcsa/presentation_buffer_area	Size of the Dynpro buffer x 2 (in bytes) Recommended: 20,000,000
	sap/bufdir_entries	Maximum number of buffer entries in the Dynpro buffer Recommended: 4,500
	zcsa/table_buffer_area	Size of the generic table buffer (in bytes)
	zcsa/db_max_buftab	Maximum number of entries in the generic table buffer
	rtbb/buffer_length	Size of the single record table buffer (in KB)
	rtbb/max_tables	Maximum number of entries in the single record table buffer
	abap/buffersize	Size of the ABAP program buffer
	rsdb/obj/buffersize	Size of the import/export buffer (in KB)
	rsdb/obj/max_objects	Maximum number of entries in the import/export buffer
	rsdb/obj/large_object_size	Estimated size of the largest object in the import/export buffer (in bytes)
	rdisp/ROLL_MAXFS	Size of the roll area (roll buffer plus the roll file) (in 8KB blocks) Recommended: 32,000 (optimal), 16,000 (minimal)
	rdisp/PG_MAXFS	Size of the R/3 paging area (paging buffer plus paging file) (in 8KB blocks) Recommended: 32,000 (optimal), 16,000 (minimal)
	rdisp/ROLL_SHM*	Size of the roll buffer (in 8KB blocks)
	rdisp/PG_SHM*	Size of the R/3 paging buffer (in 8KB blocks)
	em/initial_size_MB*	Initial size of the extended memory (in MB)
	em/max_size_MB*	Maximum size of the extended memory (in MB) (Windows NT only)
	em/address_space_MB*	The address space reserved for the extended memory (in MB) (Windows NT only)

TABLE B.2: Parameters in the Instance Profiles and Their Default Values *(Continued)*

Area	Parameter	Meaning
	ztta/roll_first*	Size of the first allocated memory area from the roll area in bytes Recommended: 1
	ztta/roll_area*	Size of the roll area in bytes Recommended: 2,000,000 (Windows NT), 6,500,000 (other systems)
	ztta/roll_extension*	Amount of memory that a work process can request in extended memory, in bytes Recommended: 2,000,000,000 (Windows NT), 1/3 of the size of the extended memory (other systems)
	abap/heap_area_dia*	Size of the local process memory (heap), in bytes, that a dialog process can request Recommended: 2,000,000,000 (default)
	abap/heap_area_nondia*	Size of the local process memory (heap) in bytes that non-dialog processes can request Default: 400,000,000
	abap/heap_area_total*	Maximum heap memory for all work processes (in bytes)
	abap/heaplimit*	If a work process requests more memory than the value of this parameter allows, the work process is automatically restarted when the processing step is completed in order to release the occupied memory. Recommended: 20,000,000

Parameters marked with * in Table B.2 are automatically set for R/3 4.0 under Windows NT by Zero Administration Memory Management (see R/3 Note 88416). If you are working with R/3 4.0 under Windows NT, you should delete these parameters from the profiles. The recommendations above apply only to R/3 in UNIX environments.

All recommendations apply to computers with a main memory size of at least 500MB for an R/3 instance or 750MB for a central R/3 System.

TABLE B.3: Other Parameters in the Instance Profiles and Their Default Values

Area	Parameter	Meaning
Alert Monitor	alert/ALERTS	File name to back up the alerts of the CCMS monitor architecture
Logon	login/ fails_to_session_end	Number of permitted failed logon attempts before SAPGUI is closed Default: 3
	login/fails_to_ user_lock	Number of permitted failed logon attempts after which a user is locked out Default: 12
	login/ failed_user_auto_ unlock	Unlock locked users the next day 1 unlock 0 remain locked
	login/min_ password_lng	Required minimum length of passwords Default: 3
	login/password_ expiration_time	Maximum validity duration of a password Default: 0 no limit
	login/no_automatic_ user_sapstar	0: If user SAP* is deleted, user SAP* with password PASS is automatically available 1: No automatically available user SAP*
	login/system_client	Default logon client
	rdisp/gui_auto_logout	Automatic logoff if a user is inactive for a specific time in seconds 0: inactive
System log	rslg/max_ diskspace/local	Maximum size of the file for the local system log
	rslg/max_ diskspace/central	Maximum size of the file for the global system log (UNIX only)
Trace	rdisp/TRACE	Log level in developer traces 0: Trace off 1: Default: Errors only 2,3: Extended trace
Batch Input	bdc/altlogfile	Directory for reorganizing the batch input log file (RSBDCREO)

APPENDIX C

Glossary

ABAP

Advanced Business Application Programming. The programming language of the R/3 System.

ABAP Dictionary

Central metadata of all objects in the R/3 System. (The term *metadata* refers to data about the data.)

ACID

Describes the basic attributes of transaction management for the database and R/3: Atomic, Consistency, Isolation, and Durability.

activity group

Subset of actions from the set of actions that were defined in the Enterprise IMG. From the activity group, you can use the Profile Generator to generate the authorizations needed by R/3 users for these actions.

ADK

Archive Development Kit. Contains tools to define related business data to a logical archiving unit (archiving object), methods for transferring the data to be archived to an archive file in the form of function modules, example programs, documentation, archive administration to start programs, data transfer, and network graphics representing the interdependencies between data that can be archived.

ADO

Application-Defined Object.

ALE

Application Link Enabling. ALE is a technology for building and operating distributed applications. The basic purpose of ALE is to ensure a distributed—but integrated—R/3 installation. It comprises a controlled business message exchange with consistent data storage in non-permanently connected SAP applications.

Applications are integrated not through a central database, but through synchronous and asynchronous communication. ALE consists of three layers: application services, distribution services, and communication services.

Alert Monitor

Graphical monitor for analyzing system states and events.

ANSI

American National Standards Institute.

API

Application Programming Interface. The software package used by an application program to call a service provided by the operating system, for example, to open a file.

APPC

Program-to-program communication within the IBM world. Based on the LU6.2 protocol.

application server

A computer on which at least one R/3 instance runs.

ArchiveLink

Integrated into the Basis component of the R/3 System, a communications interface between the R/3 applications and external components. ArchiveLink has the following interfaces: user interface, interface to the R/3 applications, and interface to external components (archive systems, viewer systems, and scan systems).

archiving object

A logical object comprising related business data in the database that is read from the database using an archiving program. After it has been successfully archived, a logical object can be deleted by a specially generated deleting program.

ASAP

AcceleratedSAP. Standardized procedural model to implement R/3.

background processing

Processing that does not take place on the screen. Data is processed in the background, while other functions can be executed in parallel on the screen. Although the background processes are not visible for a user, and run without user intervention (there is no dialog), they have the same priority as online processes.

BAPI

Business Application Programming Interface. Standardized programming interface that provides external access to business processes and data in the R/3 System.

Batch Input

Method and tools for rapid import of data from sequential files into the R/3 database.

button

Element of the graphical user interface. Click a button to execute the button's function. You can select buttons using the keyboard as well as the mouse. Place the button cursor on the button and select Enter or choose the Enter button. Buttons can contain text or graphical symbols.

CATT

Computer-Aided Test Tool. You can use this tool to generate test data and to automate and test business processes.

CCMS

Computing Center Management System. Tools for monitoring, controlling, and configuring the R/3 System. The CCMS supports 24-hour system administration functions from within the R/3 System. You can use it to analyze the system load and monitor the distributed resource usage of the system components.

CET

Client Components Enabling Technology.

client

From a commercial law, organizational, and technical viewpoint, a closed unit within an R/3 System with separate master records within a table.

CO

Customizing Organizer. Tool to administer change and transport requests of all types in an R/3 System.

Control Panel

Central tool for monitoring the R/3 System and its instances.

CPI-C

Common Programming Interface-Communication. Programming interface, the basis for synchronous, system-to-system, program-to-program communication.

CTO

Change and Transport Organizing Method used to manage changes and development in the R/3 System, as well as their transport to other R/3 Systems.

Customizing

Adjusting the R/3 System to specific customer requirements by selecting variants, parameter settings, etc.

DSA

Data Striping Array (RAID 1).

data archiving

Removing data that is currently not needed from the R/3 database and storing it in archives (see also *archiving object*).

database

A database is made up of files that are needed for permanently storing data on the hard disk and one or more database instances. Each R/3 System has only one database. There is normally only one database instance for each database. DB2/390 and Oracle Parallel Server are database systems for which a database can be made up of multiple database instances. In an R/3 System a database instance can either be alone on a single computer or together with one (or theoretically more) R/3 instance(s).

database instance

An administrative unit that allows access to a database. A database instance consists of database processes with a common set of database buffers in the shared memory.

database server

A computer with at least one database instance.

DBA

Database administrator.

DCL

Data Control Language. Language commands to control user transactions.

DDL

Data Definition Language. Language commands to define relationships.

deadlock

Blocking of multiple transactions that are each waiting for locked objects to be released.

DIAG protocol

The communication protocol between SAPGUI and dialog work processes on the instance.

dialog work process

R/3 work process used to process requests from users working online.

dispatcher

The process that coordinates the work processes of an instance.

DML

Data Manipulation Language. Language commands to query and change data.

Dynpro

The DYNamic PROgram that consists of a screen and the underlying process logic.

EDI

Electronic Data Interchange. Intercompany electronic interchange of structured data (for example, business documents) between business partners in the home country and abroad who may be using different hardware, software, and communication services.

Enterprise IMG

Company-specific Implementation Guide.

entity

Uniquely identifiable, real or imaginary. The connections between entities are described by relationships.

FDDI

Fiber Distributed Data Interchange.

firewall

Software to protect a local network from unauthorized access from outside.

front-end computer

A computer or CPU that generates and manipulates data before that data is passed to another process.

GUI

Graphical User Interface. The medium through which a user can exchange information with the computer. You use the GUI to select commands, start programs, display files, and perform other operations by selecting function keys or buttons, menu options, and icons with the mouse.

high availability

Property of a service or a system that remains in production operation for most of the time. High availability for an R/3 System means that unplanned and planned downtimes are reduced to a minimum. Good system administration is decisive here. You can reduce unplanned downtime by using preventive hardware and software solutions that are designed to reduce single points of failure in the services that support the R/3 System. You can reduce the planned downtime by optimized scheduling of necessary maintenance activities.

Hot Package

Delivered by SAP, software corrections or enhancements for a specific R/3 release.

HSM

Hierarchical Storage Management. Software and hardware for archiving data.

HTML

HyperText Markup Language.

HTTP

HyperText Transfer Protocol. Protocol used between a Web server and the Web client.

IAC

Internet Application Components.

IDA

Independent Disk Array (RAID 5).

IDES

International Demo and Education System. IDES contains multiple model companies, which map the relevant business processes of the R/3 System. Using simple user guidelines and different master and transaction data, scenarios with large data volumes can be tested. IDES is therefore well suited as a training tool to assist in instructing project teams.

IDoc

Internal Document. An IDoc type filled with real data. An IDoc is a real business process formatted in the IDoc type.

IDoc type

Internal Document SAP format, into which the data of a business process is transferred. An IDoc type is described by the following components:

- A control record. Its format is identical for all IDoc types.

- One or more records. A record consists of a fixed administration segment and the data segment. The number and format of the segments differ for different IDoc types.

- Status records. These records describe stages of processing that an IDoc can go through. The status records have the same format for all IDoc types.

IMG

Implementation Guide. A tool for making customer-specific adjustments to the R/3 System. For each application component, the Implementation Guide contains:

- All steps to implement the R/3 System

- All default settings and all activities to configure the R/3 System

- A hierarchical structure that maps the structure of the R/3 application components

- Lists of all the documentation relevant to the implementation of the R/3 System

instance

R/3 instance. Administrative unit that groups together components of an R/3 System that offer one or more services. An R/3 instance can provide the following services:

D—Dialog

V—Update

E—SAP lock management (Enqueue)

B—Background processing (Background)

S—Printing (Spool)

G—SAP Gateway

An R/3 instance consists of a dispatcher and one or more work processes for each of the services, as well as a common set of R/3 buffers in the shared memory.

The dispatcher manages the processing requests. Work processes execute the requests. Each instance provides at least one dialog service and a gateway. An instance can provide further services. Only one instance can be available that provides the service SAP lock management. In accordance with this definition, there can be two (or more) R/3 instances on an application server. This means that with two or more instances on one server, there are the same number of dispatchers.

IPC

InterProcess Communication.

IS

Industry Solution. Industry-specific applications for R/3. For example, IS-H (IS Hospital), IS-RE (IS Real Estate), or IS-PS (IS Public Sector) are ISs.

ISAPI

Microsoft Information Server API.

ITS

Internet Transaction Server. The gateway between the R/3 System and the World Wide Web.

LAN

Local area network.

LUW

Logical Unit of Work. From the viewpoint of R/3, an indivisible sequence of database operations that conform to the ACID maxims. From the viewpoint of a database system, this sequence represents a unit that plays a decisive role in securing data integrity.

MAPI

Messaging Application Programming Interface.

MIME

Multipurpose Internet Mail Extensions.

NSAPI

Netscape Server API.

OLE

Object Linking and Embedding.

OLTP

Online Transaction Processing.

OMS

Output Management System.

Operation mode

Defined number and type of work processes of one or more instances in a particular time period. Operation modes can be switched automatically.

OS

Operating system.

OSS

Online Service System. OSS is SAP's central service and support system. OSS can be used by all SAP's customers and partners.

PAI

Process After Input. Technical program processes after data is entered in a screen in R/3.

PBO

Process Before Output. Technical program processes before a screen is output in R/3.

performance

Measurement of the efficiency of an IT system. The synonym for this is *throughput*.

pop-up window

A window that is called from a primary window and that is displayed in front of that window.

port

Term used for the channel through which the R/3 System exchanges data with an external system.

Profile Generator

Automatically generates an authorization profile based on the activities in an activity group.

Q-API

Queue Application Programming Interface. The interface to buffered, asynchronous data transfer between decentralized applications and R/2 and R/3 SAP systems, based on CPI-C.

R/3

Runtime System 3.

RAID

Redundant Array of Independent Disks. Hardware-based technology that supports disk redundancy through disk mirroring and related methods.

RDBMS

Relational Database Management System.

RFC

Remote Function Call. RFC is an SAP interface protocol, based on CPIC. It allows the programming of communication processes between systems to be simplified considerably. Using RFCs, pre-defined functions can be called and executed in a remote system or within the same system. RFCs are used for communication control, parameter passing, and error handling.

SAPGUI

SAP Graphical User Interface. (*See* GUI.)

SAProuter

A software module that functions as part of a firewall system.

server

The term *server* has multiple meanings in the SAP environment. It should therefore only be used if it is clear whether it means a logical unit, such as an R/3 instance, or a physical unit, such as a computer.

session

A user's time online in an SAPGUI window.

Session Manager

The tool used for central control of R/3 applications. The Session Manager is a graphical navigation interface used to manage sessions and start application transactions. It can generate both company-specific and user-specific menus. The Session Manager is available since R/3 Release 3.0C under Windows 95 and Windows NT.

shared memory

Main memory area, which can be accessed by all work processes in an instance. Also used in the RDBMS. The term *shared memory* is also used to mean the main memory area shared by the RDBMS processes.

SID

SAP System Identifier. Placeholder for the three-character name of an R/3 System.

SQL

Structured Query Language.

SSCR

SAP Software Change Registration. A procedure for registering manual changes to SAP sources and SAP Repository Objects.

SUSE

Self-Upgrading Software Environment.

system landscape

A real system constellation installed at a customer site. The system landscape describes the required systems and clients, their meanings, and the transport paths for implementation and maintenance. Of the methods used, client copy and the transport system are particularly important. For example, the system landscape could consist of a development system, a test system, a consolidation system, and a production system.

TCP/IP

Transmission Control Protocol/Internet Protocol.

TDC

Transport Domain Controller. Application server of an R/3 System in the transport domain, from which transport activities between the R/3 Systems in the transport domain are controlled.

TemSe

TEMporary SEquential objects. Data storage for output management.

TMS

Transport Management System. Tool for managing transport requests between R/3 Systems.

TO

Transport Organizer. Tool for managing all the change and transport requests with more extensive functionality than the CO and the WBO.

Transaction code

Code (consisting of four alphanumeric characters) that is used to call an R/3 Transaction directly.

transport

Term from software logistics in R/3: Data export and import between R/3 Systems.

transport domain

Logical group of R/3 Systems between which data is transported in accordance with fixed rules. The Transport Domain Controller exercises control over the transport domain.

tRFC

Transactional RFC. Remote Function Control to which the ACID principles are applied.

URL

Uniform Resource Locator.

WAN

Wide area network.

WBO

Workbench Organizer. Tool for managing change and transport requests that are generated from the use of the ABAP Workbench.

WORM

Write Once, Read Multiple. Storage medium that can be written once and read any number of times. WORM ensures that data stored cannot be changed and that it will be intact for many years. It is primarily used for data archiving.

WP

Work process. The application services of the R/3 System have special processes, for example, for dialog administration, updating change documents, background processing, spool processing, and lock management. Work processes can be assigned to dedicated application servers.

APPENDIX

D

Bibliography

This appendix lists the books and manuals relevant to the topics covered in this book. You may find some of these information sources useful as you develop broader experience with the R/3 System.

Brand, Hartwig. *ABAP/4 Development Workbench Manuals*. Walldorf: SAP AG, 1996.

Brand, Hartwig. *SAP R/3 Implementation with ASAP: The Official Guide*. San Francisco: Sybex, 1999.

Buck-Emden, Rüdiger, and Galimow, Jürgen. *SAP Systems R/3: A Client/Server Technology*. Bonn: Addison-Wesley, 1997.

Cassidy, Pete. *High Performance Oracle 8: SQL Programming & Tuning*. Scottsdale: Coriolis Group, 1998.

Hansen, Wolf-Rüdiger. *Client-Server-Architektur*. Bonn: Addison-Wesley, 1993 (only available in German).

Herrmann, Uwe, and Lenz, Dierk, and Unbescheid, Günter. *Oracle 8 für den DBA: Edition Oracle*. Bonn: Addison-Wesley, 1998 (only available in German).

McLean, Pete. *An Introduction to RAID*. Maynard: DEC Company, 1991.

Patterson, David, and Gibson, Garth, and Katz, Randy. *A Case for Redundant Arrays of Inexpensive Disks (RAID)*. Berkeley: University of California, Berkeley Press, 1987.

Schneider, Robert D. *Microsoft SQL Server: Planning and Building a High Performance Database*. New Jersey: Prentice Hall, 1997.

Schwerin-Wenzel, Sven. *Authorizations Made Easy*. Walldorf: SAP AG, 1998.

Stürner, Günther. *Oracle 7: Die verteilte semantische Datenbank 3., erweiterte Auflage*. Weissach: DBMS Publishing, 1993 (only available in German).

Technical Committee ISO/IEC. *ISO/IEC 9075, 1992 Database Language SQL*. ISO, 1992.

Manual of Language Import. Walldorf: SAP AG, 1998.

Manual OSS: Online Service System. Walldorf: SAP AG, 1998.

R/3-Installation Guide. Walldorf: SAP AG 1998.

SAP R/3 System Manuals. Walldorf: SAP AG, 1998.

APPENDIX
E

Menu Structures

Figures E.1, E.2, and E.3 illustrate the menu structure for the main Basis administration tasks in R/3 Release 4.0.

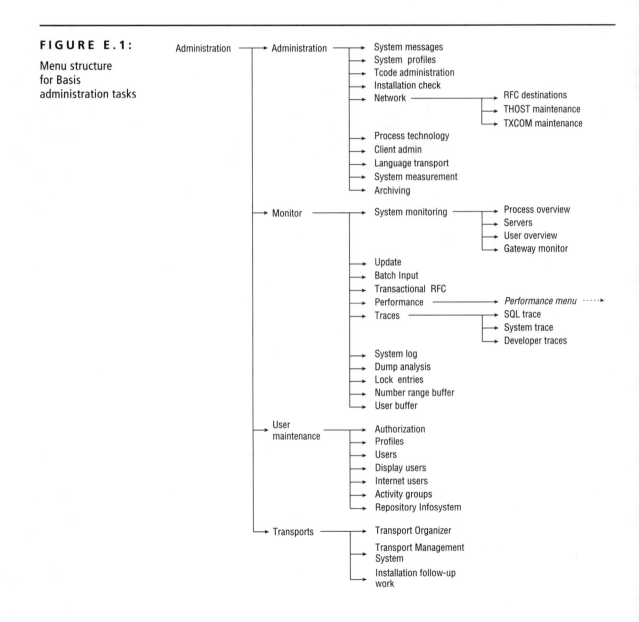

FIGURE E.1:

Menu structure for Basis administration tasks

FIGURE E.2:

Menu structure
for Basis
administration tasks

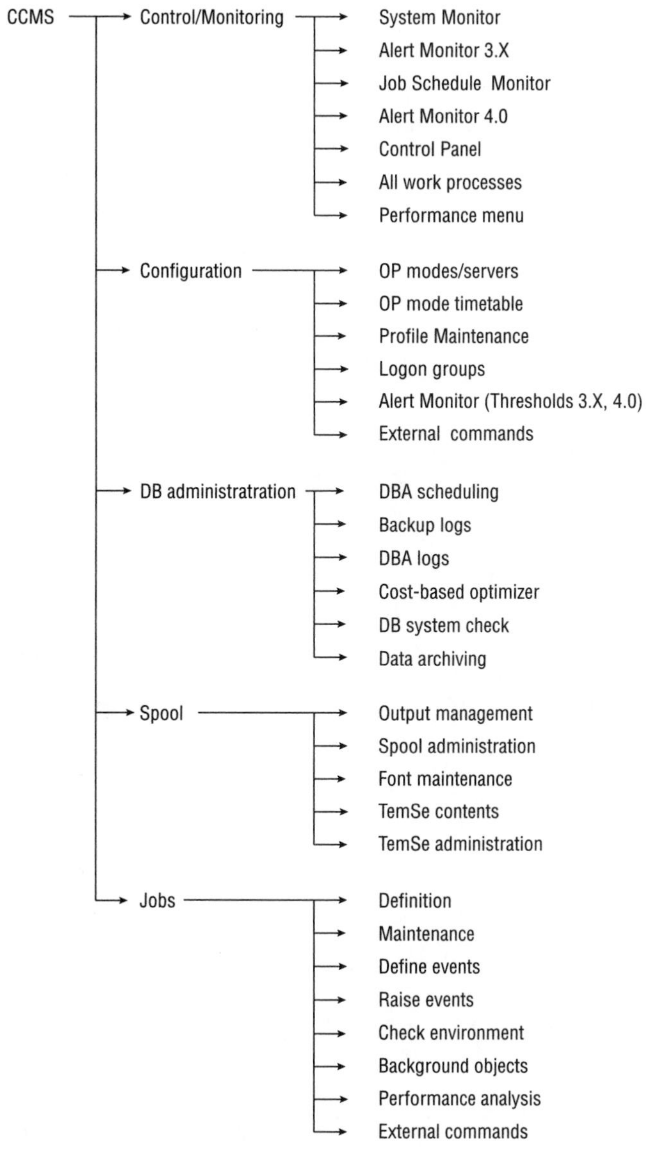

CCMS — Control/Monitoring
- System Monitor
- Alert Monitor 3.X
- Job Schedule Monitor
- Alert Monitor 4.0
- Control Panel
- All work processes
- Performance menu

Configuration
- OP modes/servers
- OP mode timetable
- Profile Maintenance
- Logon groups
- Alert Monitor (Thresholds 3.X, 4.0)
- External commands

DB administratration
- DBA scheduling
- Backup logs
- DBA logs
- Cost-based optimizer
- DB system check
- Data archiving

Spool
- Output management
- Spool administration
- Font maintenance
- TemSe contents
- TemSe administration

Jobs
- Definition
- Maintenance
- Define events
- Raise events
- Check environment
- Background objects
- Performance analysis
- External commands

FIGURE E.3:

Menu structure
for Basis
administration tasks

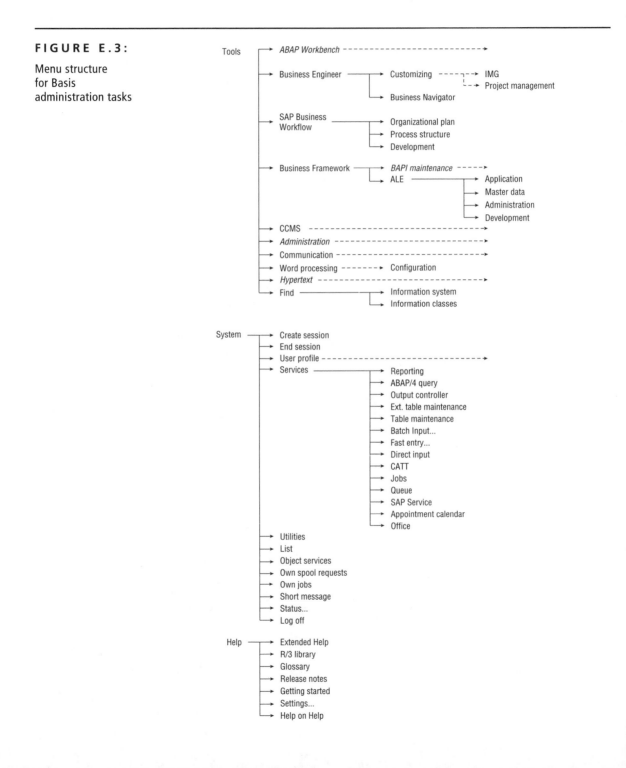

APPENDIX

F

Review Questions and Answers

Chapter 1: Technical Implementation of Client/Server Architecture in R/3

1. Which services does the application layer provide?

    A. Communication service

    B. Dialog service

    C. Spool service

    D. Update service

    E. Message service

    F. Transport service

    G. Gateway service

    H. Network service

    I. Enqueue service

    J. Background service

    K. Change service

    Answer: B, C, D, E, G, I, J

2. Which of the following statements is correct?

    A. The Dispatcher and the dialog processes should not run on the same instance.

    B. The Enqueue and the Message Server work together closely and should therefore run in one instance.

    C. The background service and the update service work together closely and should therefore never run on different instances.

    Answer: B

3. What is the gateway service for?

    A. Communication between the R/3 processes

    B. Communication between R/3 Systems and instances of an R/3 System

    C. Communication with the operating system spool

    D. Connection of external programs such as MAPI, EDI, and Telex service

    E. Communication with R/3 Systems

Answer: B, D, E

4. How many Message Servers are active in an R/3 System?

    A. 0

    B. 1

    C. 2

Answer: B

5. How many update services can be active in each instance?

    A. 1

    B. 2

    C. The number is changed automatically by the R/3 System depending on requirements.

    D. Any number depending on the available resources. The number must be determined in advance by the administrator.

Answer: D

6. Which clients and users are delivered in the standard R/3 System?

    A. Client 000 and users SAP* and DDIC

    B. Client 001 and user MUSTER

    C. Client 001 and users SAP* and DDIC

    D. Client 066 and user SUPPORT

    E. Client 066 and user EARLYWATCH

Answer: A, C, E

Chapter 2: First Steps

1. Which tools can you use in the operating system to start your R/3 System?

    A. Task Manager

    B. SAP Service Manager

    C. start SAP

    D. `startsap`

Answer: B, D

2. Which tools can you use to stop the R/3 System (depending on the operating system)?

    A. Task Manager

    B. SAP Service Manager

    C. kill

    D. `stopsap`

Answer: B, D

3. Which profiles are used for the configuration of R/3?

    A. R/3 Profile

    B. Instance profile

    C. Application server profile

    D. `DEFAULT.PFL`

E. Start profile

F. Stop profile

Answer: B, D, E

4. In which logs does R/3 document the system start?

A. `startdb.log`

B. `startsap_<computer name>_<instance number>.log`

C. `startsap.log`

D. `r3start.prot`

Answer: A, B, C

5. How could an SAPGUI to R/3 System QO1 instance 00 on computer P311 be started?

A. `sapgui -p3111/00`

B. `sapgui /H/Q01/I/3200`

C. `sapgui /H/P311/S/sapdp00`

Answer: C

Chapter 3: The Online Service System

1. What is `saprouter` used for?

A. It replaces a firewall.

B. It is used to control the establishment of remote connections to application servers in an R/3 System.

C. It is used to establish connections between front ends and the application servers in an R/3 System in the local network.

Answer: B

2. In what file do you normally maintain the SAProuter routing data?

   A. saprouttab

   B. DEFAULT.PFL

   C. autoexec.bat

   Answer: A

3. What requirements must be met in order to establish a service connection from SAP to a customer's R/3 System?

   A. The R/3 System must be registered in the OSS System.

   B. The connection data for the application computers in the R/3 System and the SAProuter in the customer's system must be maintained.

   C. The connection must be opened by the customer.

   Answer: A, B, C

Chapter 4: Installation Concepts

1. Which statement is correct? During an R/3 installation with Oracle,

   A. Multiple tablespaces are created according to the R/3 naming conventions.

   B. Exactly one tablespace is created, which is large enough to store all R/3 data.

   C. No Oracle-specific storage structures are established.

   Answer: A

2. Which statement is correct? The R/3 naming conventions

   A. Can be changed using operating system tools.

    B. Are a permanent part of various R/3 tools and therefore cannot be changed arbitrarily.

    C. Help the user find logs and messages quickly.

Answer: B, C

3. Which statement is correct?

    A. Using RAID systems increases security in case of R/3 System failure.

    B. Running the R/3 database in a RAID system is not recommended because it causes a loss in performance.

    C. RAID systems are only recommended for the data areas of the R/3 database. For performance reasons, log areas should not be run with RAID systems.

Answer: A

4. What programs are used to perform an R/3 installation?

    A. R3up

    B. InstGUI and R3Setup

    C. Sapinstall

    D. Setup

Answer: B

Chapter 5: Setting Up a System Landscape

1. For production purposes, it is recommended

    A. That at least two R/3 Systems on different computers for development/quality assurance and production are set up.

B. That as powerful a computer as possible is set up on which a central R/3 System is available for all tasks.

C. That multiple R/3 Systems run on a common, central database.

Answer: A

2. In a multi-system landscape, transport activities

A. Can only be controlled from the system that the data is being imported into or exported from.

B. Can be controlled centrally from the Domain Controller of the transport domain.

C. Can only be controlled on the operating system level using the tp program.

D. Can be controlled in a transport domain from each R/3 System in the domain.

Answer: B, D

3. What transport paths are there?

A. Direct transport path

B. Indirect transport path

C. Consolidation path

D. Delivery path

E. Diversion

Answer: C, D

4. Which program on the operating level is used to perform transports?

A. R3load

B. R3INST

C. tp

    D. dpmon

    E. sapdba

Answer: C

5. Which parameter file is used to control the transport control program?

    A. Default.pfl

    B. profile

    C. initparam

    D. TPPARAM

Answer: D

Chapter 6: Software Logistics

1. The R/3 transport system is

    A. Equivalent to copying a client.

    B. Used to exchange development and Customizing data between different R/3 Systems.

    C. Used to exchange data between different clients in one R/3 System.

Answer: B

2. A development class is

    A. A defined group of developers.

    B. Client-independent.

    C. Assigned to the object when a SAP original is changed.

    D. Assigned to a transport layer.

Answer: B, D

3. Modifications to SAP-owned objects

   A. Must be registered in the OSS.

   B. Are not permitted.

   C. Are strongly recommended to implement company-specific processes.

Answer: A

4. A repository object of an R/3 System

   A. Is automatically locked if a developer makes changes to an object. When the changes are saved, the lock is automatically removed.

   B. Can only be changed if a corresponding change request is assigned. The object is then automatically locked for changes by all users until the assigned task and the change request are released by the developer.

   C. Can only be changed if a corresponding change request is assigned. Changes to the object can only then be made by users named in the change request.

Answer: C

Chapter 7: Client Administration

1. Which of the following statements about the R/3 client concept are correct?

   A. Customizing settings are always client-independent.

   B. A client is an independently accountable business unit within an R/3 System.

   C. Each client has its own application data.

D. Each client has its own technical data, which is independent of other clients.

E. Each client has its own application tables.

F. The table field `mandt` is used to differentiate between client-dependent data within the tables with application data.

Answer: B, C, F

2. Which client copy methods does R/3 offer?

   A. Local copy

   B. Remote copy

   C. Data interchange procedure

   D. Client export

   E. Data backup

Answer: A, B, D

3. Which data can be copied in a remote client copy?

   A. Client-dependent application data

   B. Client-dependent table definitions

   C. Client-independent data

   D. All data in the R/3 System

Answer: A, C

4. What is the transaction code for checking the copy logs?

   A. SE38.

   B. There is none.

   C. SCC3.

   D. S000.

Answer: C

Chapter 8: R/3 Users and Authorizations

1. The Profile Generator:

   A. Is used to maintain and automatically generate R/3 profiles.

   B. Is used to create activity groups and corresponding authorization profiles, and to assign the users.

   C. Is an ABAP tool for generating authorization objects for programming.

   Answer: B

2. Which statement is correct?

   A. A user can only belong to one activity group.

   B. A user can belong to multiple activity groups.

   Answer: B

3. Which requirements for the use of the Profile Generator must be met?

   A. Parameter `auth/no_check_in_some_cases` must have the value Y in the instance profile.

   B. Only users DDIC and SAP* must be known in the R/3 System.

   C. The Enterprise IMG and the enterprise menu must already have been generated.

   Answer: A, C

4. Which statement is correct?

   A. The term *responsibility* is used to mean the responsibility of the user administrator for maintaining authorizations.

   B. A responsibility groups together multiple activity
      groups.

   C. The terms *responsibility* and *activity group* are always
      identical.

   D. Responsibilities are used within an activity group to
      make a distinction between identical activities used for
      different organizational levels, such as company codes.

Answer: D

Chapter 9: Background Processing

1. Which transaction is used to analyze the job logs?

   A. SE38

   B. SM37

   C. S000

Answer: B

2. Which external program is used to trigger events in the R/3
   System?

   A. sapevt

   B. sapxpg

   C. sapstart

   D. spmon

Answer: A

3. What does the status of Ready mean for a background job?

   A. Scheduling of the job was completed and saved.

   B. The job was executed and the log is ready to be printed.

    C. The job is waiting for system resources so that it can start.

Answer: C

Chapter 10: Update Service

1. Which components make up an update?

    A. V1 and V2

    B. Pre- and post-update

    C. Test and main update

Answer: A

2. Which status does an update record have if it is waiting for an update?

    A. Active

    B. Released

    C. Init

    D. Start

Answer: C

3. Which R/3 profile parameter is used to send a message to a user whose update request was canceled?

    A. `rdisp/vbmail`.

    B. A message is always sent to the user.

    C. `rdisp/vbdelete`.

Answer: A

Chapter 11: Output Configuration and Administration

1. Which access methods are there?

    A. Local access methods

    B. Remote access methods

    C. Special access methods

    D. Access methods with formatting

    E. Access methods without formatting

    F. Internal access methods

    G. External access methods

   Answer: A, B, C

2. For which authorizations does R/3 provide authorization objects?

    A. Device authorizations

    B. Display authorizations

    C. TemSe administration authorizations

    D. Authorizations for operations with spool requests

   Answer: A, B, C, D

3. Which access methods are recommended for mass printing?

    A. Local access method L for transferring to the host spool using the appropriate command interface

    B. Local access method C for direct transfer to the Print Manager of the host spool using the appropriate command interface

    C. Local access method F for front-end printing

    D. Remote access method S for work center printers through SAPLPD

    E. Remote access method U based on the Berkeley protocol

Answer: A, B

4. Which three areas are there in the R/3 spool system?

    A. User administration

    B. Authorization administration

    C. Output administration

    D. Device administration

    E. Access methods

    F. Data storage (TemSe)

Answer: C, D, F

5. What is a dedicated spool server?

    A. A selected application server in the R/3 System that is used for central spool administration.

    B. The application server assigned to an output device defined in the R/3 System. The spool service of the dedicated spool server handles the processing and administration of the spool requests passed to this device.

    C. The front-end computer (desktop) that is currently used for front-end printing.

    D. The application server in an R/3 System that is explicitly assigned to a user as a spool server for that user's spool requests.

Answer: B

Chapter 12: Data Archiving

1. What is an archiving object?

   A. CD-ROM or WORM

   B. The archiving files created by the archiving run

   C. The logical unit of physically related data and the programs needed for archiving

   Answer: C

2. What is meant by data archiving?

   A. Saving the archive logs

   B. Archiving documents such as inbound and outbound print lists, and invoices or documents from application components

   C. Removing data from the database and storing it in an archive system or on separate media

   Answer: C

3. Which tool is used in R/3 data archiving to transfer data to an archive?

   A. SAP ArchiveLink

   B. HSM (Hierarchical Storage Management)

   C. ADK (Archive Development Kit)

   D. RFC

   Answer: C

4. Which statement is correct?

   A. The entire archiving process can take place during normal R/3 operation.

B. The entire archiving process must take place while the R/3 System is stopped.

C. When the archive files are generated, no work can be done in the R/3 System.

Answer: A

Chapter 13: Data Distribution and Transfer

1. Which statement is correct? For data distribution based on ALE:

    A. A permanent connection between the partner systems is established.

    B. The partner systems are not permanently connected during data transfer.

    C. Functions of the RDBMS, for example SAPDBA, are used to exchange data.

    Answer: B

2. Which methods can be used to exchange data?

    A. CPI-C

    B. Sequential files

    C. tRFC

    D. Internet

    E. telnet

    Answer: A, B, C, D

3. What Transaction code is used for ALE monitoring?

    A. SM51

    B. STUN

    C. MM01

    D. BALE

Answer: D

4. How can tRFCs terminated due to communication errors be processed?

    A. Automatically by activating the automatic repeat option when you define the tRFC connection

    B. By scheduling the job RSARFCEX

    C. By scheduling the job RSEOUT00

    D. By resolving the error and executing the application transaction again

Answer: A, B

5. Which options exist to send IDocs?

    A. Event-driven, for example, operation mode switching

    B. Delayed, by scheduling the jobs

    C. Immediately

    D. Send individually after the IDocs are generated

    E. Collect IDocs and send them as a packet

Answer: A, B, C, D

6. What is the batch input procedure used for?

    A. To import data from sequential files into the R/3 database

    B. To process mass data in the background

    C. To import data using the transport control program tp

Answer: A

Chapter 14: Maintaining Instances

1. What is meant by an operation mode?

    A. An operation mode describes the number and type of work processes in one or more instances.

    B. An operation mode additionally comprises all the settings for the R/3 main memory areas.

    C. An operation mode denotes the status of the R/3 System: *active* means ready for operation; *DB active* means that only the R/3 database is available, and the R/3 System is stopped.

Answer: A

2. What is a logon group?

    A. All users that are assigned to the same user group comprise a logon group.

    B. A logon group is a logical unit of a subset of all application servers in an R/3 System.

    C. All users with the same tasks comprise a logon group.

Answer: B

3. Which R/3 parameters can be changed and activated while R/3 is running?

    A. None

    B. Selected parameters to assign the R/3 main memory areas

    C. Type and number of work processes

    D. All parameters

Answer: B, C

4. How do you find out the initial and the maximum swap requirements of an instance for the current configuration?

   A. Add up the appropriate parameter values in the instance profile.

   B. Perform basic maintenance of the instance profile.

   C. `sappfpar check pf=<instance profile name>`.

Answer: B, C

Chapter 15: System Monitoring

1. To which directory are the developer traces written?

   A. `\users\<sid>adm`

   B. `\usr\sap\<SID>\<instance>\work`

   C. `\usr\sap\<SID>\SYS\global`

Answer: B

2. Your R/3 System cannot be started. Where will you find information on the cause of this problem?

   A. `startdb.log`

   B. `startsap_<computer name>_<instance number>.log`

   C. R/3 log

   D. Developer traces

   E. System log

   F. SQL trace

Answer: A, B, D

3. A user informs you that his or her session was terminated with an error. Unfortunately, the user has no details about

what happened. Where would be the best place to start your analysis?

A. Do not start an analysis. Without any details, you cannot find the cause of a cancellation.

B. Check all the runtime errors that occurred in your R/3 System.

C. Check the system log.

D. Check the backup logs.

Answer: C

INDEX

Note to the Reader: Throughout this index **boldface** page numbers indicate primary discussions of a topic. *Italic* page numbers indicate illustrations.

C

E

F

J

N

S

U

V

W

X

Z

Testing Your R/3 Knowledge with the CD-ROM

The CD that comes with this book includes a test engine designed to familiarize you with the Certified Technical Consultant (CTC) exam format. The test questions are taken from the pages of the book and can help you gauge your preparedness for the real world of SAP R/3 Administration and for the CTC test.

The test contains proprietary software components and information of SAP AG and AsseT GmbH Assessment and Training Technologies.